MW00711282

Learning iOS Development

Learning iOS Development

A Hands-on Guide to the
Fundamentals of
iOS Programming

Maurice Sharp

Erica Sadun

Rod Strougo

✦✦Addison-Wesley

Upper Saddle River, NJ • Boston • Indianapolis • San Francisco
New York • Toronto • Montreal • London • Munich • Paris • Madrid
Cape Town • Sydney • Tokyo • Singapore • Mexico City

Many of the designations used by manufacturers and sellers to distinguish their products are claimed as trademarks. Where those designations appear in this book, and the publisher was aware of a trademark claim, the designations have been printed with initial capital letters or in all capitals.

The authors and publisher have taken care in the preparation of this book, but make no expressed or implied warranty of any kind and assume no responsibility for errors or omissions. No liability is assumed for incidental or consequential damages in connection with or arising out of the use of the information or programs contained herein.

The publisher offers excellent discounts on this book when ordered in quantity for bulk purchases or special sales, which may include electronic versions and/or custom covers and content particular to your business, training goals, marketing focus, and branding interests. For more information, please contact:

U.S. Corporate and Government Sales
(800) 382-3419
corpsales@pearsontechgroup.com

For sales outside the United States, please contact:

International Sales
international@pearsoned.com

Visit us on the Web: informit.com/aw

Library of Congress Control Number: 2013938698

Copyright © 2014 Pearson Education, Inc.

All rights reserved. Printed in the United States of America. This publication is protected by copyright, and permission must be obtained from the publisher prior to any prohibited reproduction, storage in a retrieval system, or transmission in any form or by any means, electronic, mechanical, photocopying, recording, or likewise. To obtain permission to use material from this work, please submit a written request to Pearson Education, Inc., Permissions Department, One Lake Street, Upper Saddle River, New Jersey 07458, or you may fax your request to (201) 236-3290.

ISBN-13: 978-0-321-86296-9
ISBN-10: 0-321-86296-1

Text printed in the United States on recycled paper at R. R. Donnelley in Crawfordsville, Indiana.

First printing: November 2013

Editor-in-Chief
Mark Taub

Senior Acquisitions Editor
Trina MacDonald

Senior Development Editor
Chris Zahn

Managing Editor
Kristy Hart

Senior Project Editors
Betsy Gratner
Jovana Shirley

Copy Editor
Kitty Wilson

Indexer
Tim Wright

Proofreader
Anne Goebel

Technical Reviewers
Gemma Barlow
Mark H. Granoff
Scott Gruby
Marcantonio Magnarapa

Editorial Assistant
Olivia Basegio

Cover Designer
Chuti Prasertsith

Senior Compositor
Gloria Schurick

To my wife, Lois, and my daughter, Karli. They gave me the time I needed to work on the book, even though it effectively meant a second job on top of my day one. You did it with love and compassion and still had energy for when I could be there.

Maurice

Contents at a Glance

Table of Contents

Foreword

It's been an amazing five years since the first edition of the *iPhone Developer's Cookbook* debuted for the new Apple iPhone SDK. Since then, new APIs and new hardware have made the task of keeping on top of iOS development better suited for a team than for an individual. By the time the iOS 5 edition of the *Cookbook* rolled around, the book was larger than a small baby elephant. We had to publish half of it in electronic form only. It was time for a change.

This year, my publishing team sensibly split the *Cookbook* material into several manageable print volumes. This volume is *Learning iOS Development: A Hands-on Guide to the Fundamentals of iOS Programming*. My coauthors, Maurice Sharp and Rod Strougo, moved much of the tutorial material that used to comprise the first several chapters of the *Cookbook* into its own volume and expanded that material into in-depth tutorials suitable for new iOS developers.

In this book, you'll find all the fundamental how-to you need to learn iOS development from the ground up. From Objective-C to Xcode, debugging to deployment, *Learning iOS Development* teaches you how to get started with Apple's development tool suite.

There are two other volumes in this series as well:

- The *Core iOS Developer's Cookbook* provides solutions for the heart of day-to-day development. It covers all the classes you need for creating iOS applications using standard APIs and interface elements. It offers the recipes you need for working with graphics, touches, and views to create mobile applications.

- The *Advanced iOS 6 Developer's Cookbook* focuses on common frameworks such as Store Kit, Game Kit, and Core Location. It helps you build applications that leverage these special-purpose libraries and move beyond the basics. This volume is for those who have a strong grasp of iOS development and are looking for practical how-to information for specialized areas.

It's been a pleasure to work with Maurice and Rod on *Learning iOS Development*. They are technically sharp, experienced developers, and they're genuinely nice guys. It's difficult to hand over your tech baby to be cared for by someone else, and these two have put a lot of effort into turning the dream of *Learning iOS Development* into reality. Maurice, who wrote the bulk of this volume, brings a depth of personal experience and an Apple background to the table.

iOS has evolved hugely since the early days of iPhone, both in terms of APIs and developer tools. *Learning iOS Development* is for anyone new to the platform, offering a practical, well-explored path for picking up vital skills. From your first meeting with Objective-C to App Store deployment, *Learning iOS Development* covers the basics.

Welcome to iOS development. It's an amazing and exciting place to be.

—Erica Sadun, April 2013

Acknowledgments

What do acknowledgments have to do with learning iOS development? I used to be likely to skim or skip this section of a book—and you might be tempted to do that as well. Who are these people? Why do I care? You care because your ability to get things done really depends on who you know. And I am about to thank people who have helped me, many of whom enjoy helping. You may know some of them or know someone who does. I am often surprised how close I am to the truly great people on LinkedIn. So read on, note the names, and see how close you are to someone who may be able to help you solve your most pressing problem.

First, my deep thanks to Erica Sadun (series editor and code goddess) and Trina MacDonald (editor) for the opportunity to write most of this book. When they asked me to contribute, my first thought was "I have never written anything this big, but how hard could it be?" I found out, and their support, along with that of Rod Strougo, Chris Zahn (please correct my grammar some more), Jovana Shirley (so *that* is production editing), Kitty Wilson (are you sure you do not know how to code?), Anne Goebel (may I use might, or might I use may?), both Olivia Basegio and Betsy Gratner (if only I were that organized), and the entire production staff (I fed them sketches; they produced the beautiful diagrams). All of you started my journey of learning to *be* an author. I have always been a helper. Developer Technical Support enabled me to help thousands. This book is an opportunity to help a wider audience. Thank you, all.

I am also deeply grateful to friends old and new for answering technical questions: Mike Engber, a superstar coder at Apple, showed me the light on blocks as well as answering other questions. Others took time to answer questions or talk about possible solutions: Thanks to Tim Burks, Lucien Dupont, Aleksey Novicov, Jeremy Olson (@jerols, inspired UX!), Tim Roadley (Mr. Core Data), and Robert Shoemate (Telerik/TestStudio). Thanks also to Marc Antonio and Mark H. Granoff for reviewing every chapter and giving suggestions and corrections on things technical. And an extra shout out to Gemma Barlow and Scott Gruby for checking the iOS 7/ Xcode 5 changes in addition to all the other feedback.

Contributors are not limited to engineers. German translations are from Oliver Drobnik and David Fedor, a longtime friend. Arabic is from Jane Ann Day...take her course; she is very good. Glyphish, aka Joseph Wain, provided the beautiful icons and user interface (UI) element graphics. Get some great icons for your app at www.glyphish.com. The 11 car photos first used in Chapter 6, "Scrolling," are courtesy of Sunipix.com.

Thanks to those at Couchsurfing (www.couchsurfing.org) for giving me time to work on this book, including our CEO Tony Espinoza, my friend Andrew Geweke, and the whole mobile design and development team: Gemma Barlow, David Berrios, Evan Lange, Hass Lunsford, Nicolas Milliard, Nathaniel Wolf, and Alex Woolf. You are a joy to serve.

Thanks to those who have taught, inspired, and challenged me along my technical journey. Listing them all would take a whole book, but some include the faculty and fellow students at the University of Calgary computer science department, as well as Dan Freedman, Scott Golubock, Bruce Thompson, Jim Spohrer, Bob Ebert, Steve Lemke, Brian Criscuolo, and many more from Apple, Palm, eBay, Intuit, Mark/Space, ShopWell, and Couchsurfing.

Then there is one man who taught me how to *be* a steward (some say leader or manager): Gabriel Acosta-Mikulasek, a coworker, then manager, and now close friend: *Querido hermano.* He now teaches leadership and living, and you could not ask for a better coach. Find him at www.aculasek.com.

Oddly, I'd like to also thank our kittens (now cats), who continually tried to rewrite content, typing secret cat code such as "vev uiscmr[//I'64." And many thanks to my family, who stood beside me and gave me the time to work, and even provided content. My 10-year-old daughter drew the *r* graphic used in Chapter 12, "Touch Basics."

—*Maurice Sharp*

About the Authors

Maurice Sharp is a 21-year veteran of mobile development at companies both large and small, ranging from Apple, Palm, and eBay to ShopWell and Couchsurfing. Maurice got his start as an intern developing the Newton ToolKit prototype, then as a Developer Technical Support (DTS) Engineer helping make the world safe and fun for Newton then Palm developers. After mastering the DTS side, he went back to coding, and he currently manages and does mobile development at Couchsurfing; runs his own consulting company, KLM Apps; and is ex officio technical advisor to some mobile-focused startups. When not living and breathing mobile, Maurice spends his time being a husband, and a father (to a precocious 10-year-old girl)—his two most important roles.

Erica Sadun is a bestselling author, coauthor, and contributor to several dozen books on programming, digital video and photography, and web design, including the widely popular *The Core iOS 6 Developer's Cookbook*, now in its fourth edition. She currently blogs at TUAW. com and has blogged in the past at O'Reilly's Mac Devcenter, Lifehacker, and Ars Technica. In addition to being the author of dozens of iOS-native applications, Erica holds a Ph.D. in computer science from Georgia Tech's Graphics, Visualization, and Usability Center. A geek, a programmer, and an author, she's never met a gadget she didn't love. When not writing, she and her geek husband parent three geeks-in-training, who regard their parents with restrained bemusement when they're not busy rewiring the house or plotting global domination.

Rod Strougo is an author, instructor, and developer. Rod's journey in iOS and game development started way back with an Apple, writing games in Basic. From his early passion for games, Rod's career moved to enterprise software development, and he spent 15 years writing software for IBM and AT&T. These days, Rod follows his passion for game development and teaching, providing iOS training at the Big Nerd Ranch (www.bignerdranch.com). Originally from Rio de Janeiro, Rod now lives in Atlanta, Georgia, with his wife and sons.

Preface

"Mobile is the future" is a phrase you hear more and more these days. And when it comes to mobile, nobody has more user-friendly devices than Apple.

You want to add iOS development to your set of skills, but where do you begin? Which resources do you need and choose? It depends on how you learn. This book is hands-on. The goal is to get you doing things as soon as possible. You start with small things at first and then build on what you already know.

The result is a book that gives you the skills you need to write an app in an easily digestible format. You can go as fast or slow as you wish. And once you are creating apps, you can turn back to specific parts of the book for a refresher.

So find a comfortable place, have your Mac and your iOS handheld nearby, and dig in!

What You'll Need

You will need a few things before you go any further in learning iOS development:

- **A modern Mac running the current or previous generation of Mac OS**—As of the writing of this book, Mac OS X Mountain Lion (v. 10.8) is the latest version with Mavericks just around the corner (not used for this book). Before Mountain Lion was Mac OS X Lion (v. 10.7). Ideally you want to use the latest OS, have at least 8GB of RAM, and lots of disk space.

- **An iOS device**—Although Xcode includes a desktop simulator for developing apps, you will need to run your app on an actual device to make sure it works correctly. It is helpful to have the same kinds of units your target customers are likely to use to make sure your app works well on all of them.

- **An Internet connection**—You will need to be able to download development resources. At some point, you might also want to test wireless app functionality. And of course, you will want to ship your app.

- **Familiarity with Objective**-C—You create native applications for iOS by using Objective-C. The language is based on ANSI C, with object-oriented extensions, which means you also need to know a bit of C. If you have programmed with Java or C++ and are familiar with C, you'll find that moving to Objective-C is easy. There is a short intro to Objective-C in Chapter 2, "Objective-C Boot Camp," but a broader understanding will help you learn more quickly.

You also need Xcode, the development tool, and some sort of Apple developer account, as discussed in Chapter 1, "Hello, iOS SDK."

Your Roadmap to iOS Development

One book can't be everything to everyone. Try as we might, if we were to pack everything you need to know into this book, you wouldn't be able to pick it up. There is, indeed, a lot you need to know to develop for the Mac and iOS platforms. If you are just starting out and don't have any programming experience, your first course of action should be to take a college-level course in the C programming language.

When you know C and how to work with a compiler (something you'll learn in that basic C course), the rest should be easy. From there, you can hop right on to Objective-C and explore how to program with it alongside the Cocoa frameworks. The flowchart shown in Figure P-1 shows you key titles offered by Pearson Education that provide the training you need to become a skilled iOS developer.

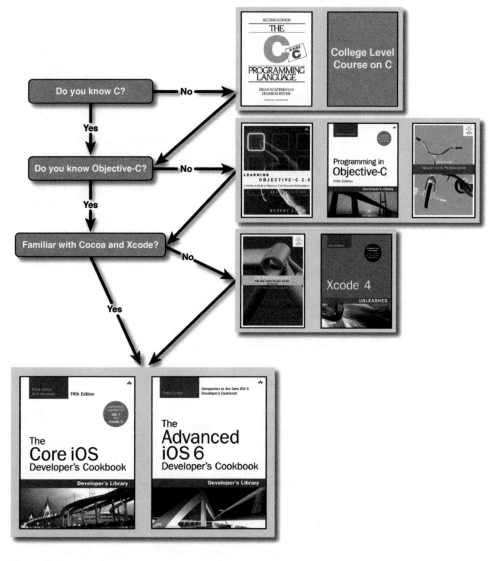

Figure P-1   A roadmap to becoming an iOS developer

When you know C, you have a few options for learning how to program with Objective-C. If you want an in-depth view of the language, you can either read Apple's documentation or pick up one of these books on Objective-C:

- *Objective-C Programming: The Big Nerd Ranch Guide* by Aaron Hillegass (Big Nerd Ranch, 2012)

- *Learning Objective-C: A Hands-on Guide to Objective-C for Mac and iOS Developers* by Robert Clair (Addison-Wesley, 2011)

- *Programming in Objective-C 2.0*, fourth edition, by Stephen Kochan (Addison-Wesley, 2012)

With the language behind you, next up is tackling Cocoa and the developer tools, otherwise known as Xcode. For that, you have a few different options. Again, you can refer to Apple's documentation on Cocoa and Xcode. See the *Cocoa Fundamentals Guide* (http://developer.apple.com/mac/library/documentation/Cocoa/Conceptual/CocoaFundamentals/CocoaFundamentals.pdf) for a head start on Cocoa, and for Xcode, see *A Tour of Xcode* (http://developer.apple.com/mac/library/documentation/DeveloperTools/Conceptual/A_Tour_of_Xcode/A_Tour_of_Xcode.pdf). Or if you prefer books, you can learn from the best. Aaron Hillegass, founder of the Big Nerd Ranch in Atlanta (www.bignerdranch.com), is the coauthor of *iOS Programming: The Big Nerd Ranch Guide*, second edition, and author of *Cocoa Programming for Mac OS X*, soon to be in its fourth edition. Aaron's book is highly regarded in Mac developer circles and is the most recommended book you'll see on the cocoa-dev mailing list. And to learn more about Xcode, look no further than Fritz Anderson's *Xcode 4 Unleashed* from Sams Publishing.

> **Note**
>
> There are plenty of other books from other publishers on the market, including the bestselling *Beginning iPhone 4 Development* by Dave Mark, Jack Nutting, and Jeff LaMarche (Apress, 2011). Another book that's worth picking up if you're a total newbie to programming is *Beginning Mac Programming* by Tim Isted (Pragmatic Programmers, 2011). Don't just limit yourself to one book or publisher. Just as you can learn a lot by talking with different developers, you can learn lots of tricks and tips from other books on the market.

To truly master Apple development, you need to look at a variety of sources: books, blogs, mailing lists, Apple's documentation, and, best of all, conferences. If you get the chance to attend WWDC (Apple's Worldwide Developer Conference), you'll know what we're talking about. The time you spend at conferences talking with other developers, and in the case of WWDC, talking with Apple's engineers, is well worth the expense if you are a serious developer.

How This Book Is Organized

The goal of this book is to enable you to build iOS apps for iOS handheld and tablet devices. It assumes that you know nothing about iOS development but are familiar with Objective-C. (Although there is a boot camp in Chapter 2, you will find it easier to learn from this book if you are more familiar with the language.) Each chapter introduces new concepts and, where appropriate, builds on knowledge from previous chapters.

Most chapters cover extra material in addition to their core content. The additional material doesn't necessarily fit with the heart of a particular chapter, but it is important in creating apps. Extra material shows you how to use specific UI elements, provides tips and tricks, explains coding practices, and provides other helpful information.

Here is a summary of each chapter:

- **Chapter 1, "Hello, iOS SDK"**—Find out about the tools, programs, and devices used for creating iOS apps. You start by installing Xcode and also learn about the Apple developer programs and how to sign up. The last two sections help when you design your app. The first covers how limitations of handheld devices inform various iOS technologies. And the last gives a tour of model differences.

- **Chapter 2, "Objective-C Boot Camp"**—An Xcode project is a container for an app's code, resources, and meta-information. In this chapter, you create your first project. You also get a quick refresher on Objective-C, the language of app development.

- **Chapter 3, "Introducing Storyboards"**—A user of your app sees only the interface. You might implement app behaviors by using incredible code, but the user sees only the effects. In this chapter, you start creating the interface by using a storyboard, a way to see all your app screens at once. You add screens and hook them together and to underlying code. The skills you get from this chapter are a core part of creating iOS apps.

- **Chapter 4, "Auto Layout"**—So far, iOS handheld devices have two different screen sizes and two different orientations for each screen size. Supporting four screen variations can be challenging. In this chapter, you learn and use auto layout, Apple's constraint-based layout engine, to more easily support multiple screen sizes. You even use it to change layouts when the screen rotates.

- **Chapter 5, "Localization"**—iOS devices are available in at least 155 countries and many different languages. As you go through the chapter, you create one app that supports three languages and many countries. You build on Chapter 4, using auto layout to adjust interface elements for different localized string lengths. You also implement language- and country-specific formatting of dates and times as well as left-to-right and right-to-left writing.

- **Chapter 6, "Scrolling"**—You typically want to present more information than fits on a handheld screen. Sometimes the best way to navigate is to scroll through content. Starting with the simplest use case, you use the built-in scroll view UI element to go from simply bouncing a screen to scrolling through elements. You add pan and zoom as well as display item numbers based on scroll position.

- **Chapter 7, "Navigation Controllers I: Hierarchies and Tabs"**—Navigating complex information can be challenging, especially on a phone's relatively small screen size. iOS provides navigation controllers to make the job easier. You start by using `UINavigationController` for moving through a hierarchy of information. Then you use more advanced features providing further customization. Next, you use a tab bar for moving between different kinds of information, and you learn how to work with view controllers that are not on the storyboard.

- **Chapter 8, "Table Views I: The Basics"**—Table views are an important part of apps on both the iPhone and iPad. After learning how they work, you create a table of cars and then implement addition and deletion of items. You go deeper, using a variation of a table for car details. While doing this, you use a picker view for dates and protocols for communicating data and state between scenes.

- **Chapter 9, "Introducing Core Data"**—Core Data provides full data management for a relatively small amount of work. In this chapter, you create a Core Data model for the app and use that data for the list of cars and car detail. Next, you use built-in objects to make managing the table view of cars even easier. You also learn ways to convert a project to use Core Data, and you become familiar with common errors.

- **Chapter 10, "Table Views II: Advanced Topics"**—There are several advanced features of table views for adding polish to apps. As the chapter progresses, you implement different features, including custom cells, sections, sorting, a content index, and searching. You also learn about `UISegmentedControl`, a bit more on debugging, and a good way to use `#define`.

- **Chapter 11, "Navigation Controllers II: Split View and the iPad"**—Apps for the iPad usually require a different design than ones for the iPhone. In this chapter, you create a universal app, one that works on both the iPhone and iPad. You build a separate interface using the iPad-only `UISplitViewController`. You learn how to adapt iPhone views to iPad and how to choose when to use them and when to create something new. In addition, you implement a singleton, a special object that can have only one instance, learn the usefulness of accessor methods, and implement custom transition animations.

- **Chapter 12, "Touch Basics"**—Almost everything a user does on iOS devices involves gestures with one or more fingers. Some features, like buttons, are easy to add. Others take more work. In this chapter, you learn the basics of gesture recognizers and add swiping through car detail views. Then you go deeper, creating a custom gesture recognizer. Finally, you add a draggable view.

- **Chapter 13, "Introducing Blocks"**—From animating views to error responders, blocks are an important tool for using system calls. You learn how to create and use blocks, and use them to add pulsing to a view. You also learn about variable scope and read-only versus modifiable variables. Finally, you replace a protocol using blocks.

- **Chapter 14, "Instruments and Debugging"**—There are two constants in app development: Initial implementations rarely perform as you expect, and there are always bugs. In this chapter, you start by fixing a performance problem using Instruments, a tool for checking performance, memory use, and other important parts of your app. Next, you learn some advanced features of breakpoints in the debugger. Then, you use both tools to solve one of the hardest types of bugs. In this chapter, you also learn about a process for finding and fixing problems, as well as a way to use background tasks.

- **Chapter 15, "Deploying Applications"**—In the final chapter, you take your app from your machine to the App Store. First, you create any required developer credentials and app security certificates. You add icons and launch images, and then you learn about useful extra functionality for your app, such as metrics and bug reporting, as well as some of the main providers. After a brief look at marketing, you get the App Store ready to receive your application, build it, and upload it. The chapter ends with a summary of resources you can use as you continue your journey of creating great iOS apps.

About the Sample Code

As you progress through this book, you develop and refine an application for valet car parking. The CarValet app is used as a practical implementation for concepts you learn. It is not meant to be an app shipped to the masses, although it could serve as a base for one.

Any chapter that involves creating code usually comes with at least two projects: a starter that incorporates code from any previous chapters in the book and a finished project, including all changes made in the chapter. For most of the book, you can use your own completed project from one chapter as the starter for the next. There are a couple places where this is not the case, and the chapter makes that plain.

Except for the very end, the sample code projects use the same unique bundled identifier: com.mauricesharp.CarValet. As a result, you cannot have multiple versions installed in the simulator or on your device at the same time. If you want to have multiple versions, you can simply add a unique string to the end of the identifier, such as com.mauricesharp.CarValet. CH05.portrait. You'll learn the significance of the bundle identifier in Chapter 15.

All the code you write and concepts you learn work with iOS 7 or later. By the end of the first day of availability, more than 35% of existing devices were using the iOS 7, the fastest adoption rate ever. That share will only increase. Adoption rates for iOS are usually very fast, typically hitting 80% or higher within a few months.

Getting the Sample Code

All the sample code is on GitHub, at https://github.com/mauricesharp/Learning-iOS-Development. The code is organized by chapter, with most folders containing starter and finished projects. Some also contain projects for interim steps, as well as folders containing new assets such as images. For example, these are the folders for Chapter 6:

- **CH06 CarValet Starter**—The finished project from Chapter 5, with no changes from Chapter 6. Use either this project or your own project from the end of Chapter 5 as a starting place for Chapter 6 additions.

- **CH06 CarValet Finished**—A project with all the changes from Chapter 6. You can use this as a reference for what changes should have been made or as a starter for the next chapter.

- **CH06 Assets CarImages**—An extra folder with image resources used in changes made during the chapter.

The code will be refreshed as needed. If you see something that needs changing, is missing, or even a way to implement something in a better way, feel free to...

Contribute!

Sample code is never a fixed target. It continues to evolve as Apple updates its SDK and the Cocoa Touch libraries. Get involved. You can pitch in by suggesting bug fixes and corrections, as well as by expanding the code that's on offer. GitHub allows you to fork repositories and grow them with your own tweaks and features, and you can share those back to the main repository using a Pull Request on GitHub. If you come up with a new idea or approach, let us know. We are happy to include great suggestions both at the repository and in the next edition of this book.

Accessing git

You can download this book's source code by using the git version control system. An OS X implementation of git is available at http://code.google.com/p/git-osx-installer. OS X git implementations include both command-line and GUI solutions, so hunt around for the version that best suits your development needs.

There are third-party git tools, as well—some free and some not. These are two of the most popular:

- **SourceTree**—A free git hub client tool available at www.sourcetreeapp.com
- **Tower**—A paid client with a polished UI at www.git-tower.com

Accessing GitHub

GitHub (http://github.com) is the largest git-hosting site, with more than 150,000 public repositories. It provides both free hosting for public projects and paid options for private projects. With a custom web interface that includes wiki hosting, issue tracking, and an emphasis on social networking of project developers, it's a great place to find new code and collaborate on existing libraries. You can sign up for a free account at http://github.com. When you do that, you can copy and modify the book repository or create your own open-source iOS projects to share with others.

Contacting the Author

If you have any comments, questions, or suggestions about this book, please e-mail me at learningios@mauricesharp.com.

This book was written using developer preview releases of both iOS 7 and Xcode. Several different versions were used, though the majority was done using DP (Developer Preview) 4. Large portions of the book were checked against DP 6, the last preview before the final release, but some earlier code does exist, especially in the CarValet sample. Check the errata for updates.

Now read through these pages, write the code, and do the challenges. By the end, you will know how to create iOS apps for handhelds and tablets.

Editor's Note: We Want to Hear from You!

As the reader of this book, you are our most important critic and commentator. We value your opinion and want to know what we're doing right, what we could do better, what areas you'd like to see us publish in, and any other words of wisdom you're willing to pass our way.

You can e-mail or write us directly to let us know what you did or didn't like about this book—as well as what we can do to make our books stronger.

Please note that we cannot help you with technical problems related to the topic of this book, and that due to the high volume of mail we receive, we might not be able to reply to every message.

When you write, please be sure to include this book's title and authors as well as your name and phone or e-mail address.

E-mail: trina.macdonald@pearson.com

Mail: Trina MacDonald
          Senior Acquisitions Editor
          Addison-Wesley Pearson Education, Inc.
          75 Arlington Street, Suite 300
          Boston, MA 02116 USA

1

Hello, iOS SDK

Developing for iOS is a joyful and fun adventure in learning Objective-C and the Apple frameworks. Nowhere else is it so easy and quick to go from an idea to an app you can hold in your hand on an iPhone, iPad, or iPod touch. With your code behind the glass touchscreen, you can turn these devices into anything you can think of. An iOS device can become a flight simulator, an interactive book, or just about anything else you can imagine. In this chapter, you take the first steps in developing for iOS by learning about the iOS Software Development Kit (SDK) and how to get the Xcode toolset installed on your Mac. (It is easy.) In the next chapter, you dive in, create your first iOS app, and get it running on the iOS Simulator.

The iOS family includes the iPhone, the iPad, and the iPod touch. Despite their relatively diminutive proportions compared to desktop systems, they use increasingly powerful multi-core CPUs to run iOS, a first-class version of OS X. iOS comes with a rich and varied SDK that enables you to design, implement, and realize a wide range of applications. For your projects, you can take advantage of the multitouch interface and powerful onboard features using Xcode, Apple's integrated development environment (IDE). In this chapter, you learn about Apple's various iOS Developer Programs and how you can join. Ready? Onward to the next step: getting the Xcode application installed on your Mac.

Installing Xcode

The first step in developing for the iOS platform is to get *Xcode*: the IDE from Apple. Xcode is the tool you use for writing Objective-C applications and compiling them for iOS devices. Apple has recently made installing Xcode as easy as possible by providing Xcode as a free download from the Mac App Store, as shown in Figure 1-1.

Figure 1-1   Xcode in the Mac App Store

To install Xcode, follow these steps:

1. Launch the Mac App Store application on your Mac.

2. Search for Xcode.

3. Click the Free button to install Xcode.

While Xcode is downloading and being installed, you can read the rest of this chapter and learn about the iOS SDK. That is all it takes to install Xcode and get on your way. The rest of this chapter covers the iOS SDK, the devices, and the development programs Apple offers. In Chapter 2, "Objective-C Boot Camp," you start your journey into the Objective-C language and application development in iOS.

About the iOS SDK

The iOS SDK comprises all the libraries you need to write iOS apps, as well as the iOS Simulator for you to try out your apps on your Mac. The SDK is included with the Xcode tool, which is used for creating iOS and Mac applications.

You can register for free for the Apple Online Developer Program and download and explore the full iOS SDK programing environment. However, as discussed in the next section, this program doesn't let you deploy your applications to an actual iOS device, such as the iPhone or iPad. If you want to do that, you need to register and become a member of Apple's iOS Developer Program. There are four program choices, described in Table 1-1.

Table 1-1   **iOS Developer Programs**

Program	Cost	Audience
iOS Developer Program–Individual	$99/Year	Individual developers who want to distribute through the App Store. The apps will appear under your name in iTunes.
iOS Developer Program–Company	$99/Year	For a company or development team that wants to distribute through the App Store. The apps will appear under the company name in iTunes.
iOS Developer Enterprise Program	$299/Year	Large companies building proprietary software for employees and distributing the apps in-house.
iOS Developer University Program	Free	Free program for higher education institutions that provide iPhone development curriculum.

Each program offers access to the same iOS SDK, which provides ways to build and deploy your applications. The audience for each program is specific. Keep in mind that if your company wants to deploy apps in the normal App Store, all you need is the iOS Developer Program–Company. The Enterprise option is available to you only if your company wants to deploy apps in a private in-house App Store.

The following sections discuss the various iOS Developer Programs in more detail.

What You Get for Free

The free program is for anyone who wants to explore the full iOS SDK programming environment but isn't ready to pay for further privileges. The free program limits your deployment options to the iOS Simulator. Although you can run your applications in the simulator, you cannot install those applications to a device or sell them in the App Store.

Although each version of the simulator moves closer to representing iOS, you should not rely on it for evaluating your application. An app that runs rock solid on the simulator might be unresponsive or even cause crashes on an actual device. The simulator does not, for example, support vibration or accelerometer readings. These and other features present on devices are not always available in the simulator. A more detailed discussion about the simulator and its differences from a real device follows later in this chapter, in the section "Simulator Limitations."

While you can download Xcode for free and without registering, joining a full program gives you access to much more, including the ability to run your code on devices, access to early releases, and even the ability to ask questions of Apple developer support engineers.

iOS Developer Program (Individual and Company)

To receive device and distribution privileges, you pay a program fee, currently $99/year, for the standard iOS Developer Program. You can join as an individual or as a company. When you have paid, you gain access to App Store distribution and can test your software on actual iOS hardware. This program adds ad hoc distribution as well, allowing you to distribute prerelease versions of your application to a set number of registered devices. The standard program provides the most general solution for the majority of iOS programmers who want to be in the App Store. If you intend to conduct business by selling applications, this is the program to sign up for.

The standard iOS Developer Program also offers early access to beta versions of the SDK. This is a huge advantage for developers who need to prepare products for market in a timely manner and to match Apple's OS and device upgrade dates. As an example, program members gained access to early versions iOS 7 and Xcode 5 in June 2013.

Caution: Going from Individual to Company Is Hard to Do

Joining the company program currently requires paperwork to prove the company is a valid corporate entity. Changing from individual to company is even harder than starting with a company membership. If you are an individual and expect to become a company, even if only for liability protection, you are better off creating the company first and then joining the Developer Program, or even joining as an individual and then creating a separate company membership later. Joining as a company does take longer, especially with the current requirement for a DUNS (Data Universal Numbering System) number.

Note

In early 2010, Apple restructured its Macintosh Developer Program to match the success of the iOS Developer Program. Currently costing $99/year, the restructured Mac program offers the same kind of resources as the iOS program: code-level technical support incidents, developer forum membership, and access to prerelease software. Neither program offers hardware discounts. The Mac Developer Program does not give access to iOS software and vice versa.

Developer Enterprise Program

The Enterprise Program, currently $299/year, is meant for in-house application distribution. It's targeted at companies with 500 employees or more. Enterprise memberships do not offer access to the Apple public App Store. Instead, you can build your own proprietary applications and distribute them to your employees' hardware through a private storefront. The Enterprise Program is aimed at large companies that want to deploy custom applications such as ordering systems to their employees.

Developer University Program

Available only to higher education institutions, the Developer University Program is a free program aimed at encouraging universities and colleges to form an iOS development curriculum. The program enables professors and instructors to create teams with up to 200 students, offering them access to the full iOS SDK. Students can share their applications with each other and their teachers, and the institution can submit applications to the App Store.

Registering

Register for a free or paid program at the main Apple developer site: http://developer.apple. com/programs/register.

Regardless of which program you sign up for, you must have access to a Mac running a current version of Mac OS X. It also helps to have at least one—and preferably several—iPhone, iPad, and/or iPod touch units. These are for testing to ensure that your applications work properly on each platform, including legacy units. What better excuse for buying that iPhone, iPad, or iPod touch you've been wanting...err, needing for business purposes?

Often, signing up for paid programs involves delays. After registering, it can take time for account approval and invoicing. When you actually hand over your money, it may take another 24 to 72 hours for your access to advanced portal features to go live. There is a very short delay for individual registration, and the delay is longer for companies.

Registering for iTunes Connect, so you can sell your application through the App Store, is a separate step. Fortunately, this is a process you can delay until after you've finished signing up for a paid program. With iTunes Connect, you must collect banking information and incorporation paperwork prior to setting up your App Store account. You must also review and agree to Apple's distribution contracts. Apple offers full details at http://itunesconnect.apple.com. Bear in mind that it can take several days until you are able to upload apps, so do not delay signing up for too long.

iTunes U and Online Courses

When you have registered for any level of iOS development with Apple, you will have access to the World Wide Development Conference (WWDC) videos that Apple releases each year. These high-quality presentations, given by Apple's own engineers, provide great insight into many of the features in iOS and examples of how to use them. In addition, there are many iPhone programming courses available for free on iTunes University (iTunes U inside iTunes) that you can use as a companion to this book.

The iOS SDK Tools

Xcode typically runs a few gigabytes in size and installs an integrated suite of interactive design tools onto your Macintosh. This suite consists of components that form the basis of the iOS development environment and includes the following parts:

- **Project Editor**—This is the heart of Xcode and provides a home for most of the features, including project file and component management, syntax-aware source editing for both the Objective-C language and iOS SDK, as well as a visual editor and a full debugger. A separate window gives access to the full range of documentation for iOS, Xcode, and other supporting documentation.

- **Interface Builder (IB)**—IB is accessed through the project editor and provides a rapid prototyping tool for laying out user interfaces (UIs) graphically, and linking those prebuilt interfaces to your Xcode source code. With IB, you use powerful visual design tools to add the visual elements of your app and then connect those onscreen elements to objects and method calls in your application. In addition to individual screens, you can lay out all your application screens in one document and define the ways each screen moves to the next. You learn about this in Chapter 3, "Introducing Storyboards."

  In Chapter 4, "Auto Layout," you learn how to use IB with another powerful feature of iOS. Auto layout is an advanced rule-based system that enables you to specify the visual relationships between views instead of worrying about pixel-perfect placement. With it, you can create one interface that adapts to different screen orientations and sizes.

- **Simulator**—The iOS Simulator runs on a Macintosh and enables you to create and test iOS apps on your desktop. You can test programs without connecting to an actual iPhone, iPad, or iPod touch. The simulator offers the same API (Application Programming Interface) used on iOS devices and provides a preview of how your concept designs will look and behave. When working with the simulator, Xcode compiles Intel x86 code that runs natively on the Macintosh rather than ARM-based code used on the iPhone. Keep in mind that performance in the simulator is likely very different than on a physical device as it is running with a very different CPU, GPU (graphics processor), and storage/disk format. Your app is likely to be much faster in the simulator and have no memory or communications problems.

- **Performance Tools**—As you run your app in the simulator or on a device, runtime debug gauges give an overview of performance including memory and CPU use. Instruments provides even more detail, profiling how iPhone applications work under the hood. It samples memory usage and monitors performance, enabling you to identify and target problem areas in your applications and work on their efficiency. As you see in Chapter 14, "Instruments and Debugging," if you tune your app as you develop, you will catch issues early and end up with the best performance. Instruments offers graphical time-based performance plots that show where your applications are using the most resources. It is built around the open-source DTrace package developed by Sun Microsystems and plays a critical role in making sure your applications run efficiently on the iOS platform.

  In addition, a static analyzer shows you places where your code might have problems. Simply run the analyzer on a single file or on your whole project to find unused variables, possible logic problems, potential memory leaks, and more.

- **Debugger**—Chapter 14 also covers the debugger. It helps you quickly find and fix problems in your code. With it, you can step through code and inspect values of variables, either in a separate display area or by just hovering the mouse pointer over the source code. You can set rich breakpoints, including conditional triggers and associated actions such as logging messages, playing source, or even running scripts. There is even a console for fine control.

- **Other Features**—Xcode provides a wide array of other features supporting the app development and deployment cycle including built-in support for branching source code control using Git, management of developer certificates and app entitlements, testing device management, and uploading apps to the store.

Together, the components of the iOS SDK enable you to develop your applications. From a native application developer's point of view: You will spend most of your time editing and debugging source, creating the interface, and running your app in the simulator. You will also spend time tuning your code in instruments. In addition to these tools, there's an important piece not on this list. This piece ships with the SDK, but is easy to overlook: Cocoa Touch.

Cocoa Touch is a library of classes provided by Apple for rapid iOS application development. Cocoa Touch, which takes the form of a number of API frameworks, enables you to build graphical event-driven applications with UI elements such as windows, text, and tables. Cocoa Touch and UIKit on iOS is analogous to Cocoa and AppKit on Mac OS X and supports creating rich, reusable interfaces on iOS.

Many developers are surprised by the code base size of iOS applications; they're tiny. Cocoa Touch's library support is the big reason for this. By letting Cocoa Touch handle all the heavy UI lifting, your applications can focus on getting their individual tasks done. The result is compact code, focused on the value provided by your app.

Cocoa Touch lets you build applications with a polished look and feel, consistent with those developed by Apple. Remember that Apple must approve your software. Apple judges applications on the basis of appearance, operation, and even content. Using Cocoa Touch helps you better approximate the high design standards set by Apple's native applications.

Before you start creating apps, make sure you look at the Apple "iOS Human Interface Guidelines" available in the Xcode documentation in the "User Interface" group, or on the web at https://developer.apple.com/appstore/guidelines.html. Also read through the legal agreement you signed for iTunes Connect. Breaking rules is highly likely to result in your app being rejected from the App Store.

Testing Apps: The Simulator and Devices

A physical iPhone, iPad, or iPod touch is a key component of the SDK. Testing on a device is vital. As simple and convenient as the iOS Simulator is, it is not the same as a real device. You want your apps to run on some or all of the iOS device family, so it's important that they run best in the native environment. An iOS device itself offers the fully caffeinated, un-watered-down testing platform you need.

Apple regularly suggests that a development unit needs to be devoted exclusively to development. Reality has proven rather hit and miss on that point. Other than early betas, releases of iOS have proven stable enough that you can use your devices for both development and day-to-day tasks, including making calls on iPhones. It's still best to have extra units on hand devoted solely to development, but if you're short on available units, you can probably use your main iPhone for development; just be aware of the risks, however small. Note that as a developer program member, you have agreed to a non-disclosure agreement (NDA) with Apple. Beware of accidentally showing Apple confidential prereleases to others.

Devices must be proactively set up for development use with Xcode's Organizer. The Organizer also lets you register your device with Apple, without having to enter its information by hand at the provisioning portal. Chapter 15, "Deploying Applications," gives detailed information on how to do this.

When developing, it's important to test on as many iOS platforms as possible. Be aware that real platform differences exist between each model of iPhone, iPad, and iPod touch. For example, two models of the fifth-generation iPod touch offer front- and back-facing cameras; one only offers a front-facing camera. The second-generation iPad and earlier as well as the original iPad-mini do not have retina screens. iPhones all have cameras, which none of the iPod touches offered until the fourth generation. Certain models of the iPad and the iPhone offer GPS technology; other models do not. A discussion of major platform device features along with some device differences follows later in this chapter.

Note

iOS developers do not receive hardware discounts for development devices. You pay full price for new devices, and you pay nonsubsidized prices for extra iPhones and iPads with carrier access. You can get significant savings by buying used and refurbished units. Depending on your country and other circumstances, you might be able to deduct the cost of units from your taxes.

Simulator Limitations

Each release of the Macintosh-based iOS Simulator continues to improve on previous technology. That said, there are real limitations you must take into account. From software compatibility to hardware, the simulator approximates but does not equal actual device performance.

The simulator uses many Macintosh frameworks and libraries, offering features that are not actually present on the iPhone or other iOS devices. Applications that appear to be completely operational and fully debugged on the simulator might flake out or crash on a device itself due to memory or performance limitations on iOS hardware. Even the smallest Mac nowadays comes with 4GB of RAM, whereas the third-generation iPad has only 1GB of RAM. Instruction set differences might cause apps to crash on older devices when they are built to support only newer versions of the ARM architecture. You simply cannot fully debug any program solely by using the simulator and be assured that the software will run bug-free on iOS devices.

The simulator is also missing many hardware features. You cannot use the simulator to test the onboard camera or to get accelerometer and gyro feedback. Although the simulator can read acceleration data from your Macintosh using its sudden motion sensor (if there's one onboard, which is usually the case for laptops), the readings will differ from iOS device readings and are not practical for development or testing. The simulator does not vibrate or offer multitouch input (at least not beyond a standard "pinch" gesture).

> **Note**
>
> The open-source accelerometer-simulator project at Google Code (http://code.google.com/p/accelerometer-simulator/) offers an iPhone application for sending accelerometer data to your simulator-based applications, enabling you to develop and debug applications that would otherwise require accelerometer input. A similar commercial product called iSimulate is available in the App Store for purchase.

From a software point of view, the basic keychain security system is not available on the simulator. You cannot register an application to receive push notification either. These missing elements mean that certain kinds of programs can be properly tested only when deployed to an iPhone or other iOS device.

Another difference between the simulator and the device is the audio system. The audio session structure is not implemented on the simulator, hiding the complexity of making things work properly on the device. Even in areas where the simulator does emulate the iOS APIs, you might find behavioral differences because the simulator is based on the Mac OS X Cocoa frameworks. Sometimes you have the opposite problem: Some calls do not appear to work on the simulator but work correctly on the device. For example, if you store or access files, the simulator is usually case-insensitive (depending on how the Mac is set up), but iOS is case-sensitive.

That's not to say that the simulator is unimportant in testing and development. Trying out a program on the simulator is quick and easy, typically much faster than transferring a compiled application to an iOS unit. The simulator lets you rotate your virtual device to test reorientation, produce simulated memory warnings, and try out your UI as if your user were receiving a phone call. It's much easier to test out text processing on the simulator because you can use your desktop keyboard rather than hook up an external Bluetooth keyboard to your system *and* you can copy and paste text from local files; this simplifies repeated text entry tasks such as entering account names and passwords for applications that connect to the Internet.

Another area the simulator shines is localization. As you see in Chapter 5, "Localization," switching languages for your app is as easy as launching the simulator with the right special flag.

In the end, the simulator offers compromise: You gain a lot of testing convenience but not so much that you can bypass actual device testing.

> **Note**
>
> The simulator supports Video Out emulation. There's no actual Video Out produced, but the simulated device responds as if you've added a compliant cable to its (nonexistent) connector. You can view the "external" video in a floating simulator window.
>
> Apple encourages new applications to use AirPlay to send the content to the user's TV via AppleTV instead of relying on cables.

Tethering

Apple is moving away from tethered requirements in iOS but has not yet introduced a way to develop untethered at the time this book is being written. At this time, all interactive testing is done using a USB cable. Apple provides no way to wirelessly transfer, debug, or monitor applications as you develop. This means you perform nearly all your work tethered over a standard iPhone USB cable.

When you are debugging a tethered unit, try to set things up to reduce accidentally disconnecting the cable. If that happens, you lose the debug session including any interactive debugging, the console, and screenshot features.

You want to invest in a good third-party dock for iPhones or iPod touches and possibly one for iPads. Look for stands that allow the cable to be connected and hold the unit at a comfortable angle for touching the screen. Even better are docks that work in both portrait and landscape. The iPad will work in the Apple doc, though only in portrait. Alternatively, the Apple folding cases that also act as stands work in both orientations.

When tethered, always try to connect your unit to a port directly on your Mac. If you must use a hub, connect to a powered system that supports USB 2.0 or higher. Most modern screens, including Apple's large display, come with built-in powered USB ports, but it pays to double check.

When it comes to the iPad, if the USB connection does not have sufficient power to charge the device, untether your device between testing periods and plug it directly into the wall using its 10W power adapter. Some USB ports provide sufficient power to charge the iPad while you're using it, but this is not a universal situation.

> **Note**
>
> When testing applications that employ Video Out, you can use the Apple-branded component and composite cables or the HDMI digital adapter. These provide both Video Out and USB connections to allow you to tether while running your applications. The Apple-branded VGA cable does not offer this option. You need to redirect any testing output to the screen or to a file because you cannot tether while using VGA output. Another common way to show apps on another device is to use AirPlay screen mirroring. It is a good idea to pick up an AppleTV and test whether your app works well with AirPlay. It can also save money compared to buying adapter cables for both the original 30-pin and newer lightning connectors.

iOS Device Considerations

Designing apps for mobile platforms such as the iPhone or iPad is not the same as designing for the desktop (or laptop). There are several extra considerations such as storage, interaction methods, and battery life. Storage limits, smaller screens, different interaction techniques, and energy consumption are important design considerations when creating your app.

With the iPhone, you are designing for a small touch-based screen with a good, but limited battery life. It is not a desktop with a large screen, a mouse or trackpad, and a physical always-on A/C power supply. Platform realities must shape and guide your development. Fortunately, Apple has done an incredible job designing a platform that leverages flexibility from its set of storage, interaction controls, and constrained battery life.

Storage Considerations

The iPhone hosts a powerful yet compact OS X–based installation. Although the entire iOS fills no more than a few hundred megabytes of space—almost nothing in today's culture of large operating system installations—it provides an extensive framework library. These frameworks of precompiled routines enable iPhone users to run a diverse range of compact applications, from telephony to audio playback, from e-mail to web browsing. The iPhone provides just enough programming support to create flexible interfaces while keeping system files trimmed down to fit neatly within tight storage limits.

Most modern devices come with at least 16GB of onboard Flash-based storage, and some have considerably more. Some older devices running iOS 7 and later have as little as 4GB. Although application size is limited (see the "Note: App Size"), the space for data is much larger. Having said that, be aware that users can check how much space an app is using and might delete hungrier apps.

Note: App Size

Each application is limited to a maximum size of 2GB. To the best of my knowledge, no application has ever actually approached this size, although there are some navigation apps that are pushing new records of deployment size, such as Navigon (1.5GB) and Tom Tom (1.4GB). Apple currently restricts apps larger than 50MB to Wi-Fi downloading. This bandwidth was set at the time that Apple announced its new iPad device and the possibility of delivering universal applications that could run on both platforms. Apple's over-the-air restrictions help reduce cell data load when media-intense applications exceed 50MB and ease the pain of long download times. The 50MB limit is also an important design consideration. Keeping your size below the 50MB cutoff allows mobile users to make impulse application purchases, increasing the potential user base. Check the iTunesConnect guide for the latest maximum size.

Data Access Considerations

Every iOS application is sandboxed. That is, it lives in a strictly regulated portion of the file system. Your program cannot directly access other applications, certain data, and certain folders. Among other things, these limitations require accessing built-in application data using system APIs including the iTunes library, calendar, photos, location services, notifications, reminders, and built-in social services such as Facebook and Twitter.

Your program can, however, access any data that is freely available over the air when the iOS device is connected to a network—including any iCloud documents it owns. Your app can also access data stored in the shared system pasteboard and data shared using a document interaction controller, which offers a limited way to share document data between applications. Apps that create or download data can send those files to applications that can then view and edit that data. In that situation, the data is fully copied from the originating application into the sandbox of the destination application.

Memory Considerations

On iOS, memory management is critical. Apple has not enabled disk swap–based virtual memory for iOS. When you run out of memory, iOS shuts down your application; random crashes are probably not the user experience you were hoping for. With no swap file, you must carefully manage your memory demands and be prepared for iOS to terminate your application if it starts swallowing too much memory at once. You must also take care concerning what resources your applications use. Too many high-resolution images or audio files can bring your application into the auto-terminate zone.

Many parts of the iOS framework cache your image data in order to speed up rendering and application performance. This caching can come at the cost of a larger memory footprint and, on retina devices, if used improperly, can generate more memory pressure on your app. Chapter 14 covers using the Instruments tool to figure out what parts of your application consume too much memory and techniques to address and resolve those issues. It also covers the debug memory gauge, a handy way to see if and when your app is approaching the memory danger zone.

Interaction Considerations

For the iPhone and iPod touch, losing physical input devices such as mice and working with a small screen doesn't mean you lose interaction flexibility. With multitouch and the onboard accelerometer, you can build UIs that defy expectations and introduce innovative interaction styles. The iPhone's touch technology means you can design applications complete with text input and pointer control, using a virtual screen that's much larger than the actual physical reality held in your palm.

Note
Almost all iOS devices support external keyboards. You can connect Bluetooth and USB keyboards to iOS devices for typing. Only a tiny fraction of devices running versions of iOS older than 3.2 have no external keyboard support.

In addition to the touchscreen, users can interact with your app using a smart autocorrecting onscreen keyboard, built-in microphone (for all units except on the obsolete first-generation iPod touch), and an accelerometer that detects current orientation as well as changes. When designing text input, look for ways you can make it easier for the user such as splitting up longer inputs into smaller fields or using auto completion. For longer text areas, make sure you use scrolling text views. Most importantly, try your interface without an external keyboard, as most users will not have one.

Focus your design efforts on easy-to-tap interfaces rather than on desktop-like mimicry. Remember to use just one conceptual window at a time—unlike in desktop applications, which are free to use a more flexible multiwindow display system.

> ### Note
> The iPhone screen supports up to five touches at a time. The iPad screen supports up to about 11 touches at a time. With its larger screen, the iPad invites multihand interaction and gaming in ways that the iPhone cannot, particularly allowing two people to share the same screen during game play. Virtual instruments are another type of app that benefits from lots of fingers. Apple has not specified the maximum number of touches for an iPad at the time of writing this book, but empirical evidence still points to 11. See http://mattgemmell.com/2010/05/09/ipad-multi-touch/.

Energy Considerations

For mobile platforms, wise use of the battery is part of any design. Apple's SDK features help to design your applications to limit CPU use and avoid running down the battery. A smart use of technology (for example, properly suspending themselves between uses) lets your applications play nicely on the iPhone and keeps your software from burning holes in users' pockets (sometimes almost literally, speaking historically). Some programs, when left running, produce such high levels of waste heat that the phone becomes hot to the touch, and the battery quickly runs down. The Camera application was one notable example.

Heavy users of the battery include the Camera app; communications, especially over phone networks; and high-precision location services that use the GPS hardware instead of Wi-Fi triangulation.

Each new generation of iOS device brings some improvement to battery life. Even so, you should continue to keep energy consumption in mind when developing your applications.

Application Considerations

With iOS multitasking, applications can allow themselves to

- Be suspended completely between uses (the default behavior)
- Be suspended with occasional slices of background processing time
- Quit entirely between uses
- Run for a short period of time to finish ongoing tasks
- Create background tasks that continue to run as other applications take control

There is built-in support for background tasks including playing music and other audio, collecting location data, and using Voice over IP (VoIP) telephony. Rather than running a simple background daemon, these tasks are event-driven. Your application is periodically called by iOS with new events, allowing the application to respond to audio, location, and VoIP updates.

Since only the current app can update the UI, Apple supports pushing data from web services. Using Push Notifications sends processing off-device to dedicated web-based services, leveraging their always-on nature to limit on-device processing requirements. Registered services can push badge numbers and messages to users, letting them know that new data is waiting on those servers. Push notifications can allow the user to launch your app or bring it to the foreground, passing a small amount of optional data while doing so.

A special kind of notification gives your app some background execution time for updating changes. And even if you do not use notifications, you can ask the system for regular background processing callbacks. These two mechanisms keep your app up to date before the user brings it into the foreground.

In addition, applications can pass control from one to the other by passing data (using the document interaction controller) and by opening custom URL schemes.

Apple strongly encourages developers to limit the amount of cell-based data traffic used by each application. The tendency of carriers to meter data usage and the overall movement away from unlimited data plans help reinforce this requirement. Applications that are perceived to use too much cell bandwidth might be rejected or pulled from the store. If your application is heavily bandwidth-dependent, you may want to limit that use to Wi-Fi connections.

Almost all device families come with Wi-Fi, mostly 802.11n. For those with cellular connections, many are at least 4G (5.8Mbps HSUPA), and LTE is usually the minimum speed for new devices.

> ### Note
> According to the iPhone Terms of Service, you may not use Cocoa Touch's plug-in architecture for applications submitted to the App Store. You can build static libraries that are included at compile time, but you may not use any programming solution that links to arbitrary code at runtime. That means your app cannot download new or replacement code from a server.
>
> That means bug fix releases need to be just that, full app releases. It also means extra code-level features available by in-app purchase need to ship with the app.

User Behavior Considerations

Although this is not a physical device-based consideration, iPhone users approach phone-based applications sporadically. They enter a program, use it for its intended purpose, and then leave just as quickly. The handheld nature of the device means you must design your applications around short interaction periods and prepare for your application to be interrupted as a user receives a phone call or sticks the phone back into a pocket, purse, or backpack. Keep your application state current between sessions and relaunch quickly to approximately the same task your user was performing the last time the program was run. This can demand diligence on the part of the programmer, but payoff in user satisfaction is worth the time invested. Apple does provide APIs for state restoration, though they are beyond the scope of this book. For more information, start with the chapter on state preservation and restoration in the iOS App Programming Guide available with the documentation that comes with Xcode.

Understanding Model Differences

When it comes to application development, many iOS apps never have to consider the platform on which they're being run. Most programs rely only on the display and touch input. They can be safely deployed to all the current family of iOS devices; they require no special programming or concern about which platform they are running on.

There are, however, real platform differences. The most obvious difference is in screen size between iPhones/iPod touches and iPads. Other differences are usually feature-based such as the types of sensors, the presence or absence of cellular-based networking, and a few other items.

These differences can play a role in deciding how you tell the App Store to sell your software and how you design the software in the first place. Should you deploy your software only to the iPhone family or only to the iPad? To the iPhone, the iPad, and the second-generation and later iPod touch? Or can your application be targeted to every platform? You can use APIs and other techniques to find out what particular features are on a given device and even enable or disable parts of your app. The next section covers some issues to consider.

Screen Size

The most obvious difference is the amount of screen space available on the iPad family versus iPhone or iPod touch. iPads have a large 1024x768 point resolution enabling the display of much more content. iPhones and iPod touches have two display geometries: The 3.5-inch screen used by earlier devices is 480x320 points while the newer 4-inch screen is 568x320.

Notice that the above resolutions are in points, not pixels. Most Apple devices now use a higher resolution retina display, doubling the number of available pixels and better matching human vision. Luckily, instead of worrying about whether the device is 480x320 (non-retina) pixels or 960x640 (retina) pixels, you can work in the world of points. For artwork, Xcode makes it easy to provide any appropriate resolutions and, at runtime, the system automatically chooses the right one.

The Apple human interface guidelines for iPad differ from those for iPhone/iPod touch. Developing for the iPad involves creating unified interfaces rather than the staged screen-by-screen design used by the earlier iPhone and iPod touch units, with their reduced window size. Applications that rely on the greater screen scope that the iPad provides may not translate well to the smaller members of the device family.

Although the retina screens on the newer iPhones and iPod touches look great, their screen dimensions are either 3.5- or 4-inches diagonal. That geometry, combined with the physical realities of the human hand and fingers, prevents these units from providing the same kind of user interaction experience that is possible on the iPad. The interaction guidelines for the newest units remain in lock step with the earlier members of the iPhone and iPod touch family.

Camera

Most applications can assume there will be at least one camera. In most cases, there will be front- and back-facing cameras, though it is still wise to check at runtime. Although some very early devices had no camera (earlier iPod touches or the first-generation iPad), those devices make up a very small percentage of the market, and none of them run iOS 7. There are also devices with just a back-facing or a front-facing camera. The 16GB fifth-generation iPod touch is an example of the latter.

The cameras are useful. You can have the camera take shots and then send them to Flickr or Twitter. You can use the camera to grab images for direct manipulation, augmented reality, and so forth. The iOS SDK provides a built-in image picker controller that offers camera access to your users. There are also ways to capture still images, capture video, play movies, and stream content.

Audio

All iOS devices have headphone jacks and all but the very oldest have speakers as well. The same is true of microphones. The SDK provides ways to capture and play back audio.

The microphones and speakers are also used for accessibility features such as the VoiceOver screen reader. You can build descriptions into your graphical user interface (GUI) elements to enable your applications to take advantage of VoiceOver, so your interfaces can describe themselves to visually impaired end users.

Telephony

It may seem an overly obvious point to make, but the iPhone's telephony system, which handles both phone calls and SMS messaging, can and will interrupt applications when the unit receives an incoming telephone call. Sure, users can suspend out of apps whenever they want on the iPhone, iPad, and iPod touch platforms, but only the iPhone has to deal with the kind of transition that's forced by the system and not a choice by the user.

In addition to phone calls suspending your app, the user is able to open your app while on a call. When that happens, iOS adds a special top bar indicating the status of the call. Make sure to test your interface with the bar open as well as the bar being open then closing. The simulator lets you toggle the in-call status bar on and off.

Consider how the different kinds of interruptions might affect your application. It's important to keep all kinds of possible exits in mind when designing software. Be aware that the choice to leave your app might not always come from the user, especially on the iPhone. Applications that use audio need to take special care to restore the correct state after phone call interruptions.

Another fallout of telephony operations is that more processes end up running in the background on iPhones than on iPod touches and iPads, even those iPads that provide cellular data support. These processes do reduce the amount of free memory, though for modern devices, the effect is minimal. Having said that, it still pays to test your app on cellular-enabled devices.

Core Location and Core Motion Differences

Core Location depends on three different approaches, each of which might or might not be available on a given platform. These approaches are limited by each device's onboard capabilities. Wi-Fi location, which scans for local routers and uses their MAC addresses to search a central position database, is freely available on all iPhone, iPad, and iPod touch platforms.

Cell location, however, depends on an antenna that is available on the iPhone and on suitably equipped iPad models. This technology triangulates from local cell towers, whose positions are well defined from their installations by telephone companies.

The final and most accurate strategy, GPS location, depends on appropriate hardware. Most modern iPhones and iPads come with the hardware, though as of the writing of this book, no iPod touches do. You can use built-in calls to check for the presence of the hardware.

The third-generation iPhone 3GS introduced a built-in compass (via a magnetometer) along with the Core Location APIs to support it. The iPhone 4 and iPad 2 added a three-axis gyro, which provides pitch, roll, and yaw feedback, all of which can be solicited via the Core Motion framework. Most modern iPhone and iPad devices have both the compass and gyro. Modern iPod touches have only the gyro as of the writing of this book.

Vibration Support and Proximity

Vibration, which adds tactile feedback to many games, is limited to iPhones. The iPad and iPod touch do not offer vibration support. Nor do they include the proximity sensor that blanks the screen when holding an iPhone against your ear during calls. The UIDevice class offers direct access to the current state of the proximity sensor.

Processor Speeds

All modern devices come with fast Apple-designed ARM processors. The CPU includes a good amount of fast access RAM for code execution. To save power, some devices run the CPU at slower speeds (underclocked), and all have the ability to suspend parts of the hardware. Some earlier devices had relatively slow processors and much less execution space though they make up an ever-decreasing part of the market. Targeting iOS 6 or later will avoid those early devices.

The important thing is to run your app on a representative sample of the kinds of devices you are targeting. Make sure it performs well on the devices your customers will use. This is especially important if you plan to support iPhones prior to the 4 as well as first-generation iPads.

If your application isn't responsive enough on the older platforms, consider working up your code efficiency. There is no option in the App Store at this time that lets you omit earlier generation iPhone devices from your distribution base, although setting your minimal required iOS version to 6.0 or higher will automatically exclude most older devices.

There are a few places you can look for an idea of the market share for each version of iOS. When a new version is released, check the Apple-oriented press, such as the following sites:

- **MacOSRumors:** www.macrumors.com
- **MacWorld:** www.macworld.com
- **TUAW:** www.tuaw.com

You can also check with data analysis and mobile information companies, though you might have to dig to find the information:

- **Canalys:** www.canalys.com
- **Chitika:** chitika.com
- **Flurry:** www.flurry.com/index.html
- **Gartner:** www.gartner.com/technology/home.jsp
- **IDC:** www.idc.com

Finally, app developer David Smith regularly updates what OS versions are used in his app:

- http://david-smith.org/iosversionstats/

OpenGL ES

OpenGL ES offers a royalty-free cross-platform API for 2D- and 3D-graphics development. It is provided as part of the iOS SDK. Most devices support OpenGL ES 2.0 with the newest support version 3.0. Some very early units supported only OpenGL ES 1.1, but you are unlikely to encounter them.

> **Note**
>
> Devices and features remain a moving target. Apple continues to introduce new units and make changes to iOS. As new devices are introduced, check Apple's information pages, especially the technical specs. For iOS, make sure you read the release notes. In addition, you can look for summary pages on the Internet. One good source is Wikipedia: http://en.wikipedia.org/wiki/List_of_iOS_devices.

iOS

One obvious difference is the version of iOS running on any given device. iOS device users are quick to upgrade to new releases. It took comparatively little time for most devices to upgrade from iOS 3 to 4, then 4 to 5, and 5 to 6. Although there are some models that cannot upgrade to iOS 7, they make up a rapidly shrinking percentage of the total number of units.

There are definitely differences in functionality between various versions of the OS. For example, in addition to the new look, iOS 7 introduces UI Motion, UI Dynamics, and Text Kit. All three offer ways to increase engagement with your user. Usually it is a decision of supporting the current version plus the one before—in this case, iOS 6 and 7. It is fairly easy to test for the availability of features and enable or disable access in your app. The largest difference is the user experience, though it is fairly easy to create interfaces that work on both 6 and 7 if you use the built-in UI elements.

Ultimately, what you support should depend on what your potential customers are using. If they are all using devices with iOS 7, there is no need to support 6. This book focuses on iOS 7, though with the exception of some specific features, everything will work in iOS 6. In addition, using auto layout, covered in Chapter 4, makes adapting your interfaces to each iOS much easier.

> **Note**
>
> Apple expanded the iOS version of Objective-C 2.0 starting with the 4.0 SDK to introduce blocks. Blocks are a technology that have been around for decades in languages such as Scheme, Lisp, Ruby, and Python. Blocks allow you to encapsulate behavior as objects, so you can pass that behavior along to methods as an alternative to using callbacks. This new feature is introduced in Chapter 13, "Introducing Blocks."
>
> Other features, such as literals, better property declarations, and fast enumeration, make Objective-C even more powerful. You work with all these features as you progress through the book.

Summary

In this chapter, you have taken the first steps in learning to create applications for iOS. You have downloaded and set up Xcode and covered some of the basics of the devices and Apple's developer program. Through the rest of the book, you continue your journey into the world of creating iOS apps. Each chapter focuses on important skills for some area of development. Though the territory might be unfamiliar, the book provides a focused map to guide you through.

In the next few chapters, you learn the Objective-C language and create your first application in Xcode. From there, you continue to expand your knowledge of iOS development, including user interface elements, adapting to screen size and language, performance tuning, debugging, and how to ship your app. When you are ready, turn the page to start writing your first iOS app.

Objective-C Boot Camp

The first step in learning any programming language is to write a Hello World program. In this chapter, you start by creating an iOS Hello World program and get a quick tour of Xcode, the main tool for developing iOS apps.

Next you learn the fundamentals of Objective-C. With that base, you explore classes and objects, the main building block of apps. While doing that, you create the CarValet project, practice building classes, and learn about properties.

You end the chapter exploring subclassing by working through a guided challenge. By the time you have finished the chapter, you will have the beginnings of the CarValet project and enough Objective-C knowledge to work through this book.

Building Hello World the Template Way

Xcode's preconfigured templates offer the easiest path to creating a Hello World–style sample application. In the following steps, you create a new project, edit it to say "Hello World," and run it on the iOS Simulator. As you build your first Xcode project, you get a general introduction to this key tool, as well as discovering how to create and navigate a project.

Creating the Hello World Project

Launch Xcode and you will see the Xcode welcome page shown in Figure 2-1. (If you have dismissed this page, you can bring it back up by choosing Window > Welcome to Xcode or pressing Cmd-Shift-1.) Click Create a New Xcode Project. You can also create a new project in Xcode by choosing File > New > Project (or pressing Cmd-Shift-N). The template selection window shown in Figure 2-2 appears. By default, the template selection window is embedded in a large new window, called a *workspace*. Workspaces include all of Xcode's editing and inspector features in a single window.

Figure 2-1   Xcode welcome window

In the template selection window shown in Figure 2-2, select Application under the iOS menu on the left side, select Single View Application, and click Next.

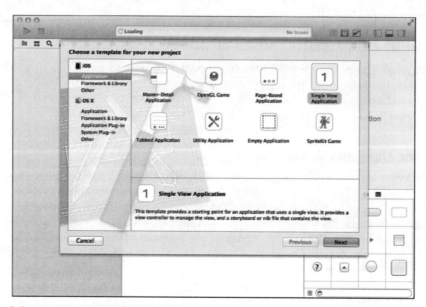

Figure 2-2   Xcode template selection window

Caution: Screenshots and Functionality May Vary

Xcode is updated on a regular basis. This means the instructions might vary slightly from the actual items in Xcode or on Apple websites. When you encounter this situation, there is usually some obvious way to accomplish the same action. Check for controls or items that have the same name in a different position. Also look for similar names in similar areas. If this does not work, check the book website (www.informit.com/title/9780321862969) for updates and, failing that, please send feedback.

The Xcode project options panel is up next, as shown in Figure 2-3. Follow these steps in this window:

1. For Product Name, enter HelloWorld.

2. Set Company Identifier to your company, using reverse domain-naming notation. For example, Maurice's is com.mauricesharp or com.klmapps, Rod's is com.strougo, while Erica's is com.sadun. If you have no identifier, Apple suggests using edu.self.

3. Click Next.

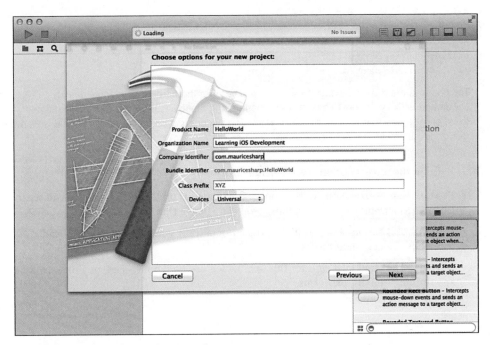

Figure 2-3   Xcode project options panel

Class Prefix lets you specify a prefix to include with your classes that Xcode will automatically add to your class definitions. Using prefixes is a good way to avoid conflicting with current or future iOS system classes. For example, if you created the class `SlideMenuViewController`, and a system update adds a class with the same name, at best your application would fail to build. Worse, your app could end up creating instances of the system class instead of your own, and that could lead to very nasty bugs. If you specified a prefix of "MS," Xcode would create a file and class called `MSSlideMenuViewController`, avoiding the potential conflict. This book does not use prefixes to keep names shorter. You should add one based on your developer or company name.

Pro Tip: Prefix Formats

The most typical class prefixes are a short string of capitalized letters (Apple recommends three characters), usually the initials of you or your company. This is the style you usually find inside companies or for open source software. However, it is not the most readable. The following are some variations of a symbol for an imaginary slide menu class I did not write. Try just glancing at the items in the list, much like you would when scanning through code. See which ones are easier to recognize quickly:

```
SlideMenuViewController
MSSlideMenuViewController
MS_SlideMenuViewController
msSlideMenuViewController
ms_slideMenuViewController
```

The chances are the all caps prefix with no separator is the hardest to identify quickly. Lowercase is likely the next easiest, then those using a separator. When you use class prefixes, choose one that makes it easy to work with symbol names. In the long run, you will save lots of development and debugging time.

Other items in the project options panel include the following:

- **Product Name**—The name of the app, as it will appear on the device. As you will see in Chapter 15, "Deploying Applications," you can change this later.

- **Organization Name**—Used as part of the automatically generated source file header comments for copyright attribution.

- **Devices**—The target platform for this app, which can be iPhone, iPad, or Universal for an app running on both platforms.

The last Xcode panel asks you for the location to save your Hello World project. If you want, Xcode can also set up a local git repository for your project. For this Hello World example, leave the Source Control box unchecked. Choose a folder and click Create, as shown in Figure 2-4.

Figure 2-4   Xcode project folder location panel

After you click Create, you should see your new Hello World project opened in Xcode, along with several files Xcode generates for you. As of this point, you have a fully functional, if not particularly interesting, app. If you click the Run button right now, your app will show a blank white screen with a status bar at the top.

A Quick Tour of the Xcode Project Interface

You will spend a lot of time developing apps in Xcode. Figure 2-5 shows Xcode after expanding the project files and selecting the ViewController.m file.

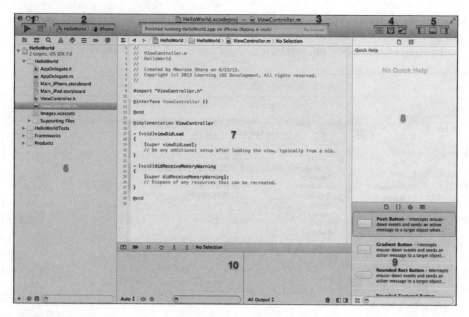

Figure 2-5   Parts of the Xcode project interface

The following is a quick tour of the Xcode interface. Later chapters go into more detail on different parts. The following numerals correspond to the numerals shown in Figure 2-5:

1. Pressing the Run (left-hand) button compiles and launches your app in the simulator or on a device. Pressing and holding Run gives you other options, such as testing or analyzing your project. The right-hand button stops a running app, a build, or whatever action you have kicked off.

2. In this two-sided popup, the left side is for selecting and editing schemes, or what you want to run and how to run it. On the right side, you select where you want to run your app: in one of the simulators or on an attached device.

3. The status area shows the result of the previous action or the progress of the current one. Actions include building the app, running the app, or even downloading the app to a device.

4. The Editor buttons let you configure what shows up in the editor (the area labeled 7 in Figure 2-5). The left-hand button, selected in the figure, shows just one item, the main editor area. The Assistant button in the middle divides the editor area into two and shows any related file, typically the header file, on the right. The final button shows

source code differences, including the ability to look at different versions, on the right. This is useful if you are using a source code repository to track your changes. Note that you cannot show both the Assistant and Source code views at the same time.

5. This area controls the general layout of the workspace views in Xcode. The first button shows or hides the Navigator (area 6 in Figure 2-5). The second button controls the Debugger (area 10). The final one shows Utilities (areas 8 and 9).

6. The Navigator shows you different views of the project. The icons at the top control the type of view. In Figure 2-5, the folder icon is selected, so the area is showing the file and group-based project navigator. The others are a project symbol navigator, the magnifying glass for project-wide search, the alert triangle for build issues, and then a unit test navigator, a debug navigator, breakpoints list, and finally a log view.

One point of confusion can be the difference between what is shown in the file and group navigator versus what is in the Finder. The two can be different. In the Navigator, groups are represented by folder icons, but these are not the same as the folders in the Finder. If you want the groups and Finder folders to be the same, you need to add those folders in the Finder and save source files in the right place.

7. The Editor is where you will spend most of your time. Currently, it is showing the source editor. It can also display Interface Builder, the data model editor, or runtime debug gauges.

8. The utilities area shows different types of utilities including: file information; quick help (currently selected); inspectors for data model details; view attributes such as color, button title, or image; and size, including screen size and constraints.

9. At the bottom of the utilities area is the libraries area. Here you can find drag-and-drop components for building an app in Interface Builder, code snippets, and even pictures and other media. Note that you might see only the row of library selector icons at the bottom of the utilities area. To expand the library, click and drag the library selector bar up.

10. The debugger area has three main pieces. The top bar has controls for pausing and stepping through a running app on the left, and the current selection or file on the right side. The bottom is divided into two main areas, one for inspecting variables and the other for the console. You will see more of this throughout the book, especially in Chapter 14, "Instruments and Debugging."

Now that you have an understanding of Xcode, it is time to start creating your first app.

Adding the Hello World Label

By default, Xcode creates a project that is set to run on the iPhone or iPad; when you create a project, the next one uses your previous settings. New projects start with all the classes and supporting files you need to create your application. This includes a basic home screen with no content. When you run a new project, it shows a blank white screen.

The quickest way to see Hello World on the screen is to add a label to your project. With your project open, follow these steps (see Figure 2-6):

1. Check that the project is set to run in the simulator by looking at the right side of the scheme popup menu (area 2 in Figure 2-5.) If the right-hand side does not say "iPhone Retina (4-inch)," click on that side of the scheme menu and choose that item. Note that the dropdown menu has two parts: The left side is the scheme popup, and the right allows you to choose where the app will run. You will be adding the Hello World label only to the iPhone storyboard; therefore, it is important that you run your app on the iPhone simulator instead of the iPad.

2. Click and select the `Main_iPhone.storyboard` file in the Xcode Project Navigator. Interface Builder opens in the editor area.

   In the rare circumstance that the Interface Builder view does not open, check to make sure you do not have the third button, for showing source code control file differences, selected (refer to area 4 of Figure 2-5). If the source code control button is not selected, try selecting an `.m` or `.h` file and then choosing the storyboard file again. If that still does not work, quit Xcode and relaunch it.

3. In the bottom-right search panel, type `label` and drag the label object onto the storyboard canvas.

4. Type `Hello World` into the Text field in the attributes inspector shown in the Utility area on the left of the Xcode workspace. Adjust the label so it looks nice. Figure 2-6 shows the label horizontally centered in the top part of the view controller.

5. Click the Run button to compile and run your Hello World app.

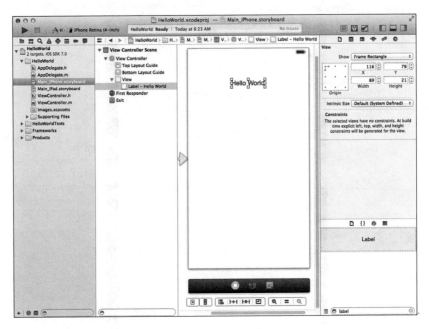

Figure 2-6   Adding the Hello World label via Interface Builder in Xcode

When you run your Hello World app, you should see the iPhone Simulator (see Figure 2-7). If you see the iPad Simulator, remember to switch the run destination to the iPhone Simulator by using the Scheme popup menu.

This is all it takes to create a simple Hello World program. You didn't even have to write any code. In the next section, you learn some Objective-C basics, and you come back to this Hello World app and add some code to learn and practice Objective-C.

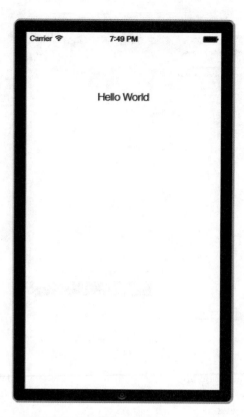

Figure 2-7   Hello World app running in the iPhone Simulator

Fitting the Simulator to Your Screen

The simulator shown in Figure 2-7 is a full-size, 4-inch retina display and can be quite large, especially if you are working on a laptop screen. You can change the size of the displayed screen using the Simulator Window > Scale menu.

Objective-C Boot Camp

To become a proficient iOS developer, you need to learn Objective-C, the main programming language of iOS and the Mac. Objective-C is a powerful object-oriented language that lets you build applications leveraging Apple's Cocoa and Cocoa Touch frameworks. In this chapter, you learn basic Objective-C skills that help you get started with iOS programming. You learn about interfaces, methods, and more. To round things out, you get to practice what you have learned by adding some custom classes to your Hello World application.

> **Note**
>
> This section covers enough Objective-C for you to understand the code shown in this book and to implement the challenges at the ends of most chapters. However, there is a lot more to Objective-C than we can cover in such a small section, and a lot of it is important in writing production-quality apps. A good source for learning Objective-C is *Learning Objective-C 2.0: A Hands-on Guide to Objective-C for Mac and iOS Developers*, 2nd edition, by Robert Clair. You can also use *Objective-C Programming: The Big Nerd Ranch Guide* by Aaron Hillegass, which has more advanced coverage.

The Objective-C Programming Language

Objective-C is a strict superset of ANSI C. C is a compiled, procedural programming language developed in the early 1970s at AT&T. Objective-C, which was developed by Brad J. Cox in the early 1980s, adds object-oriented features to C. It blends C language constructs with concepts that originated in Smalltalk-80.

Smalltalk is one of the earliest and best-known object-oriented languages. It was developed at Xerox PARC as a dynamically typed interactive language. Cox layered Smalltalk's object and message-passing system on top of standard C to create his new language. This approach allowed programmers to continue using familiar C-language development while accessing object-based features from within that language. In the late 1980s, Objective-C was adopted as the primary development language for the NeXTStep operating system by Steve Jobs' startup computer company, NeXT. NeXTStep became both the spiritual and literal ancestor of OS X, and through that, of iOS.

Objective-C 2.0 was released in October 2007 along with OS X Leopard, introducing many new features, such as properties and fast enumeration. In 2010, Apple updated Objective-C to add blocks, a C-language extension that provides anonymous functions and lets developers treat code like objects. (You see more in Chapter 13, "Introducing Blocks.") In the summer of 2011, Apple introduced Automatic Reference Counting (ARC). This extension greatly simplified development, allowing programmers to focus on creating application semantics rather than worry about memory management. (To be precise, ARC is a compile time extension, not a language extension.) More recently, Objective-C has expanded to include literals (how you define static objects) and subscripting (how to access elements in arrays and dictionaries). Apple continues to improve the Objective-C language, so keep your eye on the release notes of new iOS and Xcode updates.

Object-oriented programming brings to the table features that are missing in ANSI C. An *object* is a data structure that is associated with a publicly declared list of function calls. Every object in Objective-C has *instance variables*, which are the fields of the data structure, and *methods*, which are the function calls the object can execute. Object-oriented code uses these objects, variables, and methods to introduce programming abstractions that increase code readability and reliability. You might sometimes see instance variables referred to using the contraction *iVars*, and the term *messages* instead of methods.

Objects are defined using a *class*. You can think of a class as a template for what the final object should be like: how to check state (instance variables) and what behaviors (methods) it supports.

Classes usually do not do much by themselves. Their main use is creating fully functional objects. Each of these objects is called an *instance*, that is, a functional entity based on the template provided by the class. "Instance variables" are called that because they only exist in an instance of the class, not in the class itself. When you typed the text "Hello World" into the field in step 4, you set the value of the `text` instance variable for a `UILabel` object. The `UILabel` class does not have any `text` variable to set. All the work and code of creating the label instance was done for you.

Object-oriented programming lets you build reusable code units that can be decoupled from the normal flow of procedural development. Instead of relying on process flow, object-oriented programs are developed around the custom data structures provided by objects and their methods. Cocoa Touch on iOS and Cocoa on Mac OS X offer a massive library of these custom objects. Objective-C unlocks that library and lets you build on Apple's toolbox to create effective, powerful applications with a minimum of effort and code.

> **Note**
>
> iOS Cocoa Touch class names that start with NS, such as NSString and NSArray, harken back to NeXT. NS stands for NeXTStep, the operating system that ran on NeXT computers. Apple acquired NeXT in 1996.

Calling Functions: a.k.a. Message Sending

Objective-C is a superset of the C programming language, and as such, it follows mostly the same syntax. The one item that confuses most people learning Objective-C is the message-passing syntax used to invoke, or run, a method implemented by an instance of a class. Unlike function calls that use the `function_name(arguments)` syntax, messages are sent to objects using square brackets.

A message tells an object to perform a method. It is the object's responsibility to implement that method and produce a result. The first item in the brackets is the receiver of the message—that is, the object implementing the method; the second item is the method name and possibly some arguments to that method that together define the message you want sent. In C, you might write this:

```
printCarInfo(); // This function prints out the info on the default car
```

but in Objective-C, you use this:

```
[self printCarInfo]; // This method prints out the info on the default car
```

In C, the object on which you want to run the function is assumed to be the current object. In some languages, you would see `this.printCarInfo()`. In Objective-C, `self` identifies the current object, much as `this` does.

In other languages, you can call a function on another object by using something like `someOtherObject.printCarInfo()`, assuming that `someOtherObject` has the `printCarInfo()` function. In Objective-C, you would use this:

```
[someOtherObject printCarInfo]; // This method prints out the info on the default car
```

Despite the difference in syntax, methods are basically functions that operate on objects. They are typed using the same types available in standard C, in addition to Objective-C types. Unlike with function calls, Objective-C places limits on who can implement and call methods. Methods belong to classes. And the class interface defines which of the methods are public, or declared to the outside world.

It starts to look different when a function has one or more arguments. Suppose you had to pass the car object `myCar` to the `printCarInfo` method. In C, you would write this:

```
printCarInfo(myCar); // Print the info from the myCar object
```

In Objective-C, you would write this:

```
[self printCarInfo:myCar]; // Objective-C equivalent, but with poor method name
```

In Objective-C, you are encouraged to interleave the method names with the parameters, so you would likely rename the `printCarInfo` method to this:

```
[self printCarInfoWithCar:myCar]; // More clear as to which car it will print out
```

Taking our example a step further, suppose you have to pass along the font size to use in displaying the information. In C, you would type this:

```
printCarInfo(myCar,10); // Print the info using a font size of 10
```

In Objective-C, you would use this:

```
[self printCarInfoWithCar:myCar withFontSize:10]; // Print using a font size of 10
```

You can see right away how much clearer the Objective-C method call is when you read through your code. Let's take it one step further. Now assume that you have three parameters: the car object, the font size of the info, and a Boolean denoting whether the text should be bold or not. In C, you would use this:

```
printCarInfo(myCar, 10, 1); // Using 1 to represent the value of true in C
```

In Objective-C, you would use this:

```
[self printCarInfoWithCar:myCar withFontSize:10 shouldBoldText:YES];
```

> **Note**
>
> In Objective-C/Cocoa, the Boolean type is provided by `BOOL`. Unlike C, the standard values for a `BOOL` are `YES`/`NO` rather than true/false. Though you could import the standard C library and use that Boolean type, it is not recommended.
>
> The interleaving of the method name with the parameters works to make the Objective-C message passing (or function calling in C) easy to read and understand. In C and other languages, you have to always reference the function definition to determine what each parameter is supposed to be and their order. In Objective-C, it is clear and right in front of you. You get to really appreciate this when you use some of the `UIKit` method calls, which take five or more parameters.

In Objective-C, the parameters of a method are separated by the colon (`:`) character, with a part of the method name included between the parameter values. Your method can return a value or an object, the same way a C function can return a value. In C, you would use this:

```
float mySpeed = calculateSpeed(100,10); // returns the speed based on distance / time
```

In Objective-C, your method call would look like this:

```
float mySpeed = [self calculateSpeedWithDistance:100 time:10];
```

> **Note**
>
> If the Objective-C method declaration and message-passing syntax are not clear to you, do not worry. In the next section of this chapter, you get ample opportunity to practice.
>
> Apple provides the following diagram and text to illustrate the parts of Objective-C method calls. For more information, see https://developer.apple.com/library/ios/#referencelibrary/ GettingStarted/RoadMapiOS/Languages/WriteObjective-CCode/WriteObjective-CCode/ WriteObjective-CCode.html.

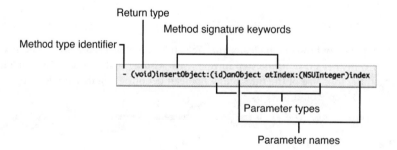

Methods bring one more powerful feature in addition to making the arguments clear. A method has access to everything defined in the class. In other words, it can access any instance variables or methods implemented by the instance of its class. In this sense, how a method works is transparent to the calling object. The implementation of a particular method or even the whole class can completely change without requiring a change anywhere else. This can be very useful as you upgrade or replace features of your app: perhaps making them more efficient, updating for new hardware features, or even completely replacing how you handle communications.

Classes and Objects

Objects are the heart of object-oriented programming. You define objects by building classes, which act as object creation templates. In Objective-C, a class definition specifies how to build new objects that belong to the class. To create a car object, for example, you define the Car class and then use that class to create new objects on demand. As in C, implementing a class in Objective-C is done in two places: a header file and implementation file. The header file specifies how the outside world can interact with the class: the instance variables and their types, and the methods with their arguments and any return types. It is like a contract promising how instances of your class will interface with other objects. The implementation file is how your class will provide values for instance variables or respond when a method is called. The implementation file can, and usually does, have private variables and methods in addition to the public ones declared in the header file.

Each class lists its public instance variables and methods in a header file using the standard C .h convention. For example, you might define a SimpleCar object like the one shown in Listing 2-1. The Car.h header file shown here contains the interface that declares how a SimpleCar object is structured.

Listing 2-1   **Declaring the** SimpleCar **Interface (**SimpleCar.h**)**

```
#import <Foundation/Foundation.h>
@interface SimpleCar : NSObject {
    NSString *_make;
    NSString *_model;
    int _year;
}

@property float fuelAmount;

- (void)configureCarWithMake:(NSString*)make
                       model:(NSString*)model
                        year:(int)year;
- (void)printCarInfo;
- (int)year;
- (NSString*)make;
- (NSString*)model;

@end
```

Class, variable, and method names use camel case in Objective-C. Instead of creating identifiers_like_this, in Objective-C, you would use identifiersLikeThis. Classes start with an initial capital letter, while other names start with lowercase. You can see this in Listing 2-1. The class name, SimpleCar, starts with an initial capital. The instance variable fuelAmount, is camel case, but starts with a lowercase letter. The methods, declarations starting with a minus sign toward the bottom of the listing, also use camel case. One example is the following:

```
- (void) printCarInfo
```

In Objective-C, the @ symbol is used with certain keywords. Two of the items shown here (@interface and @end) delineate the start and end of the class interface definition. This class definition describes an object with five methods and four instance variables.

Of the four variables, only fuelAmount is *public*, meaning it is available outside of an instance of the SimpleCar class. The three inside the curly braces can only be used by an instance of SimpleCar or any subclasses. The three variables could be defined inside the .m implementation file, but then they would only be available to the SimpleCar class. This is a problem if you want subclasses such as ElectricCar to share these variables.

Two of the private variables, _make and _model, are strings. Objective-C usually uses the NSString object-based class instead of the byte-based C strings defined with char *. As you see throughout this book, NSString offers far more power than C strings. With this class, you can find out a string's length, search for and replace substrings, reverse strings, retrieve file extensions, and more. These features are all built into the object libraries for iOS (and Mac OS).

Both the private _year variable and the public fuelAmount are simple types. One is an int, and the other a float.

Using a leading underscore character (_) is a common practice in Objective-C to differentiate between an instance variable and its *getter* method. You know that using x = _year; is getting the value directly from the instance variable, whereas x = [self year]; is calling the getter method - (int)year;, which might do some needed computation or calculation before returning the value. A *setter* method is like a getter, except it is used for setting the value of an instance variable. Again, you use setters to perform any extra work such as updating an onscreen count. You learn more about creating and using getters and setters below as well as throughout the book.

The first public method is the following:

```
configureCarWithMake:model:year:
```

This entire three-part declaration, including the colons, is the name, or *selector* (sometimes also called *signature*), of that single method. That's because Objective-C interleaves parameters inside the method name, using a colon to indicate each parameter. In C, you'd use a function such as setProperties(char *c1, char *c2, int i). Objective-C's approach, although heftier than the C approach, provides much more clarity and self-documentation. You don't have to guess what c1 and c2 mean because their use is declared directly within the name:

```
[myCar configureWithMake:c1 model:c2 year:i];
```

Every method has a return parameter. `printCarInfo` returns `void`, `year` returns `int`, while both `make` and `model` return `NSString*`. As in C, these refer to the type of data returned by the method. `void` means the method returns nothing. In C, the equivalent function declaration to the `printCarInfo` and `year` methods would be `void printCarInfo()` and `int year()`.

Using Objective-C's "method name interspersed with arguments" approach can seem odd to new programmers but quickly becomes a much-loved feature. There's no need to guess which argument to pass when the method name itself tells you what items go where. You see this a lot in iOS programming, especially when you use calls to `respondsToSelector:`, which lets you check at runtime if an object responds to a particular message.

Notice that the header file in Listing 2-1 uses `#import` to load headers rather than `#include`. When you import headers, Objective-C automatically skips files that have already been added. You can therefore add duplicate `#import` directives to your various source files without penalties.

Defining the Implementation

The `.h` file tells the outside world how to interact with a class of an object. The `.m`, or implementation file, contains the code that powers an object. Listing 2-2 shows some of the implementation for the `SimpleCar` class.

Listing 2-2   **Implementation of** `SimpleCar` (`SimpleCar.m`)

```
#import "SimpleCar.h"
@implementation SimpleCar

- (void)configureCarWithMake:(NSString*)make
                       model:(NSString*)model
                        year:(int)year {
    _make = [make copy];
    _model = [model copy];
    _year = year;
}

- (void)printCarInfo {
    NSLog(@"--SimpleCar-- Make: %@ - Model: %@ - Year: %d - Fuel: %0.2f",
            _make, _model, _year, [self fuelAmount]);
}

- (int)year {
    return _year;
}

- (NSString*)make {
    return [_make copy];
```

```
}

- (NSString*)model {
    return [_model copy];
}
@end
```

Implementation files are usually paired with a header, so the first thing is importing that header, in this case `SimpleCar.h`. Most classes import other headers and possibly declare constants or other things. The main part of the class implementation is between `@implementation` and `@end`.

`configureCarWithMake:model:year:` sets values for each of the private instance variables. Except for `fuelAmount`, it is not possible to individually set a value for the current car. It is possible to read values for any individual element using the accessor methods such as `-(int) year` defined toward the bottom of Listing 2-2. Because the header used `@property` for `fuelAmount`, the setter and getter methods, as well as the underscore version of the variable are created for you. You will see more about that in the "Properties" section later in the chapter.

The first method sets the value of the three non-public instance variables. `printCarInfo` prints the current values of all instance variables to the log. The final three methods are getters for the private instance variables.

One thing you might notice is that both the configuration method and getters work with copies of the string. This is a common defensive practice to avoid other code accidentally changing the value of the string. This makes sense when you realize each variable is a pointer to an `NSString` object. If you assign it to the string argument, it is pointing to the same memory location as the original owner of the string. If that original owner changes the value of the string, the car object gets that new value because it is pointing to the same address.

Assigning and returning copies of strings results in new objects at different memory locations. Those copies can be changed without changing the car's make or model. Note that the only time you need to worry about this is for long-lived instance variables. Temporary strings and objects do not need to be copied.

Creating Objects

You have learned that a class defines one or more objects. How does a class become an object at runtime? To create an object, you tell the class to allocate enough memory for a new object and return a pointer to that memory location. You then tell the new object in that newly allocated memory to initialize itself. You handle the memory allocation by calling the `alloc` method, and the initialization occurs when you call the `init`. If you were creating an instance of the `SimpleCar` object, you could use the following two lines of code:

```
SimpleCar *myCar = [SimpleCar alloc];
[myCar init];
```

Although it might not seem like a lot of code, it is something you will type often. Luckily, Objective-C supports *nesting* of message sends. This means you can use the result of one method as the receiver of another one. The return value of the set of nested messages comes from the last message.

In the previous code, the first line allocates the memory for the car object and returns a pointer to that object. The second line takes the allocated car and initializes it. The init method returns the initialized object, though the second line of code does not need to use the return value as myCar is already pointing to the right object. With nesting, you can shorten the two lines into one:

```
SimpleCar *myCar = [[SimpleCar alloc] init];
```

Here, the source code sends the message alloc to the SimpleCar class resulting in a new car object, and then sends the message init to the newly allocated SimpleCar object and returns the initialized car. This nesting is typical in Objective-C.

The "allocate followed by init" pattern you see here is the most common way to instantiate a new object. The class SimpleCar performs the alloc method. It allocates a new block of memory sufficient to store all the instance variables listed in the class definition, zeros or nils out any instance variables, and returns a pointer to the start of the memory block. The newly allocated block is an instance and represents a single object in memory.

Some classes, like views, use custom initializers such as initWithFrame:. As you will see later in this chapter, you can write custom initializers such as initWithMake:model:year: fuelAmount:. The pattern of allocation followed by initialization to create new objects holds universally. You create the object in memory and then you preset any critical instance variables.

Inheriting Methods

Objects inherit method implementations as well as instance variables. A SimpleCar is a kind of NSObject, so it can respond to all the messages that an NSObject responds to. That's why myCar can be allocated and initialized with alloc and init. These two methods are defined by NSObject and can be used to create and initialize any instance of SimpleCar, because it is derived from the NSObject class. All objects in Objective-C eventually inherit from NSObject, at the top of their inheritance tree.

Tip: Inherited Methods

If you look in the .h file for your Hello World AppDelegate or ViewController class, you will find that AppDelegate inherits from UIResponder and ViewController from UIViewController, which in turn inherits from UIResponder. If you select and right-click UIResponder and select Jump to Definition, Xcode shows you the declaration for UIResponder, and there you can see that it, too, inherits from NSObject.

As another example, when you have arrays in your app, you will likely use NSArray or NSMutableArray, a kind of NSArray that allows you to add or delete items. All array methods can be used by mutable arrays, their child class. You can count the items in the array, pull an object out by its index number, and so forth.

> ### Caution
>
> Some classes are not "subclassing" friendly. They are implemented as a *class cluster*; that is, the class itself creates objects of some other type of class, depending on some criteria. NSArray and NSString are both examples of clusters. They use different classes to create objects in the most memory-efficient way. All such classes are clearly marked in the documentation. Check before subclassing a system class.

A subclass can implement a method with the same selector as its superclass. Invoking the method on the subclass object calls the new method. Depending on how the method is implemented, it either specializes or overrides the behavior of the superclass. *Specializing* means you also let the superclass method run. You do this by sending the message to the *super* object, a special identifier that stands for the superclass. *Overriding* means you do not send the message to your superclass; that behavior never occurs.

A good example is initialization. You need to make sure every class in the inheritance chain gets a chance to initialize itself, though your method needs to worry only about calling its own superclass. Initialization methods always contain a line in this form:

```
self = [super init];
```

This sets the current object instance to whatever the superclass creates. Initializing the rest of your object follows.

> ### Warning: Initialize the Superclass First
>
> It is very important to call the superclass initialization method before doing anything specific to your class. If you try to manipulate your object first, nothing provided by any superclass, including NSObject, is set up. Although instance variables might return a value and method calls might work, the object is in an undefined state. At best, you will get a crash during initialization. More likely, you will get some random crash or strange behavior at a later date. You learn how to write a correct init method later.

Pointing to Objects

You have learned that creating objects is easy to do with classes. When you have a newly created (allocated) and initialized object, the next step is to reference and use your new object. In Objective-C, you use the * character to denote that a variable is a pointer to an object. You saw this in Listing 2-2, where the _make, and _model variables were declared. The _make and _model variables both point to objects (NSString) and require a * before the variable name.

Other variables are primitive types, not objects. The variable itself, or more precisely, the memory location, holds the value instead of the address of the object. The _year variable is an example of a primitive type (int), so it does not require a * character.

To send a message to an object, you leave out the * character. In the following code snippet, the myCar object is created as an instance of the SimpleCar class, and its printCarInfo method is called.

```
SimpleCar *myCar = [[SimpleCar alloc] init];
[myCar printCarInfo];
```

If you wanted to create another pointer to the same SimpleCar instance, you could use this:

```
SimpleCar *sameCar = myCar;
```

or this:

```
id sameCar = myCar;
```

id is a special type that translates to NSObject *, which already includes the * character, denoting a pointer to an object.

It is important to realize that myCar and sameCar point to the same object. If you change the make, model, and year using the sameCar pointer, then [myCar printCarInfo] shows the new values.

The CarValet App: Implementing Car Class

Now it is time to practice creating methods, variables, and classes in Objective-C. To start, create a project for the CarValet app. As you continue through this book, you will take this app from these simple beginnings to a full iOS app, one that runs on iPhone and iPad using native user interface elements and other parts of iOS.

The first step is creating the CarValet project. You do this in the same way you created HelloWorld:

1. In Xcode, choose File > New > Project (or press Cmd-Shift-N).

2. Select an iOS Single View Application template, the same one you selected in Figure 2-2 when you created the HelloWorld project. Choose Next.

3. In the next panel, enter CarValet for the name of the app. Make sure Devices is set to Universal. The Organization and Company Identifier fields should be prepopulated with whatever you entered for HelloWorld. Change those fields if needed and select Next.

4. Save the project and Xcode opens the project in a new window. If you already have a project open, there may be an Add To option at the bottom of the Save panel. If so, make sure the selected option is something like Don't Add to Any Project or Workspace.

> **Note**
>
> The code for this example—and all the other examples in this chapter—is found in the sample code for this book. See the Preface for details about downloading the book's sample code from GitHub.

Just like HelloWorld, your CarValet project already comes with two classes provided by the Xcode template: the `AppDelegate` and `ViewController` classes. Now you add a `Car` class representing a simple automobile:

1. To start, right-click the CarValet folder in the Navigation window and select New File. You could also choose File > New > File from the menu or press Cmd-N.

2. In the new file dialog, select Cocoa Touch under iOS and then select Objective-C Class, as shown in Figure 2-8; then click Next.

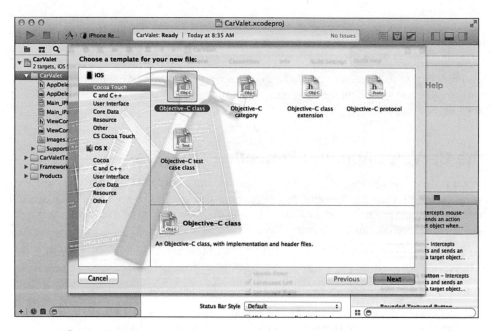

Figure 2-8   Selecting Objective-C as the file type for the `Car` class in Xcode

3. In the following panel, enter `Car` for the Class field and `NSObject` in the Subclass Of field, as shown in Figure 2-9. You are creating a `Car` class, which inherits from `NSObject`. Click Next to show the save panel.

4. There is one more area at the bottom of the save panel allowing you to specify Target membership. For now, the important thing is to make sure the CarValet target is checked, as shown in Figure 2-10. When you are sure the box is checked, click Create to have Xcode create the `Car` class and place it inside your project.

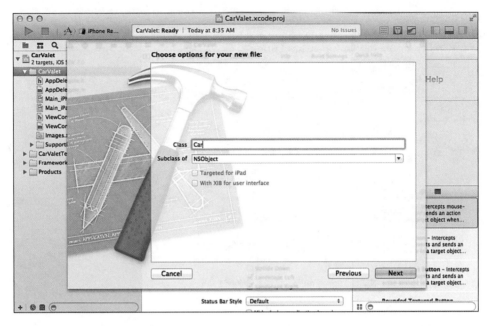

Figure 2-9   Setting the class name as Car and inheriting from NSObject

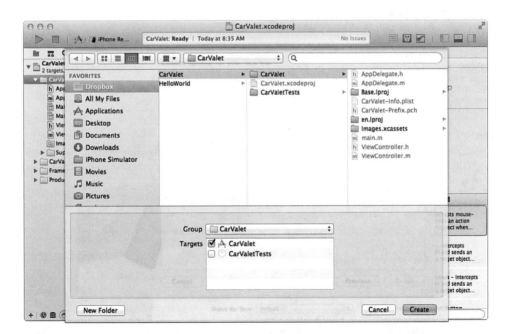

Figure 2-10   Setting the target for the Car class in Xcode

With the `Car` class created, Xcode automatically opens to the `Car.m` implementation file. You need to switch to the header file in order to add the instance variables for the `Car` class. Edit the `Car.h` header file so that it matches Listing 2-3.

Listing 2-3   `Car.h` **Header File**

```
//   Car.h
//   CarValet

#import <Foundation/Foundation.h>        // 1

@interface Car : NSObject {              // 2
    int       _year;                     // 3
    NSString *_make;                     // 4
    NSString *_model;                    // 5
    float     _fuelAmount;               // 6
}

- (id)initWithMake:(NSString *)make      // 7
            model:(NSString *)model
             year:(int)year
       fuelAmount:(float)fuelAmount;

- (void)printCarInfo;                    // 8
- (float)fuelAmount;                     // 9
- (void)setFuelAmount:(float)fuelAmount;
- (int)year;                             // 10
- (NSString*)make;
- (NSString*)model;

@end
```

The first two lines are comments. In Objective-C, two forward-slashes (//) tell the compiler to ignore the text that follows. They can be used for single line or inline comments. You can use a combination of forward-slash and asterisk to enclose a comment block—that is, multiple lines of comments:

```
// this is a one line comment
// and so is this, even though it follows the last one
[MyObject doSomething]; // and this is an end of line comment
/*
  And finally a lot of comments started by a forward-slash and asterisk
  that can include lots of lines and ends with an asterisk then forward-slash.
*/
```

The first non-comment line imports the Foundation framework, the workhorse of iOS and Mac OS. Here you find everything from arrays and dictionaries to dates and predicates, from URL connections and JSON parsing to the most important object of all, NSObject. Next is the @interface declaration for the Car class. You can see that Car inherits from NSObject via the :NSObject tag.

The statements between @interface and @end define the class. Inside the brackets of the @interface declaration, you can see the four instance variables that will hold the information needed by the Car object. The methods define how to send messages to a car.

Here's what happens in the numbered lines in Listing 2-3:

1. Import the Foundation Framework.

2. Define the interface for the Car object, a subclass of NSObject.

3. _year is the year the car was manufactured. This is stored as an integer, a primitive non-object type.

4. _make is the make of the car, stored as an NSString object.

5. _model is the model of the car, stored as another NSString object.

6. _fuel is the amount of fuel in the Car's tank, stored as a floating-point value.

7. The initWithMake:model:year:fuelAmount: method initializes a newly allocated object and sets the car's make, model, and year, as well as the fuel in the tank. It is a custom init method as described earlier.

8. The printCarInfo method prints out the Car's information to the debugging console.

9. This pair of methods, fuelAmount and setFuelAmount:, are the getter and setter for the _fuelAmount instance variable.

10. The remaining three methods are getters for the other private instance variables.

The initWithMake:model:year:fuelAmount: method is a clear example of how method names and parameters are interleaved in Objective-C. These four parameters take in values of type NSString*, NSString*, int, and float. Notice the hyphen that starts both method declarations. It indicates that the methods are implemented by object instances. For example, you call [myCar printCarInfo] and not [Car printCarInfo]. The latter sends a message to the Car class rather than an actual car object instance. You see uses of class versus object methods (indicated by + rather than -) later in the book, though a full discussion is beyond the scope of this book.

Method calls can be long. For example, the following call initializes an iOS UIAlert object:

initWithTitle:message:delegate:cancelButtonTitle:otherButtonTitles:

Each parameter specifies different items that show, or optionally show, in the alert box, including a title, a message, a title for the cancel button, and other button titles. Another parameter specifies a *delegate*.

The use of a delegate is another common pattern in iOS and provides a way for two objects to communicate using a defined set of messages (called a *protocol*). These messages form a contract between the provider of the protocol and the delegate. Basically, the delegate promises to implement the messages, and the provider promises to use them appropriately. A protocol is defined separately from a class; they are two different kinds of things. Any class can choose to use the protocol as either the delegate or the implementer.

`UIAlert` uses this pattern to inform the delegate what button the user presses. As you go through the book, you see more complex uses of the delegate pattern by system objects. You also implement that pattern for some of the objects you build—that is, you create protocols and add the delegate code to objects.

> ### Tip: Switching Between Header and Implementation Files
>
> In Xcode, the keyboard shortcut Ctrl-Cmd-Up arrow allows you to move to the next counterpart, and the Ctrl-Cmd-Down arrow allows you to move to the previous counterpart. This shortcut makes it very easy to quickly switch between your header and implementation files.

Implementing `Car` Methods

Together, a header file and an implementation file store all the information needed to implement a class and use it with the rest of an application. The implementation source code is usually contained in an `.m` (either for *i*mplementation or *method*) file. As the name suggests, the methods file of a class provides the implementation of the methods and how the class will carry out its functionality.

In a larger class, in addition to the methods defined in the `.h` file, you would likely implement other supporting non-public methods. Unlike public methods, you do not need to declare the private methods before you define them. The compiler is smart enough to figure out where private methods are, even if you implement them after code that uses them. You will see more on this as you work through this book.

In addition, you can declare local instance variables that are visible only to the object. You do this inside curly braces below the `@implementation` statement. For example, you could add a local lemon flag:

```
@implementation Car {
    BOOL    isALemon;
}
```

For most objects with instance variables, one of the first methods you typically implement is `init`. Create a first version of this method by copying the bold code in Listing 2-4 to the `Car.m` implementation file.

Listing 2-4   `Car.m` **Implementation File** `init` **Method**

```
//  Car.m
//  CarValet
```

```
#import "Car.h"

@implementation Car

- (id)init {
    self = [super init];        // 1
    if (self != nil) {          // 2
        _year = 1900;           // 3
        _fuelAmount = 0.0f;     // 4
    }
    return self;                // 5
}
```

Here's what happens in the numbered lines in Listing 2-4:

1. The first task is calling init on the superclass (NSObject). This ensures that any initialization required by NSObject is complete before the Car class–specific initializations are carried out.

2. A check is made to ensure that self was in fact initialized. If so, the rest of the object is set up.

3. The _year instance variable is set to 1900 as a default.

4. The _fuelAmount is set to 0.0f as a default. Although not strictly necessary, including f at the end of the number tells the compiler this is a float rather than some other type of floating point value.

5. The value of self returned. Note what is returned depends on the check in step 2. If the superclass returned nil, nil is returned. Otherwise the now-initialized Car object is returned.

At this point, the Car object is initialized, but it still does not respond to the custom initializer starting with initWithMake:, the printCarInfo, or any of the other method calls. If you tried to call those methods, you experience a runtime crash, with a message in the Console half of the Debug Area saying "unrecognized selector sent to instance."

Sending a Message to nil and Sending an Unrecognized Message (Selector)

In Objective-C, the terms *sending a message* and *performing a selector* mean basically the same thing: calling a method on an object. While it is perfectly safe to send any message to nil, trying to send a message to an object that does not implement the message results in a runtime crash. This is a common mistake newcomers to Objective-C make, and as you see later in the book, there are ways to check that an object or a class will respond to a message (selector) before you send it. Also note that the message can be implemented anywhere in the inheritance tree. That is, the message can be defined either in the specific class or any class that object inherits from.

Add the next two methods, the custom initializer and `printCarInfo`, by adding the contents of Listing 2-5, the `init` method in the `Car.m` implementation file.

Listing 2-5   `Car.m` **Implementation** `initWithMake:...` **and** `printCarInfo` **Methods**

```
- (id)initWithMake:(NSString *)make                              // 1
           model:(NSString *)model
            year:(int)year
      fuelAmount:(float)fuelAmount {

    self = [super init];                                          // 2
    if (self != nil) {                                            // 3
        _make = [make copy];                                      // 4
        _model = [model copy];
        _year = year;
        _fuelAmount = fuelAmount;
    }

    return self;                                                  // 5
}

- (void)printCarInfo {
    if (!_make) return;                                           // 6
    if (!_model) return;

    NSLog(@"Car Make: %@", _make);                                // 7
    NSLog(@"Car Model: %@", _model);
    NSLog(@"Car Year: %d", _year);
    NSLog(@"Number of Gallons in Tank: %0.2f", _fuelAmount);
}
```

Here's what happens in the numbered lines in Listing 2-5:

1. `initWithMake:...` allocates a new object and then assigns each value passed into the `Car` object's properties.

2. Call the superclass initializer method first.

3. Check if the superclass was able to initialize the object and, if so, initialize the rest of the object. If not, `self` will be `nil`.

4. Now set all the instance variables for this `Car` object.

5. At this point, `self` will either be `nil` if the superclass failed to initialize or an initialized car object. Note that returning `nil` is the correct thing to do if initialization failed.

6. Only print if `Car` has a make and model defined.

7. Use NSLog to print the values to the console.

NSLog is a wrapper around the C printf function. As a wrapper, it uses some of the same formatting cues as printf. %d is used for integers, %f for float values, and %@ for objects. You can see the full list of printf flags in the Xcode documentation.

The Real Open Curly Brace Convention

The listings in this book put the open curly brace ({) for methods right after the method name. This is done for space and is not the typical coding convention. Instead, the curly brace is on a line by itself. You can see this in any Xcode autogenerated code such as that in ViewController.m.

Base Initializer

Everything done by the custom init method in Listing 2-4 can be done by the custom initializer in Listing 2-5. Instead of duplicating effort, simplify the first method by replacing it with the following code:

```
- (id)init {
    return [self initWithMake:nil model:nil year:1900 fuelAmount:0.0f];
}
```

initWithMake:model:year:fuelAmount: allows the caller to specify values for all the public instance variables—that is, to completely specify the initial state of a new car object. Any other initialization method can call the complete one. This is another common pattern in Objective-C. initWithMake:... is called a *base initializer*, as it is the basic one that any other customized initializer can call. You will see this pattern used throughout the book.

Accessors

The last five methods declared in the .h file are used for accessing information about the car, in this case, instance variables. Add the code in Listing 2-6 to the bottom of Car.m.

Listing 2-6 Car.m **Implementation of Accessor Methods**

```
- (float)fuelAmount {
    return _fuelAmount;                    // 1
}

- (void)setFuelAmount:(float)fuelAmount{
    _fuelAmount = fuelAmount;              // 2
}

- (int)year {                             // 3
    return _year;
}
```

```
- (NSString*)make {
    return [_make copy];
}

- (NSString*)model {
    return [_model copy];
}
```

Here's what happens in the numbered lines in Listing 2-6:

1. Return the current value of the _fuelAmount instance variable.

2. Set the value of the _fuelAmount instance variable to the fuelAmount argument.

3. Define the remaining instance variable getters. Each one returns the value of the related instance variable.

Usually, each of the public instance variables would be hidden by getters and setters. The variables themselves would be declared in the .m file, so only their car object could directly access them. Even in this simple class, that means eight extra methods to declare and define, a lot of repetitive code. Luckily, there is a better way.

Properties

Properties let you define instance variables and let the compiler take care of creating the *accessor methods*—that is, methods that access (get or set) variables or information. The compiler also generates the underscore version of the variable. Declaring a property is simple:

```
@property float fuelAmount;
```

This tells the compiler to create one instance variable and two methods:

```
float _fuelAmount;
- (float)fuelAmount;
- (void)setFuelAmount:(float)fuelAmount;
```

You might have noticed that the variable and method declarations are identical to the ones in Listing 2-3.

The compiler generates the underscore version of the variable for you. Any non-car objects have to use the getter and setter. The variables and method implementations are added at compile time. And if you need to do something special, just implement the particular accessor method in the .m file and the complier uses that instead.

Update the Car object to use properties by following these steps:

1. Open Car.m file in the editor and remove the implementations of the fuelAmount, setFuelAmount:, year, make, and model methods.

2. Open Car.h and remove the declarations for the methods you removed in step 1.

3. Change the part of the header file defining the instance variables to look like the
following (the new code is in bold; make sure you remove the underscores):

```
@interface Car : NSObject

@property int year;
@property NSString *make;
@property NSString *model;
@property float fuelAmount;

- (id)initWithMake:(NSString *)make
```

Using properties might sound redundant. After all, the class definition shown in Listing 2-3
defines the accessors and the underscore instance variables are private. So why use properties?
It turns out that there are more advantages to using properties over using publicly declared
methods than saving space, especially encapsulation and dot notation.

Encapsulation

Encapsulation allows you to hide implementation details away from the rest of your application, including any clients that use your objects. The object's internal representation (instance
variables) and its behaviors (methods, and so on) are kept separate from the way the object
declares itself to the outside. You are free to completely change the internal implementation
as long as the publicly declared details stay the same. Properties provide ways to expose object
state and other information in a well-structured and circumscribed manner.

Properties are not, however, limited to use as public variables. They play an important role in
class definitions as well. Properties allow you to add smart proactive development techniques,
including lazy loading and caching, to the rest of a class implementation. That's why classes
can be property clients as well as providers.

In addition to hiding details, encapsulation enables reusing the same code in other projects.
A well designed `Car` class is not limited to CarValet. You could use it for a car collector app,
dealership inventory tracker, or even a game. As you develop more apps, careful use of encapsulation results in a collection of plug and play classes that shorten your development cycles.
And classes are not limited to data representation; they can also implement interface behaviors,
custom views, and even server communications.

Dot Notation

Dot notation allows you to access object information without using square brackets. Instead
of calling `[myCar year]` to read the value of the `year` instance variable, you use `myCar.year`.
Although this might look as if you're directly accessing the `year` instance variable, you're not.
Properties always invoke methods. These, in turn, can access an object's data. So you're not
breaking an object's encapsulation because properties rely on these methods to bring data
outside the object.

Using `my.year` results in a call to `[myCar year]`. By using properties, the compiler will automatically generate the required accessor methods. If you need to do something special, such as check a remote web server, define the `year` accessor method in the `.m` file and the compiler will use your method instead of generating one.

Due to method hiding, properties simplify the look and layout of your code. For example, you can access properties to set a table's cell text via the following:

```
myTableViewCell.textLabel.text = @"Hello World";
```

rather than this more cumbersome code:

```
[[myTableViewCell textLabel] setText:@"Hello World"];
```

The property version of the code is more readable and ultimately easier to maintain. For those used to using dots for indicating structure, it is important to remember that dots are invoking methods, not just traversing an object hierarchy.

To practice using dot notation, replace the implementation of `printCarInfo` with the code in Listing 2-7.

Listing 2-7   `Car.m` **Updated Implementation** `printCarInfo`

```
- (void)printCarInfo {
    if (self.make && self.model) {                                    // 1
        NSLog(@"Car Make: %@", self.make);                            // 2
        NSLog(@"Car Model: %@", self.model);
        NSLog(@"Car Year: %d", self.year);
        NSLog(@"Number of Gallons in Tank: %0.2f", self.fuelAmount);
    } else {                                                          // 3
        NSLog(@"Car undefined: no make or model specified.");
    }
}
```

The key changes in Listing 2-7 are the following:

1. Change the two checks and return to checking that both the make and model are non-nil.

2. Use dot notation for printing each of the variable values to the log.

3. If there is no make or model, update the log.

The code in Listing 2-7 is easier to read even after adding extra functionality for printing something when the car is not fully specified. It is also clear that the variables are object-level items instead of just a local variable. Although that is less relevant in such a short method, imagine looking through code that is much longer.

You could make the same type of change to the initializer, though there are risks, especially if you use custom accessors. And using dot notation in custom accessors can be the most dangerous of all—see the following sidebar, "Why Use Underscore: No Dot, No Accessor."

Why Use Underscore: No Dot, No Accessor

One common source of errors is using dot notation either in a properties custom accessor or in a method that could call the custom accessor. A simple example:

```
- (void) setMake:(NSString*)newMake {
    if (![newMake isEqualToString:self.make) {
        self.make = newMake;
    }
}
```

This code is a custom setter for the make attribute. It checks to see if the new make is the same as the old make, and if not, sets the car's make to the new one. But there is a lurking problem.

The call to `self.make = newMake` translates into:

```
[self setMake:newMake];
```

The result is a recursive call to the same setter, which in turn calls the same setter, and so on. An infinite recursion—well, at least until your app crashes.

The correct thing to do is use the underscore version of the variable in the setter. The assignment becomes:

```
_make = newMake;
```

The safe thing is for setters and getters to use the underscore version of the iVar they set or return. Any `init` method as well as custom initializers should also use the underscore version.

Creating and Printing Cars

You now have a `Car` class in your CarValet project, but it is not called or used anywhere in your app. Open up the `ViewController.m` implementation file and follow these steps:

1. Add the `#import "Car.h"` statement below the last import at the top of the `ViewController.m` file.

2. Add the `viewWillAppear:` method in Listing 2-8 below the `viewDidLoad` method.

Listing 2-8 `ViewController.m` `viewWillAppear:` **Method**

```
- (void)viewWillAppear:(BOOL)animated {
    [super viewWillAppear:animated];

    Car *myCar = [[Car alloc] init];              // 1
    [myCar printCarInfo];                         // 2
```

```
    myCar.make = @"Ford";                                // 3
    myCar.model = @"Escape";
    myCar.year = 2014;
    myCar.fuelAmount = 10.0f;


    [myCar printCarInfo];                                // 4


    Car *otherCar = [[Car alloc] initWithMake:@"Honda"   // 5
                                        model:@"Accord"
                                         year:2010
                                   fuelAmount:12.5f];
    [otherCar printCarInfo];                             // 6
}
```

The method `viewWillAppear:` is called each time this `ViewController`'s view is about to be displayed on the screen. It is a convenient location to create and call your `Car` object. Here's what happens in the numbered lines in Listing 2-8:

1. The `myCar` object is allocated and initialized as an instance of the `Car` class.

2. The `printCarInfo` method is called, but because `make` and `model` are `nil` (uninitialized), it will print the car undefined message. If you look back at Listing 2-7, inside the `printCarInfo` method, you can see the `if` statement which checks that `make` and `model` are not `nil` and the resulting message when they are.

3. The `make`, `model`, `year`, and `fuelAmount` are set. The `NSString` values are prefixed with the @ character before the double quote, and the float value has a trailing `f`.

4. The `printCarInfo` method is called a second time, and this time `make` and `model` are set so the information for the Ford will print.

5. A new car is created using the custom initializer to set values.

6. Unlike the call to `printCarInfo` after the plain `init` in step 2, this call prints out the Honda's details as both `make` and `model` are defined.

When you run the code you will see something like the following in the console:

```
2013-07-02 08:35:44.267 CarValet[3820:a0b] Car undefined: no make or model specified.
2013-07-02 08:35:44.269 CarValet[3820:a0b] Car Make: Ford
2013-07-02 08:35:44.269 CarValet[3820:a0b] Car Model: Escape
2013-07-02 08:35:44.270 CarValet[3820:a0b] Car Year: 2014
2013-07-02 08:35:44.270 CarValet[3820:a0b] Number of Gallons in Tank: 10.00
2013-07-02 08:35:44.270 CarValet[3820:a0b] Car Make: Honda
2013-07-02 08:35:44.271 CarValet[3820:a0b] Car Model: Accord
2013-07-02 08:35:44.271 CarValet[3820:a0b] Car Year: 2010
2013-07-02 08:35:44.272 CarValet[3820:a0b] Number of Gallons in Tank: 12.50
```

Properties: Two More Features

The current version of CarValet is all you need for the next chapter. This section covers two different variations of the project. Each variation comes with the sample code for this chapter.

Some of you might be wondering if it is a good idea to change the make, model, and year of a car after it has been created. So far, you have been using properties in their default read and write configuration. However, it is easy to set a property to read only. All you have to do is add a little extra when declaring a property. The general form of the property declaration is the following:

```
@property <(qualifier1, qualifier2, ...)> <type> <property_name>;
```

You have already used the `type` and `property_name`. The make of a car has a `type` of `NSString*` and a `property_name` of `make`. Qualifiers let you change a number of things including setting a property as read only, specifying different levels of object ownership for memory management, and even changing the name of the default setters and getters. Another qualifier is covered later in this chapter.

If you do not specify qualifiers, the property is created with defaults: read and write, owned by the object declaring the property, and default setter and getter names. If you want a different behavior, all you need to do is change the defaults.

Creating read-only properties is as simple as including the `readonly` qualifier. Setting `make`, `model`, and `year` to read only is done by changing their declarations in the `.h` file:

```
@property (readonly) int year;
@property (readonly) NSString *make;
@property (readonly) NSString *model;
```

Do this and try to build the project. You get three errors in the `ViewController.m` file that you are trying to set the value of read-only properties. Fix the errors by removing or commenting out the code in `ViewController.m` and setting read-only values.

But say you wanted the properties to be read only outside the class, but read/write inside. That is also easy as you can re-declare property inside the `.m` file. You add or override class interface declarations by adding the following code to the `Car.m` file just before the `@implementation` statement:

```
@interface Car ()
@property (readwrite) int year;
@property NSString *make;
@property NSString *model;
@end
```

A car object uses the new definitions of the instance variables. Note that you do not need to specify `readwrite` as that is the default.

To see this working, add a method to update the `make` attribute by following these steps:

1. Open `Car.h` and add the following method declaration below `printCarInfo`:

```
- (void)shoutMake;
```

2. Open `Car.m` and add this method just below `printCarInfo`:

```
- (void)shoutMake {
    self.make = [self.make uppercaseString];
}
```

3. Open `ViewController.m` and remove the calls to create and print the first `myCar` object.

4. Add a call to `shoutMake` and another to `printCarInfo` to the end of `viewWillAppear:`. The end will now look like (new code in bold):

```
    ...
                                    fuelAmount:12.5f];
    [otherCar printCarInfo];

    [otherCar shoutMake];
    [otherCar printCarInfo];
}
```

When you run the code, the last call to `printCarInfo` shows the car make in all caps. You can convince yourself everything works as expected by trying to set the `make` of a `myCar` in `viewWillAppear:`. You get an error that you are trying to set the value of a read-only value.

Custom Getters and Setters

In another variation, sometimes you do not want the default getters and setters generated by the compiler. As an example, suppose you want `self.fuelAmount` to return liters instead of gallons, but only if a new property, `showLiters`, is `YES`. You also want to access this new property using `isShowingLiters`.

It only takes one line in `Car.h` to add the property. Add the following code below the existing properties:

```
@property (getter = isShowingLiters) BOOL showLiters;
```

The qualifier sets a different name for the getter. Instead of using `aCar.showLiters` to check the value of the variable, you use `aCar.isShowingLiters`, a more descriptive name. Setting the value still uses `aCar.showLiters`:

```
if (aCar.isShowingLiters) {
    aCar.showLiters = NO;
}
```

Similarly, you can change the name of the setter like this:

```
@property (setter = setTheFuelAmountTo:) float fuelAmount;
```

However, a custom setter behaves a bit differently than a custom getter. You need to send a message to use the custom setter. This works:

```
[aCar setTheFuelAmountTo:20.0f];
```

but this does not:

```
aCar.setTheFuelAmountTo = 20.f;
```

Atomic and Nonatomic

With the new property defined, it is time to override the getter for `fuelAmount`. Add this code to the end of `Car.m`, just below `printCarInfo`:

```
- (float)fuelAmount {
    if (self.isShowingLiters) {
        return (_fuelAmount * 3.7854) ;
    }
    return _fuelAmount;
}
```

This custom getter returns liters instead of gallons if `isShowingLiters` is `YES`. (Of course, the formula only works for U.S. gallons, not U.K. ones, but world harmony of measurement standards is beyond the scope of this book.) Note this is another case where you must use the underscore version of the instance variable to avoid an infinite loop. See the sidebar, "Why Use Underscore: No Dot, No Accessor."

After you add that method, you will notice a yellow warning triangle noting something about a "writable atomic property...." A what? In this case, the warning is quite correct. Another property qualifier is the atomicity of the variable. That is, can there be only one object accessing the variable at any one time (*atomic* or synchronous access), or can multiple objects on different threads access the object at the same time (*nonatomic* or asynchronous access)?

When you develop in a multithreaded environment, you can use the `atomic` property to make sure assignment works as expected. When you set an object as `atomic`, the compiler adds code to automatically lock objects before they are accessed or modified and unlock them after. This ensures that setting or retrieving an object's value is performed fully, regardless of concurrent threads. However, it is also incredibly expensive and runs the danger of an infinite wait for unlock.

All properties are atomic by default; however, you can use the `nonatomic` property qualifier, a generally far safer and more performant alternative:

```
@property (nonatomic) NSString *make;
```

Marking your properties `nonatomic` does speed up access, but you might run into problems if two competing threads attempt to modify the same property at once. Atomic properties, with their lock/unlock behavior, ensure that an object update completes from start to finish before that property is released to a subsequent read or change, but they should be used only where required.

Some argue that accessors are not usually the best place for locks and cannot ensure thread safety. An object might be set to an invalid state, even with all atomic properties.

In practice, most properties are marked as `nonatomic` and other mechanisms are used to deal with possible issues of thread-safe access. For a deeper discussion, see the chapter on properties in *Learning Objective C 2.0*, second edition, by Robert Clair.

Get rid of the error by changing the declaration of the `fuelAmount` property in `Car.h` (and while you are there, you can add the `nonatomic` qualifier to all your properties, including `showLiters`):

```
@property (nonatomic) float fuelAmount;
```

Now you need to test that the change works. Once again, you only need to add a couple of lines to the end of `viewWillAppear:` in `ViewController.m`:

```
otherCar.showLiters = YES;
[otherCar printCarInfo];
```

When you run the code, you will see a Honda with 12.50 gallons in the tank and then printed again with 47.32 gallons. Gallons!? But that is the subject of Challenge 3 at the end of the chapter.

Subclassing and Inheritance: A Challenge

While gas and diesel cars continue to improve their use of fuel, your customers are demanding that you model a hybrid car. Your job is to create a `HybridCar` class that inherits from `Car` and adds a method to return the number of miles until the car's battery and fuel are empty. You can name this method `-(float)milesUntilEmpty`.

Hint

Don't forget to track the miles per gallon (MPG) so you can calculate the distance until the car is empty. For example, the 2013 Toyota Prius hybrid gets 42MPG. If there were 10 gallons left in the tank, the car would have a theoretical range of 402 miles until the tank was empty.

Think about it for a few minutes.

Do you have a solution worked out?

Go to the following section to see how you did.

Inheritance and Subclassing

In Objective-C, each new class is derived from a class that already exists. The Car class described in Listings 2-3 through 2-7 inherits from NSObject, the root class of the Objective-C class tree. Each subclass adds or modifies state and behavior that it inherits from its parent, also called its "superclass." The Car class adds several instance variables and methods to the vanilla NSObject it inherits from.

The HybridCar class inherits from Car and adds functionality to calculate the distance the car can travel until empty, based on the MPG that the hybrid car is capable of. Listings 2-9 and 2-10 show one possible way to implement the HybridCar class. The sample code for this chapter contains a project with the code from Listings 2-9 to 2-11 in the folder "CarValet HybridCar."

Listing 2-9   HybridCar.h **Header File**

```
//  HybridCar.h
//  CarValet

#import "Car.h"

@interface HybridCar : Car

@property (nonatomic) float milesPerGallon;

- (float)milesUntilEmpty;

- (id)initWithMake:(NSString *)make
             model:(NSString *)model
              year:(int)year
        fuelAmount:(float)fuelAmount
               MPG:(float)MPG;

@end
```

First, notice how small the .h file is. All the file needs to do is specify the differences between a Car and a HybridCar—in this case, one property and two methods. The property stores how many miles per gallon the hybrid car gets. milesUntilEmpty returns how many miles the car should be able to travel on the current contents of the fuel tank (fuelAmount), and the custom initializer adds an MPG argument, to set milesPerGallon.

Listing 2-10 shows a possible implementation file for the HybridCar class.

Listing 2-10   HybridCar.m **Implementation File**

```
//  HybridCar.m
//  CarValet
```

```objc
#import "HybridCar.h"

@implementation HybridCar

- (id)init
{
    self = [super init] ;

    if (self != nil) {
        _milesPerGallon = 0.0f;
    }

    return self;
}

- (id)initWithMake:(NSString *)make
             model:(NSString *)model
              year:(int)year
        fuelAmount:(float)fuelAmount
               MPG:(float)MPG {
    self = [super initWithMake:make model:model year:year fuelAmount:fuelAmount];

    if (self != nil) {
        _milesPerGallon = MPG;
    }

    return self;
}

- (void)printCarInfo {
    [super printCarInfo];

    NSLog(@"Miles Per Gallon: %0.2f", self.milesPerGallon);

    if (self.milesPerGallon > 0.0f) {
        NSLog(@"Miles until empty: %0.2f",
            [self milesUntilEmpty]);
    }
}

- (float)milesUntilEmpty {
    return (self.fuelAmount * self.milesPerGallon);
}

@end
```

There are at least two major ways to implement the `init` method of a subclass when both the class and superclass have a base initializer. One is to call the base initializer of the subclass with some default values. The main body would look something like the following:

```
return [self initWithMake:nil model:nil year:1900 fuelAmount:0.0f MPG:0.0f];
```

However, there is a hidden bug and/or maintenance cost for doing this. Imagine there are several subclasses of `Car`, perhaps for hybrids, electrics, and diesels. And perhaps even subclasses of the subclasses such as `GasElectricHybrid`, `DieselElectricHybrid`, and so on.

You decide to change the default year of manufacture to `0` in order to easily detect missing values. If the `init` method of each subclass uses that class's custom initializer, you have to change the value in every subclass. Miss one and you have introduced a bug. If, instead, the `init` methods use `[super init]` and then set default values specific for the subclass, you only need to make the change in one place.

The `initWithMake:...MPG:` used here is a great example of a subclass custom initializer extending the superclass method with additional functionality—in this case, setting `milesPerGallon`. First, it calls the superclass's `initWithMake:...` method to initialize the `Car` attributes, then initializes the specific `HybridCar` value.

Because there are new attributes for the car, `HybridCar` specializes the `printCarInfo` method. The first thing is calling the `Car` version of this method—that is, the superclass. After that, the information specific to the hybrid is printed. Specialization is a powerful part of inheritance, allowing each class to do only the work it needs to. When combined with encapsulation, it lets the developer of a class focus on just that class, utilizing any public methods and properties up the inheritance chain to speed development.

The `milesUntilEmpty` method calculates how many more miles the car can go until the tank is empty. It uses a simple formula multiplying the MPG times the gallons of fuel in the tank. In a real hybrid vehicle, the algorithm would likely be much more complex.

The last step is to add an instance of the `HybridCar` class to the CarValet `ViewController`. You need to add the `#import "HybridCar.h"` at the top of the `ViewController.m` file and then the contents of Listing 2-11 inside the `viewWillAppear:` method.

Listing 2-11   **Adding a Hybrid Car to the** `ViewController.m`

```
HybridCar *myHybrid = [[HybridCar alloc] initWithMake:@"Toyota"
                                  model:@"Prius"
                                  year:2012
                                  fuelAmount:8.3f
                                  MPG:42.0f];

[myHybrid printCarInfo];
```

The `myHybrid` instance is created and set with `make`, `model`, `year`, and `MPG`. The hybrid's info is printed, and then `NSLog` is called to display how many miles the car can travel until empty. If you run your Hello World app, you should see the following in your Debug console:

```
2013-07-03 08:39:45.458 CarValet[9186:a0b]  Car Make: Toyota
2013-07-03 08:39:45.458 CarValet[9186:a0b]  Car Model: Prius
2013-07-03 08:39:45.459 CarValet[9186:a0b]  Car Year: 2012
2013-07-03 08:39:45.459 CarValet[9186:a0b]  Number of Gallons in Tank: 8.30
2013-07-03 08:44:39.419 CarValet[9346:a0b]  Miles Per Gallon: 42.00
2013-07-03 08:44:39.419 CarValet[9346:a0b]  Miles until empty: 348.60
```

There are many different ways that the `HybridCar` class could be defined and implemented. Take some time to create a few variants. The key is to start becoming comfortable with Objective-C syntax. You can get more practice working on the challenges at the end of this chapter. As you continue through this book and move on to writing apps of your own, the Objective-C syntax and patterns will become second nature to you.

Summary

This chapter provided an abridged, high-octane introduction to Xcode, Objective-C syntax, objects, classes, properties, and inheritance. It also gave you practice with creating projects, using Xcode, as well as Objective-C concepts.

This is also a chapter you can refer back to as you go through this book. To get the most value, try testing all the material discussed in this chapter directly in Xcode. Mess around with the examples. Hands-on experience is the best way to gain critical skills you need for iOS development.

Learning Objective-C takes more than just a chapter. If you're serious about learning iOS programming, and these concepts are new to you, consider seeking out single-topic books that are dedicated to introducing these technologies to developers new to the platform. Consider *Learning Objective-C 2.0: A Hands-on Guide to Objective-C for Mac and iOS Developers*, 2nd edition, by Robert Clair, or *Programming in Objective-C*, 5th edition, by Stephen G. Kochan. For Xcode, look for versions of *Xcode 4 Unleashed*, 2nd edition, by Fritz F. Anderson or *Xcode 4 Developer Reference* by Richard Wentk updated for Xcode 5 (though even the Xcode 4 versions are valuable). Apple has an excellent Objective-C 2.0 overview at http://developer.apple.com/Mac/library/documentation/Cocoa/Conceptual/ObjectiveC/Introduction/introObjectiveC.html.

During this chapter, you created the CarValet project. In the next chapter, you build on this project and learn about storyboards, a way to graphically create all the screens for your app, and hooking them together. You also learn more about Objective-C as well as several important techniques when coding for iOS.

Challenges

1. Update the `printCarInfo` method to print the string "Car undefined: no make specified." if just `make` is `nil`; "Car undefined: no model specified." if just `model` is `nil`; and keep printing "Car undefined: no make or model specified." if both are `nil`. You can create test car objects using variations of the call to `initWithMake:model:year:fuelAmount:` from Listing 2-5 for checking your code.

2. Create a subclass of `Car` called `ElectricCar`. Take some time to design what that class might look like: the instance variables, modifications to existing methods, and any unique methods. When you have done that, either implement or read on for some possible approaches.

   There are a few ways you could design the class for an electric car. Part of the choice depends on how much you want to inherit from the `Car` class. Of the instance variables describing a car, only `fuel` could be an issue. An electric car has a charge. You could reuse fuel and pretend it is the charge. If you reuse the variable, then all you have to do is change `printCarInfo` and add a method for the amount of charge left. You could also add an instance variable for distance per kilowatt hour and use that in calculating the remaining distance the car can travel.

3. In the "Custom Getters and Setters" section, you saw how to return U.S. gallons or liters from `fuelAmount`. But `printCarInfo` always prints "gallons." Modify `printCarInfo` so that it prints "gallons" when `isShowingLiters` is `NO` and "liters" when it is `YES`.

   When `printCarInfo` is working for liters, change `Car` so that it can print results in U.S. gallons, U.K. gallons, or liters. You will need a way to set which type of fuel is being shown. If you use `BOOL`s, remember that more than one can be set to `YES`.

3

Introducing Storyboards

Unlike the simple HelloWorld example and CarValet app you started in Chapter 2, "Objective-C Boot Camp," most apps include multiple screens. Each screen may include buttons, labels, images, and even custom views. It is possible to create each screen in code: allocating each visual element, setting appropriate bounds, and configuring any specific properties such as text, state, and color. For many, a visual editor is a much better fit for matching design concepts to actual interface layout, saving a lot of effort.

Storyboards enable you to lay out your screens and the major ways users move from one screen to another. This chapter introduces you to the process of designing and laying out a storyboard. You start by exploring the scene, a single interface element that presents a complete and coherent user view. From there, you add more scenes, learning different ways to transition from one scene to the next and building a complex and nuanced app along the way. Finally, you learn and practice some ways to pass data between different scenes, an important part of the development process.

By the time you finish this chapter, you'll know what it takes to architect apps with multiple scenes and to design the ways a user moves about the different scenes.

Storyboard Basics

To a user, the interface *is* your app. It is the primary gateway between the user and the functionality—the logic and data—powering your app. You design and implement the experience by creating informative and utilitarian elements, both the screens and the content of those screens. Each screen you design can do a number of things:

- Display information, such as the number of car objects in the CarValet app
- Enable actions, such as creating new cars by touching a button
- Request input, such as specifying the make of a car
- Show the result of user activities by updating the displayed car or switching to a screen that enables the user to edit cars

Every time someone uses an app, that user experiences a story. The story might focus on organizing their lives (Calendar), interacting with friends (Mail, social apps, and so on), or making the world safe against bad pigs (you know which apps those are).

App design happens on multiple levels. The best apps include holistic goals—not just how users interact with the pieces of information or activities, but how they interact with the app as a whole. Like a story, an app can be divided into scenes of naturally grouped activities of information. In Contacts, for example, there are scenes for looking at everyone and finding people, seeing someone in detail, and for editing someone.

Xcode supports this method of design with *storyboards*. With them, you can create and see all the scenes in your app and the flow between them. You edit storyboard files using a visual Layout editor that can have multiple controllers and manage connections between them. With the editor, you set the following:

- The container class (view controller) for each screen
- How a screen looks (the view objects)
- The transition from one screen to another
- How all the screens flow together to make your application

Scenes

The combination of a view controller and the view objects it contains is called a *scene*. You already created and modified a scene in the HelloWorld example in Chapter 2. Because you specified a Universal app when you created the project, Xcode created iPhone and iPad storyboards, each with an initial scene. As part of the example, you added a static label to the iPhone scene (refer to Figure 2-6).

Designing and building storyboards is a central part of app development. Many apps can use just one or two storyboards, one for each major supported form factor: handheld and tablet. And for those that are more complex, it is possible to use multiple storyboards for a form factor, flowing from one to the other, though that is beyond the scope of this book.

Storyboards fit well into the design process. First, you identify app functionality, divide the app into scenes for related functionality, and establish the flows between scenes. Then you conceptualize, build, and debug scenes, turning the design into the graphical user interfaces (GUIs) and the code that powers them.

In this chapter, you update the CarValet app so that it enables the user to create, view, and modify cars. The number of ways to divide and implement these three simple tasks is immense, if not infinite. For example, you could have one scene for adding cars, another for viewing them, and a third for editing. Or you could have a slight variation with a read-only editing overview scene that opens to a different scene depending on the type of value being edited: one scene for the text-based model and make, another for the year, and one more for the fuel level; and as you will do here, combine adding and viewing into one scene, with another scene for editing.

iOS provides a wealth of predefined user interface (UI) elements, and you can create many more. During this chapter, you learn about a few more elements in addition to the label, so your design will be relatively simple. As you progress through this book and add more elements to your toolset, your storyboard will grow more complex. For now, your app provides two scenes: one for adding and viewing cars and the other for editing a specific car.

A Note on User Experience

At this stage of the book, the goal is learning the basic pieces you need to create fully featured apps. Because of that, the focus is on learning how to use important elements such as storyboards and basic view classes, and hooking them together.

The emphasis is on using the individual elements, not on creating an app with the iOS 7 look and feel. Some of that comes in later as you start to put together what you have learned, though some elements, such as translucency, scrolling under bars, dynamics, and Text Kit, are more advanced topics.

Scene 1: Creating the Add/View Scene

Your first scene enables the valet attendant to create cars and view individual cars. Open either the project you used for Chapter 2 or use the CH03 CarValet Starter project from the sample code for this chapter.

Creating a scene is done in roughly three phases: add the visual elements, connect those elements to view controllers, and then implement scene behaviors using those elements. In practice, this tends to be an iterative process.

Step one is adding views to create the add/view car scene.

Adding the Add/View Visual Elements

Select Main_iPhone.storyboard from the list of files in the Project Navigator in Xcode. Xcode opens a Storyboard editor similar to Figure 3-1. The storyboard files were added when Xcode created the project from the Single View project template. As of the release of Xcode used for this book, all project templates except Empty add storyboard files.

Looking at the left side of Figure 3-1 just next to the Project Navigator, you can see that the storyboard already contains one scene called View Controller Scene. Again, Xcode created this along with ViewController.m and ViewController.h, the class for the scene's view controller. These classes and storyboards provide a jumping-off point for implementing your design. They also provide an example of how Xcode helps you by creating starting points for adding your new elements and classes.

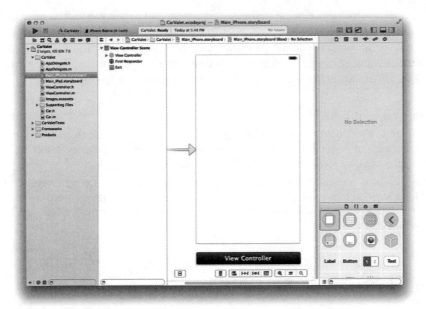

Figure 3-1   The Storyboard editor

The application already works: build and run the app in the iPhone Simulator. Make sure the simulator will use the larger phone form factor by checking the right-hand side of the scheme popup. It should say iPhone (Retina 4-inch). If the menu shows something else, change the selection, and run the app again if it is already running.

The simulator shows a blank screen with a status bar that looks like the screen in the Storyboard editor. But how did the system know which scene to show first, when most storyboards have multiple scenes? The answer is the gray arrow on the left side of the Interface Builder (IB) window in Figure 3-1. It points to the scene to show when the app has finished launching.

Adding the First Label: Xcode Guides

Informational labels provide important pieces of information to the user. If the app is about parking cars, "How many cars are parked?" and "How many cars have I ever parked?" are important questions to answer. For now, the label answers the second question. To change from a blank screen, add the first visual element for the interface: the label showing the total number of cars.

The goal is for the label to be at the top of, and stretch across, the width of the app screen—but not right at the top or the full width. The Apple User Interface Guidelines recommend white space around various elements, including labels. Xcode helps conform to these guidelines by showing dashed blue guidelines as you move elements around the current screen. This includes snapping elements to those guidelines.

To see this in action, lay out the Total Cars label following these steps:

1. From the palette of objects on the lower right, drag a `UILabel` into the scene.

2. Move the label until the top and left of the label are flush with the top and left Xcode guidelines. The left side of Figure 3-2 shows the label and the guidelines before the mouse is released.

3. Now grow the right side of the label until it is flush with the right guideline. Make sure the top and left edges of the label are still flush with their respective guideline. The right side of Figure 3-2 shows how things look just before you release the mouse.

4. Change the text and set the label font to Headline, as shown in Figure 3-3. The text and numbers are placeholders to help you lay out the interface. Your app updates them as values change at runtime. The font shows the text is important information.

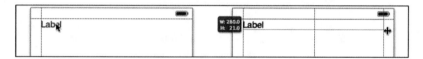

Figure 3-2   Using Xcode guides to align the Total Cars label

Run the project again, and you see the Total Cars: 999 label that you just created.

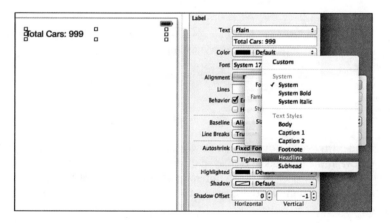

Figure 3-3   Adding the first label

In the CarValet app, the parking valet needs to create and view cars. Your app must supply critical information to help the valet do the job. Table 3-1 lists the visual elements needed, along with each element's purpose and class. This table provides an excellent example of the kinds of information to capture and produce as you design apps. Always take care to document the purpose of visual elements as well as their relationships and behaviors. Although things can and will change as you create your apps, you'll find documented information like Table 3-1 to be invaluable in speeding up your implementation.

Use Table 3-1 to add the remaining elements to your scene. When you are finished, your scene should look like the interface shown in Figure 3-4.

Table 3-1   **Visual Elements in the Add/View Scene**

Visual Element	Purpose	Class
Total Cars	Displays the total number of parked cars—that is, the number of Car objects.	UILabel
New Car	Park a car by adding a new Car object.	UIButton
Divider	Provides visual separation between the areas for adding a car and viewing a car. Adding the divider can be challenging. A step-by-step guide follows the table.	UIView
Current Car Number	Shows the index of the currently displayed Car object.	UILabel
Car Information	Displays the details for the current car.	UILabel
Previous	Lets the valet look through cars by updating Car Information with details for the previous car, if any.	UIButton
Next	Updates Car Information with details for the next car, if any.	UIButton

You might wonder why you want a divider view. Without the divider, users find it difficult to differentiate between the two sets of displayed information. Labels help here, but they don't help enough. Without dividers, users may interpret each big header label as a different part of the same kind of information. See the sidebar "Adding the Visual Divider" for help adding it to your view controller.

Figure 3-4   Scene 1 visual elements

Adding the Visual Divider

Using dividers is a common visual separation technique for categories of information. A divider differentiates the material on one side from the material on the other. The following steps enable you to add a divider to your scene (see Figure 3-5):

1. Drag a `UIView` element onto the scene and leave it selected.
2. In the Attributes inspector on the right of the storyboard area, set the background color to Light Gray, as shown in Figure 3-5.
3. Set the left edge of the view to the default inset from the main view. Then drag the right side to the default inset from the main view's right edge. You can use the left and right guidelines in Xcode shown previously in Figure 3-2.
4. Change to the Size inspector and set the height to 2 points. The Size inspector icon looks like a ruler. In Figure 3-1, it is the fifth icon at the top of the utilities area on the right side of the Xcode project window.
5. Move the view until it is about halfway between the bottom of the Add Car button and the top of the Car Number label. Again, use the guidelines to make sure it stays centered. Another trick is to get the view close to where you want it and then use the arrow keys for fine movement. The arrow keys work with the selected view.
6. After you let go of the divider view, check to make sure the left and right edges are the correct inset from the main view. Also check that the divider still has a height of 2 points. Keep adjusting things until everything looks right.

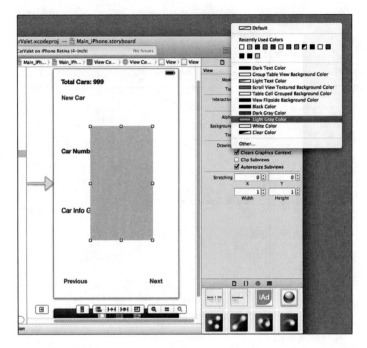

Figure 3-5   Setting the divider view background to light gray

When you have completed the layout, run the app to see your changes. If the screen still does not look balanced, try adjusting the layout and re-running the app until things look right.

Adding the Initial Add/View Behaviors

Every UI element you add to your app must show or do something relevant. Yes, some elements—such as the divider view and decorative images—serve other purposes. These decorations are useful only when used with items that show information, allow action, or show results of an action.

The interface you are working on now displays the total number of cars, the index of the car shown, and its detailed information. It also provides actions: creating a car and going to the next or previous car. Before you can create the code to respond to buttons or update labels, you need a way to know when the button is touched. You also need references to any labels you will change.

IBAction and IBOutlet

You use IB to add behaviors and link to displayed items by using the IBAction and IBOutlet identifiers. Their names give you hints about what they are for. Actions do something, and outlets connect things together. And both start with IB; they are not Objective-C types, but instead enable Xcode to create stand-ins that IB uses for connecting visual elements to properties and user actions to methods.

IBAction identifies methods that a UI element can call, usually in response to a user doing something with the interface. Buttons are touched, switches are toggled, or sliders are changed; the user interacting with a control on the screen can call an action.

IBOutlet identifies properties for UI elements. When connected, you use the property for updating labels, setting a value for a slider, or even hiding and showing views. Those same properties can be used to read user input: text from fields, whether a switch is on or off, or where a dragged view is.

When you design your app, you set up how things are connected and what kinds of actions they may take. After you lay out your interface, you create the actions and outlets to connect the code you write with the views the code updates or reads. For CarValet, the valet creates new cars, sees the information for a car, or types in a new make or model.

You need to update the labels with numbers or information. You also need to enable the user to create cars or navigate through them.

Creating an Outlet

You create outlets by Ctrl-dragging from a UI element to a source file, usually the class header. To learn how this is done, create an outlet for the total number of cars label.

First, open the `Main_iPhone.storyboard` file and then show the Assistant editor, either by selecting the middle button from the three editor buttons in the Xcode toolbar, selecting View > Assistant Editor > Show Assistant Editor, or pressing Cmd-Option-Return.

By default, the Assistant editor shows the appropriate matching file for whatever is in the Main editor window. When the main window is IB, it is the header file for the active view controller class. Right now, there is only one scene with a view controller class of `ViewController`, so `ViewController.h` is shown in the Assistant.

Creating the connection happens in two steps: first, dragging out the new connection and then naming the connection. Add an `IBOutlet` for the Total Cars label using these steps:

1. Make sure that `ViewController.h` is showing in the Assistant editor.

   If not, you can use the file popup at the top of the Assistant editor to change files. Click in the area highlighted in green in the top screen shot of Figure 3-6 and choose Automatic > ViewController.h.

2. Right-click (or Ctrl-click) and drag from the Total Cars label in IB to the properties area in `ViewController.h` in the Assistant editor, as shown in the top of Figure 3-6.

3. In the popup that appears, make sure the Connection type is Outlet and then enter `totalCarsLabel` for the name. The filled-out popup is shown in the middle of Figure 3-6.

4. Press Connect in the popup, and the property shown in the bottom of Figure 3-6 is created.

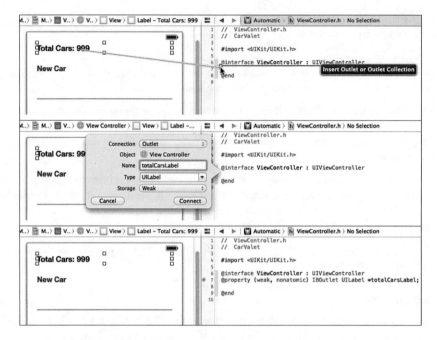

Figure 3-6   Creating and connecting an `IBOutlet`

You can now use the `totalCarsLabel` property to access the label object in your scene. Setting the text is as simple as the following:

```
self.totalCarsLabel.text = @"New text!";
```

Creating an Action

Creating actions is almost identical. The only change is how you fill out the popup that appears after you have dragged out the connection. Add an `IBAction` for the New Car button using these steps:

1. Make sure you are viewing the iPhone storyboard in the Main editor and `ViewController.h` in the Assistant. If not, look at step 1 in the earlier section, "Creating an Outlet."

2. Right-click (or Ctrl-click) the New Car button and drag to the methods area in `ViewController.h`. The convention is to group properties in the upper part of the class interface definition and methods in the lower part, as shown in the top part of Figure 3-7.

3. In the popup that appears after you release the mouse, set the Name of the method to `newCar` and the Connection type to Action, as shown in the middle of Figure 3-7.

4. The bottom part of Figure 3-7 shows the resulting declaration of the action method. A corresponding action method shell is created in the `.m` file.

If you forget to choose Action, it takes two steps to fix the problem. See the sidebar, "Important: Fixing a Forgotten Action Choice," for more information.

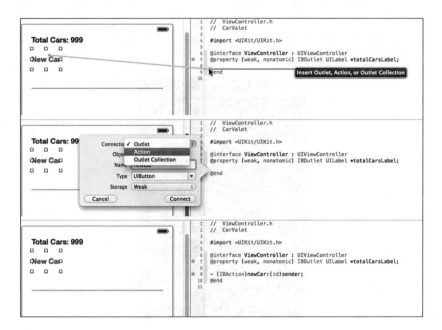

Figure 3-7   Creating and connecting an `IBAction`

Important: Fixing a Forgotten Action Choice

It is inevitable: You are specifying your outlets and actions, and you forget to choose Action for a button. Now your `newCar` method is an outlet instead. Your first attempt at a fix is to delete the `newCar` property and hook things up again.

Everything looks fine, but then you try to run the app. The result is a crash with something like the following near the top of a long stack trace in the console:

```
2013-07-21 14:20:10.180 CarValet[9257:a0b] *** Terminating app due to uncaught
exception 'NSUnknownKeyException', reason: '[<ViewController 0x8aa22e0>
setValue:forUndefinedKey:]: this class is not key value coding-compliant for the
key newCar.'
```

The clue is in the last part of the message. Something about "not key value coding-compliant for the key `newCar`." That says there is a class property called `newCar` that the view is trying to hook up at runtime. It happens because deleting the property from the `.h` file does not update the information in IB. It is still trying to hook up the `newCar` outlet to the New Car button.

To fix this, you have to remove the IB information. In this case, you connected the outlet to the `ViewController` class, so that is where the problem lies:

1. In the Storyboard view, find the `ViewController` class in the left-hand list of view items and view controllers and then right-click or Ctrl-click that item.

   Note that you can also do this using the yellow view controller symbol below the scene on the main IB canvas.

2. A popover that looks like Figure 3-8 appears. Find the item with the yellow warning triangle and click the "x" next to that item.

Figure 3-8   Fixing a forgotten Action choice

Now you can build and run, and the app works correctly.

This mistake is not limited to beginners. It is one that even experienced iOS programmers make on a somewhat regular basis. Remember how to fix this one; you will need it.

Scene 1: Finish Adding Outlets and Actions

Now you can practice creating outlets and actions by adding connections for the rest of the UI elements in scene 1.

Table 3-2 is another example of helpful information you can record as you design your screens and behaviors. It shows the UI elements, how they are connected to your code, and the name of each connection. Use this table to set up outlets and actions for your add/view scene. In addition, practice creating an Outlet instead of an Action so you remember how to fix it (see the sidebar, "Important: Fixing a Forgotten Action Choice").

Table 3-2 **Actions and Outlets for the Add/View Scene**

Element	Type	Name
Total Cars label	IBOutlet	totalCarsLabel
Car Number label	IBOutlet	carNumberLabel
Car Info label	IBOutlet	carInfoLabel
New Car button	IBAction	newCar:
Previous Car button	IBAction	previousCar:
Next Car button	IBAction	nextCar:

As you added outlets, you might have noticed a new qualifier in the created properties:

`@property (weak, nonatomic) IBOutlet UILabel *totalCarsLabel;`

weak indicates object ownership and helps the compiler add code for memory management. It is important to understand what these memory qualifiers mean.

A Brief Diversion on Memory Management

iOS devices have a set amount of physical RAM, and unlike desktop systems, there is no virtual memory system making storage space appear to be infinite. Instead, iOS gives you the tools you need to easily manage the memory used by your app.

Each app gets a fixed amount of memory while it is running. The important part is not the exact amount—there is usually enough for quite complex apps—the important part is how you manage the memory. The reason is the system watchdog, an aptly named part of iOS that keeps an eye on all running applications and terminates any memory hogs.

Every object you allocate, from view controllers to cars, requires memory. And every object has a lifetime: It is created, used, and then no longer needed. After that last stage happens, the system can safely free up, or reclaim, the memory used by that object. But how do you indicate you are done with an object? More importantly, what if your class is not the only one using the object? Safe removal of the object means that nothing needs it, that nothing has a reference; or put another way, that no other object owns or needs the one to be freed.

iOS keeps track of how many other objects need a particular instance, and when that number reaches zero, it frees up the memory. In most cases, you do not need to do anything for this to work.

One simple example is creating temporary variables. Look at the following method:

```
- (void)usesATempString:(NSString*)inString {
    NSString *tempString = [inString copy];
    // do things with tempString
}
```

The `tempString` object is created from a copy of the method argument `inString`. `copy` creates a whole new object including allocating any required memory. But how does the system know when to free up the memory used by `tempString`?

The answer lies in how many other objects are referencing `tempString`. In the previous code, the string is allocated and used inside the method. No other objects refer to `tempString`, so it can be safely freed up when the method is done. The `usesATempString:` method is the only owner of `tempString`.

However, as you create custom view controllers with outlets or create larger model objects, the relationships get more complicated. There can be multiple users of a car object or several places referencing a view controller. You need a way to tell the OS the relationship between an instance and the objects it uses.

Memory-related property qualifiers are used for this purpose. You specify the relationship between the instance and object it uses using one of two qualifiers: strong or weak. (There are a few other qualifiers, but they are rarely used and Xcode often adds them for you.)

strong is the default qualifier and means ownership. The system cannot free the object until the owner is done with it. Generally, it says either: "I created this object and when I am done with it (or I am freed up), the system can free it," or "I did not create this object, but I need it and you have to at least wait until I am done with it."

Owners are done with objects when one of three things happens: The owner sets the variable holding the object (the reference) to `nil`; the owner sets the reference to another object; or the owner itself is freed up.

weak means the object is not owned, so it can be freed up as needed. This can sound dangerous, especially if your reference had a valid object and then that object gets freed. To deal with this situation, when the system frees an object with a weak reference, it sets the reference to `nil`. That way, you do not accidentally try to access memory in an unknown state. This is handy, especially because sending a message to a `nil` object works. For methods with return values, it just results in `nil`.

Tip: To Type Defaults or Not to Type Defaults?

That is the question. Whether 'tis nobler in the code to suffer the bugs and problems of forgotten defaults, or to write extra words and, by writing, stop bugs... Okay, enough Shakespeare parody. The question is whether to include defaults, such as strong for a property, in your code.

Along with almost all the professional coders I know, I find it better to include them for two important reasons. When they are not there, you inevitably have to refer to the docs for the defaults. Worse, treating a property as weak when it is really strong—effectively pretending your object is not the owner when it really is—can lead to memory leaks that are hard to find as well as other possible memory issues.

As an example, Car might include a reference to the valet that parked it. The car object does not own the valet object, and there may not even be an assigned valet yet. The property is weak both because of ownership and because it is optional. A method that returns the name of the valet can deal with this situation with code such as the following:

```
NSString *valetName;
if (self.valet != nil) {
    valetName = self.valet.name
} else {
    valetName = @"No valet.";
}
```

If there is a valid valet object, the name is set to the name attribute of that valet. If not, the string is set to "No valet."

Warning: Memory Leaks and Retain Cycles

A leak happens when the memory is no longer needed, but it is not possible for the system to free that memory. Even with the sophisticated memory management in iOS, leaks can occur and are usually due to *retain cycles*. This happens when two objects have strong references to each other. Because strong references are set to nil only when the owning object is freed up, the two-way reference can never be set to nil. Each object is waiting for the other to be deallocated.

For example, imagine a screen showing all cars that then shows a viewer for an individual car. The individual car viewer can also show an editor. The classes are set up so that the editor can inform the viewer when it is done:

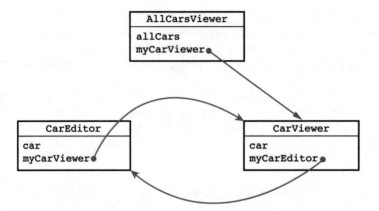

The viewer and editor both have `strong` references to each other. When the editor is done, it lets the viewer know; the viewer closes the editor but fails to set `myCarEditor` to `nil`.

The system closes the car editor but is unable to free up the memory because some other object, in this case the car viewer, still has a `strong` reference. If the viewer opens another editor, the old one can be deallocated. This happens because assigning a new editor to `myCarEditor` tells the system that the viewer is no longer interested in the old one. However, it is now tied to the new one.

But that is not the full cause of the memory leak. That happens at the `AllCarsViewer` level, and here is how:

- The all cars viewer opens an individual car viewer.
- That car viewer opens an editor.
- The editor closes, and, as you have seen, the editor cannot be deallocated.
- The car viewer closes, and the all cars viewer correctly cleans up by setting `myCarViewer` to `nil`.

At this point, the system is unable to free up the memory for the car viewer because another object, the car editor, has a `strong` reference. And the car viewer has a `strong` reference to that same car editor. Worse, there are no other references to either the viewer or editor because `myCarViewer` is now `nil`.

The result is two objects in memory, the viewer and editor, that cannot be deallocated. This can get especially tricky when it is not a simple object-to-object cycle where object A retains object B that also retains A. The more typical situation is a chain of objects, where the retain cycle happens between two or more of those objects at different levels of the hierarchy.

For more information, see "Retain Cycles" in *Learning Objective-C 2.0,* Second Edition, by Robert Clair, page 337.

Adding New Cars

Apps often show counts of things. CarValet displays the total number of cars. To show a total car count, you need to keep track of all `Car` objects. To display information for a particular car, you need to track the current car. Counting objects and displaying information are common display tasks in apps. You could accomplish them by using a reference to an actual `Car` object, or you could simply use an index into the array of cars. Remember that simpler is generally better and less error-prone. Open `ViewController.m` and change it so it looks like Listing 3-1, where the changes are shown in bold.

Listing 3-1   **Adding and Initializing State Instance Variables**

```
//  ViewController.m
//  CarValetScenes

#import "ViewController.h"

#import "Car.h"

@implementation ViewController {
    NSMutableArray *arrayOfCars;              // 1
    NSInteger displayedCarIndex;             // 2
}

- (void)viewDidLoad {
    [super viewDidLoad];

    arrayOfCars = [[NSMutableArray alloc] init]; // 3

    displayedCarIndex = 0;                   // 4
}
```

Here's what happens in the numbered lines in Listing 3-1:

1. Use a mutable array to keep track of all the `Car` objects.

2. Specify the array index for the car displayed in the lower area.

3. Initialize the array of cars to an empty array.

4. Display the first car created.

Now that you have a place to hold new cars, you need to create them. The shell of `newCar:` was created for you when you set up the IBAction. You can tell that a method is an IBAction by looking at the declaration in either in the `.h` or `.m` file. The first part always looks like this:

```
- (IBAction)
```

When you drag a connection from a button to a view controller, Xcode looks through the controller's source for `IBAction` and presents a list of those methods (among other things).

Actions that create new objects are very common in apps. Replace `newCar:` with Listing 3-2. The method shows a simple way to both create an object—in this case, a car—and update status.

Listing 3-2   `newCar:`

```
- (IBAction)newCar:(id)sender {
    Car *newCar = [[Car alloc] init];                        // 1

    [arrayOfCars addObject:newCar];

    NSString *totalCarText;
    totalCarText = [NSString stringWithFormat:@"Total Cars: %d",   // 2
                            [arrayOfCars count]];

    self.totalCarsLabel.text = totalCarText;                 // 3
}
```

Here's what happens in the numbered lines in Listing 3-2:

1. Create a new car with default values and add it to the array.
2. Create a new total car string based on the current number of cars.
3. Update the string displayed to the valet.

Run the app. Because there are initially no cars, the label still says Total Cars: 999. This is a common mistake for first-time app coders. You could initialize the number to 0. Another solution is to create one car when the view loads, a technique you might use in your own apps.

You just finished adding code to create a new car from a button tap. You can simulate a tap by calling `newCar:` and not specifying a sender. To do this, add the following line to `viewDidLoad:` just after initializing `arrayOfCars`:

```
[self newCar:nil];
```

Now build and run the app again. The label shows Total Cars: 1.

Adding Car Display Behaviors

Displaying object information is another common task. A `UILabel` displays the string from its `text` attribute in the interface, using whatever font, size, and color you specify. When the `text` attribute changes, the label updates.

You need four things to use `UILabel` for displaying changing information: a label, a connection to that label, a string to display, and code to set the label's text.

You have already added the car information label to your scene. You have also created a connection, an IBOutlet, to that label. Adding a description for a car can be done in a few ways. One is by adding a public method. Another is using a read-only property and custom getter. Implement the property and getter by following these steps:

1. In Car.h, add the following property declaration below fuelAmount (see Challenge 5 later in the chapter):

```
@property (readonly) NSString *carInfo;
```

2. Open Car.m and add this code for the custom getter just below initWithMake:...

```
- (NSString *)carInfo {
    return [NSString stringWithFormat:
                @"Car Info\n    Make: %@\n    Model: %@\n    Year: %d",
                self.make ? self.make : @"Unknown Make",
                self.model ? self.model : @"Unknown Model",
                self.year];
}
```

carInfo constructs a string with newlines "\n" between each category of information. The string either includes the make and the model or indicates that they are unknown. (See the following sidebar, "The Ternary Operator," for how this works.)

The Ternary Operator

The ?: ternary operator used in this section defines a simple if-then-else conditional expression:

```
NSString *what = self.which ? @"Something" : @"Nothing";
```

This line checks if self.which evaluates to YES or NO. Note that non-nil is the same as YES, and nil the same as NO. If it is NO, it sets what to the string "Something"; otherwise to "Nothing". It is a shorthand way of writing the following code:

```
NSString *what;
if (self.which) {
    what = @"Something";
} else {
    what = @"Nothing";
}
```

Now that you can get a string describing the car information, you need a way to update the text of the car number and info labels. You could just set the text of each label every place you need to update information. However, you know that updating the displayed car information can happen from multiple places. When that happens, it is good design practice to abstract out the relevant code.

Abstracting out, or centralizing, commonly called code is a good way to reduce the overall amount of code in an app, as well as making maintenance and updates easier. If you change the way car information is displayed at a later date, you need to change only one routine in addition to making any interface changes. Without abstraction, you could be making multiple changes—and probably missing some.

Abstract out the display of car information by adding the `displayCurrentCarInfo` method from Listing 3-3 just above `newCar:`.

Listing 3-3 `displayCurrentCarInfo`

```
- (void)displayCurrentCarInfo {
    Car *currentCar;
    currentCar = [arrayOfCars objectAtIndex:displayedCarIndex];    // 1

    self.carInfoLabel.text = currentCar.carInfo;                   // 2

    NSString *carIndexText;                                        // 3
    carIndexText = [NSString stringWithFormat:@"Car Number: %d",
                                    displayedCarIndex + 1];
    self.carNumberLabel.text = carIndexText;
}
```

Here's what happens in the numbered lines in Listing 3-3:

1. Load the object for the currently displayed car. Note that production code should check that `displayedCarIndex` is a valid index.

2. Get the car description using the `carInfo` property.

3. Update the number in the car label. Note that 1 is added to the current index. See the "Index Versus Count" sidebar for an explanation.

Index Versus Count

Array indexes begin at 0, but people think of the first item as being, well, first. Displaying the index as car number would show a 0 for the first car. This is an error that happens frequently.

To add confusion, the `count` method returns the number of objects in the array. It is effectively 1-based. If there are two cars in the array, you use an index of 1 for the second element, but `count` returns 2 for the number of items.

Just remember this: "Index is 0-based; `count` is 1-based."

When the view opens, you create a car. When data is created or changed, it is good UI practice to show that data, in this case the car, to the user. Call `displayCarInfo` in `viewDidLoad`, just after the line that sets `displayedCarIndex` to 0:

```
[self displayCurrentCarInfo];
```

When you run the app this time, it almost works, but the car display label shows only "Car Info," the first line of the string returned by carInfo. By default, a label is set to display one line of text. For tall labels that you know can show multiple lines and that need to show as much information as possible, set the lines to 0. This tells UILabel to show as many lines as can fit:

1. Open the storyboard.

2. Select the car display label. If needed, change the height so it roughly matches the height of the label shown in Figure 3-9.

3. In the attributes panel on the right-hand side of the storyboard, change the number of lines from the default of 1 to 0, as shown in Figure 3-9.

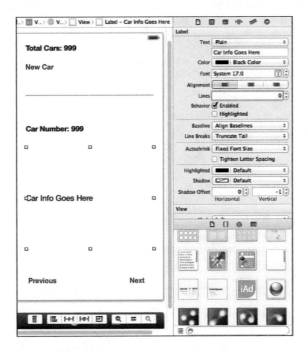

Figure 3-9   Changing label line count

Setting the number of lines to 0 for a UILabel tells iOS to use as many lines as needed to display the text. Since the string returned by carInfo includes newline characters, the information for the selected car needs multiple lines. Run the app again to see the change.

Adding Previous and Next Car Buttons

You have given the user a way to create cars, and the app shows users car detail. But at the moment, you are always showing the same car. Now it is time to let the user choose which car to view. iOS has lots of ways to do this, and in Chapter 8, "Table Views I: The Basics," you learn to use one of the most common ones. For now, you use Previous and Next buttons to switch cars.

Previous and Next car buttons work by changing the index of the current car, displayedCarIndex, to a new element in the arrayOfCars. Then they update the displayed info with the routine you wrote earlier. The only real difference between the buttons is that Previous subtracts 1 from the current index, and Next adds 1. Instead of writing two sets of code that do almost the same thing, you can use the power of abstraction to write one method that takes a new desired index, makes sure the new index is valid, and then updates displayedCarIndex if the updated new index is different.

changeDisplayedCar: is called by previousCar: and nextCar:. Add the code from Listing 3-4 above newCar:.

Listing 3-4   changeDisplayedCar:

```
- (void)changeDisplayedCar:(NSInteger)newIndex {
    if (newIndex < 0) {                          // 1
        newIndex = 0;
    } else if (newIndex >= [arrayOfCars count]) {  // 2
        newIndex = [arrayOfCars count] - 1;
    }

    if (displayedCarIndex != newIndex) {          // 3
        displayedCarIndex = newIndex;
        [self displayCurrentCarInfo];
    }
}
```

Here's what happens in the numbered lines in Listing 3-4:

1. Make sure the new index is a valid index. If the index is less than 0, make it 0.

2. If newIndex is beyond the end of arrayOfCars, set it to the last element. Remember that "Index is 0-based; count is 1-based."

3. Update the display only if the index has changed. Although code execution savings are not really necessary in this simple case, reducing code execution is a good habit to form. Anything you can do to preserve battery power ultimately benefits the user.

Now use changeDisplayedCar: in the action methods (see Listing 3-5).

Listing 3-5   **Next and Previous Action Methods**

```
- (IBAction)previousCar:(id)sender {
    [self changeDisplayedCar:displayedCarIndex - 1];
}

- (IBAction)nextCar:(id)sender {
    [self changeDisplayedCar:displayedCarIndex + 1];
}
```

`changeDisplayedCar:` is an example of code consolidation. Another example is `displayCurrentCarInfo`. Using less code has some important advantages:

- Easier to maintain and debug

- Generally performs better

- Results in smaller applications and faster development

Another simple consolidation you can implement is setting the two count-based labels. Each displays a base string with a variable number. Look for consolidation opportunities when you start designing app behaviors. You can also do it as you refine the design and include things like a data model and more specific scene behaviors. For now, you are going through a more iterative process. Some things are well specified and others are not. As you implement, you make changes to the design and vice versa...you iterate the design and implementation.

Listing 3-6 shows a method for updating both count labels. Add `updateLabel:withBaseString:count:` to your app above `displayCurrentCarInfo`, and make the changes to the other methods that are shown in bold.

Listing 3-6   **Adding** `updateLabel:withBaseString:count:`

```
- (void)updateLabel:(UILabel*)theLabel
     withBaseString:(NSString*)baseString
              count:(NSInteger)theCount {
    NSString *newText;
    newText = [NSString stringWithFormat:@"%@: %d", baseString, theCount]; // 1

    theLabel.text = newText;                                               // 2
}

- (void)displayCurrentCarInfo {
    Car *currentCar;
    currentCar = [arrayOfCars objectAtIndex:displayedCarIndex];

    self.carInfoLabel.text = [currentCar carInfo];

    [self updateLabel:self.carNumberLabel
```

```
                withBaseString:@"Car Number"
                        count:displayedCarIndex + 1];
}

- (IBAction)newCar:(id)sender {
    Car *newCar = [[Car alloc] init];

    [arrayOfCars addObject:newCar];

    [self updateLabel:self.totalCarsLabel
        withBaseString:@"Total Cars"
                count:[arrayOfCars count]];
}
```

Here's what happens in the numbered lines in Listing 3-6:

1. The format string @"%@: %d" creates a string with the contents of baseString, followed by a colon and a space, and then the integer value of theCount. See the "Formatted Strings" sidebar for more information.

2. Sets the label to the newly generated string.

Run the app and try all the features. You can create new cars and look at each car. Try looking at the first car and tapping Previous, and then try looking at the last car and tapping Next. The last two actions test behavior that is just out of bounds. In this case, trying to show an element just before the beginning of the array of cars and an element just past the end. These kinds of tests are great for catching code errors because they are the ones most likely to result in some sort of crash.

Formatted Strings

You use dynamically created strings for many purposes, such as displaying updates to data, generating URLs, and greeting a user by name. Using stringWithFormat:, a class method on NSString, is the most common way to create formatted strings.

A format string is like a normal string, except there are placeholders for values of objects and variables. A string can be simple, with just one variable, or very complex, including multiple placeholders, newlines, and other special characters.

This is the basic syntax of the message:

```
[NSString stringWithFormat:FormatString, arg1, arg2, ...];
```

The number of arguments is dynamic and must equal the number of placeholders in the string.

FormatString is an Objective-C string that has special placeholder characters for different types of values. For example, @"An Integer: %d\nString: '%@'" replaces the %d with the value of an integer variable and the %@ with the contents of a string object or the description of any object. The \n sequence inserts a newline.

> All placeholders start with a percent symbol, then optional formatting, then a character that specifies the type of value. For example, in %0.2f, f specifies a floating-point value, and 0.2 displays only two decimal places of accuracy.
>
> You can read more about format strings in the Apple documentation. Search for "String Format Specifiers."

The add/view scene contains most of the elements it needs. Xcode set the container class to ViewController, a custom subclass of UIViewController, when the project was created. You added the following visual elements:

- UILabels such as the total car count

- UIButtons to add cars and show details about different cars

- One UIView to provide some visual separation

The outlets, methods, and instance variables you create give the interface life.

Scene 2: Adding an Editor

In this section, you practice another core task in app development: laying out and coding a scene, and then hooking the new scene into an existing interface. For the edit scene, you add a new scene to the storyboard, add the views for displaying and editing a car, and create a custom controller for that scene. Next, you implement the transition to and from the view/edit scene.

If the valets using your app parked only one type of car, what you have already might be enough. Instead, cars can vary in make, model, and year, and your app needs to help the valet identify cars by using these criteria. You need a scene for editing cars.

The process you use for adding a new scene goes like this:

1. Create an object for managing the new scene. This is a subclass of one of the built-in iOS view controllers.

2. Add an iOS view controller of the same built-in type to the storyboard.

3. Set the class of this new controller to the one you set up in step 1.

4. Add the view elements to the new scene on the storyboard.

5. Create any actions or outlets needed by the scene.

6. Write the code to make it work and make sure it works.

At some point in the process, you also need to add any required transitions. Sometimes that happens at the end, and sometimes it happens earlier. Also, sometimes the controller is dragged out and some or all of the visual elements are added before the Objective-C class is added.

Now you need to create a container class. Make a new Cocoa Touch Objective-C Class file called `CarEditViewController`, a subclass of `UIViewController`. Make sure it is added to the `CarValet` target.

Now add the new scene:

1. Select `Main_iPhone.storyboard` to open the storyboard.

2. Drag a view controller object from the object palette onto the canvas as shown in Figure 3-10.

3. In the Identity inspector, set Class to `CarEditViewController` (see Figure 3-11).

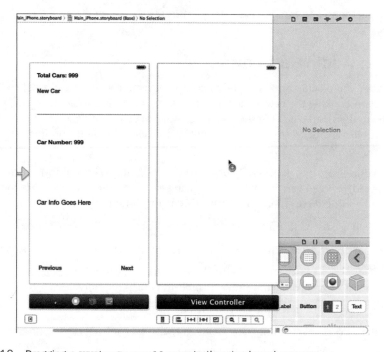

Figure 3-10   Dragging a `UIViewController` onto the storyboard canvas

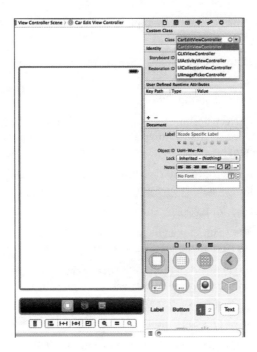

Figure 3-11   Setting the Scene 2 custom class

Adding the Editor Visual Elements

Any app that shows values probably needs to edit at least some of them; this is true of CarValet. To edit a car, you need to show and change values. `UILabel` can only display values. `UITextField` enables the user to edit text. Anything that can be changed to and from text can be edited, including strings, numbers, and dates. A good rule of thumb is that any text string or non-object value `stringWithFormat:` can create is editable with `UITextField`.

Like `UILabel`, `UITextField` uses the `text` attribute for what is displayed. You can use it to display a string—say, the current make of a car—as well as read whatever changes the user made. Text fields come with lots of handy behaviors, including support for keyboards, copying, pasting, undoing, and even placeholder strings that suggest what to type.

When you design editing screens, part of the design involves how an object is edited. This might seem strange at first, but mobile devices, especially handheld ones, don't have an abundance of room. As you move through the book, you learn different ways to edit, but for now, you can present all the fields on one screen.

You need to add nine more visual elements to the project: one for the Car Number label, and two for each attribute so your scene looks like the one in Figure 3-12. To get some practice, try doing this before you continue reading.

As you tried adding the visual elements, you might have found yourself following these steps in the Storyboard editor for `CarEditViewController`:

1. Drag out a `UILabel` for the car number. Set the text to Car Number: 999 and set the font to Headline.

2. Drag out a `UITextField` on the right-hand side of the view.

3. With the text field selected, show the Attributes inspector and look for the Clear Button list and set it to Appears While Editing. The x clear button then shows in the active field if there is any content.

   If you are doing this step after adding all the text fields, select all the text fields. You can do this by holding the Cmd key and tapping on each view.

4. Drag out the `UILabel` for `Make:` on the left-hand side.

5. Right-align the label. Again, if you are doing this after initially laying out all the views, select the four labels next to the text fields and then change the alignment.

6. Adjust the label and text field so they are vertically centered in relation to each other. Make sure there is vertical separation between them and the Car Number label.

7. Select the label and field you just created and duplicate them (by selecting Edit > Duplicate the menu or pressing Cmd-D).

8. Move the new label and field combination down until IB indicates the correct vertical spacing. Now make sure the label and edit fields are vertically centered with the corresponding label and edit fields above. Change the label to `Model:`.

9. Duplicate the line two more times to make the `Year:` and `Fuel:` lines.

10. Adjust the spacing to make the view look less crowded. Figure 3-12 uses 25 points of vertical space between text fields.

Note: Why Make the Labels Less Crowded?

In step 10, you adjust the labels to look less crowded. Why do you need to do this? It is important for two reasons. First, when items are too close together, it is hard for the user to easily differentiate what they are. This happens because of how the eye and brain work together to interpret things. Look at a very crowded picture and try to find something. It is difficult, which is why the "find these items in this picture" puzzles are challenging.

When things are difficult to differentiate, the user gets frustrated and might pick a different app. Apple has a set of recommendations for minimum distances. IB supports these by "snapping" objects to dashed lines that show up as you move objects closer together. These distances are minimums.

The other reason for adjusting labels so they don't look crowded is that fingers are big. A cursor on a laptop or desktop is very small and can easily hit targets that are 5 to 10 points square. Fingers are much larger, so Apple recommends that targets be much larger. For example, the minimum recommended view button size is 44×44 points, with 8 points between adjacent ones.

As you design your interfaces, pay attention to visual separation. It is one thing that differentiates well-designed, easy-to-use apps from all the rest.

The combination of a label and the adjacent text field is very common. Text fields are taller than labels, so the rule of thumb is to first add the field and then the label. Also, the text field is used to set vertical spacing.

You can make it easier to check your changes by setting the initial scene shown by the app to the editor:

1. Open `Main_iPhone.storyboard`.

2. Find the gray starting arrow next to the original view controller scene. This is the arrow shown in Figure 3-1.

3. Click and drag the arrow so it points to the new car edit scene.

4. When the new scene highlights, release the arrow. It is now pointing to the editing scene.

Run the app and see how the screen looks. If it seems unbalanced or crowded, use the editor to adjust the spacing. This cycle of running and adjusting is very common in development. UI designers (sometimes you) regularly do this to tweak position, graphics, colors, and font sizes.

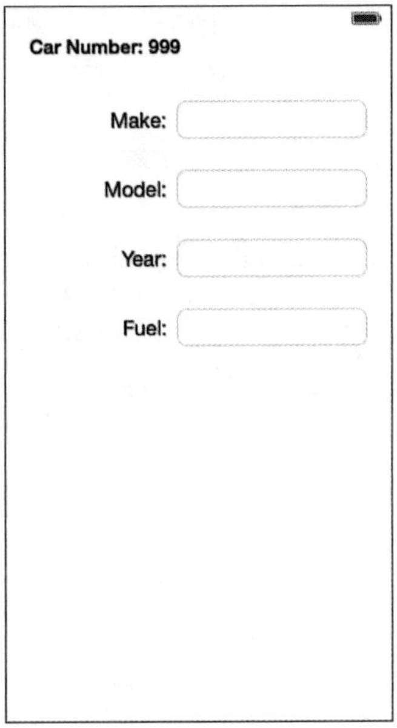

Figure 3-12   Scene 2 visual elements

Adding Editor Behaviors

You need a reference to each field so you can populate and read the text. As before, you add the behaviors in two steps: First, you add the outlets and actions, and then you implement the behaviors. You use Table 3-3 for setting the outlets and actions. As before, you want to open the storyboard with the Assistant editor showing `CarEditViewController.h`.

Table 3-3   `CarEditViewController.h` **Outlets**

Element	Property Name
Car number	`carNumberLabel`
Make field	`makeField`
Model field	`modelField`
Year field	`yearField`
Fuel field	`fuelField`

To set values for the Car Number label and the text fields, you need a reference to the car object being edited as well as the car number. The add/view scene needs to communicate data to the edit scene. The first approach is to add public properties to the edit view controller class.

Modify `CarEditViewController.h` so it looks like Listing 3-7. The new code is in bold.

Listing 3-7   **Public Properties for Edited Car**

```
//  CarEditViewController.h
//  CarValetScenes

#import <UIKit/UIKit.h>

@class Car;                                         // 1

@interface CarEditViewController : UIViewController

@property (nonatomic) NSInteger carNumber;
@property (strong, nonatomic) Car *currentCar;      // 2
```

```
@property (weak, nonatomic) IBOutlet UILabel *carNumberLabel;
@property (weak, nonatomic) IBOutlet UITextField *makeField;
@property (weak, nonatomic) IBOutlet UITextField *modelField;
@property (weak, nonatomic) IBOutlet UITextField *yearField;
@property (weak, nonatomic) IBOutlet UITextField *fuelField;

@end
```

Here's what happens in the numbered lines in Listing 3-7:

1. `@class` specifies a forward reference. See the "Forward References" sidebar.

2. The controller uses the strong memory qualifier as it needs to make sure the edited car is not removed from memory.

Forward References

Before you can declare the type of an instance variable or property, the compiler needs to know about that type. A view controller header file already imports the common iOS header files so you have access to all those class definitions.

There are two ways to use a new class in a declaration. The first is to import the header file for the new class type. To create a `Car` property, you would `#import "Car.h"`.

Another way is to declare a *forward reference* to the `Car` class. `@class Car;` tells the compiler that `Car` is a valid class and will be defined elsewhere. Typically, you use `@class` in an .h file and `#import` in an .m file.

There are three reasons to use forward references. The first is to speed up building your code. In the small projects you have done so far, there is really no issue. But in larger projects with trees of subclasses, Xcode has to process each imported file in a header. It is possible to have many imported classes that are processed for each header file, even though there are only one or two implementation files that need the class.

The second, and less common, reason is to avoid circular references. This happens when two classes end up referring to an instance of each other. That is, `ClassA` needs to include a property of type `ClassB`, and `ClassB` has a property of type `ClassA`. Usually, the problem is not so obvious, and the properties are declared in subclasses of other classes.

The final reason is to provide flexibility and reusability. You read more on this in the section "Exchanging Data Using a Protocol."

The safest practice is to use `@class` in .h files and `#import` in .m files.

Add code to `CarEditViewController.m` to import `Car.h`. Then use Listing 3-8 to change `viewDidLoad:` to set the text of the Car Number label and populate the data fields.

Listing 3-8   `CarEditViewController.m viewDidLoad:`

```
- (void)viewDidLoad {
    [super viewDidLoad];

    NSString *carNumberText;
    carNumberText = [NSString stringWithFormat:@"Car Number: %d",
                        self.carNumber];
    self.carNumberLabel.text = carNumberText;

    self.makeField.text = self.currentCar.make;                     // 1
    self.modelField.text = self.currentCar.model;
    self.yearField.text = [NSString stringWithFormat:@"%d",         // 2
                        self.currentCar.year];
    self.fuelField.text = [NSString stringWithFormat:@"%0.2f",      // 3
                            self.currentCar.fuelAmount];
}
```

Here's what happens in the numbered lines in Listing 3-8:

1. `make` and `model` are both string-based attributes, so they can be set directly.

2. Use a formatted string for the integer value representing the year.

3. Because `fuel` is a `float`, using the format code `@"%0.2f"` limits the resulting string to two decimal places. (As you see in Chapter 5, "Localization," this is not a localization safe way of formatting a number.)

The goal of the scene is for the valet to edit a car. This means updating the properties of the `Car` object. For now, it happens when the view disappears. Listing 3-9 shows `viewWillDisappear:`, which is a method that gets called each time the view disappears. Add that method below `viewDidLoad`. The implementation reads the text fields to update `currentCar`.

Listing 3-9   `CarEditViewController.m viewWillDisappear:`

```
- (void)viewWillDisappear:(BOOL)animated {
    [super viewWillDisappear:animated];

    self.currentCar.make = self.makeField.text;                     // 1
    self.currentCar.model = self.modelField.text;
    self.currentCar.year = [self.yearField.text integerValue];      // 2
    self.currentCar.fuelAmount = [self.fuelField.text floatValue];  // 3
}
```

Here's what happens in the numbered lines in Listing 3-9:

1. `make` and `model` are strings, so you can set them directly.

2. Set `year` by converting the contents of the year field to an integer value.

3. Set `fuelAmount` by converting the contents of the fuel field to a float value.

When you run the code, the fields are set but the data is wrong. Number fields are set to `0`, and strings are empty. This is because the default value for `carNumber` is `0`, and `currentCar` is `nil`. Remember that accessing a property really calls a method. Sending a message to a `nil` object does not result in an error. Instead, it returns `nil`. The text field interprets an argument of `nil` as an empty string. The number formats show the value for the memory address value for `nil`, `0x00000000`.

Tap in each of the fields. iOS automatically brings up the default keyboard. Part of a good user experience is using the right element for the right job. A text field can show several different types of keyboards. To help the user enter numbers, change the type of keyboard for year and fuel:

1. Open the Storyboard editor and select the Year field.

2. Make sure the Attributes inspector is open and then select Number Pad from the Keyboard popup shown in Figure 3-13.

3. Click on the Fuel field and select Decimal Pad.

As you set the keyboards, note the other kinds provided by the system, including ones for e-mail addresses and URLs. As you create apps, it is important to choose the right type of keyboard for two reasons. First, it enables the user to quickly and easily enter data. Second, certain keyboards can help reduce errors. For example, a number keyboard means the user is unable to accidentally type in alpha characters.

Try the app again. First, tap in the Make field and then the Year field. The keyboard changes automatically for each field.

Figure 3-13   Setting the number pad keyboard

Hooking It All Together

You have laid out a new scene, set up the connections, and added behaviors. Now you need to add the edit scene into the flow of the app. Hooking scenes together is a common task in development. As you will see, it is more than just pointing from one to another. There can be data sharing or other types of behaviors associated with movement. The first step in hooking it all together is to add a button to the add/view scene that transitions to the edit scene:

1. Open the Storyboard editor and move the gray first scene arrow back to the add/view scene.

2. Drag out a button and set the title to Edit. The best way to do this is double-clicking the "Button" text on the storyboard layout view to select the title text, and then typing in the new title. When you do this, Xcode automatically resizes the button element to best fit the new text.

3. Center the button vertically between the Previous and Next buttons. Do this by dragging the button until you see both the vertical center and horizontal alignment guides, as shown in Figure 3-14.

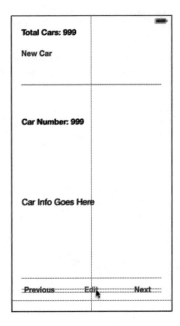

Figure 3-14   Aligning the Edit car button

In apps with more scenes, keeping track of the current scene, where the user came from, and the path back is very important and can be very complex. Luckily, iOS provides navigation controllers to manage the transitions. You learn a lot more about different controllers in Chapters 7, "Navigation Controllers I: Hierarchies and Tabs," and 11, "Navigation Controllers II: Split View and the iPad."

Carry out the following steps to add a `UINavigationController` (see Figures 3-15 and 3-16).

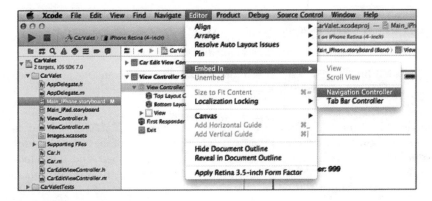

Figure 3-15   The Embed In menu

1. Open the storyboard and select Scene 1. One way to quickly do this is to click in the black object bar below the scene.

2. Embed the scene in a navigation controller. At the time this book is being written, this is done by selecting Editor > Embed In > Navigation Controller, as shown in Figure 3-15.

Figure 3-16   The new navigation controller

After embedding the new navigation controller, the first two controllers on the storyboard look like Figure 3-16. There are three important changes to note here:

1. Xcode moves the first screen arrow to the inserted navigation controller.

2. A relationship link is added between the navigation controller and the add/view scene.

3. The navigation controller adds a title bar to the scene.

Double-click in the title bar of the add/view scene to set the title to CarValet. Now run the app and notice how the title bar obscures the Total Cars label and part of the New Car button, as shown in the left side of Figure 3-17. The label and button are still there, and, if you look carefully at the title bar, you see the label underneath. In iOS 7, the title bar is slightly transparent, providing the users context as to where they are in the app.

Move all the view elements down, as the view does not scroll. You want to do that in roughly four steps:

1. Move the top of the car info view down.

2. Select the view elements above the car info view: the Car Number label, divider, New Car button, and Total Cars label. You can do this by pressing and holding the mouse below the Car Number label and dragging up to the top of the view, as shown in Figure 3-18.

3. Move these elements down until the top of the Total Cars label is about 8 points below the title bar.

4. Now adjust the top of the Car Info label so it is the default distance from the bottom of the Car Number label. The final layout will look like the right side of Figure 3-17.

Figure 3-17   Scene 1 before and after

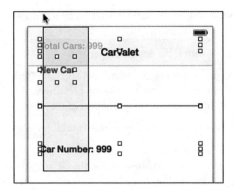

Figure 3-18   Selecting the view elements under the title bar

Transitions

Apps usually show standard graphical transitions when moving from one scene to another. iOS provides full support for those transitions.

Add a transition between the add/view scene and the edit scene when the valet taps the Edit button. To create the transition, Ctrl-drag from the Edit button to the edit scene. Choose Push from the popup that appears, as shown in Figure 3-19. Note that the title of this popup title is Action Segue. *Segues* are the objects that implement transitions. Figure 3-20 shows an arrow between the two scenes. That is how storyboards show segues. In code, they are represented by an instance of the `UIStoryboardSegue` class.

When you connect the scenes, Xcode automatically embeds the edit scene in the top-level navigation controller. This is why a title bar is added to the edit scene. Set the title of the scene to Edit. Also move all the contents of the view, the Car Number label and label/edit field pairs, down below the title bar.

Figure 3-19   The action segue popup

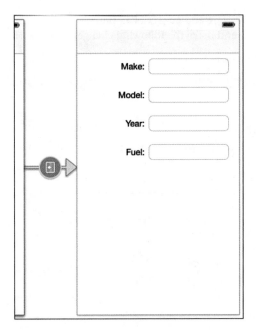

Figure 3-20   The segue connection

Run the app and tap the Edit button. The navigation controller brings the edit scene on from the left. It also adds a Back button to the title bar. Tap that to go back to the add/view scene. You learn more about the navigation bar, including how to add your own buttons, in Chapter 7.

Before you continue, update the views in the car edit scene so they are below the navigation bar.

The Magic Method: `prepareForSegue:sender:`

When you transition from one scene to another, there is usually some sort of transfer of information. The user is going somewhere to do something or view something. In the case of the CarValet app, the valet is editing and updating car data, but the technique described next also applies to many other apps.

You need to get the information to the new scene after the segue has been started but before the new scene gets to `viewDidLoad:`. This is exactly what `prepareForSegue:sender:` is used for. It is called after each segue is initiated but before the results of that segue occur. The most important thing to remember is that `prepareForSegue:sender:` is sent to the view controller currently on the screen, not the incoming one.

To pass a car, set the `carNumber` and `currentCar` properties in the incoming `CarEditViewController` and make the following changes to `ViewController.m`:

1. Import `CarEditViewController.h`.

2. Add the code shown in Listing 3-10 to `ViewController.m`, just above `viewDidLoad`.

Listing 3-10   `ViewController.m prepareForSegue:sender:`

```
- (void)prepareForSegue:(UIStoryboardSegue *)segue
                sender:(id)sender {
    if ([segue.identifier isEqualToString:@"EditSegue"]) {        // 1
        CarEditViewController *nextController;

        nextController = segue.destinationViewController;         // 2
        nextController.carNumber = displayedCarIndex + 1;         // 3

        Car *currentCar = arrayOfCars[displayedCarIndex];        // 4
        nextController.currentCar = currentCar;                   // 5
    }
}
```

Here's what happens in the numbered lines in Listing 3-10:

1. Set up the edit scene only if this is the edit segue.

2. Get the edit scene view controller from the segue. A segue has properties for the source and destination controllers. That is, for the controller currently on the screen (source) and the incoming one (destination).

3. Set the car number property, remembering that the index is 0-based.

4. Use the Objective-C subscripting instead of the `objectAtIndex:` message.

5. Find and set the right `Car` object.

To call the code inside the `if` statement, you need to set the identifier of the segue. To do that, open the Storyboard editor, select the segue that connects to the edit scene, and open the Attributes inspector. The segue is the arrow with the round type identifier shown between the two scenes in Figure 3-20. Set Identifier to `"EditSegue"`, the same string used in Listing 3-10.

Run the app, tap Edit, and then tap into the Make field. You see a screen like the one shown in Figure 3-21. Type in a make, model, and year and then tap the CarValet app's Back button.

Nothing changes. You might think things are broken, but actually, the car is saved. To see this, add another car, tap Next, and then tap Previous. The car detail screen shows the changes you made.

Before adding code to update the add/view display after an edit, there is a slight formatting issue with the edit scene. The lines with labels and edit fields appear to be off center. To make the view look balanced, line up the colons of the labels with the colon in the Car Number label. Good-looking apps are appealing partly because they show things lined up. A quick way to do this is the Guides feature in Interface Builder. With it, you create horizontal and/or vertical guides for aligning visual elements. Using Guides in combination with Snap to Guides (which you access by selecting Editor > Canvas > Snap to Guides) makes aligning views easy.

When a view is selected, you create a horizontal guide by selecting Editor > Add Horizontal Guide, or Cmd-Shift-hyphen. For a vertical guide, use Editor > Add Vertical Guide or Cmd-Shift-backslash. Drag the new guide to the desired position, using the displayed point location: a number displayed on each side of the guide, one showing the distance from the top or left, and the other showing the distance from the bottom or right. Figure 3-22 shows a guide with numbers. When you are done, drag the guide out of the view.

> ### Note: Why Are Add Horizontal/Vertical Guides Disabled?
>
> Adding a guide requires selecting a view. If the menu items are disabled, it is because you do not have an appropriate view selected. The easiest way to do this is to select the correct view in the left-hand column of view elements in the Storyboard editor.

Figure 3-21   Editing a car

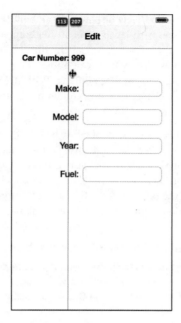

Figure 3-22   Using a vertical guide for layout

Why Not Segue Back?

Your first thought for telling the add/view scene to update may be to segue back. Unfortunately, this does not work. Each segue creates a new view controller. Instead of going back to the same add/view view controller instance that opened the edit scene, you would go to an entirely new view controller with just one car. Even worse, the original edit scene would not be disposed of, and each edit/return cycle would create two more controllers that take up memory.

You can update the add/view scene in at least three ways:

- Add a `currentCarUpdated` method to `ViewController` and a link to the `ViewController` object in `CarEditViewController`. Call the update method when the edit scene disappears.

- Use a protocol to tell `ViewController` to update.

- Use the unwind segue mechanism that first appeared in iOS 6.

The first option works but also significantly reduces code reusability and modularity. Each view controller object needs to know too much about the other, so they cannot be separated. Using protocols eliminates this problem, as discussed in the following section.

Improving the Storyboard: Take 1

Most apps have some need to exchange data with and/or trigger behaviors in other objects. Doing so can lead to interdependent code that is hard to maintain and reuse. Instead, you can use *protocols*.

Protocols increase the maintainability, reusability, and flexibility of your code. You can think of a protocol as a contract between a requestor and a provider. The provider, or delegate as it is usually called, agrees to implement a set of methods that the requestor can call. Each method is usually used for one of three purposes:

- To request data from the delegate, such as a `Car` object
- To inform the delegate of a change in state that enables saves, cancels, and/or redisplays data
- To perform a specific behavior, such as paging someone to fetch the car

The main advantage of protocols is reusability. Any class can be a delegate, as long as it implements the required methods. Similarly, any class can use the protocol methods to request information or initiate behaviors.

For more information on protocols, see the section on protocols on page 231 in *Programming in Objective-C 2.0*, 2nd edition, by Stephen G. Kochan, published by Addison Wesley. Alternatively, read the section on protocols in Apple's Objective-C documentation.

How Protocols Help

One of the advantages of object-oriented programming is encapsulation. You take the behaviors that make up your application, divide them out into components that interact together, and create objects for those components.

Some components might be pieces of the interface or views. Others could be parts of the underlying data or model. And still others, controllers, hook the two together. But those divisions are not quite enough. As you create more applications, you find yourself doing the same kinds of things over and over again.

One example is a series of related screens: One shows a set of data objects, the cars; another shows the detail for just one object, a car detail view; and another lets you edit attributes of that car, a make or year editor.

The typical first-time way to solve this common pattern is to hand around references to both the object and any relevant screens. The detail screen gets a reference to the overview, the Attribute editor gets a reference to the detail screen, and so on.

Then each class implements methods for other classes to call. The overview has a method for updating a car, as does the detail view. The detail view has a method for updating fields. Soon you end up with a spaghetti bowl of interrelated methods, attributes, and screens. A change in one place can have significant impacts on others. The code is not flexible, and it is difficult to maintain.

Even worse, the classes become specific to the type of data they show, the set of classes used, and the interface flows. They are not reusable.

> Using protocols is one way to fix that. A protocol defines how one kind of object talks to another: What information do I want? What information and status will I send? and What actions can I perform? Protocols can also specify which messages a delegate must support and which are optional.
>
> Using protocols allows you to untangle the spaghetti. Changes are easy to make because you know exactly how one class, screen, or object talks to another one. You can change the entire implementation code for the provider or user of the protocol, as long as they both conform to the protocol. And as you progress, you start to abstract out common types of needs into classes you can use for many projects.
>
> Using protocols makes all this much easier, especially when you realize that an object can be the delegate of, and/or implementer of, more than one protocol.

Exchanging Data Using a Protocol

One common use of protocols is to exchange data. The editor, or requestor, needs information, and the delegate provides and perhaps updates it. In this section, you design a protocol.

In this case, your car editor needs to know both the car object and number. The add/view scene, or delegate, needs to be informed when the car is changed so you can update the display. That makes three methods for the protocol:

- carToEdit returns the car object to edit.

- carNumber returns the number (not the index) of the edited car.

- editedCarUpdated tells the delegate that editing is done.

Now create a new Objective-C protocol called CarEditViewControllerProtocol and add it to the project. Set the content of the file to Listing 3-11. Creating a protocol file is just like creating a class, except you choose the "Objective-C protocol" file template.

Listing 3-11   CarEditViewControllerProtocol.h

```
//   CarEditViewControllerProtocol.h
//   CarValetScenes

#import <Foundation/Foundation.h>                    // 1

@class Car;

@protocol CarEditViewControllerProtocol <NSObject>   // 2

    - (Car*)carToEdit;                               // 3

    - (NSInteger)carNumber;
```

```
    -  (void)editedCarUpdated;

@end
```

Here's what happens in the numbered lines in Listing 3-11:

1. Import any headers for types used in the protocol. `Foundation.h` defines many of the core Cocoa types, including `NSInteger`.

2. `@protocol` is the directive for declaring a protocol. The next part is the protocol name, followed by any included protocols. In this case, `CarEditViewControllerProtocol` has access to any methods declared in the `NSObject` protocol, such as `self`, `class`, and `description`.

3. The method declarations are specified the same way as public class methods.

A forward reference is used for the `Car` object. Protocols are some of the most common places to use the `@class` directive. One reason is to prevent circular references. The other is to increase flexibility and reusability. The protocol does not care about the properties or methods of `Car`. This means you can use the protocol in another project that has a completely different `Car` class. All that matters is the name of the class.

When your protocol is defined, change the requestor to use it. For CarValet, start by changing the include file. In `CarEditViewController.h`, remove the `carNumber` property and then make the changes shown in bold in Listing 3-12.

Listing 3-12   **Protocol Changes to** `CarEditViewController.h`

```
#import <UIKit/UIKit.h>

#import "CarEditViewControllerProtocol.h"

@class Car;

@interface CarEditViewController : UIViewController

@property (weak, nonatomic) id <CarEditViewControllerProtocol> delegate;

@property (strong, nonatomic) Car *currentCar;
```

The second-to-last line in Listing 3-12 is an important part of the protocol mechanism. `id` is a placeholder reference for any class of object. This means that any class, including ones you have not even thought of yet, can be a delegate for the protocol. Although the edit scene requires `Car` to have certain properties, you still have lots of flexibility in how the object is implemented. You can reuse the editor scene in other projects. Also note that you do not use an asterisk when declaring a variable of type `id`. The declaration is supposed to be `delegate`, not `*delegate`.

Using angle brackets around `CarEditViewControllerProtocol` after the type indicates that whatever the class of `delegate`, it must conform to the protocol. That is, it must implement all the required methods of the protocol.

Now update `viewDidLoad` in `CarEditViewController.m` to match Listing 3-13. The changes are in bold. The class has access to the protocol because it is included in the corresponding .h file.

Listing 3-13   `CarEditViewController.m` **Modified** `viewDidLoad`:

```
- (void)viewDidLoad {
    [super viewDidLoad];

    NSString *carNumberText;
    carNumberText = [NSString stringWithFormat:@"Car Number: %d",
                        [self.delegate carNumber]];                        // 1
    self.carNumberLabel.text = carNumberText;

    self.currentCar = [self.delegate carToEdit];                           // 2
    self.makeField.text = currentCar.make;
    self.modelField.text = currentCar.model;
    self.yearField.text = [NSString stringWithFormat:@"%d",
                                    currentCar.year];
    self.fuelField.text = [NSString stringWithFormat:@"%0.2f",
                                    currentCar.fuelAmount];
}
```

Here's what happens in the numbered lines in Listing 3-13:

1. The car number is now returned from the delegate.

2. Call the delegate for the edited `Car` object.

The final modification tells the add/view scene to update itself. You add a call to `[self.delegate editedCarUpdated]` at the end of `viewWillDisappear:`.

Modifying the `ViewController` Class

Now that you have finished the requestor, it is time to update the delegate.

`CarEditViewController` now expects all data to be communicated through the protocol. It also lets the delegate know when editing has finished. You need to enable `ViewController` to be a delegate for the protocol.

Modify the top of `ViewController.h` by adding the bold code from Listing 3-14.

Listing 3-14   **Adding the Protocol to** `ViewController.h`

```
#import <UIKit/UIKit.h>

#import "CarEditViewControllerProtocol.h"

@interface ViewController : UIViewController
<CarEditViewControllerProtocol>
```

`<CarEditViewControllerProtocol>` says that `ViewController` supports—that is, conforms to—your protocol. Of course, you have not yet implemented any support. And this shows one of the ways Xcode helps you check that your code is complete.

Look in the status area in the center of the Toolbar (refer to area 3 in Figure 2-5), and you see a yellow warning triangle on the right side. This says that compiling your code causes warnings. Now open `ViewController.m` and look at the `@implementation` line. Xcode shows a warning. Click on the warning to find more details. It shows an incomplete implementation error because the protocol methods are missing.

Add the protocol methods shown in Listing 3-15 just above `newCar:`.

Listing 3-15   **Implementation of** `CarEditViewControllerProtocol`

```
- (Car*) carToEdit {
    return arrayOfCars[displayedCarIndex];          // 1
}

- (NSInteger) carNumber {
    return displayedCarIndex + 1;                    // 2
}

- (void) editedCarUpdated {
    [self displayCurrentCarInfo];                    // 3
}
```

Here's what happens in the numbered lines in Listing 3-15:

1. Edit the car currently displayed to the valet.

2. Make the number to display one larger than the index.

3. When the car information changes, update the displayed information.

The final step is to set `ViewController` as the protocol delegate. The best place to do this is `prepareForSegue:sender:`, as it is called early enough in the transition. Change the body of the method to match Listing 3-16.

Listing 3-16 **The New** prepareForSegue:sender:

```
if ([segue.identifier isEqualToString:@"EditSegue"]) {
    CarEditViewController *nextController;

    nextController = segue.destinationViewController;
    nextController.delegate = self;
}
```

This time, running the app works as expected. The valet can add cars, edit them, and see the changes when returning to the add/view scene.

Improving the Storyboard: Take 2

iOS 6 introduced a better way to return data to the view controller that initiated the segue: You simply add a special type of IBAction to your view controller. Usually an action method has an argument that looks like (id)sender, or it has no argument at all. By changing the argument to (UIStoryboard*)segue, you create a special type of action, one that can accept segues.

As you saw earlier in this chapter, prepareForSegue:sender: is sent only when one scene initiates a transition to another. It is a forward segue. This other kind of action is the opposite: It is sent when a scene wants to go back to the previous one. It *unwinds* the segue that first opened the scene, and it opens the previous scene without creating a new one.

To see this in action, add the code in Listing 3-17 to the bottom of ViewController.m.

Listing 3-17 **Unwind Segue Action for** ViewController.m

```
- (IBAction)editingDone:(UIStoryboardSegue*)segue {
    [self displayCurrentCarInfo];
}
```

Now you need to trigger the unwind action. In the storyboard, add a Done bar button item to the title bar in your car edit scene, as shown in Figure 3-23. Navigation bar buttons are smaller versions of their cousins, and there are many different kinds provided by the system.

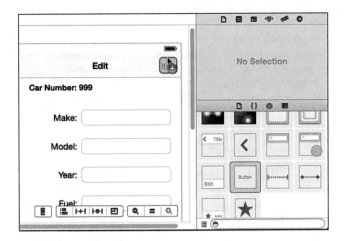

Figure 3-23   Adding a Done bar button item

Use the Attributes inspector to set the bar button item style to Done, and the identifier Done. As you are changing the identifier, look at the Identifier list for the many types you can add to future apps.

Now Ctrl-drag from the bar button to the exit segue item in the bar below the scene. Xcode dynamically generates a list of possible exit segues by looking in scenes that could have opened the current scene. Any unwind segues—that is, any IBAction method with a UIStoryboardSegue argument—are shown as possible targets for the exit. Your project has only one originating scene, but others can have complex trees of scenes.

Figure 3-24 shows the Action Segue popup with editingDone: selected.

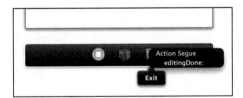

Figure 3-24   The exit segue

To prove that this works, add the following line to the end of editCarUpdated in ViewController.m:

```
NSLog(@"\neditedCarUpdated called!\n");
```

This causes editedCarUpdated called! to print to the console.

> **Pro Tip: What Is** `"\n"`**?**
>
> The NSLog statement has a weird-looking string (shown in bold): `"\neditedCarUpdated called!\n"`. In addition to the information printed out in the console, there are a couple of two character sequences: `"\n"`. Those are escape sequences, special characters you can use for a non-printable character, in this case, a newline. That is why the message shows up on a different line from the date and time of the log item. Using newlines can be a handy way to provide visual separation for items.

Run the project and try these two things:

1. Edit a car and touch the Back button. The console should show something like this:

   ```
   2013-03-16 20:28:14.115 CarValetScenes[45542:c07]
   editedCarUpdated called!
   ```

2. Edit a car, make some changes, and touch Done. The edit scene slides out, but the car does not appear to be updated. Move to the previous or next car and then move back to the just edited car. The displayed information is now correct.

The unwind action is sent before the car is updated in the `viewWillDisappear:` method of `CarEditViewController`. Once again, `prepareForSegue:sender:` is the magic method. Make the following changes so the displayed car detail is updated when returning to the add/view scene:

1. Open the Storyboard editor and select the Unwind Segue from Done to Exit from the list of scene objects on the left. The segue is shown selected on the left side of Figure 3-25.

2. Use the Attributes inspector on the right to give the segue the identifier `EditDoneSegue` as shown in Figure 3-25.

3. Add the `prepareForSegue:sender:` shown in Listing 3-18 to `CarEditViewController.m`. The car object update code is identical to that in `viewWillDisappear:`.

Listing 3-18   `CarEditViewController.m prepareForSegue:sender:`

```
- (void)prepareForSegue:(UIStoryboardSegue *)segue
                  sender:(id)sender {
    if ([segue.identifier isEqualToString:@"EditDoneSegue"]) {
        self.currentCar.make = self.makeField.text;
        self.currentCar.model = self.modelField.text;
        self.currentCar.year = [self.yearField.text integerValue];
        self.currentCar.fuelAmount = [self.fuelField.text floatValue];
    }
}
```

After checking for the right segue, the method updates the values in the car object. There is no need to call the `editingDone:` action, as that is taken care of by the segue mechanism. The Back button continues to work, using `viewWillDisappear:animated:`.

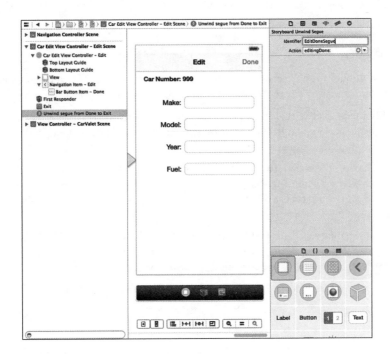

Figure 3-25   Setting the exit segue identifier

Now when you run the app and touch Done, everything works as expected.

Summary

In this chapter, you have used storyboards to create an application UI. You have created individual scenes and the transitions between them. You have also learned different ways to share data between scenes, which is something you will do in almost every application you write.

Using the Storyboard editor makes it easy to create and manage the many scenes that make up a typical application. You can change the flow of scenes, and you can zoom out to see an entire application at a glance.

As you worked through the chapter, you practiced using other useful development skills and tools, including code consolidation, forward references, protocols, and using guides to help layout and align view elements. You also learned about `UITextField`, a class you will use many times as a simple way to display and update content.

The interface in this chapter is designed for a 4-inch retina display. There is also a 3.5-inch display, as well as portrait and landscape in both display sizes. In Chapter 4, "Auto Layout," you learn a more powerful way to lay out your interfaces once so that they automatically adjust to many different screen sizes and orientations.

Challenges

1. Add an About This app scene. It can be triggered from an About button in the add/view scene or, for a more advanced challenge, an Info button in the navigation bar.

2. Modify the project so that it uses only the segue and unwind segue mechanisms to share data and updates. *Hint:* Start by removing the changes made to add the CarEditViewControllerProtocol.

3. Add behavior to the detail area of the add/view scene that disables the Previous and Next car buttons when there is no previous or next item. *Hint:* UIButton inherits from UIControlItem that has a BOOL property called enabled. YES enables the button, NO disables it.

4. Add the capability to cancel editing of a car. *Hint:* You need to have UI elements for saving and canceling as well as associated behaviors. It is possible to replace the Back button. It is also possible to have multiple segues with different names.

5. Update the property declarations in Car.h to include default properties.

4

Auto Layout

Apps on the iPhone and iPod touch can display their content in either portrait or landscape. And the devices come with either 3.5-inch or 4-inch displays. This makes four different layouts: portrait and landscape in each of two screen sizes. The interface you built in Chapter 3, "Introducing Storyboards," is specifically for 4-inch portrait displays.

Even with a visual editor, creating an app to support four different layouts can be a challenge, especially when you have dynamic screen elements and, as you will see in Chapter 5, "Localization," even different lengths for labels when the language changes. The result can be lots of customization code, as well as multiple view controllers for the same screen on your storyboard.

Auto layout is a constraint-based engine that lets you describe the relationships between views. Auto layout takes those descriptions, or constraints, and figures out how to position and size your app views for the current screen size and orientation. With it, you can create just one view controller per screen and tame the code.

This chapter shows you how to incorporate auto layout into your app design and development process. You start by discovering the key concepts of auto layout and using them to design constraints for your add/view scene. Next, you go through the process of modifying add/view to work in portrait for both screen sizes. You do this using practical design, layout, and debugging techniques. Finally, you create your own constraints and use the power of dynamically updating a controller's constraints to add landscape support.

By the time you are done with the chapter, you will have the tools you need to design and add auto layout to any scene; you will be able to create apps that adapt to different device sizes and orientations.

Auto Layout Basics

When there is just one screen size in one orientation, designing a scene means determining what view elements are needed, then placing those elements in the view, or perhaps, in a hierarchy of views. Adding rotation increases the complexity, though it is still manageable. But as soon as you add different screen sizes in addition to interface orientations, things get more complex. Earlier versions of iOS gave you some flexibility in specifying how views adjusted when their container changed size, but usually layouts with view dependencies or mildly complex hierarchies took code. Often that code required complex calculations and updating of many views.

For example, consider running an app on different-height portrait displays. You need to know the difference in height, which views can move and/or resize, and how far they can move and/or resize. Then you need to choose which views actually move and/or resize. If the difference in height requires moving more than one view, you probably need to write code.

Rotating between portrait and landscape is even more complex. To understand this, think about the portrait interface of your favorite iPhone app that supports rotation. Now imagine how the individual view elements move as the device is rotated to landscape and back again. Look at this on a device as the rotation happens and note how much movement happens. You can see that there is a lot of work going on in a continuously changing environment. Each view goes through multiple steps. And even though the interim steps are done for you, imagine calculating the end position and size of each view. There could be so much recalculation that it would be easier to create a different layout.

Figure 4-1 shows differences in the view car area for the CarValet app in the two portrait screen sizes. The highlighted rectangles show where the two screens differ. In this case, the difference in screens is entirely contained in one text view. This works because the smaller screen size has more than enough room to show all the car details. As you create more complex apps, you rarely find just one view that can absorb the difference. You usually have to start by identifying the areas with the greatest flexibility in size, then the next greatest, and so on until you have enough of a size difference to effectively display on each screen size.

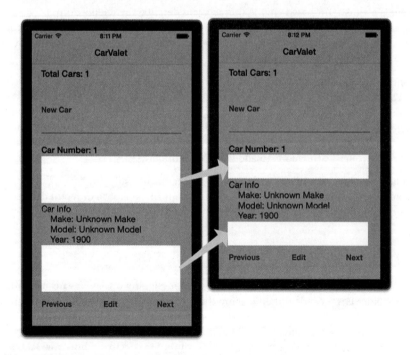

Figure 4-1   Changes in the view car area for different screen heights

Assuming that the layout is created for a 4-inch screen, you need to detect a 3.5-inch screen, calculate the difference in size, move the buttons, and resize the Car Info label. Some pseudo-code for implementing the changes follows:

```
if (!is4InchDisplay && (deltaHeight > 0.0)) {
    carInfoLabel.frame.size.height = deltaHeight / 2.0;
    previousButton.frame.origin.y -= deltaHeight;
    editButton.frame.origin.y -= deltaHeight;
    nextButton.frame.origin.y -= deltaHeight;
}
```

This is not valid Objective-C; real code would be longer. Even the pseudo-code does a lot of work for this simple case, and it is not immediately clear what the code is doing. Worse, any modification to the visual layout requires code modification.

It would be easier for you to describe how the views, or in this case groups of views, are related. The description uses three groups: Add car contains the total cars label and new car button; the separator view is by itself; and the view car group contains the rest of the elements:

- The add car group height is fixed, and it is the iOS standard distance from the top of its container.
- The separator view is a fixed distance from the top of its container and it has a fixed height.
- The view car group is the standard distance from the bottom and sides of the container view, and the top is a fixed distance from the divider view.

These descriptions create a view car group that can grow or shrink, based on the height of the screen. The "standard distance" refers to the recommended insets and spacing given by Apple. Since the view car group can change, you need to specify how the component views are related. The Car Info label has enough white space on top and bottom to adjust for the screen height:

- The Car Number label is fixed to the top of its container view (the view car group).
- Each button is fixed to the bottom of its container view.
- The top of the Car Info label is the standard distance from the bottom of the Car Number label, and the bottom is the standard distance from the top of the Previous button.

When the view car group grows or shrinks, the Car Number label and buttons stay fixed. The Car Info label changes height as needed. With some other descriptions, you can specify the entire scene.

With auto layout, you can create these kinds of descriptions, and iOS uses them to figure out how to position and size your views for the current screen size. The system takes care of adapting your interface to different screen heights and orientations. You can even force the system to recalculate if, for example, views are expanded or inserted.

Each relationship is a constraint for how one attribute of a user interface (UI) element is related to an attribute on another. It takes more than one constraint to express all the relationships between two views. For all the power of auto layout, there are only a few new methods and just one class, NSLayoutConstraint, for describing the constraints.

Constraints

The descriptions in the preceding section are constraints on the relationship between views. Sometimes the relationship is contained in the same view, sometimes between siblings, and sometimes between a view and its container. You can even specify relationships between views in different containers. For instance, you can say that the New Car button is the same width as the Previous button.

Pixels and Points

Before looking at constraints, it is important to understand the difference between pixels and points. *Pixels* are the physical hardware-addressable elements that show individual elements of color on the screen. They determine the resolution of the screen, and the number of pixels in a given area, or pixel density, determines how sharp objects on the screen appear.

To date, iOS units come with two pixel densities: normal and retina. Because retina has twice the pixel density, an image will show up correctly in normal density but at only half the size on retina. There are similar issues for correctly placing other screen elements, such as views. And there are screens with many different pixel densities. Writing code to deal with all possibilities would be a lot of effort.

Instead, Apple uses *points*, a pixel-independent representation of the drawing area of the screen. They take care of all the hard work for you. Coordinates on the screen, distance between elements, and values for constraints are all expressed in points, not pixels. And images can be provided in both normal and retina versions.

Constraint Relations

The simplest kind of constraint relates a feature of one view to itself, such as a fixed height of 44 points. You can express that constraint in an equation like this (note that this is not Objective-C code yet, just a way to think about constraints):

```
View1.height == 44.0
```

A more common relationship is the relationship of an attribute of one view to the attribute of another, such as the top of view 1 is in the same location as the bottom of view 2:

```
View1.top == View2.bottom
```

Look carefully at the two pseudo-code constraint relationships. They are not using the assignment operator, =. Instead they are using the equality operator, ==. This is an important part of constraints. They are not an assignment. The system can find a solution by changing either or both sides of the statement. For example, in the relationship above, the system can change both the top of View1 and the bottom of View2. As you will see later, this is a powerful way to build adaptive interfaces, especially as it is possible to indicate which constraints must be satisfied versus a relative ordering of those that the system can change.

In the examples in the previous section, there are places where the constraint relationship adds an offset, typically the standard separator distance. This would be the equation for the bottom of the view car group in the first constraint in the preceding section:

```
ViewCarView.bottom == ContainerView.bottom - StandardSystemDistance
```

Constraints define how the attribute of one view is related to the attribute of another view. Attributes are ways to describe view geometry and include the following:

- The `leading` and `trailing` edges of the view. These are alternatives to `left` and `right` when the relationship sense needs to change between left-to-right languages and right-to-left ones such as Hebrew or Arabic. For example, in English, `leading` is `left`, and `trailing` is `right`. In Arabic, `leading` is `right`, and `trailing` is `left`. You use these attributes in Chapter 5.

- The `left`, `right`, `top`, and `bottom` edges of the view.

- The `width` and `height` of the view.

- `centerX` and `centerY` for the X and Y centers of the view.

- The `baseline` of the view. This is used in views that show text, and is a typographical term corresponding to an imaginary line drawn under the bottom of characters that have no descenders. (When you are writing on a piece of lined paper, the descender is the piece of a letter that goes below the line. For example, *a* has no descender, but *p* and *g* do.)

This is the more general form of the constraint equation:

```
view1.attribute == (view2.attribute * scaleFactor) + offset
```

`view1.attribute` and `view2.attribute` are the two views and their attributes, `scaleFactor` is the amount of the second value to use, and `offset` is a constant added to the relationship. For example, relationship 1 above has two constraints. The first specifies the height of the view. Assuming that the height is `102` points, this is the constraint equation:

```
addCarView.height == 102.0
```

Notice that no other view is needed for the relationship. The scale factor is effectively `0`.

An example of using the scale factor is doubling the width of a view:

```
someView.width == someView.width * 2.0
```

In this case, the `offset` is `0`.

Finally, the relationship does not have to be equal. It can also be one of the following:

- Less than or equal to
- Greater than or equal to

For example, if you want to give the car info label a minimum height, you could show this with the following:

```
carInfoLabel.height >= MinimumHeightForContent
```

The formula is a way to think about how constraints are specified. Though you can make a call that creates the constraints using all the elements of the formula, it is the hardest way to do so. The next section shows an easier way to create constraints.

Creating Constraints

Now that you know what constraints are, how do you create them? You can create them in three ways:

- Using Interface Builder (IB)
- Using Visual Constraint Language (VCL)
- Specifying all the parts of the relationship equation

IB requires the least work to create constraints, VCL requires more work, and specifying the relationship equation takes the most work. You can even have IB automatically create the minimum number of constraints needed for a layout, but you are likely to want to change things. For this chapter, you use IB to create your own constraints by using visual tools.

For the last two ways of creating constraints, you use class methods of NSLayoutConstraint. In VCL, you use strings in a special format to specify how two views are related. One visual description usually results in multiple constraints. When you use the third method to create constraints, you create each part of just one relationship equation in a format that is long and difficult to read.

Exploring Constraints in IB

The best way to see how constraints are created in IB is adding some of your own. To do that, create a new single view application project in Xcode named LayoutTest. Remember, to create a project, you can choose File > New > Project or press Cmd-Shift-N.

When the project opens, select Main_iPhone.storyboard and select the File inspector. You do this either by selecting View > Utilities > Show File Inspector, pressing Cmd-Option-1, or selecting the utilities area and then the left-most icon in the control tab at the top of the utilities area. (In Figure 2-5, the utilities area is indicated by the number 8.)

The Use Autolayout box is checked. By default, storyboards are created with auto layout turned on. You could turn it off by unchecking the box.

Drag a UILabel onto the scene and align it with the lower left Xcode guidelines, as shown in Figure 4-2. Make sure the simulator target is a 4-inch retina iPhone and run the app. You see the label in the lower-left corner.

Stop the app, change the target to a 3.5-inch retina iPhone, and run the project again. The label is gone. To convince yourself the label is still around, use IB to change the top coordinate to 488. You can do this by selecting the label, opening the Size inspector, and changing the Y value.

You can confirm the label is in the correct place by selecting the label, moving the mouse out of the label, and holding down the option key. You should see something like Figure 4-3. The combination of lines and numbers tells you the distance between that edge of the label and the edge of the container. For example, the label is 80 points from the bottom of the screen and 20 from the left, or leading edge.

Run the app again in the 3.5-inch retina iPhone simulator. This time you can see part of the label at the bottom of the screen.

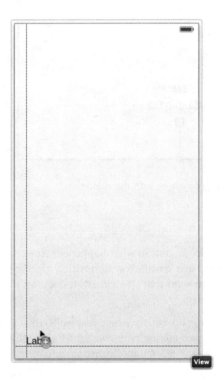

Figure 4-2   Aligning the label

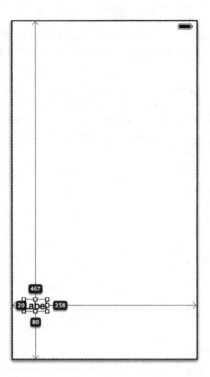

Figure 4-3   Showing distance to edges with the option key

Pixel-Perfect Help

The storyboard is set to use auto layout, so what happened? Xcode was trying to do what you asked. By placing the label at a specific location with a specific width and height, you are telling Xcode that is where you want that UI element. It does not matter how big the device is or what the screen orientation is.

To make sure the element shows up exactly where you want, the compiler generates the appropriate constraints. When you start adding your own constraints, they will take priority. That is, the compiler will not generate any placeholder constraints to override yours.

You may think this is not helpful, but actually it is exactly what you want. By making sure that elements are pixel-perfect until you say otherwise, you can quickly prototype layouts and easily try different combinations of constraints.

To see this, add a constraint for the distance between the label and the bottom of its container. Do this by selecting the label and then choosing Editor > Pin > Bottom Space to Superview, as seen in Figure 4-4.

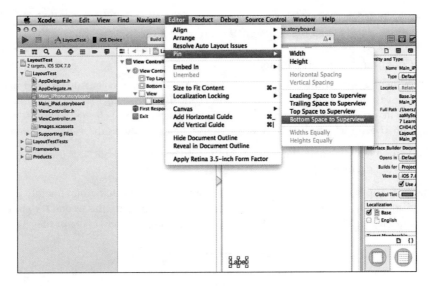

Figure 4-4   Using the Editor menu to set a constraint

You can tell the new constraint was added in one of three ways. Figure 4-5 highlights each way:

- There is a new Constraint item in IB's left-hand list of view elements.
- The selected label on the IB canvas shows an i-beam for the constraint.
- The Size inspector for the label shows the constraint.

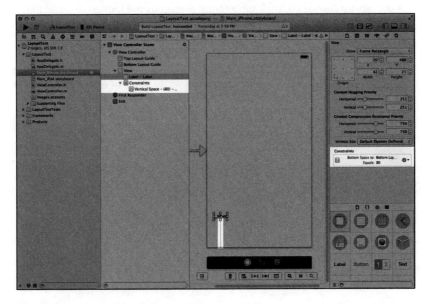

Figure 4-5   The three ways IB shows constraints

Now run the app, first on the 3.5-inch and then the 4-inch displays. You will see that the label is now the same height from the bottom of the screen on both displays.

Adding Constraints from the Toolbar

The Editor menu is one of three ways to add constraints in IB. The toolbar at the lower right of the IB canvas provides another way. Shown in Figure 4-6, the toolbar is divided into three groups. The first group has only one item and lets you quickly toggle all the view controllers on the canvas between the 4-inch and 3.5-inch screens. The figure shows the 4-inch screen setting.

The third group lets you zoom the contents of the storyboard in and out. It is used for getting an overview of larger storyboards.

The middle group is for constraints. Each of the first three items in that group roughly corresponds to an item in the Editor menu: The first item is for alignment, the second for pinning, and the third for resolving auto layout issues. Resolving issues is covered later in the chapter.

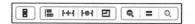

Figure 4-6   IB toolbar

Most of the alignment constraints are relationships between siblings. Two of them are used for centering a single view horizontally or vertically in a container. To see this, perform the following steps:

1. Drag another UILabel into the scene.

2. Double-click the label and change the string to "Center Y."

3. With the label still selected, click the alignment item in the toolbar to show the alignment popup.

4. Check the boxes for vertical and horizontal centering in the container. (You can see these options checked near the bottom of Figure 4-7.)

5. Open the Update Frames popup and choose to update Items of New Constraints as shown in Figure 4-7.

6. Click the button to add the constraints.

The label moves to the center of the screen and shows two blue i-beams, one for each constraint. Now use the popup to align the leading edges of both labels:

1. Select the Center Y label, then the original label.

2. Open the alignment popup on the toolbar and check Leading Edges.

3. Again select the popup to update frames of new constraints.

4. Add the constraint.

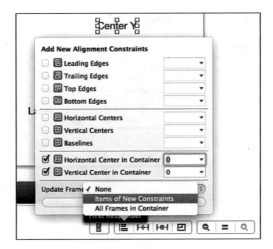

Figure 4-7   The alignment constraint popup

The original label moves over until its left (or leading) edge is aligned with the centered label. In addition, a new constraint i-bar is added between the leading edge of both labels.

The Pin Toolbar Item

The second item in the constraints section of the toolbar has the same items as those in the Editor > Pin submenu. But just like the alignment popup, the pin popup gives you much more flexibility. To see this, add another label and align it to the top leading edge of the container:

1. Add a UILabel to the scene.

2. Select the label and change the name to "Top Label."

3. With the label still selected, click the Pin item in the middle group in the toolbar to open the pin popup shown in Figure 4-8.

4. Use the dropdown triangle in the value boxes to set the Standard Value for the top edge constraint, also shown in Figure 4-8.

5. Now set the distance for the leading edge to the standard value.

6. Set the popup to update the frames of any items with new constraints and add the new constraints.

The new constraints are added and the label moves to the top-left area of the scene.

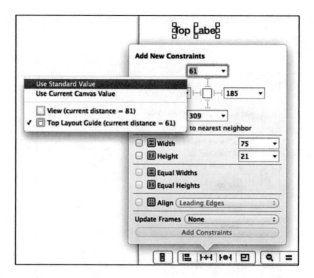

Figure 4-8   The pin constraint popup

The third item in the toolbar constraint area is for resolving constraint issues. You will see more on this later in the chapter. The last item of the group is how changes in constraints flow through the hierarchy when views are resized and is beyond the scope of this book.

Changing Constraint Values

Using the toolbar constraint popups is a great way to add both the constraints and any constants such as the standard distance from a container or an offset between two views. But what happens when you need to change those values?

One way is to select the view and open the Size inspector. Try this by selecting the Center Y label. The Size inspector shows you a list of all the related constraints. On the right side of each constraint is a gear that brings up a constraint editing dropdown shown in Figure 4-9. From here, you can delete or edit the constraint. What you can edit depends on the constraint. You will see more detail as you continue through this chapter.

Another way to edit constraints is double-clicking on a constraint on the IB canvas:

1. Select Top Label.

2. Make sure the Attributes inspector is selected in the utilities area.

3. There are two constraints, one to the left of the label, one on top. Double-click the left constraint.

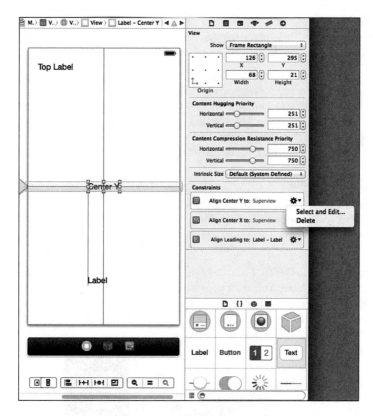

Figure 4-9   Constraints in the Size inspector

After you double-click, two changes happen as shown in Figure 4-10. The first is a quick editor pops up close to the selected constraint. You can see that editor on the left side of the figure. This editor is useful for quickly changing attributes shared by all constraints. On the left side, the Attributes inspector adds any constraint-specific editable items. As you work through the chapter, you learn more about the generally editable attributes as well as items associated with some types of constraints.

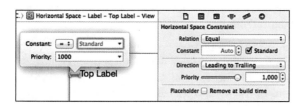

Figure 4-10   Popup constraint editor

In addition to editing constraints, you can use the details to verify that the constraints are giving you the correct positioning for the current screen size and rotation. Distances between views as well as edge alignments are also shown by using the Option key, just as you did previously.

This is because the Option key shows you the distances between the selected view and the view currently under the cursor. In Figure 4-3, there was only one other view...the superview. Now that you have more than one view, try selecting one of them and then hold down the Option key and move the mouse over other views. You will see the information change as you move between sibling views and the parent, or superview.

Dragging Out Constraints

The final way to specify constraints in IB is Ctrl-dragging (or right-mouse-button-dragging) from a view. When you complete the Ctrl-drag, IB offers a popup with possible choices for constraints. You can select one constraint or hold down the Shift key to select multiple constraints.

Try Ctrl-dragging from the Center Y label toward the right edge of the scene and let the mouse up soon after it exits the label. You see a constraints popup like the one on the left side of Figure 4-11. The right side of the figure shows the result of Ctrl-dragging from the bottom label and releasing in the Center Y label.

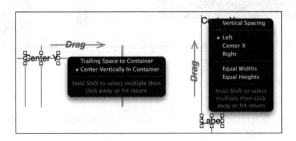

Figure 4-11   The Ctrl-drag constraint popup

Each popup shows the constraints that make sense given the direction of the drag and partici-pating views. The left side of Figure 4-11 shows only two possible constraints: one from the trailing edge of the label to the trailing edge of the container of that label and the other to center the label in a vertical direction.

The right side of Figure 4-11 shows more options because the views are siblings. The first two sections of the popup are all constraints based on vertical relationships. The first section sets a vertical distance constraint. The next section keeps the original label at the same distance and sets how the positioning of the views is related, aligning their left, center, or right locations. The third section is not related to either vertical or horizontal relationships. Instead, it sets views to the same width or height.

In both popups, you see a white circle in front of a constraint. This indicates an existing constraint between the views. For example, on the left side of Figure 4-11, the dot is for the labels' vertical centering constraint. On the right side, the white dot says there is already an align-left constraint between the two views.

Now try clicking and dragging in a diagonal line from the label on the bottom of the scene and releasing in the label on the top. When you do this, you get a constraint popup with a much larger selection of constraints, as seen in Figure 4-12.

Figure 4-12   Constraints for a diagonal drag

Ctrl-dragging is the fastest way to add constraints. The list of constraints shown in the menu depends on a combination of three things:

- The general direction of the drag

- The distance dragged

- The view where the drag ended

Xcode uses these three things to generate a likely list of possible constraints. In general, drags in a roughly horizontal direction show horizontal constraints. Drags in a vertical direction show vertical constraints, and diagonal drags show both types of constraints. Double-clicking the newly created constraint lets you quickly modify constants or other constraint-specific information.

Now it is time to use these skills and add constraints to CarValet.

Perfecting Portrait

There are models of the iPhone and iPod touch with different screen heights. Auto layout lets you create one set of constraints that works for all geometries and sizes. Right now, your layout is pixel-perfect for a 4-inch portrait display. In this section, you add constraints so it works with both 4-inch and 3.5-inch portrait displays.

Designing and adding constraints are part of the flow of designing and creating your user experience (UX). Figure 4-13 shows the general phases. First, you design your screen mockups, usually as part of the initial app specifications. When you start development, you do simple initial layout without using constraints. This is what you have done up to now with CarValet. In practice, initial designs tend to be modified during implementation, so it is best not to invest too much time creating constraints until the interface is fairly stable.

Eventually you start designing and adding the constraints. As you test your interface in various screen sizes and orientations, you usually find some problems. This gives you a cycle of adding some constraints, trying them, debugging, tuning, and then adding more constraints.

At some point, you have all the constraints you need as part of a fully functional app. At that point, you ship the app, as well as do any ongoing maintenance...and start designing the next release.

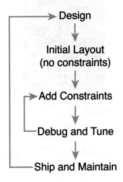

Figure 4-13   Constraint editing cycle

Thinking in Constraints

If you want to effectively use constraints, you need to change the way you think about designing and laying out your interface. The typical way is to think about the rectangles enclosing view elements in a coordinate system. Design is a matter of translating the look into the right coordinates and adding any code or additional layouts to adjust the look for different screen sizes and orientations.

With constraints, you think about your interface in a completely new way: How do the visual elements on your screen relate to each other? The goal is to find a set of constraints (relationships between views) that enable iOS to adapt the views to any of the supported screen sizes and orientations. It is not just how one view relates to another but also how to group views and how those groups relate. This can include relationships of views in one hierarchy to views in another.

Although this sounds complex, the key is to focus on the relationships. The constraints come from those relationships. And the easiest way to express the relationships is in language.

Before you start a design, it is important to understand that the set of constraints for a screen must meet two conditions. First, the constraints should combine to specify one and only one layout for a given screen size—that is, they should not be *ambiguous*. Second, the constraints must not *conflict*.

With conflicting constraints, there is no way to satisfy the highest *priority* constraints. Each constraint has a priority between 0 and 1000. 1000 is the default value and means the constraint must be satisfied. For instance, the Previous button cannot be both a fixed width at a priority of 1000 and a width that adapts to content also at a priority of 1000. Reducing the priority on either constraint or removing one constraint resolves the conflict. Conflicts cause runtime exceptions that might crash your app. Xcode usually gives warnings about possibly conflicting constraints, usually as you develop, as well as during compilation.

Ambiguity can be harder to find at design time. Unlike conflicts, the constraint system can position the affected views. However, it can position them in more than one way. A typical way ambiguity shows up is that when you change orientation and then change back, one or more views are not in the same place they were before the rotation.

As you will see when you start adding constraints, IB provides robust tools to identify both conflicts and ambiguity.

What Makes a Complete Specification

How do you know when you are done with your layout? For auto layout to unambiguously position all the views in an interface, it needs to find an origin and size for every view. To do that, every view must be part of one or more relationships that specify four constraints: two for the system to calculate the horizontal position and size, and two for the vertical position and size.

As you saw earlier in this chapter, constraints can be built using many parts of the view geometry. Table 4-1 shows what constraints unambiguously specify the Total Cars label. The completeness table is another example of an excellent tool for design. You can create tables like this for any level in the view hierarchy of a scene. Although there can be cross-hierarchy relationships, you should focus on checking completeness for one level of a hierarchy before moving deeper to the next one. As you will see later, IB shows constraints with problems in orange and uses blue for complete ones.

A good rule of thumb is to start checking completeness for the children of the main view, and after that is done, move on to checking the hierarchies of each child. In computer algorithm terms, you perform a depth-first traversal.

Table 4-1   **Constraint Completeness for the Total Cars Label**

Axis and Metric	Total Cars Label Attribute	Related View Attribute
Horizontal position	Leading edge	Standard distance from the leading edge of the superview
Horizontal size	Width	Wide enough to display the string in the label
Vertical position	Top	Standard distance from the top of the superview
Vertical size	Height	Tall enough to display one line in the current font/size

The Total Cars label can act as an anchor view—that is, a view with completely specified constraints for any given screen size, usually near an edge or edges of the screen or group. You can use it to help specify other views, such as the New Car button. When designing constraints, looking for anchor views is a good starting point.

As you look at the constraints, you might wonder how the system knows how to set the width and height of the label—especially since you could change the text of any label at runtime.

Intrinsic Content Size

The content of certain UI elements has a natural size. For images, it is the size of the image; for labels, the amount of space required to display the text in the current font; switches have their own size, and so on. This natural, or *intrinsic*, size is used by the constraint system when figuring out the width and/or height of a view.

In Table 4-1, both the width and height have an intrinsic value: the amount of space required to show the text for the label in the font used by the label.

UView includes an intrinsicContentSize method returning a CGSize—that is, a width and a height. The default is to return UIViewNoIntrinsicMetric—that is, no intrinsic value, for each component. Some view system classes that override the method include UILabel, UIImageView, UISwitch, and UIButton.

Adding/Viewing Cars: Designing and Implementing the Constraints

Before you added any constraints to LayoutTest, you moved the label, ran it on a 3.5-inch screen, and only saw part of the label. Figure 4-14 shows CarValet running on the smaller screen. This is because Xcode adds compile time constraints for any views you have not constrained. These added constraints are just enough to make sure your interface matches exactly what is on the IB canvas, resulting in the bottom row of buttons being cut off. You need to design a set of constraints that works on both screen sizes, something you could do as you design your UX.

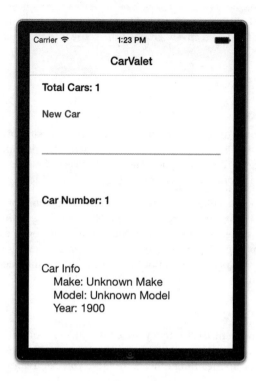

Figure 4-14   CarValet on a 3.5-inch screen

The following is a good process for integrating constraints into the design of an interface:

1. Specify what the user can do on the screen (that is, what the behaviors are).

2. Choose visual elements that support the behaviors and create a rough layout.

3. Break up the visual elements into relevant groups, based on screen functionality. There might be only one group if the behavior is simple.

4. Do an initial design of how the visual elements are arranged in the groupings.

5. Design how the groupings relate to each other in the different layouts: portrait and landscape in both 3.5- and 4-inch screen sizes. For now, you look at only a general solution to landscape, and you work on a more detailed design later.

6. Iterate through steps 3, 4, and 5 until you have something that works on the target layouts. Sometimes this may change steps 1 or 2.

7. Express the constraints in natural language.

Steps 1 and 2, and possibly 3 and 4, are part of any UX design; the rest are constraint-specific.

You designed the scene behaviors in Chapter 3 (step 1). The interface elements already exist (step 2), and you have already effectively grouped the scene into three parts (step 3):

- An add car group
- A separator view
- A view car group

The separator view is not connected with any behaviors. It is the kind of visual element used to support visual clarity. Other kinds of nonbehavioral elements can provide decoration or other ways of potentially delighting the customer. The key is to keep these elements to a minimum. Think carefully about each one and be clear on why it is being added.

In a normal project flow, designing the constraints along with groups of views would be done before writing any constraint-related code. Ideally, it is done before laying out the scene, though more often it is done after the layout becomes stable. Although early design is not always possible, and the scene might be modified as the app progresses, doing more upfront design work can save a significant amount of time laying out the interface, as well as in debugging constraints later on.

The Three Add/View Car Groups

Modifying your add/view scene to effectively use constraints for portrait is a good exercise in adding constraints to an existing scene. It also gives some practice in designing the constraints, solving interim problems, and learning other techniques you can use for your own projects.

There are only two views in the add car group, and they each have simple relationships. The Total Cars label is at the top on the leading (or, in English, left) side. The bottom of the New Car button is attached to the bottom of the area and aligned with the leading edge. This layout should work for both portrait and landscape, with the only difference being how wide and tall the area is.

The separator view is even simpler. It is a 2 points high (portrait) or wide (landscape) line that separates the add and view areas. It stretches across the view along the appropriate axis for portrait or landscape. The separator is visually halfway between the add and view car groups.

There is no direct way of specifying that an attribute of a view is halfway between two other views, so you have three basic options here:

- If the attribute of the halfway view is between two views with fixed positions on the relevant axis (or axes), you can use a spacing constraint between the closest appropriate edge of a fixed view and the edge of the separator. For the vertical axis, the constraint would be from the top to bottom or the bottom to top edges. The constant value of the constraint corresponds to the distance.
- You can insert a new container view that is pinned to the relevant sides of the two views, put the halfway view inside the new container, and set a constraint to center it horizontally and/or vertically in this new container.

- You can calculate the constraint yourself at runtime and either update an existing constraint or add a new constraint to the appropriate container view. This might involve removing some of the automatic constraints that IB added or even ones you added in code.

In this case, you can use the first solution because the top of the add view area is a fixed distance from the top of the container. And as you will see, the view car area has a variable height based on the height of the screen. The distance from the bottom of the add car group to the separator is the same as the distance from the separator to the top of the view car group.

Halfway Approach 2: The Invisible Pinned Container

Sometimes you can use an invisible container view for correctly placing a view element halfway between two others. Follow these steps to do this for portrait in the add/view scene:

1. Add a `UIView` to the top-level view container between the add car and view car groups.
2. Add a constraint to pin the top of the new view to the bottom of the add car group.
3. Add a constraint to pin the bottom of the new view to the top of the view car group.
4. Set the width of the new view to be equal to the add group.
5. Move the separator view inside the new view and add constraints to set the separator height to `2.0` and set the width to the same as the container view.
6. Add a constraint to vertically center the separator in the new container.
7. Set the background color of the new container to the main background color. If the background color is not consistent, you can set it to clear, though there is a slight performance penalty when you do this.

When you use IB to visually edit the constraints, you might end up with more views and constraints than when you specify them in code. However, it can be more obvious and easier to maintain.

The view car group is slightly more complex than the add car one. The Car Number label is at the top on the leading edge. What do you do about the Car Info label and buttons? The expectation for iOS applications is that controls for data element navigation and editing are near the bottom of the data they control. Based on that, it would make sense to have the buttons "attached" to the bottom of the container and evenly spread out.

That leaves the Car Info label. In portrait view on both screen sizes, there is considerably more vertical space than needed to show the info. This indicates a prime location for adding or removing vertical space. In Figure 4-1, the Car Info label grows or shrinks based on the vertical screen size. In landscape, there is enough vertical space to show the Car Number label, Car Info label, and button row. That just leaves the question of horizontal space, and as you see later, there is enough.

There is one more important decision to make before designing the constraints. Does it make sense to encapsulate the views for each functional group in their own container? In other words, do you add a `UIView` for the add car group and put the Total Cars label and New Car button in that view? Similarly, do you add a `UIView` for the view car group and move all the related labels and buttons inside?

The answer lies in what happens in landscape. It is easiest to put the add car group on the leading edge of the screen, the view car group on the trailing edge, and the visual separator between them. You could do this by changing the relevant constraints for every label, button, and the separator, but that is a lot of work. It is better to minimize the number of changing constraints. In this case, it is easier to change the constraints on the container views which minimizes the changes required by the subviews of those groups.

Designing the Top-Level View Constraints

Now that you have a rough idea of the top-level constraints and view area groupings, it is time to start designing the constraints. You work down the hierarchy—that is, start with the top-level views and groups of views, move to the visual elements that make up those groups, and so on. The goal is to create descriptions of the constraints in your native written language that include all the relevant parts of the constraint equation.

As mentioned earlier, you should look for anchor views, specify their constraints, and keep adding more descriptions until you have a complete specification: a set of unambiguous descriptions that have no conflicts. You can perform this cycle for the top-level groups, then for the views in each group hierarchy, and finally for any cross-hierarchy constraints.

The simplest description for the three areas is that the add car group should be anchored to the top of the superview, the view car group anchored to the bottom of the superview, and the separator halfway between the two. That is a good start, but it is not precise enough to implement. If you look at both screen sizes in Figure 4-1, you see a few important details:

- **Description 1:** The add car group is the standard distance from the top and sides of the superview.
- **Description 2:** The add car group is a fixed height.
- **Description 3:** The separator is a fixed distance from the bottom of the add car group and the standard distance from the sides.
- **Description 4:** The view car group is the standard distance from the bottom and sides of the superview.

In most cases, these descriptions are sufficient to create constraints. For example, description 1 contains three pseudo-constraint equations:

```
AddCarGroup.top == AddCarGroup.Container.top + StandardSystemDistance
AddCarGroup.leading == AddCarGroup.Container.leading + StandardSystemDistance
AddCarGroup.trailing == AddCarGroup.Container.trailing - StandardSystemDistance
```

Some parts of the description are missing important details, such as the actual height in description 2 and the distance in description 3. You can get those numbers by looking at the Size inspector for the elements in IB or selecting the relevant view, holding down the Option key, and moving the mouse over the target views. More importantly, the list does not give a complete list of constraints. For example, although there is a constraint for the bottom of the view car group, there is no indication of the top or height.

One way to know if you have a complete set of constraints is to make a completeness table similar to Table 4-1 showing each view and the constraints that specify horizontal and vertical position and size. Table 4-2 does this for the three top-level views. After you make such a table, you can quickly see what constraints are missing.

Table 4-2   **Constraints for Top-Level Views**

Axis and Metric	Attribute	Related View Attribute (Description)*
Add Car Group		
Horizontal position	Leading edge	Standard distance from the leading edge of the superview (1)
Horizontal size	Trailing edge	Standard distance from the trailing edge of the superview in combination with Horizontal position (1)
Vertical position	Top	Standard distance from the top of the super-view (1)
Vertical size	Height	Fixed height of 102 points (2). Note that the height is based on the visual balance of the screen on both 3.5- and 4-inch displays.
Separator View		
Horizontal position	Leading edge	Standard distance from the leading edge of the superview (3)
Horizontal size	Trailing edge	Standard distance from the trailing edge of the superview in combination with Horizontal position (3)
Vertical position	Top	22 points from the bottom of the add car group (3)
Vertical size	Height	MISSING
View Car Group		
Horizontal position	Leading edge	Standard distance from the leading edge of the superview (4)
Horizontal size	Trailing edge	Standard distance from the trailing edge of the superview in combination with Horizontal position (4)
Vertical position	Bottom	Standard distance from the bottom of the superview (4)
Vertical size	Height	MISSING

* The numbers in parentheses refer to descriptions 1-4 given earlier in this section.

You can see from Table 4-2 that there are missing constraints for both the separator view and the view car area. Adding a description for the height of the separator is easy:

- **Description 5:** The separator is a fixed height of 2 points.

The view car group is the most challenging because the height can vary depending on the height of the screen. So far, each group has one constraint that determines the height. Using a single fixed height constraint for the view car area would mean switching constants for the 3.5- and 4-inch screens. But that defeats the purpose of using constraints. Imagine if Apple released an iPhone with a 5-inch screen. Suddenly your constraints would stop working, as the view car area would be too short. It is better if the system does the work for you.

And that is where the answer lies. The constraint system does not just read a set of constant value constraints; it uses the constraint equations to find a solution that works. This is very powerful when you understand that the runtime can change values on both sides of the equations. It is not just answering a set of questions with known left-hand-side values. It is solving a set of equations, finding values for both sides that result in positions and sizes for all views. For the mathematically inclined, the runtime is solving a system of linear equations.

The system might go through constraints multiple times, trying out combinations that work to satisfy the left- and right-hand sides of each equation. (Okay, it is more technical than this, but you get the idea.) This means you can use multiple constraints that are combined to specify one or more of the positions or sizes.

Here is one description you could add that, when combined with description 4, allows the system to consistently calculate the height:

- **Description 6:** The top of the view car area is a fixed height (22 points) from the bottom of the separator view.

This works because there is enough information to calculate the height. Both the top and bottom locations are specified in relation to anchor views. Because the superview is the top level app view, it is fully specified. Because of this, setting the bottom of the car view group in relation to the superview is also fully specified.

Figuring out the height relies on a chain of relations to an anchor view. The add car group has a fixed height and is anchored to the top of the superview, the root view of the application. Then the separator is a fixed distance from that group. Next, the separator has a fixed height, so the bottom of the separator is unambiguously specified relative to the enclosing root view. Now the top of the view car group is set a fixed distance from the bottom of the separator. Both the top and bottom of the view car group are fully specified. The height is a simple matter of subtraction:

```
viewCarArea.height = viewCarArea.bottom.y - viewCarArea.top.y
```

Use `CH04 CarValet Starter`: A Brief Excursion in Becoming Modern

In 2012, Apple introduced Modern Objective-C, a set of syntactical shortcuts that make code clearer and easier to write. Up until now, the code in this book has used whatever syntax helped in learning a concept.

By this point, you have seen the longer syntax for things such as creating arrays, accessing items in arrays, and the `alloc/init` pattern. From now on, the code in this book uses the Modern Objective-C syntax. All source files in `CH04 CarValet Starter` have been updated to Modern Objective-C, including updating the properties in `Car.h`.

Note that if you want to check or convert a project, you can use Edit > Refactor > Convert to Modern Objective-C Syntax.

Implementing the Top-Level View Constraints

You have designed a set of constraints for a screen, including how to effectively use invisible view containers to create subgroups. Now it is time to create those constraints in the UI. Again, you start with the top-level constraints and work your way down.

Table 4-2 along with descriptions 5 and 6 from the previous section specify the constraints you need to add. Start by adding the container view for the add car area. Ideally you would have designed the grouping views before starting work with IB. That way you can add the top level grouping views and then add their children. This example is likely to be more work than your own projects because you would have started with the grouping views. Instead, you have to create the groups and move in existing views:

1. Open `CH04 CarValet Starter` project and select the `Main_iPhone.storyboard` file.

2. Add a `UIView` to the main view controller and drag it into the upper-left corner of the main view below the navigation bar.

3. With the view still selected, open the pin constraint popup from the IB toolbar.

4. Figure 4-15 shows setting the constraints for the Add Car grouping view:

    - The top of the view is the standard distance from the container, as are the leading and trailing edges.

    - The height is fixed at `102`.

    - Update Frames is set to update items of new constraints.

5. When your pin popup matches the one in Figure 4-15, click to add the constraints. You should see the Total Cars label and Add Car buttons disappear on the IB canvas. This is because the new view is opaque, higher in the hierarchy, and occupies the same space.

    Note that if the grouping view disappears or you see other strange behaviors, such as red or orange lines, press Undo twice and make sure the view is really at the top left. The pin popup sets constraints to the nearest neighbor, and you want to make sure that neighbor is the root view of the controller.

6. On the left-hand list of views in IB, double-click the name of the new view and change it to Add Car Group. Then move the new view to the top of the hierarchy. When you do this, the Total Cars label and New Car button appear.

7. Still using the left-hand list of views, move the Total Cars label and New Car button into the newly added view. When you move the elements in, they are centered in the container. You set constraints for them later.

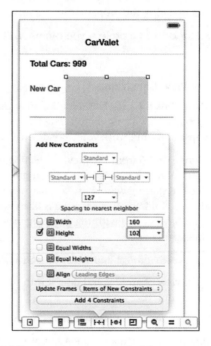

Figure 4-15   Setting the Add Car grouping view constraints

Next, set up the constraints for the separator view based on Table 4-2 and description 5. Once again, the pin constraint popup makes this easy, allowing you to set all three constraints:

- Standard distance from the leading edge
- Standard distance from the trailing edge
- 22 points from nearest top neighbor above the separator, that is, the add car group

The configured pin popup will look like Figure 4-16.

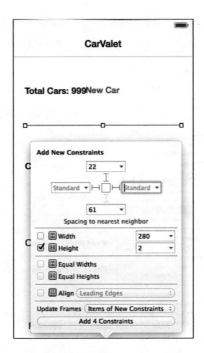

Figure 4-16   Setting the separator view constraints

Now add the view and associated constraints for the view car group. The constraints are based on Table 4-2 and description 6:

- The leading, trailing, and bottom edges of the grouping view are the standard distance from the superview.

- The top edge of the grouping view is 22 points from the bottom of the separator view.

To use the pin constraint popup, follow these steps:

1. Drag a UIView to the main view controller so that its left and bottom edges are the standard distance from the superview.

2. Move all the components of the view car group into the grouping view. These are all top-level views except for the add car group and the view separator.

3. With the View Car grouping view selected, open the pin constraint popup.

4. Enter 22 for the top space to nearest neighbor constraint. This is to the separator view.

5. Choose Standard Value for the left (leading), right (trailing), and bottom distances.

6. Make sure to choose to update frames of new constraints and add the constraints.

When you have finished, the top-level views and their constraints should look like those shown in Figure 4-17.

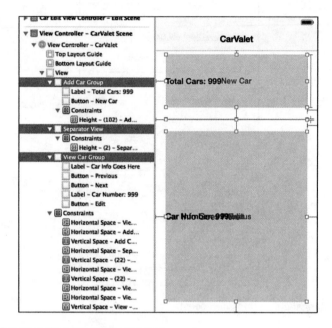

Figure 4-17 Top-level view constraints finished

Previewing Constraints

The grouping views and constraints have all been added to a 4-inch screen. Now you need to make sure they will work with a 3.5-inch one. There are three basic ways to so this:

1. Run the app on a 3.5-inch screen simulator and/or device.

2. Change the view controller in IB to a 3.5-inch size.

3. Use the IB Preview mode to show how the constraints will work with any desired device screen sizes and orientations.

Of the three methods, running on a physical device is a critical step before you release an app. However, during development you can get a good idea from running on the simulator. You can choose both a real device and different simulator sizes using the right side of the scheme popup (see item 2 in Figure 2-5).

As you are adding the constraints, you can get quick feedback either by switching the view controller on the IB canvas between the two screen sizes (number 2 previously) or by using a preview window (number 3).

On the canvas, you can change the size and orientation of an individual view controller using the Attributes inspector shown on the left side of Figure 4-18. Just select the view controller and then select the appropriate value from the size and/or orientation popup. The view controller changes in IB, and views are updated based on their constraints.

The other way to quickly toggle between the two screen sizes is with the screen-size toggle button. Clicking the button toggles the size of all top-level view controllers on the current IB canvas. The right side of Figure 4-18 shows the button as it looks when displaying the two different screen sizes.

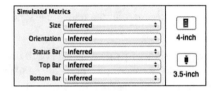

Figure 4-18   Toggling screen size and orientation for view controllers

The most flexible way to view the effect of constraints is using the assistant editor preview mode. This will show you how the current controller will look in one selected screen size and orientation. Additionally, the preview dynamically updates as you change constraints in the main IB editing window.

You can change the size, orientation, or even iOS version of the device screen in a preview pane, and you are not limited to just one preview. With a large screen, you can view the IB editor and then at least two preview panes, one for each size. In fact, the larger screens let you show not only sizes but rotations as well.

Before you open a preview pane, use the attributes editor to set the background color of each grouping view to light gray. This helps you see how they do or do not resize as you change screen size.

Opening Two Assistant Previews

The easiest way to open the assistant preview is by choosing where the view opens. You can select where a view opens using the placement panel, an Xcode helper that opens whenever you hold Option-Shift when choosing to open a new view.

To show the preview, select the related files icon in the upper left of the IB window, hold down Option-Shift, and select the Preview item for the file you are editing. Figure 4-19 shows selecting the preview item with the related files icon in the upper left. The icon has been highlighted to make it stand out.

When you have selected the preview while holding Option-Shift, you are shown the placement panel seen at the top of Figure 4-20. This panel gives you a great deal of flexibility when opening any new views.

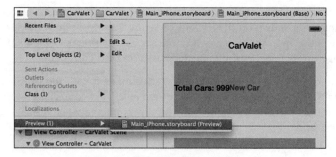

Figure 4-19   Opening an assistant preview from the related files menu

There are three basic parts to the placement panel. The title of the panel is the file you are placing. On the bottom of the panel is a description of what the placement panel does if you press Return. You can dismiss the panel at any time by pressing Escape.

The middle area lets you choose where to place the contents of the file. You can replace the content of an existing pane, put the content in a new pane by selecting an area with a +, or even in a whole new window by selecting the background item with the +.

The blue area on the left-hand panel is the current IB window. You want to open the preview in a new assistant pane, so select the area with the + to the right of the blue area. The bottom of Figure 4-20 shows what the placement panel looks like after selecting this area. Notice that the text on the bottom of the panel has changed to say it will open a new assistant editor. Also note that you can use the placement pane when opening any file, not just preview windows.

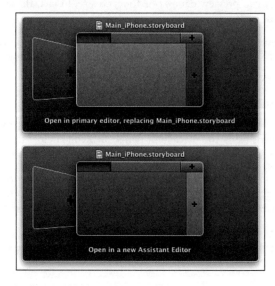

Figure 4-20   Placing the first assistant preview panel

After you press Return, a preview is added in an assistant pane next to the existing IB canvas, as shown in Figure 4-21. The main contents of the new pane look similar to the canvas. Updating items on the canvas updates the preview pane. To see an example, select the Total Cars label in the add car group and use the pin constraint popup to set the distance to the top of the super-view to 0. Make sure that you choose to update frames for new constraints.

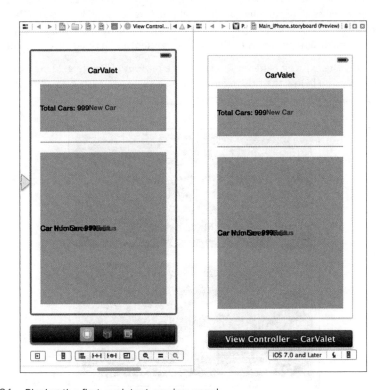

Figure 4-21   Placing the first assistant preview panel

Because the set of constraints for the label are ambiguous, there are many different things the label could do, including disappear off the screen. The key is that it does it in both the canvas and the preview.

The preview pane also has some differences in the surrounding controls. The first things to notice are two small buttons in the upper right. The one with the + lets you add another assistant editor below the current one. The other button with the "x" closes the pane.

The true power of preview comes from the control bar at the bottom of the pane. Try clicking the far-left button. Just like the Size button on the main IB canvas, this switches the preview between 4- and 3.5-inch screens. The middle button rotates the screen. The first button shows the screen as it would look on different OS versions. This is useful if your app needs to support iOS versions, such as iOS 6.1, that use different interface elements for things like buttons.

A simple way to save time as you add constraints is to show a preview of both the 3.5- and 4-inch screens. You do this by opening a second preview pane and placing it below the first one. This is done in almost the same way as adding the first preview pane, except when the placement panel comes up.

Figure 4-22 shows the resulting panel before and after selecting the location for the new pane. Notice that the initial state of the placement panel is different from Figure 4-20. This time there is a pane with a star. The star is how the placement panel indicates that you are opening the same thing and can either shift focus to the existing content pane or add another copy.

Select the + below the existing pane, as shown on the bottom of Figure 4-22, and a new preview pane opens up below the existing one. Each preview pane can have different settings, though they are all previewing the same thing.

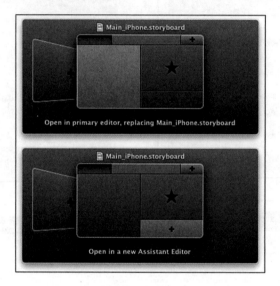

Figure 4-22   Placing the second assistant preview panel

One important thing to remember about preview panes is that they only show the results of constraints added in IB. They do not show any constraints added or changed in code. For that, you need to use the simulator or a device.

Designing and Implementing the Add Car Constraints

You have finished adding the constraint relationships for the top-level groups. Now you can add relationships for their subviews. The process of completing all constraints for the highest level and then working down the hierarchy is one you will use repeatedly. It is the most effective way both to create the initial constraints, as well as flow through changes.

The views in your add car area seem to have simple constraints. The Total Cars label is pinned to the top and leading edge of the container and is high enough for one line of content. The New Car button is pinned to the bottom and leading edge of the container and is high and wide enough to show the button title and be an effective touch target.

Finding Constraint Issues

You have already added one of the constraints for the views in the add car group when you pinned the total cars label top edge to the top edge of the superview. At the moment, the constraints do not work. IB shows you when there are constraint issues in three main ways. First, when you select the total cars label, the i-bar for the top constraint is orange, indicating there is an issue.

The second way is by showing a triangular yellow caution icon in the address bar above the IB canvas. Because there are also constraint issues with the contents of the view car group, you can already see this caution icon in the address bar above the IB canvas in Figure 4-21. The icon is roughly in the middle of the top bar in the figure and looks the same as each of the yellow triangles in Figure 4-23.

Clicking the icon brings up a list of issues, as you can see in Figure 4-23. Selecting the line for the Total Cars label selects that label. You can also navigate through the issues using the forward and backward buttons on either side of the yellow caution icon in the address bar.

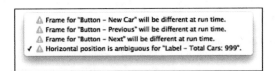

Figure 4-23   Constraint issues in the IB view list

The third way is a red circle with a white arrow in IB's left-hand list of view controllers, as shown on the left in Figure 4-24. Clicking the arrow shows details for any constraints that have issues, as shown on the right in the figure. There is an item in that list for every view that has some sort of problem.

Figure 4-24   Constraint issues in the IB view list

Each item includes the view with the issue, a brief description of the issue, and a quick fix button (the red octagonal button with the circle). Clicking the quick fix button opens a popup with a recommended fix and a button to either apply the fix or cancel.

You can get general information and help on the problem by moving the mouse over the item. When you do that, an info button appears, as seen after the words "Missing Constraints" in Figure 4-24. Clicking that usually gives you a short description of the issue as well as general approaches to find and/or solve the issue.

To complete the constraints for the children of the add car and view car groups, you need to know about two more types of constraints: the content hugging priority and the content compression resistance priority.

Constraints and View Content

As you saw earlier, elements containing strings, images, and so on, have an intrinsic content size, a size that best fits the content. When you build apps with labels, buttons, and other elements, you need to think about how auto layout will display that content, especially as the size of the container changes. As you see in Chapter 5, strings can be especially tricky as you adapt the interface to different languages. The question is how to specify constraints related to content.

Open the Size inspector for the Total Cars label shown in Figure 4-25. Roughly in the middle are two areas called Content Hugging Priority and Content Compression Resistance Priority.

Content hugging tells the system how important it is to avoid excess padding around the content along a particular axis. This is usually used for views that contain strings or images. For the Total Cars label, you want the view to be as wide as required to show the string but no wider. In other words, you want to hug the content in the horizontal direction.

Content compression resistance refers to staying large enough to show all the content along an axis. If you want a label to show as much of the string as possible, increase the vertical content compression resistance, and then set Lines to 1 in the Attributes inspector to make sure only one line of text is shown. If the resistance is too low, your string is likely to get clipped. Instead of showing "Total Cars: 23," it might show "Tota..."

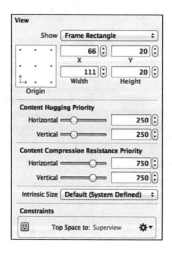

Figure 4-25   Content constraint priority editors

The most important thing to understand about priority is that only the relative difference matters, not the magnitude. The system only looks for values that are different from the norm, and it stack ranks those values only if there is a conflict. For example, if there are three labels with compression resistance priorities of 751, 752, and 753, and the system can satisfy all those requirements, the priorities are ignored. If the system can satisfy only one content hugging request, the one with a priority of 753 wins. It makes no difference if the priority is 999 instead of 753; only the relative value matters.

The only time the actual value makes a difference is when resolving competing constraints. In other words, it does not matter if you set the horizontal content hugging priority of the Total Cars label to 251 or 1000, unless there are other content hugging priorities that interact with the label.

The safest practice is to use an increment or decrement of 1 unless you know there is some possible conflict. This applies to both content hugging and compression resistance.

If you are not sure that the label is showing the content at the intrinsic size, there is one more step to using either of these settings. Tell IB to set the current size to fit the content by selecting the element and either choosing Editor > Size to Fit Content from the menu or pressing Cmd-=. This ensures the system will use the priorities as part of adjusting the element.

You use the following steps to set up the constraints for the Total Cars label and New Car button:

1. Use the pin constraint popup to set the leading edge of the total cars label to the leading edge of the container. That is, set the distance constraint for the left edge to 0. Again, remember to update frames.

   Notice that setting the leading edge constraint turns both constraints blue and the orange arrow disappears from the left-hand views list. That means the constraints completely specify how to position and size the label.

2. With the label selected, use the Size inspector to increment the content hugging and content compression resistance by 1 for each axis. This says the label should be just as large as it needs to be to show the label, and no larger.

3. Select the New Car button and open the pin constraint popup.

4. Set both the leading edge and bottom edge constraints to 0. That is, to no distance between the button and the nearest neighbor, in this case, the superview.

5. Increment the horizontal and vertical compression resistance but not the content hugging resistance. This allows you to set equal widths for buttons if needed, providing larger and consistent tap targets.

Designing and Implementing the View Car Constraints

When you adapt an interface to different screen sizes, you need to enable some view or views to grow or shrink. In your app, the view car area is a good example of a complex view group that adapts to changes in screen height. Most of the constraints are straightforward.

The Car Number label constraints are identical to the Total Cars label; however, there is one issue. Because all the views are centered in the view car group, how do you make sure you select the right view before applying constraints?

The answer is using another Xcode key combination: Hold Ctrl-Shift and click in the center of the stack of views in the view car group. You get a popup similar to the one in Figure 4-26 that lets you choose one of the views in that location.

Figure 4-26   View selector popup

Select the Car Number label from the popup and set it to the same constraints as the Total Cars label. Use the pin constraint popup to set the top and leading constraints to 0. Then set the content hugging and compression priorities.

Select the Previous Car button and set it to the same constraints as the New Car button from the add car group. The Next Car button is almost identical: The bottom edge is adjacent to the bottom of the container, but it is the trailing edge of the Next Car button adjacent to the superview's trailing edge. Add those constraints. Remember to add both the pin constraints and the content compression resistance priorities.

Caution: Pin Popup Constrains to Nearest View

Sometimes using the pin constraint popup does not place the target view where you expect. This is because the constraints are to the *nearest* view for that particular constraint, not to the parent. That is, if you want the bottom of view A constrained to the parent, and there is some view B between the bottom of view A and the parent, the pin popup sets the bottom constraint to view B. You might encounter this with the Next Car or Edit buttons.

If this problem occurs, undo the constraints and move the view you are trying to constrain so that there are no other views between it and the target of the constraint. You can also try adding one constraint at a time, again moving the view closer to the target view.

One last caution: This chapter was created using a pre-release version of Xcode 5. One of the things that changed in Xcode 5 pre-releases was the way IB created constraints. Those of you who register your book can check for errata and/or supplemental content.

Now select the Edit button. You need to use the pin and align popups to correctly position this view. This time you are going to do something slightly different with each popup—you are not going to update frames for new constraints:

- Use the align constraint popup to horizontally center the button in the container, and remember, do not update frames.

- Open the pin constraint popup and set the distance to nearest bottom neighbor (the superview) to 0. Leave update frames set to none and add the constraint.

When you add the centering constraint, the vertical centering constraint appears in orange. There were also some orange rectangles. Pinning the button to the bottom turns the centering constraint blue but results in another orange line with a number, as well as another orange rectangle, as shown in Figure 4-27. (Note that the background for the grouping view is set to white to make the figure easier to see. Your grouping view should still be light gray.)

This is how IB tells you that there is a conflict between the existing frame and the frame that is generated by the relevant constraints. IB also uses a yellow circle with an arrow, much like the red one on the left side of Figure 4-24. Yellow indicates the constraints are incomplete, versus red, which indicates a conflict or other serious issue. Clicking the yellow arrow shows problem details similar to the right side of Figure 4-24.

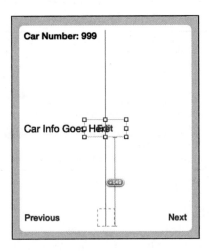

Figure 4-27   Orange constraint problems in IB

The problem detail shows that the Edit button is a misplaced view. It also shows you the specific values with problems. Looking at the expected and actual y values, you can see where the +149 in Figure 4-27 comes from. The view is 149 points away from where it should be.

There are a few ways you can fix this issue. One is to remove or undo the added constraints and then redo them, making sure to update frames. However, there are at least two other ways to fix the issue. This is important because sometimes you end up with misplaced views because of how constraints interact.

Because you are already viewing the problem detail, another way to fix the constraints is to click the yellow triangle with the circle that is part of the misplaced view detail. Doing this gives you a popup with a number of choices:

- **Update frame**—Update the frame in IB to match the constraints.

- **Update constraints**—Update the constraints to match the existing frame.

- **Reset to suggested constraints**—Sets the constraints based on what the system thinks they should be.

There is also an option to apply any changes to all views in the container. This last choice can have ripple effects through all your existing constraints and should be used with care.

Resolve Auto Layout Issues Popup

The fastest way to resolve constraints is using the third item in IB's constraint toolbar. It is next to the pin constraint popup and has a black circle instead of a +. When you open the Auto Layout Issues button with the Edit button selected, you see something similar to Figure 4-28.

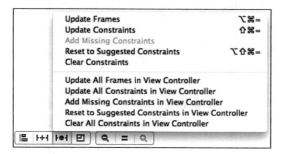

Figure 4-28   Auto layout issues popup

The top choices are the same as those in the popup you opened by clicking on the yellow triangle in the problem details area. The bottom choices affect the entire view controller, not just the particular view or groups of views you are working with.

If your view controller is already laid out the way you want and you have not yet added any constraints, the bottom part of this menu is a quick way to have Xcode add a complete set of constraints that results in the current layout. Of course, it might not support other screen sizes or orientations, but it can provide a good starting point. Combined with the item to reset to suggested constraints, it provides a great way to explore what sets of consistent constraints look like and how various modifications affect the view controller as a whole.

For now, all you need to do is update the frames. Choose the top item in the popup menu or press Cmd-Option-=. The Edit button moves so that it is centered at the bottom of the view car group container. Use the Size inspector to check the constraints for the Edit button to confirm they are what you wanted: centered horizontally in the container with the bottom edge at the same place as the bottom edge of the container.

Adjusting for Screen Height

You are close to making portrait work for both screen sizes. The top-level views already resize correctly. Adjust the size of your preview pane by clicking the far-left screen height button. The app almost looks correct. The only issue is the car info area. The height of that area has not changed, so the centered car info placeholder text is shown toward the bottom of the view car group.

Because there is more than enough space on the smaller screen to show car info, all you need to do is set the constraints for the car info label so that it changes height when its container, the view car group, changes height.

You do that by attaching the top and bottom of the label to other view elements in the group. When the view car group gets shorter, the Edit button moves up because it is attached to the bottom of the group. If the bottom of the car label is related to the top of the Edit button, it too will move up.

Use the pin constraint popup to set the leading and trailing edge constraints to 0 and the top and bottom edge constraints to standard. Remember that a shortcut for setting a constraint to standard is deleting the current contents of the value for that constraint. Make sure to update frames.

Now use the Size inspector to reduce the Content Hugging Priority to 249 in the vertical direction. Finally, with the Car Info label selected, use the Layout Issues item to update Frames.

When you add those constraints, the preview pane changes to show the Car Info label in the center of the car view group. You now have a set of portrait constraints that works for both screen sizes.

Edit Car: An Initial Look

Most of the work of adapting your edit car scene is left for the Challenges at the end of this chapter. You might think there is little work because there appears to be plenty of room on both screen sizes for all the fields. And there is—until you tap in a field. A tap in a field brings up the keyboard and drastically reduces the space you have to work with.

On the 4-inch display, there is space between the bottom of the last label and the top of the keyboard. That is not the case with the 3.5-inch display. Based on what you already know, you could change both screens to use standard Apple spacing both between the title and first text entry line and then between the text entry lines. That would work on the smaller screen. Alternatively, you could dynamically change the constraints based on the size of the screen.

Neither of these is a great alternative, especially because in landscape, it is not possible to prevent the keyboard from covering up input lines.

It is possible to create code that sets up a way to shift the input lines up and down based on some user event, such as a button press. However, this does not really give the user control of which input lines he or she is seeing, and it doesn't even give an indication that there could be more input lines above or below. The solution is to scroll the view with the input lines, which you do in Chapter 6, "Scrolling." For now, leave the portrait layout as it is.

Adding Landscape

Some apps support only one orientation. However, you will write apps supporting both portrait and landscape. In this section, you add support for rotating between two orientations, in the process learning more about designing and using constraints. You will also add constraints using both VCL and create individual constraints. In an actual project, you would choose which orientations to support and then design the scenes and their constraints before implementing the screens. Here, you get the additional experience of adapting an existing portrait interface to landscape.

The CarValet project is already enabled for both landscape left and right, as you can see in Figure 4-29. Quickly check how the app will appear in landscape using a preview pane. Adjust the screen to 3.5 inches high and rotate the screen using the rotation arrow in the control bar. As you can see in Figure 4-30, although the add car group is fine, the view car group has almost no room.

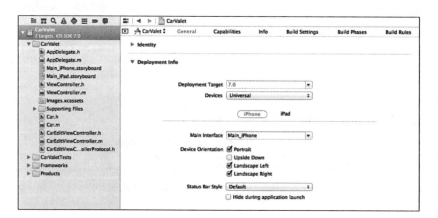

Figure 4-29   Supported app orientations

In this case, auto layout is using the same constraints you built earlier to lay out the land-scape screen. The add car and separator areas are at fixed locations and sizes. The view car area adjusts to the new vertical height. Inside the view area, the Car Number label and buttons are in fixed positions relative to the area's top and bottom, and the Car Info label adjusts based on the height—or in this case, lack of height. In other words, the constraints do not work for landscape. You need to design new constraints for landscape and put them in place at the right time.

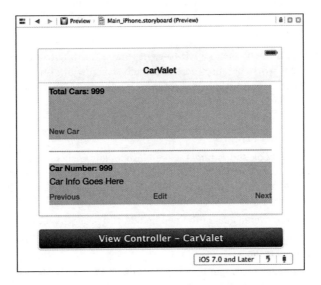

Figure 4-30   Preview pane landscape

The right time for updating has to do with enabling the system to build the rotation anima-tion. When the device rotates, the system remembers the current layout, gives you a chance to change the constraints, generates a new layout, and then creates animations for views that changed location and/or size. Putting the right constraints in place requires two steps:

1. Remove any constraints that do not work for landscape.

2. Add any constraints required to generate the landscape interface.

Rotating back to portrait means reversing the process: Remove the landscape-specific constraints and add back the portrait-specific ones. You can use the `willAnimateRotationTo-InterfaceOrientation:duration:` method of `UIViewController` for removing and adding constraints, but first you need to know what constraints to change.

Adding and Viewing Cars: Designing the Landscape Constraints

Sometimes landscape might have different functionality from portrait, as in the Apple Stocks and Calendar apps. Each of these apps has two different scenes, each with its own constraints. In your app, landscape has the same behavior, visual elements, and grouping as portrait, so there is just one scene. Either way, you design landscape constraints the same way you do portrait constraints.

Your first design decisions are how the add and view groups look in portrait and where the separator view goes. When you know the desired layout, you can design the constraints and see how they differ from portrait.

The simplest approach is to change to a left-to-right (that is, leading-to-trailing) layout from a top-to-bottom one. This works because there is enough screen width on a 3.5-inch device to show all the visual elements and still leave sufficient white space. Figure 4-31 shows your target landscape layouts on 4- and 3.5-inch screens.

Mocking Up Apps and Screens

In several places, this book shows target screen layouts in the simulator. Figure 4-31 is a good example. It is important to understand that the scene was not originally designed using Xcode and the simulator. Before writing a line of code or even creating the project, the app went through a design process that included the following:

- Writing down the overall goal of the app and its target audience.
- Creating an outline of app functionality that was then expanded and broken down into major functional tasks.
- Grouping the functionality into possible screens and the associated actions for those screens (including navigational actions).
- Creating sketches of the UI, starting with simple wireframes on paper and then mockups in Keynote as they became closer to finalized. A great help for mocking up screens is a set of iOS UI elements in Photoshop made freely available by Teehan+LAX. A big thanks to Geoff and Jon. You can find the files at www.teehanlax.com/tools/.
- AppCooker is an iPad tool for mockups and more. The app takes you from idea to demo-capable mockup. It also has tools for designing the icons, prototyping the App Store listing, figuring out pricing, and more. You can find more info on the App Store and at www.appcooker.com.
- Briefs is a similar tool for Mac OS and includes an iOS App for showing the mockups. You can find information at http://giveabrief.com.

The previous tasks are not so much a sequential flow of steps as a back and forth. During design, some small Xcode projects might be used to test particular functionality or a certain look. However, architecting, designing, and implementing the code for the app does not start until some level of product specifications and mockups exist.

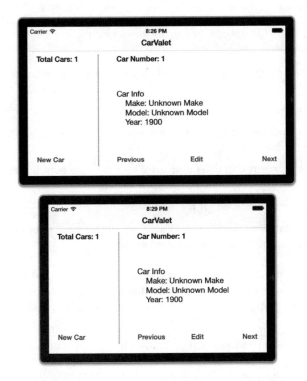

Figure 4-31   Landscape layout

The next step would normally be to design the constraints starting at the top of the view hierarchy and working your way down the hierarchy of each container. If you want more practice designing constraints, take some time to design all the constraints for landscape before continuing.

Constraint Differences for Top-Level Views

Your groups of views make the landscape design process easier. Keep this in mind when you design groups in other apps, by thinking how the information can be presented in both portrait and landscape. When done well, groups minimize the number of constraints you need to change as your app switches between portrait and landscape.

When you have groups, designing the landscape constraints focuses on the changes you need at each level in the view hierarchy. You need to identify portrait constraints that do not work and create landscape constraints that are missing. At this stage of design, you can still use language-based descriptions of constraints. Later on, you will need to find and create actual constraint objects.

The obvious change for the three top-level views is that the layout now goes from leading to trailing. Any constraints that position or size the views for a top-to-bottom layout do not work. For each view, follow these steps:

1. Identify constraints that "attach" the view to its container, both horizontally and vertically.

2. Create the constraints needed for the new orientation.

3. List the constraints from step 1 that do not work or that need to be changed and eliminate any duplicate constraints created in step 2.

4. Identify the constraints that determine the size of the view both horizontally and vertically.

5. Create the constraints needed for the new orientation.

6. List the constraints from step 1 that do not work or that need to be changed and eliminate any duplicate constraints created in step 5.

For the add car group, the attached sides in portrait are top, leading, and trailing. For landscape, they need to be top, leading, and bottom. That makes one difference between portrait and landscape: For landscape, you have to remove the trailing edge constraint and add the bottom one.

The add car group has one size constraint that makes it `102` points high. There are two problems with this constraint. It prevents the system from calculating the correct height using the top and bottom constraints, and it also conflicts. A view cannot be both the standard distance from the top and bottom of its container and be fixed at `102` points high. That makes one more change: Remove the fixed height for landscape.

The separator view changes to a vertical orientation with a fixed width. Every constraint that contains the separator view needs to change. It needs to be the standard distance from top and bottom, a fixed width of `2` points, and the leading edge will be a fixed distance from the trailing edge of the add car group.

The view car group is still used to adapt to different screen sizes, but this time the change is in horizontal space—in the width not the height. In portrait, the area is the standard distance from the top, bottom, and trailing edge of its container. In landscape, it needs to be attached to the top, bottom, and trailing edge.

In portrait, the vertical size of the view car group is calculated. The top of the group is a fixed distance below the separator view. The bottom is the standard distance from the bottom of the screen, though this coordinate will vary depending on screen size. In landscape, the vertical size is calculated from attachments to both top and bottom. The horizontal size is variable. You need to replace the vertical relationship with the separator view with a horizontal one.

Table 4-3 shows how the constraints differ between portrait and landscape. It is also an example of another useful design tool for your own projects. In some cases, constraints for one orientation are not required, and the attribute is calculated. In Challenge 1 at the end of the chapter, you use information from Table 4-3 to show how the constraints for the top level grouping views are complete.

Table 4-3   **Comparing Portrait and Landscape Constraints**

Constraint	Portrait	Landscape
Add Car Group		
Height	Fixed height of 102 points	Calculated
Bottom	Calculated from top location and height	Standard distance from container
Top	Standard distance from top of container	Same
Leading edge	Standard distance from leading edge of container	Same
Trailing edge	Standard distance from trailing edge of container	Calculated from leading edge position and fixed width
Width	Calculated from leading and trailing edge locations	132 points
Separator View		
Width	Calculated from leading and trailing edge locations	2 points
Height	2 points	Calculated from the top and bottom locations
Leading edge	Standard distance from container	2 points from add car group
Trailing edge	Standard distance from container	Calculated from horizontal position and width
Top	22 points from bottom edge of add car group	Standard distance from container
Bottom	Calculated from top location and fixed height	Standard distance from container
View Car Group		
Top	22 points from the top of the separator view	Standard distance from container
Bottom	Standard distance from container	Same
Leading edge	Standard distance from container	40 points from container from trailing edge of separator view
Trailing edge	Standard distance from container	Same
Width	Calculated from leading and trailing positions	Calculated from the leading and trailing positions

With the top-level view constraints done, it is time to check constraints for the children of those views. Before reading on, take some time to look at the constraints and jot down what, if any, changes are required.

The label and button for the add car group stay in their same relative positions. The same is true for the view car group. The Car Number label stays at the top, the buttons are evenly spaced along the bottom, and the Car Info label fills up the space between (less the standard distances from the label and buttons). There are no changes or additions.

This is why using views to group areas can save a lot of time and effort. For the cost of two invisible views and a few extra constraints, you have significantly reduced the work to handle rotation. Without those groups, you would have to remove and add constraints for every label and button as well as the separator.

Finding the Constraint Objects to Change

Next, you need to create references to all the portrait constraints you identified in the last section. You need a reference to any portrait constraints in Table 4-3 that change or need to be removed. When you use auto layout to handle rotation, most of the time changing constraints means you remove ones that do not work and add new ones. Sometimes you can simply change a constant value for a constraint without removing it. For this project, you are only removing some constraints and adding others.

The constraint itself is not quite enough. Removing a constraint requires sending a message to the view that owns the constraint. That same view reference is used to add the constraint back.

As you saw earlier, constraints are attached to, or owned by, the lowest common parent in the hierarchy. This means a constraint affecting more than one view could be attached to either of those views or somewhere higher up the chain.

The easiest way to find the owner for a constraint is to select the constraint and then look at the left-hand list of view elements in IB. The constraint is highlighted in the left-hand list, which is expanded as necessary. The constraint is under the Constraint item for a particular view, the owning view.

As you saw in the earlier section, "Changing Constraint Values," there are multiple ways to select a constraint. In this case, use the Size inspector to find and select the fixed height constraint for the add car group. When selected, the left-hand list changes as shown in Figure 4-32. You now know the constraint is attached to the add car area because it shows up in the Constraints list for that view. You have found one constraint and one unique view.

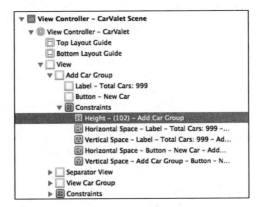

Figure 4-32   Selected fixed height constraint

Find the next constraint, the trailing edge for the add car group, by selecting it on the IB canvas:

1. Select the add car group view.

2. Select the i-bar for the trailing edge constraint.

3. Look at the left-hand list.

This time the constraint is attached to the root view. That makes a total of two constraints and two unique views. The other two portrait constraints for the add car group are calculated, so there are no more to find.

The separator view has six lines in the table of which four are uniquely portrait constraints. Select the separator view and then select the 2-point height constraint. It is attached to the separator view. Select each of the other three constraints in turn and you see they are all attached to the root view. That makes three views and six constraints.

Finally, find the two portrait constraints for the view car area. Both constraints are attached to the root view. This makes a total of eight constraints and three views.

Adding References to the Changing Constraints

You have already used IBOutlets for dragging connections to IB objects. This does work, but it can be hard to maintain as the UI is changed over time and the constraints change. It also can increase coding errors as you forget to use all eight outlets in every place.

It would be easier if you could group constraints together by their attached view. You can do this with a special type of IBOutlet called an IBOutletCollection. These outlets collect multiple item references in an array. You need one collection for each view that has constraints to remove.

The general way to define an IBOutletConnection in code is the following:

```
@property <Optional Property Qualifiers> IBOutletConnection(CollectionElementClass)
<Variable Declaration>
```

The optional first part is used to declare property qualifiers such as weak. Next is the definition of the collection. The optional class in parentheses tells the compiler what kind of elements can be in the collection. When you drag out connections in IB, it only lets you connect to elements of any class you set. If you specify UIView, you can connect to any kind of views, including buttons, labels, and just plain views. If you specify UIButton instead, you can only connect to buttons. The final part declares the actual variable and must be some kind (class or subclass) of NSArray.

Add the following properties to ViewController.h between the existing property and method declarations. The new code is shown in bold:

```
@property (weak, nonatomic) IBOutlet UILabel *carInfoLabel;

@property (strong, nonatomic) IBOutletCollection(NSLayoutConstraint)
                              NSArray *addCarViewPortraitConstraints;
@property (strong, nonatomic) IBOutletCollection(NSLayoutConstraint)
                              NSArray *separatorViewPortraitConstraints;
@property (strong, nonatomic) IBOutletCollection(NSLayoutConstraint)
                              NSArray *rootViewPortraitConstraints;

- (IBAction)newCar:(id)sender;
```

Each new property is an outlet collection that can contain an array of NSLayoutConstraint objects. There is one collection for each view containing constraints you need to remove: addCarViewPortraitConstraints for the add car group, separatorViewPortrait-Constraints for the separator view, and rootViewPortraitConstraints for the root view of ViewController.

Add each of the constraints you have found to the correct outlet collection. The simplest way to do this is to show all the constraints in the left-hand list of view elements in IB, and then click and drag from the dot next to each property in the .h file to the relevant constraints. Figure 4-33 shows adding the leading edge constraint of the separator view to rootViewPortraitConstraints.

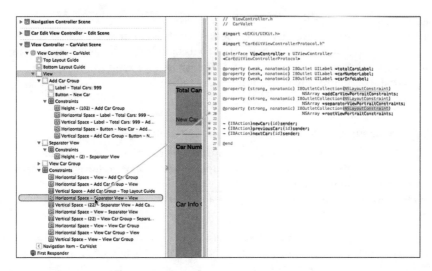

Figure 4-33   Adding the leading separator constraint to the collection

Another way to access the properties of a view controller is by Ctrl-clicking or second-mouse-button-clicking the view controller in the left-hand list. You can use the circles in this floating view instead of the .h file. You can also use it to confirm the outlet collections are correct.

When you have added all the constraints, the Outlet Collections area looks something like Figure 4-34. The order of the items might be different, depending on the order in which you added the constraints. The important thing is that all the constraints are there in the correct collections. Note that all the other areas in the view have been collapsed, as shown by the left-pointing triangles next to items such as Triggered Segues and Outlets.

Figure 4-34   Collections of removable portrait constraints

Why use collections for the add car and separator views if there is only one constraint for each of them? There are two main reasons. First, you can use the same code for whatever operations you perform. This allows you to abstract out what will become an increasingly common operation. The second reason is to allow for future changes that result in the need to remove multiple portrait constraints. If you had just used an outlet, you would need to change both the property type and all associated code.

Creating Landscape Constraints: Visual Constraint Language

For more complex layouts, you are likely to create your own constraints. You cannot do this in IB because any constraint you create is attached to an existing view, at least as of the writing of this book. You create your own constraints in code by using either VCL, or a method that has arguments for each component of the constraint equation. Both ways use methods of the `NSLayoutConstraint` class.

`constraintWithItem:attribute:relatedBy:toItem:attribute:multiplier:constant:` is the least preferred way of creating a single constraint. As the length of the method signature implies, there are lots of arguments—one for each part of the constraint relationship equation. You get a lot of control, but you sacrifice readability and maintainability.

VCL is much easier to use and far more readable. VCL uses strings to construct horizontal or vertical constraints, and each string can result in multiple constraints. Here is a simple example:

```
@"H:[addCarView]-2-[separatorView]"
```

Expressed in language, this string says that the leading edge of the separator view is 2 points from the trailing edge of the add car view. VCL is a step between using IB and using code to create each constraint.

The VCL string creates leading/trailing or left/right (horizontal) or top/bottom (vertical) constraints depending on the letter at the start of the string: `H:` is horizontal, and `V:` is vertical. Names in square brackets refer to specific views. A dash (-) by itself refers to the standard distance. A number between two dashes is a specific value. `-2-` makes the leading edge (`[`) of the separator view 2 points after the trailing edge (`]`) of the add car view. You can also specify values for a particular view by including them in parentheses inside the reference to a view. In the previous string, `(2)` sets the width of the separator view.

Using VCL makes it much easier to see what constraints you are generating, and takes up less space than the more complex single constraint creation method. It is the preferred way for creating constraints in code. Unfortunately, there are some constraints that cannot be expressed in VCL.

The Cocoa Auto Layout Guide, part of the Xcode documentation, contains a full guide to the syntax and parts of VCL. For a deeper discussion, see *Auto Layout Demystified* by Erica Sadun. The description of VCL begins in the section "Visual Format Constraints" though the whole book is useful for understanding other ways to use auto layout.

The previous format string specifies two of the four separator view constraints from the Landscape column in Table 4-3. That leaves the two vertical constraints to set the standard distance from the top and bottom of its container. In a format string, a pipe symbol (|) stands for the container view. You have already seen the symbol for standard distance, and this is a vertical constraint string:

```
@"V:|-[separatorView]-|"
```

The string generates two constraints. One sets the top of the separator view to the standard distance from the top of its container view. The other sets the bottom of the separator view the standard distance from the container's bottom.

Now you need the two add car view constraints. The first constraint places the view's bottom the standard distance from its container:

```
@"V:[addCarView]-|"
```

The second constraint sets the width to 132 points:

```
@"H:[addCarView(132)]"
```

Finally, there are three constraints for the view car area that can be implemented with two strings. The first is a vertical constraint for the top edge:

```
@"V:|-[viewCarView]"
```

And the second is the horizontal constraints for the leading edge position:

```
@"[separatorView]-40-[viewCarView]-|"
```

You might think there are two typos in the last string. However, it points out a couple things about visual constraint strings. First, the default constraint axis specified by a string is horizontal. Although you can put H: in the string, you do not need to. The second is that adding a constraint that already exists has no effect. In this case, the string specifies that the trailing edge of the view car area should be the standard distance from its superview. This constraint is already specified using IB and is not removed when a rotation occurs.

VCL Versus Full Specification

You might wonder what the difference is between using VCL and the longer class method. @"H:[addCarView(132)]" is one of the constraint strings you used earlier. The following is the same constraint, using the more complete class method:

```
NSLayoutConstraint *constraint;
    constraint = [NSLayoutConstraint
                constraintWithItem:addCarView
                attribute:NSLayoutAttributeWidth
                relatedBy:NSLayoutRelationEqual
                toItem:nil
                attribute:nil
                multiplier:0.0
                constant:132.0];
```

As you can see, there is considerably more code, and it is harder to read. The format string makes the relationships very clear, almost at a glance. The preceding code is hard to read and not nearly as easy to translate into language. Worse, if you need to change the width, or even the relationship, you would be changing several arguments. The string makes it immediately obvious what to change and how to change it.

Having said that, there is far more flexibility with the complete method. There are relationships you can specify that are impossible to create using either IB or VCL. One simple example is access to the multiplier for things like scaling or even pulsing a view.

Creating Landscape Constraints: Code

Whenever you switch between constraints, you need a reference to each constraint. In CarValet, when the device rotates back to portrait, you remove any landscape constraints you added. That means keeping a reference to any generated landscape constraints. And as with the portrait constraints, you need to associate each constraint with a view. Your first task is to figure out which view hosts each of the new landscape constraints.

To find the host view, you look for the lowest view in the hierarchy that contains both members of the constraint relationship. The simplest case is a constraint with only one member, such as specifying a fixed size. The most complex is where the members are in different hierarchies, such as an equal-width constraint between the New Car and Edit buttons. In this case, the host is the main view, or root view, of `ViewController`. Table 4-4 shows all the format strings, their member views, and the lowest view in the hierarchy that contains all those members.

Table 4-4   **Container Views for Visual Format Strings**

Format String	Component Views	Container View
`"H:[addCarView]-2-[separatorView]"`	Add car view, separator view	Main (root) view
`"H:[separatorView(2)]"`	Separator view	Separator view
`"V:|-[separatorView]-|"`	Main view, separator view	Main view
`"V:[addCarView]-|"`	Add car view, main view	Main view
`"H:[addCarView(132)]"`	Add car view	Add car view
`"V:|-[viewCarView]"`	Main view, view car view	Main view
`"[separatorView]-40-[viewCarView]-|"`	Main view, view car view	Main view

One thing to notice is there are multiple ways to specify constraints. As an example, you could combine the first and last items in Table 4-4 into one string for a few reasons as all the constraints:

- Along the same axis (horizontal)
- Attached to the main view
- Specify related views, including a shared view

The modified string would be as follows:

```
@"|-[addCarView]-2-[separatorView]-40-[viewCarView]-|"
```

This string has some extra information, but it also very clearly specifies the horizontal contents of some portion of the view: an add car view the standard distance from the leading edge of the superview, followed by 2 points of space, a separator view, then 40 points of space, and a view car view that is also the standard distance from the trailing edge.

One important thing to notice is the string does not contain the width for the separator view. The ones generated by the string are all attached to the container view. But the width of the separator view is a relationship between the separator view and itself. The constraint is attached to the separator view.

Adding the Landscape Constraints

There are only two unique hosts for the landscape constraints: the add car and main views. You need to add two arrays to `ViewController.m` to hold the constraints. Declare the arrays just after the implementation; the new code is shown in bold:

```
@implementation ViewController
{
    NSMutableArray *arrayOfCars;
    NSInteger displayedCarIndex;
    NSArray *rootViewLandscapeConstraints;
    NSArray *addCarViewLandscapeConstraints;
    NSArray *separatorViewLandscapeConstraints;
}
```

Before you can use a VCL string to generate constraints, you need references to any used views. You use these references to generate what is called a *dictionary of variable bindings*. This dictionary sets up a binding between a text-based view name and a reference to a `UIView` object. You need a reference to each unique view in the Component Views column of Table 4-4.

Add an `IBOutlet` for connecting each component view in the variable-binding dictionary. `viewController.view` is already a reference to the main view, so you only need three outlets. Note that you could declare these variables elsewhere using properties. The changes are shown in bold:

```
    NSArray *addCarViewLandscapeConstraints;

    __weak IBOutlet UIView *addCarView;
    __weak IBOutlet UIView *separatorView;
    __weak IBOutlet UIView *viewCarView;
}
```

Since you do not own the UIView objects, you use __weak to avoid retain loops, as you saw in the section "A Brief Diversion on Memory Management" in Chapter 3. Now use IB to drag connections from each of the three new outlets to the associated view. Connect the following:

- addCarView to the add car group view
- separatorView to the separator view
- viewCarView to the view car group view

You can use the same popup panel shown in Figure 4-34 to make the connections. When you bring up the panel, expand the Outlets section if it is not already expanded. You see each of the new outlets in that list. Drag from the dot to the appropriate view in either the list on the left of IB or on the canvas. If you use the canvas, make sure you are connecting to the right view. Check the name of the item added in the popup after the connection. It should correspond to the name in the left-hand column of views.

To generate constraints from a string, you use constraintsWithVisualFormat:options: metrics:views:. It is important to remember that each call creates an array of constraints, even if it is an array of one. The more complex class method shown earlier creates an individual constraint object. Add the setupLandscapeConstraints method from Listing 4-1 to ViewController.m.

Listing 4-1   setupLandscapeConstraints **Method**

```
- (void)setupLandscapeConstraints {
    NSDictionary *views;                                              // 1
    views = NSDictionaryOfVariableBindings(addCarView,
                                           separatorView,
                                           viewCarView);
    NSMutableArray *tempRootViewConstraints = [NSMutableArray new];   // 2

    NSArray *generatedConstraints;                                   // 3

    generatedConstraints =                                           // 4
            [NSLayoutConstraint
            constraintsWithVisualFormat:@"H:[addCarView]-2-[separatorView]"
            options:0
            metrics:nil
            views:views];
    [tempRootViewConstraints addObjectsFromArray:generatedConstraints]; // 5

    generatedConstraints =
            [NSLayoutConstraint
            constraintsWithVisualFormat:@"V:|-[separatorView]-|"
            options:0
            metrics:nil
            views:views];
```

```
[tempRootViewConstraints addObjectsFromArray:generatedConstraints];

generatedConstraints =
        [NSLayoutConstraint
         constraintsWithVisualFormat:@"V:[addCarView]-|"
         options:0
         metrics:nil
         views:views];
[tempRootViewConstraints addObjectsFromArray:generatedConstraints];

generatedConstraints =
        [NSLayoutConstraint
         constraintsWithVisualFormat:@"V:|-[viewCarView]"
         options:0
         metrics:nil
         views:views];
[tempRootViewConstraints addObjectsFromArray:generatedConstraints];

generatedConstraints =
        [NSLayoutConstraint
         constraintsWithVisualFormat:@"[separatorView]-40-[viewCarView]-|"
         options:0
         metrics:nil
         views:views];
[tempRootViewConstraints addObjectsFromArray:generatedConstraints];

rootViewLandscapeConstraints = [NSArray                          // 6
                              arrayWithArray:tempRootViewConstraints];

addCarViewLandscapeConstraints =                                 // 7
        [NSLayoutConstraint
         constraintsWithVisualFormat:@"H:[addCarView(132)]"
         options:0
         metrics:nil
         views:views];

separatorViewLandscapeConstraints =                              // 8
        [NSLayoutConstraint
         constraintsWithVisualFormat:@"H:[separatorView(2)]"
         options:0
         metrics:nil
         views:views];
}
```

Here's what happens in the numbered lines in Listing 4-1:

1. Set up a dictionary of variable bindings used in generating constraints from the strings.

2. Create a temporary mutable array to hold generated constraints that are attached to the main view.

3. Set up a reusable reference to the returned array of generated constraints.

4. Generate the constraints associated with the first string in Table 4-4. Notice that the views dictionary can contain more views than needed for a constraint string. That makes it possible to set up one views dictionary for the whole method.

5. Add the generated constraints to the temporary array of main view constraints. Then generate the rest of the main view constraints, adding each new set to the temporary array.

6. Initialize the `rootViewLandscapeConstraints` instance variable to the contents of the mutable array of generated constraints.

7. Initialize the `addCarViewLandscapeConstraints` instance variable to an array containing the width constraint for the add car view.

8. Initialize the `separatorViewLandscapeConstraints` instance variable to an array containing the constraint for width of the separator view.

Since the visual elements of the screen are static, you need to set up the landscape constraints only once. Add a call to `[self setupLandscapeConstraints]` in `viewDidLoad:`, just after the call to `[super viewDidLoad]`.

Putting It All Together

You have all the elements you need to respond to device rotations: You know the set of constraints unique to portrait and to landscape, you know what views each constraint is attached to, and you have references to the constraints. When a rotation occurs and the new orientation is landscape, you remove the portrait constraints and then add the landscape ones. When the new orientation is landscape, you remove the landscape constraints and add back portrait.

`willAnimateRotationToInterfaceOrientation:duration:` is called when the device rotates. First, check the orientation and then add and remove the appropriate constraints. Use Listing 4-2 to update your project.

Listing 4-2   **Changing Constraints for Device Rotation**

```
- (void)willAnimateRotationToInterfaceOrientation:
             (UIInterfaceOrientation)toInterfaceOrientation
                             duration:(NSTimeInterval)duration {
    [super willAnimateRotationToInterfaceOrientation:toInterfaceOrientation
                       duration:duration];
```

```
    if (UIInterfaceOrientationIsPortrait(toInterfaceOrientation)) {            // 1
        [self.view removeConstraints:rootViewLandscapeConstraints];            // 2
        [addCarView removeConstraints:addCarViewLandscapeConstraints];
        [separatorView removeConstraints:separatorViewLandscapeConstraints];

        [self.view addConstraints:self.rootViewPortraitConstraints];           // 3
        [addCarView addConstraints:self.addCarViewPortraitConstraints];
        [separatorView addConstraints:self.separatorViewPortraitConstraints];

    } else {                                                                   // 4

        [self.view removeConstraints:self.rootViewPortraitConstraints];        // 5
        [addCarView removeConstraints:self.addCarViewPortraitConstraints];
        [separatorView removeConstraints:self.separatorViewPortraitConstraints];

        [self.view addConstraints:rootViewLandscapeConstraints];               // 6
        [addCarView addConstraints:addCarViewLandscapeConstraints];
        [separatorView addConstraints:separatorViewLandscapeConstraints];
    }
}
```

Here's what happens in the numbered lines in Listing 4-2:

1. After calling the superclass method, find out what the new orientation is. UIInterfaceOrientationPortrait is a system macro that is true for any portrait orientation.

2. This is portrait, so remove the landscape constraints, starting with the main view. It is fine to call removeConstraints: with constraints that are not already attached to the view.

3. Add all the portrait constraints. Adding an existing constraint is ignored.

4. If it is not portrait, it is landscape.

5. Remove any portrait-specific constraints.

6. Add the landscape-specific constraints.

Run the app in the simulator and rotate the device. Everything should work. This is also a good time to see a common error when there are conflicting constraints. To do this, you need to modify the code entered from Listing 4-2.

The current code removes any old constraints and then adds any new ones. Instead, modify the code to first add the new constraints and then remove the old ones. The first modification is to move the three lines starting with numbered line 2 below the three lines starting with numbered line 3. Similarly, move the three lines starting with numbered line 5 below the three starting with number line 6.

Now run the app in the simulator and rotate the device to the left and watch the debugger output. As the device rotates, the debugger output window shows an error message with a lot of content. And when the screen is rotated, it does not look quite right.

First, look at the debugger output. The key line is the following:

```
2013-08-15 11:01:36.633 CarValet[55429:a0b] Unable to simultaneously satisfy
constraints.
```

This is a warning that at least two of the constraints conflict. Because the app does not crash, the system is able to layout the screen. The body of the error shows how it was able to recover by breaking a constraint:

```
Will attempt to recover by breaking constraint
<NSLayoutConstraint:0xa163120 V:[_UILayoutGuide:0xa162800]-(NSSpace(8))-
[UIView:0xa11b740]>
```

As long as the system can recover, your application continues to work. If the system cannot recover, your application crashes.

To find the source of the error, look at the main body of the debugger message (the part between the key and breaking constraints line previously):

```
Probably at least one of the constraints in the following list is one you don't
want. Try this: (1) look at each constraint and try to figure out which you
don't expect; (2) find the code that added the unwanted constraint or
constraints and fix it. (Note: If you're seeing
NSAutoresizingMaskLayoutConstraints that you don't understand, refer to the
documentation for the UIView property translatesAutoresizingMaskIntoConstraints)
(
    "<NSLayoutConstraint:0x8c9f4a0 V:[_UILayoutGuide:0x8c9eb80]-(NSSpace(8))-
[UIView:0x8c9b2e0]>",
    "<_UILayoutSupportConstraint:0x8c990b0 V:[_UILayoutGuide:0x8c9eb80(52)]>",
    "<_UILayoutSupportConstraint:0x8c9a700 V:|-(0)-[_UILayoutGuide:0x8c9eb80]
(Names: '|':UIView:0x8c9e970 )>",
    "<NSLayoutConstraint:0x8c594b0 V:|-(NSSpace(20))-[UIView:0x8c9b2e0]   (Names:
'|':UIView:0x8c9e970 )>"
)
```

If you see this message at other times, especially as you are developing your app, it might be an indication that your current constraints are ambiguous, incomplete, or incorrect. Narrowing down the problem requires finding the views that are having issues. The error message only gives you pointer addresses. However, there is a trick you can use to figure out which view is which.

Doing that requires getting the app to pause when the constraint problem is first reported. For that, you will use a special type of breakpoint that stops the app whenever an exception occurs. For now, just follow the directions to set the breakpoint. You see more about breakpoints, exceptions, and related information in Chapter 14, "Instruments and Debugging."

Refer to Figure 4-35 and follow these steps:

1. Select the debug navigator in the left panel. You should see something like the top part of Figure 4-35, minus the popup menu.

2. Click the + button on the lower left.

3. Use the menu that appears to add an exception breakpoint. The menu is shown on the bottom of Figure 4-35.

4. An All Exceptions breakpoint appears in the navigator panel nested below the CarValet project.

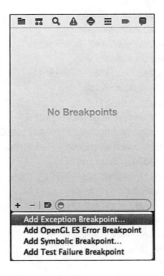

Figure 4-35   Adding an all exceptions breakpoint

Now stop and re-run the app from Xcode. The simulator should already be rotated to the left so the app should stop. If the simulator is in portrait once the app is running, rotate it to the left. You get the same kind of error as shown earlier, with a list of conflicting constraints and all the views identified by the current memory address.

Now enter this text at the debugger prompt, which looks like "(lldb)," and press Return:

```
po [[UIWindow keyWindow] _autolayoutTrace]
```

This prints out a sideways hierarchical list of all the views in the current window. Each view includes its type and, more importantly, its memory address. The output looks similar to the following:

```
*<UIWindow:0x8c58420> - AMBIGUOUS LAYOUT
|    <UIView:0x8c4dd00>
|    |    <UIView:0x8c911a0>
|    |    <UIView:0x8c94a10>
```

```
|    |      <UIView:0x8c94ac0>
|    |      <UIView:0x8c94b50>
|    *<UILayoutContainerView:0x8c8f3a0>
|    |    *<UINavigationTransitionView:0x8c91930>
|    |    |    *<UIViewControllerWrapperView:0x8ca0690>
|    |    |    |    *<UIView:0x8c9e970>
|    |    |    |    |    *<UIView:0x8c9b2e0> - AMBIGUOUS LAYOUT
|    |    |    |    |    |    *<UILabel:0x8c9b370>
|    |    |    |    |    |    *<UIButton:0x8c99d40> - AMBIGUOUS LAYOUT
|    |    |    |    |    |    |    <UIButtonLabel:0x8caea80>
|    |    |    |    |    *<UIView:0x8c9ea00> - AMBIGUOUS LAYOUT
|    |    |    |    |    *<UIView:0x8c9dc50>
|    |    |    |    |    |    *<UILabel:0x8c9dce0>
|    |    |    |    |    |    *<UIButton:0x8c9ae00>
|    |    |    |    |    |    |    <UIButtonLabel:0x8caddf0>
|    |    |    |    |    |    *<UIButton:0x8c9a5e0>
|    |    |    |    |    |    |    <UIButtonLabel:0x8cad170>
|    |    |    |    |    |    *<UILabel:0x8c9e1d0>
|    |    |    |    |    |    *<UIButton:0x8c9aa20>
|    |    |    |    |    |    |    <UIButtonLabel:0x8cabcc0>
|    |    |    |    |    *<_UILayoutGuide:0x8c9eb80> - AMBIGUOUS LAYOUT
|    |    |    |    |    *<_UILayoutGuide:0x8c9f050> - AMBIGUOUS LAYOUT
|    |    <UINavigationBar:0x8c87d70>
|    |    |    <_UINavigationBarBackground:0x8c8d300>
|    |    |    |    <_UIBackdropView:0x8c87ff0>
|    |    |    |    |    <_UIBackdropEffectView:0x8c4e230>
|    |    |    |    |    <UIView:0x8c900c0>
|    |    |    |    <UIImageView:0x8c8d600>
|    |    |    <UINavigationItemView:0x8c88420>
|    |    |    |    <UILabel:0x8c888a0>
|    |    |    <_UINavigationBarBackIndicatorView:0x8c97670>
```

You can use the list to find each view in the error message. For instance, the last constraint in the error list is this string:

```
"<NSLayoutConstraint:0x8c594b0 V:|-(NSSpace(20))-[UIView:0x8c9b2e0]    (Names:
'|':UIView:0x8c9e970 )>"
```

This string refers to a vertical constraint between two views. The top edge of the first one with a class and memory address of UIView:0x8c9b2e0 is 20 points from the top of its container. The second listed view is the superview: UIView:0x8c9e970.

Looking at the hierarchy, you can see that the first view is the add car group, a UIView with a label and a button. The other is the main view, the one containing each of the three groups. There are other views listed, including the top-level window and system-generated views for handling the transition animation between portrait and landscape.

There are also two views with a class of _UILayoutGuide, one of which is listed in three of the conflicting constraints. And that guide is the source of the problem. Make sure that you change back the code to the original Listing 4-2.

Constraining to the Top or Bottom of Containers

When you first added the constraints for the add car group in the "Implementing the Top-Level View Constraints" section, you used the pin constraint popup to set it a standard distance from its container. But actually, it was not a relative to the container but to the closest neighbor. And it is not the neighbor you think.

Look at the left-hand list of views in IB, and you see two special views just below the view controller. These are the top and bottom layout guides. They are there because the actual top of the container view is usually underneath any bars shown in the interface, including the navigation bar.

You can see this by finishing the rotation. For now, the easiest way to do this is to disable the all exceptions breakpoint you just created. For that, open the breakpoint navigator and click the breakpoint symbol next to the All Exceptions breakpoint. It will turn from a dark blue to a lighter grayed-out color.

Now rerun the app and rotate to landscape if needed. Look carefully at the navigation bar, and you should see the top of the separator, as well as the Total Cars and Car Number labels, under the bar.

The added constraints use the pipe symbol for the top of the container view. But when you laid out the views in IB, you actually were not constraining them to the top of their superview. Pin constraints work with the nearest neighbor in the relevant direction.

The nearest neighbor at the top of the view is really the Top Layout Guide. This is a special item that lets older interfaces that do not support a true full screen still work with constraints. It is a special system-created view whose bottom edge is aligned with the bottom edge of the navbar.

The source of the ambiguity is trying to align the top of the add car group with both the top layout guide and the top of the main view. You can see this in the body of the ambiguous constraints error. In order, the constraints mean the following:

1. Set the top edge of the add car group 8 points below the top guide: `UILayoutGuide:0x8c9eb80`.

2. The top guide is 52 points high.

3. The top edge of the guide is 0 points from the top edge of the superview.

4. The top edge of the add car group is also 20 points from the top of the superview.

The top edge of the add car group cannot be both 52 and 20 points from the top edge of the superview.

Fixing the issue means changing both the IB and VCL constraints to use the same top for constraints. Later you use the full superview, including space under the navigation bar. For now, change the VCL constraints to use the top layout guide.

This is as easy as adding the top layout as a member of the dictionary of variable bindings for views and using that view where you currently use the pipe (|) for the top of the main super-view. Make the following changes in `setupLandscapeConstraints`:

1. Replace the definition of the view dictionary near the top of the method with the following code:

```
id topGuide = self.topLayoutGuide;
id bottomGuide = self.bottomLayoutGuide;
views = NSDictionaryOfVariableBindings(topGuide,
                                       bottomGuide,
                                       addCarView,
                                       separatorView,
                                       viewCarView);
```

2. Change the VCL string for the second constraint by replacing the pipe with `[topGuide]`. The string will look like the following:

```
@"V:[topGuide]-[separatorView]-[bottomGuide]"
```

3. Make the same change for the next constraint in the list. The constraint string will be as follows:

```
@"V:[topGuide]-[addCarView]-[bottomGuide]"
```

4. Finally, change the fourth constraint string to the following:

```
@"V:[topGuide]-[viewCarView]"
```

Before you run the app, change the background color of the add and view car groups back to default using the Attributes inspector in IB. After that, run the app and try rotating. This time everything should work correctly with the landscape screen looking like one of those in Figure 4-31.

Note that `topLayoutGuide` only exists in iOS 7. Using it means you cannot build and run this code on earlier iOS versions. There are ways to check the version at runtime for conditionally executing code, but that is beyond the scope of this book.

One Last Problem to Solve

You have adapted each scene of CarValet for both portrait and landscape. No matter what scene is showing, changing the device orientation rotates the views to their new positions. But there is still one last issue to solve. To see the issue, follow these steps:

1. Run the app.

2. Edit a car.

3. On the edit screen, rotate to landscape.

4. Tap the back button.

Although your add/view scene is in landscape, the layout is completely wrong. This happens because rotation messages are only sent to visible view controllers. When the rotation happens, the add/view scene is not being shown. No rotation messages are sent, so the set of constraints is for the last orientation—in this case, portrait. As you saw previously, those constraints do not work for landscape.

The solution is to keep track of the last orientation shown by the view controller and check it against the current device orientation when the view is shown. If the two orientations are not the same, you can perform the appropriate rotation before displaying. You therefore need to add orientation detection to the add/view scene:

1. Open `ViewController.m` and add a new instance variable inside the curly braces below the `@implementation` statement. This tracks what orientation the view constraints are set up to show, with YES meaning portrait and NO meaning landscape:

   ```
   BOOL    isShowingPortrait;
   ```

2. Add the following lines of code to `viewDidLoad:`, just after the call to the superclass method:

   ```
   UIInterfaceOrientation currOrientation = [[UIApplication sharedApplication]
                                           statusBarOrientation];
   isShowingPortrait = UIInterfaceOrientationIsPortrait(currOrientation);
   ```

3. Modify `viewWillAppear:` to the code in Listing 4-3 to `ViewController.m`. This is where the real work takes place. This code detects the device orientation, compares it against the current orientation for the view controller, and updates the layout if needed.

4. Modify `willAnimateRotationToInterfaceOrientation:duration:` by adding the bold code shown in Listing 4-4. The new code keeps `isShowingPortrait` up to date with the current view controller orientation.

Listing 4-3 `viewWillAppear:` **for** `ViewController.m`

```
- (void)viewWillAppear:(BOOL)animated {
    [super viewWillAppear:animated];

    UIInterfaceOrientation currOrientation = [[UIApplication sharedApplication]
                                            statusBarOrientation];         // 1
    BOOL currIsPortrait = UIInterfaceOrientationIsPortrait(currOrientation); // 2

    if ((isShowingPortrait && !currIsPortrait) ||                           // 3
        (!isShowingPortrait && currIsPortrait)) {
        [self willAnimateRotationToInterfaceOrientation:currOrientation     // 4
                                    duration:0.0f];
    }
}
```

Here's what happens in the numbered lines in Listing 4-3:

1. Find the current device orientation.

2. Is the current device orientation portrait?

3. Is the last orientation for the controller different from the current device orientation? For more advanced programmers, the if statement could XOR (that is, exclusive or) the two variables instead of the longer statement:

   ```
   if (isShowingPortrait ^ currIsPortrait)...
   ```

4. The orientations are different, so use the existing method to update the layout. The duration is 0 because there is no animation. All the changes take place before the view appears to the user.

Listing 4-4   willAnimateRotationToInterfaceOrientation:duration:

```
- (void)willAnimateRotationToInterfaceOrientation:
              (UIInterfaceOrientation)toInterfaceOrientation
                                    duration:(NSTimeInterval)duration {
...

      [separatorView addConstraints:self.separatorViewPortraitConstraints];

      isShowingPortrait = YES;

   } else {

...


      isShowingPortrait = NO;
   }
}
```

Run the code again and go through the same steps that caused the problem. The main screen now has the correct layout. It also works if you start from the main screen in landscape and rotate to portrait in the edit view.

You can add the same code to any view controllers that might be offscreen when the device is rotated.

Summary

Auto layout minimizes the amount of work and code you need for creating interfaces that adapt to different screen sizes and orientations. You can use the techniques you learned here in every app you write.

In this chapter, you used auto layout to adapt your app to different screen sizes and orientations. You designed the constraints with a method you can use in any application. As part of the method, you learned how to use grouping views and hierarchies to minimize the work of adapting layouts. You also learned how to tell if a set of constraints is complete. You used the design to create constraints in IB, again using the idea of hierarchy and groups to make implementation easier.

When you added landscape, you created constraints in code, using both VCL and the more complex single-constraint class call. Along the way, you used IBOutletCollection, a special kind of collection that is useful for a group of related connections. In this chapter, you used collections for related constraints, but you can just as easily use collections for views you want to show or hide, to update, or even move with a fancy graphics effect.

As you continue to work with auto layout, you will discover there is much more you can do, up to and including animations. *Auto Layout Demystified* by Erica Sadun goes much deeper into many aspects of auto layout as well as providing great tools for implementing and debugging.

Auto layout is also helpful for localization. Chapter 5 explores the basics of localization and why leading/trailing is different from left/right.

Challenges

1. Create a table that shows how the landscape constraints for the top-level views are complete. You can base it on Table 4-2, although you might want to put the vertical constraints before the horizontal ones. Use Table 4-3 as a source of information.

2. Create a design for the landscape version of the edit car scene.

3. Use the design from Challenge 2 to create the required landscape constraints. Then make a list of what portrait constraints need to be removed and what landscape constraints need to be added.

4. Implement rotation of the edit car scene using the work from Challenges 2 and 3.

5. Add constraints to make all the buttons equal widths. Hint: You cannot use the canvas to select views in different hierarchies; try the left-hand list.

5

Localization

At this writing, the Apple App Store is available in 155 countries. In most of those countries, English is not the native language. Even if there are people who speak English in a country, it is still best to show your app in a customer's native language. That person can always choose to show it in English. And even English is not just English. There's British English, American English, Australian English, Canadian English...and they all have differences.

iOS provides ways to localize entire screens, some or all of your strings, or even just an individual image. Thanks to auto layout, most apps can focus on strings and perhaps on updating some layout constraints.

In this chapter, you add two more languages to the CarValet app and look for places where constraints might need to change. You start by exploring localization and prepare your app and scenes for localization. As part of this, you find strings that could cause problems.

German is the first language you add. As you localize, you update some interface elements and constraints. Then you reverse your perspective on writing by adding Arabic, including delving into locales by localizing numbers and dates. While doing that, you find out that there are really four ways to set the locale of a device.

When you are done, you will be able to create apps that are ready for localization from the start, which is much easier than retrofitting existing apps.

Localization Basics

When you want an app to support many languages, you need to write only one app. iOS makes it easy to dynamically update your interface based on the user's language preferences.

To find those preferences, in the simulator or on a device, open the Settings app, tap General, and then tap International. You should see a screen like the first one in Figure 5-1. Tap Language and then scroll through the list. When you choose an item from the list, the system updates the interface with the new language. The same choice enables apps to update. The third screen, which appears after you tap Region Format on the International screen, allows you to change how numbers and dates are presented.

Figure 5-1   International settings

You localize an app by using two basic iOS mechanisms: redirection and formats. Each mechanism is used to present different types of localized content. Redirection is for user interface (UI) elements, resources, and strings. Formats are for showing and reading numbers and dates. Occasionally, there is also code to write outside of these mechanisms as you see when localizing for Arabic.

Redirection

Whenever you load a resource, the system uses an indirection step to check for a local version. Resources can include storyboards, XIB (IB interface definition) files, sounds, images, and tables of strings. If a localized version is found, the system uses it; if not, the system uses a default value. You add new languages by adding files and data for that language.

A project starts with English localization. Figure 5-2 shows the project view from the Chapter 5 starting version of CarValet. In the Info panel is a category called Localizations with two items. One is a language—in this case, English.

For CarValet, there is also a "language" called Base. This is considered the default localization. If the device is running in Swahili, and the system cannot find the localized version of a string, picture, or other item, it uses whatever is in Base. That happens because the checkbox to use a base localization is checked. If it were not checked, the system would still use redirection by looking at the top level of the app bundle. (App bundles and how they are organized is beyond the scope of this book because Xcode manages them in all but the most complex cases, and using Base localization is strongly recommended.)

The localizations area also has buttons to add (+) and delete (–) localizations. As you can see, both English and Base already have two localized files. So far you have done no work to localize, so what and where are these files?

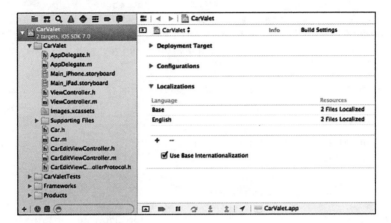

Figure 5-2   Project-level localization

To find those files, look in your project folder in the Finder for a folder called `Base.lproj`. The two files inside that folder are both storyboard files, one for iPhone and one for iPad. So far, you have only edited the iPhone version.

When you add another language, another folder is created. Any content specific to the new language goes inside the new language folder. Every folder has a similar name, `<LanguageCode>.lproj`:

- `<LanguageCode>` is the internationally recognized two-letter code for the language.

- `lproj` means "language-specific project directory."

When you add German later in this chapter, a folder called `de.lproj` is added. `de` is the internationally agreed-on, two-letter code for German, or "**De**utsch." You can find some of the two-letter codes in the iOS documentation. The letters are part of the larger ISO 639.2 standard, available at www.loc.gov/standards/iso639-2/php/code_list.php.

Any time the system needs to load a resource, the first place it looks is the language-specific project directory folder (`lproj`) for the current device language. If the system doesn't find anything, it looks in the base localization. This redirection step makes localization much easier for you.

String Tables

If you want to present an entirely different set of scenes on the iPad after adding Chinese to your product, add an iPad storyboard file with the same name to the Chinese folder, `zh.lproj`. In your project, the iPad storyboard is called `Main_iPad.storyboard`. A Chinese-specific story-board would have the same file name and be in the Chinese folder. On an iPad set to China, iOS looks in that folder first and finds the specific Chinese storyboard. For any other language, it checks in the language folder and does not find a storyboard file, so it uses the default, or English, storyboard.

For most apps, different screens are rarely needed. Usually most of the work is localizing the strings displayed to the customer. Again, this is done by redirection, using a different type of file, called a *string table*.

Each string table consists of pairs of lines in a string table, which are at the heart of string local-ization. Each pair looks like this:

```
/* Documentation about SomeStringKey */
"SomeStringKey" = "ALocalizedSomeString";
```

The first line in each pair is documentation to help translators figure out what the localized string should be. The second line is like a dictionary with a key and a value. `"SomeStringKey"` is a key to identify the particular localized string. Some people use the native language equivalent of the string, such as "Previous" or "Edit." The recommended key name, such as `"PreviousButtonTitle"` or `"EditButtonTitle"`, helps identify what the string is for.

`"ALocalizedSomeString"` is the localized version of the string. Unlike with localized storyboard files that the system finds, you write the code to get a localized string using `NSLocalizedString`. The two arguments correspond to the line pairs in a string table file:

```
NSLocalizedString(SomeStringKey, SomeStringDocumentation);
```

- `SomeStringKey` is the key side shown on the second line of the preceding code example.

- `SomeStringDocumentation` is the documentation string shown on the first comment line.

When you ask for a string this way, the system goes through a few steps:

1. It looks for a file called `Localizable.strings` in the `lproj` folder for the current device language.

2. If it finds the file, it looks for `SomeStringKey`, and if it finds it, the system returns the associated string.

3. If the system does not find either the file or string key, the system looks for the key in the `Localizable.strings` file in the Base localization folder and returns the associated string.

You might wonder why there needs to be documentation for every localized string. Languages can have many features and may require different words and/or modifiers, depending on the use of a particular concept. Languages can have any, some, or all of the following features:

- **Gender specificity**—Nouns can be feminine, masculine, or neutral, and modifiers (verbs, adverbs, and so on) have to match gender.

- **Number matching**—Different words, conjugations, or other elements are required if the noun is singular or plural.

- **Tense matching**—Different words, conjugations, or other elements are required if the noun is past, present, and/or future tense. In addition, languages may have only two tenses or even no tense.

- **Modifications for statement versus question**—Different words, conjugations, or other elements are required if the sentence is a question rather than a statement.

- **Modifications for yes or no**—Different words, conjugations, or other elements are required if an answer is a yes or a no.

For example, German has both gender and number matching. The word *car* is gender neutral, so a car is *das auto*, while more than one are *die autos*. If you are talking about a make, those are usually masculine, such as *der Porsche*, with multiple makes still using *die*. Japanese includes statement versus question, yes versus no, and tense modifications. *Arigato gozaimasu* is "Thank you for what are you are doing"; *Gozaimashita* makes it "for what you have done"; *Wakarimasuka* is "Do you understand?"; *Wakarimasu* is "I understand"; and *Wakarimashita* is "I do not understand."

You call NSLocalizedString (or, as you see later in this chapter, one of its variants) any time you need to display something to the user. This includes setting the text of buttons, labels, and other static elements. It does add some extra code to initializing views, but the one line works for displaying strings from any of your app's localized languages.

The final part is creating the string tables. Apple provides a way to build the table from the command line by using genstrings, which looks for calls to NSLocalizedString or variants. The string table is built using the key and documentation arguments. Adding a new localization makes a copy of the existing default string table.

Formats

When you localize an app, you are really localizing four things:

- **The language displayed in your interface**—In the United States, the title for a button to show the next car is Next; in German, it is *Nächstes*.

- **The order in which you display text items and some controls**—This comes up in two main ways: sort orders and order of words or visual elements. The last part comes from languages that are read right-to-left. You learn more about this later in the chapter.

- **Specific graphical elements or even whole scenes that may need to change—** All but whole scenes is made much easier using the language project folder mechanism discussed earlier.

  Changing whole scenes is very rare and is usually due to one of two things: String length and/or localized iconography make it impossible to adjust the layout using constraints or due to cultural differences.

- **The formats for dates, numbers, and other items—**In the United States, dates are month/day/year; in Canada or the UK, it is day/month/year. German reverses the use of the comma and period in decimal numbers: `1.000,1` is one-thousand point 1. The system provides classes and convenience methods for converting numbers and dates to and from localized strings.

Only some of these things are controlled by the selected language. In addition to setting a language for a device, a user can set a regional format or locale. This is done through the right-hand screen in Figure 5-1.

The locale is set independently of the language. It is perfectly fine for a user to set the language to (U.S.) English and locale to the United Kingdom or even to German. A locale specifies conventions for displaying numbers, date and time formats, and other things.

Most apps show generated numbers and dates as part of their interface. Apps may also parse entered number or date strings. Unlike static strings, you cannot translate numbers and dates in advance. In the physical world, how to display or read information varies from country to country and even from region to region in a country. On iOS, it varies by locale.

There are many rules for how to display numbers, ranging from where separators go and what character to use for the separator and decimal points, to the characters used for the numbers themselves. Dates are far more complex and can vary in the order of elements displayed, separators used, and even the number of months.

An example of order of display is showing the day, month, and year. In the United States, the standard is to display "month, day, year" or "mm/dd/yyyy." In Canada, just next door, the order of days and months is reversed, though the separators are the same—that is, "day, month, year" or "dd/mm/yyyy." In China, it is "year, month, and day" with a special character after each element, then a space, and no other separator.

Calendars also differ. Most of the West uses the Gregorian calendar. Japan uses the Imperial calendar, based on the reign of the current emperor. The Gregorian year 2013 represents a year almost 2,000 years in the future in the Imperial calendar. On the Hebrew calendar, 2013 is more than 3,000 years in the past. The English language setting offers a choice of three calendars: Gregorian (the one you are probably used to), Japanese, or Buddhist.

iOS providers two key classes that let you simplify displaying the correct format and parsing input in your apps:

- `NSNumberFormatter` is used to display and read numbers formatted for a locale.
- `NSDateFormatter` is used to display and read dates and times formatted for a locale.

Other classes are used for calculating dates and time units:

- `NSDate` represents a date in the current calendaring system. It is really just a point in time wrapped in methods.

- `NSCalendar` represents a calendaring system that includes information on the number of days in a week, months in a year, or days in a particular month.

- `NSDateComponents` is used for initializing dates from pieces and for time and date math. You can read or write the individual components of a date by using the current calendar as well as add or subtract different units of time.

  You should never do math assuming that there are 60 seconds in a minute, 60 minutes in an hour, and 24 hours in a day. Doing so is fraught with problems such as leap years and variations in daylight savings, not to mention different calendars.

- `NSTimeZone` represents a time zone and is important in the correct display of dates and times.

You will look at formats in more detail as you internationalize your app. Notice the word *internationalize* in the last sentence. There are two processes involved in adding a new language to your app:

- *Localization* is the process of preparing an application for other languages. This is when you set up the default language `lproj` folder, localize strings and generate string tables, and prepare for other types of content that can change as the language changes.

- *Internationalization* is configuring the content and files for a specific country. It is adding a language's `lproj` folder and setting up, for example, strings for German or the special graphics for Japan.

The next section guides you through localizing the CarValet app.

Preparing the App for Localization

To prepare the CarValet app for other languages, you need to know the following:

- All the static strings that are displayed and where they are defined

- All the dynamic strings that are displayed and where they are created

- All places that display dates and where they are defined or created

- All places that display numbers and where they are defined or created

- All places that parse dates or numbers entered by the user and that are read from the interface

- Any culturally specific graphics and where they are defined (for example, an upside-down triangle is used to represent a stop sign in Japan)

For CarValet, there are very few strings shown and only two places where numbers are read. Figure 5-3 shows both of the related screens. All the strings to localize are highlighted in green, display only numbers in red, and numbers that are both displayed and read in blue. The Done button is not highlighted as it is a system button so iOS does the localization for you.

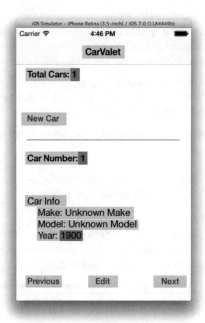

Figure 5-3   Strings and numbers to localize

For other apps, you need to know some other information:

- All places where lists of ordered strings are presented
- All places attempting to autocomplete entered text
- All places searching strings, especially for user display
- All places requiring access to strings on a character-by-character basis, such as finding the position of a character or iterating through characters

The first item is because sort orders can vary widely between different countries and locales. Most of the rest are because a character might not be a character. The key to understanding this is, well, a key: 🔑

The key emoticon is not just one character. Although it may only take one "key" press from a special keyboard, it is really a number of elements that combine to make one user-visible character, or glyph. The same is true of many languages. Not just an obvious one such as Korean, but even French, where multiple key-presses combine to make an accented character.

Although most of this is beyond the scope of this book, the basic approach is to use methods for `NSString` that are locale-specific as well as checking text input for completed user-visible glyphs versus marked, or in-progress, glyphs.

For CarValet, the next step is to add code to read language-specific strings. The code you add is then used to generate the first string table. You can use the `CH05 CarValet Starter` project provided with the sample code or continue with your project from the previous chapter.

Setting Up Localization for the Add/View Car Scene

The existing `InfoPlist.strings` string table is for localizing items from `CarValet-Info.plist`, such as the application name. You need a different string table to localize the interface.

The first step is to add the calls to read localized strings. You call `NSLocalizedString` with a key to the string table and an argument documenting the meaning of the UI element. Make the following changes in `ViewController.m`:

1. In `displayCurrentCarInfo`, change the `withBaseString:` argument in the call to the `updateLabel:withBaseString:andCount:` method:

   ```
   withBaseString:NSLocalizedString(
       @"Car Number",
       @"Label for the index number of the current car")
   ```

2. Similarly, change the `withBaseString:` argument in the `newCar:` method:

   ```
   withBaseString:NSLocalizedString(
       @"Total Cars",
       @"Label for the total number of cars")
   ```

The calls to `NSLocalizedString` contain enough information to create a string table. Instead of manually creating one, you use `genstrings` to generate the table from your `.m` file(s):

1. Open the Terminal application on your Mac.

2. Navigate to your code directory. The easiest way to do this is to type `cd` and a space at the command line in the Terminal window and then drag the CarValet folder from the Finder (the one at the same level as the `CarValet.xcodeproj` file) into the Terminal window. A long path name appears. Press Return in the Terminal window, and you are in the project folder. You can easily confirm this by typing `ls` and pressing Return to list the contents of the directory. You should see all the `.m`, `.h`, and other files, as well as the `en.lproj` folder.

3. Use `genstrings` to generate the English strings localization file. In the Terminal window, type the following command and then press Return:

   ```
   genstrings -o Base.lproj *.m
   ```

-o indicates the output folder, and *.m tells genstrings to look in each .m file for possible localized strings—that is, code that uses any of the NSLocalizedString macros.

After you complete these steps, the Base.lproj folder has a new file called Localizable.strings that contains the UI string table. Notice that you are setting up the base localization, the default for any localization item not defined in a specific language. Add that file to your project, in the Supporting Files group. Take a quick look at the project localization screen you saw in Figure 5-2. The base localization now has three files instead of two.

> ### Tip: Version Control Is Your Friend
>
> It is something that happens to all of us: The main string file has many lines, all with great symbols and comments for the localization team. Then you update the file for some new strings using genstrings and use the wrong arguments. Your work is gone.
>
> Version control is the friend that saves you hours of work. Minimally, make sure you check the box to use GIT when you create your project. Commit often. Small commits are much easier to work with than large ones. It is not a matter of if, but when.

The contents of the strings file look something like Listing 5-1.

Listing 5-1   Localizable.strings **File**

```
/* Label for the index number of the current car */
"Car Number" = "Car Number";


/* Label for the total number of cars */
"Total Cars" = "Total Cars";
```

Each of the entries in the Localizable.strings file corresponds to a unique string defined by NSLocalizedString. The key is the same as the first argument, and the comment is the same as the second argument. It might look strange that the file has the resulting string equal to the key, but that is because this is the English localization. For German, the first translation line would look like this:

```
"Car Number" = "Nummer des Autos";
```

As mentioned earlier, it is best to use a descriptive key. Change the two calls to NSLocalizedString to use NSLocalizedStringWithDefaultValue, a related macro for specifying a default value, among other things. Change the call in displayCurrentCarInfo to this:

```
withBaseString:NSLocalizedStringWithDefaultValue(
            @"CarNumberLabel",
            nil,
            [NSBundle mainBundle],
            @"Car Number",
            @"Label for the index number of the current car")
```

And change the one in `newCar:` to this:

```
withBaseString:NSLocalizedStringWithDefaultValue(
                @"TotalCarsLabel",
                nil,
                [NSBundle mainBundle],
                @"Total Cars",
                @"Label for the total number of cars")
```

Run `genstrings` again and then look at `Localizable.strings`. This time you see the following:

```
/* Label for the index number of the current car */
"CarNumberLabel" = "Car Number";

/* Label for the total number of cars */
"TotalCarsLabel" = "Total Cars";
```

Run the project in the simulator, and you do not see any differences. Now open the `Localizable.strings` file and change the right-hand side of the `"CarNumberLabel"` label to `"Car NumberCar Number"`:

```
"CarNumberLabel" = "Car NumberCar Number";
```

When you run the app again, you see the new string in the lower view car area.

Faking Localization with Double Strings

You might be surprised how long button titles or labels are in other languages. Unlike English, some languages use compound words or require an adjective and/or a definite article to modify a noun.

An example is the Edit button. In German, the text is *Bearbeiten*, which is more than twice as long as the English equivalent. Other buttons and labels might have similar issues. A good approach is to test your interface by doubling your default strings.

You could do this by manually changing your strings, although this is both tedious and prone to errors. (Imagine forgetting to change a string back before shipping.) Luckily, Xcode provides an easier way.

When you click the Run button, Xcode looks at the current scheme to figure out what to build and where to run. You can configure the arguments passed to the app before it launches. This might seem like a strange thing to do, but for debugging it can be a great help, including doubling all localized strings.

You add command-line arguments by editing the scheme (area 2 in Figure 2-5). Follow these steps to the option to double localized strings:

1. Choose Edit Scheme... from the scheme dropdown. You access the dropdown by clicking the right side of the scheme for the area. You should see the scheme editing pane.

left

2. Make sure the Debug is selected in the ~~left~~ list and then choose the Arguments tab in the ~~left~~ area.

right

3. Click the + button under the Arguments Passed on Launch list in the top part of the tab. It should be above the Environment Variables area.

4. Enter the following text in the editing field that appears. (Make sure to include the initial dash character.) When you are done, the pane should look like Figure 5-4:

   ```
   -NSDoubleLocalizedStrings YES
   ```

5. Make sure the box is checked and click OK to dismiss the pane.

Figure 5-4   The scheme-editing pane

Now run the project. On the main screen, any localized strings such as the Car Total and Number labels are localized, as are button strings. Xcode doubles the button titles for you.

Doubling the strings shows you that most of the main screen is likely to be fine with longer strings. You can also see that some buttons might be too big. Remember that you set the bottom row of buttons to be equal in width. They are all as wide as the largest button. That works well in this app for English but might not work for other languages. For now, you can take the string-doubling effect as a warning that you might need to make changes. You look at this in more detail when you add German. This is a good chance to think about how you might solve the problem of providing the same functionality where there is not enough room for all three text-based buttons.

To stop doubling strings, go back to the scheme-editing pane and uncheck the box next to the NSDoubleLocalizedStrings argument. Run your app again and your strings are back to normal.

With the labels localized, there are four other types of content on the page: button titles, the current car info, the screen title, and numbers. First, you need to localize button titles.

Localizing Buttons

To change a button title, you need a reference to the button object. The easiest way to get this is to use IB to add an IBOutlet-based property for each button. You localize the text in the view controller's `viewDidLoad:` method. (Note that there is another way to localize any storyboard elements. See the "`ibtool`: Another Way to Localize Storyboard Strings" sidebar.)

Here's how you add a property for the New Car button:

1. Open the `Main_iPhone.storyboard` file in the editor.

2. Open the Assistant editor to show `ViewController.h` next to IB.

3. Ctrl-drag the New Car button to the `ViewController.h` file and add an IBOutlet property, as shown in Figure 5-5.

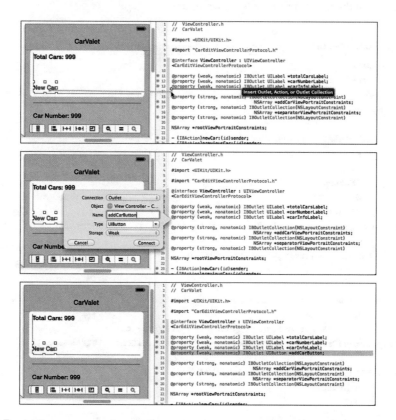

Figure 5-5   Adding a property for a button

The top part of Figure 5-5 shows Ctrl-dragging a connection from the button to the header file. The middle shows naming the outlet `addCarButton`. The bottom shows the newly added property. Note that the created property line is not normally selected. This was done afterward to make the new property easier to see.

> ### Caution: Why `addCarButton` and Not `newCarButton`?
>
> You might wonder why the property for the button titled New Car is not called `newCarButton`. `new`, like `alloc` or `init`, is the standard beginning for the name of a method that returns an object owned by the caller. Since you are creating a property, the compiler creates the accessor methods, including one called `newCarButton`. But that method returns a button owned by the view, not by the object using the accessor. The compiler detects the problem and gives an error.

Use the same technique to set up properties for `previousCarButton`, `nextCarButton`, and `editCarButton`. When you are done with that, add the code in Listing 5-2 to the `viewDidLoad` method. The new code is shown in bold.

Listing 5-2   Changes in `ViewController.m viewDidLoad`

```
- (void)viewDidLoad {
    [super viewDidLoad];

    NSString *local;                                                    // 1

    local = NSLocalizedStringWithDefaultValue (                         // 2
            @"NewCarButton",
            nil,
            [NSBundle mainBundle],
            @"New Car",
            @"Button to create and add a new car");
    [self.addCarButton setTitle:local forState:UIControlStateNormal];   // 3

    local = NSLocalizedStringWithDefaultValue(
            @"PreviousCarButton",
            nil,
            [NSBundle mainBundle],
            @"Previous",
            @"Title for button to go to the previous car");
    [self.previousCarButton setTitle:local forState:UIControlStateNormal];

    local = NSLocalizedStringWithDefaultValue(
            @"NextCarButton",
            nil,
            [NSBundle mainBundle],
            @"Next",
```

```
            @"Title for button to go to the next car");
  [self.nextCarButton setTitle:local forState:UIControlStateNormal];

  local = NSLocalizedStringWithDefaultValue(
          @"EditCarButton",
          nil,
          [NSBundle mainBundle],
          @"Edit",
          @"Title for button to go to edit the current car");
  [self.editCarButton setTitle:local forState:UIControlStateNormal];
...
```

Here's what happens in the numbered lines in Listing 5-2:

1. Set up a temporary string reference for the current localized title.

2. Set the temporary string to the localized title for the Add Car button.

3. Set the title of the default state for the Add Car button to the localized string.

Next, you add entries for the new strings to `Localizable.strings`. Use the terminal to run `genstrings`. Although you could update the strings file manually, this takes longer. Use the same command as you did before:

```
genstrings *.m -o Base.lproj
```

`ibtool`: Another Way to Localize Storyboard Strings

`ibtool` is another command-line tool like `genstrings` that works with storyboard and XIB files. It finds all strings from any standard UI element including button titles, labels, navigation items, and others. It is an advanced tool with lots of flexibility. Using the tool as part of the full project life cycle is beyond the scope of this book. What follows provides a basis for further exploration.

You can use it to generate a strings file. It uses the values in the storyboard or XIB as the default value, though you cannot specify the key or translation documentation. That means you have to go into the strings files and add the documentation yourself.

An example of the first few items from the current `Main_iPhone.storyboard` is as follows:

```
/* Class = "IBUIButton"; normalTitle = "Edit"; ObjectID = "9bN-1d-QVT"; */
"9bN-1d-QVT.normalTitle" = "Edit";

/* Class = "IBUILabel"; text = "Car Info Goes Here"; ObjectID = "Ebi-7G-Bnk"; */
"Ebi-7G-Bnk.text" = "Car Info Goes Here";

/* Class = "IBUINavigationItem"; title = "CarValet"; ObjectID = "Eva-kX-rHD"; */
"Eva-kX-rHD.title" = "CarValet";
```

As you can see, the comment is great to locate the particular element but not so good if you are the person trying to localize the string into some other language. The keys are strange-looking, but that is okay because they are part of the mechanism for matching strings to elements.

Localization is done the same way as elsewhere in this chapter: putting the localized string on the right-hand side in a file for that language.

Running the tool is done from the command line. If you wanted to generate the strings file for the `Main_iPhone.storyboard` file in the `Base.lproj` folder, you would change into that directory, and then use the following command:

```
ibtool Main_iPhone.storyboard --generate-strings-file Main_iPhone.strings
```

The first part is the file to localize. `--generate-strings-file` tells `ibtool` what to do and what the name of the strings file should be. Because you are already in the `Base.lproj` folder, the strings file is generated in that folder. You could add it to your project as part of the localization.

This book uses `genstrings` and the `NSLocalizedStrings` macros for localizing all strings, including those in storyboards or XIB files. If you want to experiment with `ibtool`, you can get full documentation by opening a terminal window and typing the following command:

```
man ibtool
```

By reading the manual page and exploring the options, you can turn `ibtool` into a handy addition to your project life cycle.

Now it is time to localize the car info area. All that content is generated from the car model.

Localizing Strings in the Car Model

`Car` objects return display strings from `carInfo`. The method is currently based on a simple format string with hard-coded values for the title, separator, categories, placeholder values, and year. For now, you can add elements to the format string for localized values.

The rule of thumb is that the sentence is the most appropriate unit of localization. It gives a translator the best chance of matching gender, number, and tense. In this case, the information is singular: There is just one car. Gender for words can vary but sentences will make it clear if a word should be female, male, or neutral. Tense should not be an issue as the information is all in the present tense.

Change the `carInfo` method in `car.m` to the code in Listing 5-3 and then run `genstrings` to regenerate the `Localizable.strings` table.

Listing 5-3   **New** `carInfo:` **Method in** *Car.m*

```
- (NSString*)carInfo {
    NSString *infoLabel = NSLocalizedStringWithDefaultValue(
                    @"CarInfoLabel",
                    nil,
                    [NSBundle mainBundle],
                    @"Car Info",
```

```
                              @"Label for the information of one car");

        NSString *makeLabel = NSLocalizedStringWithDefaultValue(
                         @"CarInfoMakeLabel",
                         nil,
                         [NSBundle mainBundle],
                         @"Make",
                         @"Make Label for the make of one car");

        NSString *modelLabel = NSLocalizedStringWithDefaultValue(
                          @"CarInfoModelLabel",
                          nil,
                          [NSBundle mainBundle],
                          @"Model",
                          @"Model label for the model of one car");

        NSString *yearLabel = NSLocalizedStringWithDefaultValue(
                          @"CarInfoYearLabel",
                          nil,
                          [NSBundle mainBundle],
                          @"Year",
                          @"Year label for one car");

        NSString *unknownMake = NSLocalizedStringWithDefaultValue(
                           @"UnknownMakePlaceholder",
                           nil,
                           [NSBundle mainBundle],
                           @"Unknown Make",
                           @"Placeholder string for an unknown car make");

        NSString *unknownModel = NSLocalizedStringWithDefaultValue(
                           @"UnknownModelPlaceholder",
                           nil,
                           [NSBundle mainBundle],
                           @"Unknown Model",
                           @"Placeholder string for an unknown car model");

        return [NSString stringWithFormat:
                @"%@\n    %@: %@\n    %@: %@\n     %@: %d",
                infoLabel, makeLabel,
                self.make ? self.make : unknownMake,
                modelLabel,
                self.model ? self.model : unknownModel,
                yearLabel, self.year];
}
```

You do the work to localize the year near the end of the chapter.

Setting Up Localization for the Edit Car Scene

Now is your chance to experiment with setting up localization. Change the `CarEditViewController` class by doing the following:

- Change how the main label showing the car number is generated.

- Add properties to access each of the labels next to the edit fields. Use Table 5-1 for the name of the properties for each field. These names will be used in Listing 5-4.

- Localize the field labels. (Remember that you are just localizing the word, not the separator.)

Table 5-1   Property Names for Elements of the Edit Car Scene

Property Name	Field
CarMakeFieldLabel	The label beside the Make field
CarModelFieldLabel	The label beside the Model field
CarYearFieldLabel	The label beside the Year field
CarFuelFieldLabel	The label beside the Fuel field/

The Done button in the navigation bar at the top of the screen is localized by the system so there is no work for you to do.

Add the new properties and the code to set localized values for all the labels on the screen. After you do that, regenerate the string table. If you used any duplicate keys such as `CarNumberLabel`, genstrings gives you a warning including any action taken:

```
Key "CarNumberLabel" used with multiple values. Value "Car Number" kept. Value
"CarNumberLabel" ignored.
```

Generally, this is what you want as it enables using the same key wherever a particular string is used. To give you an idea of how things could look, this is the strings file from the sample code after adding localization to the car edit scene:

```
/* Label for the line to enter or edit the Fuel in a car */
"CarFuelFieldLabel" = "Fuel";

/* Label for the information of one car */
"CarInfoLabel" = "Car Info";

/* Make Label for the make of one car */
"CarInfoMakeLabel" = "Make";

/* Model label for the model of one car */
"CarInfoModelLabel" = "Model";

/* Year label for one car */
```

```
"CarInfoYearLabel" = "Year";

/* Label for the line to enter or edit the Make of a car */
"CarMakeFieldLabel" = "Make";

/* Label for the line to enter or edit the Model of a car */
"CarModelFieldLabel" = "Model";

/* Label for the index number of the current car */
"CarNumberLabel" = "Car Number";

/* Label for the line to enter or edit the Year of a car */
"CarYearFieldLabel" = "Year";

/* Title for button to go to edit the current car */
"EditCarButton" = "Edit";

/* Button to create and add a new car */
"NewCarButton" = "New Car";

/* Title for button to go to the next car */
"NextCarButton" = "Next";

/* Title for button to go to the previous car */
"PreviousCarButton" = "Previous";

/* Label for the total number of cars */
"TotalCarsLabel" = "Total Cars";

/* Placeholder string for an unknown car make */
"UnknownMakePlaceholder" = "Unknown Make";

/* Placeholder string for an unknown car model */
"UnknownModelPlaceholder" = "Unknown Model";
```

The sample code from this chapter implements localizing labels with the code in Listing 5-4. The changes are in bold.

Listing 5-4   **Changes in** `CarEditViewController.m` `viewDidLoad`:

```
- (void)viewDidLoad {
    [super viewDidLoad];

    NSString *labelFormat = @"%@:";                              // 1
    NSString *local;                                             // 2

    local = NSLocalizedStringWithDefaultValue(                  // 3
```

```
                    @"CarMakeFieldLabel",
                    nil,
                    [NSBundle mainBundle],
                    @"Make",
                    @"Label for the line to enter or edit the Make of a car");
        self.carMakeFieldLabel.text = [NSString
                                    stringWithFormat:labelFormat, local];

        local = NSLocalizedStringWithDefaultValue(
                    @"CarModelFieldLabel",
                    nil,
                    [NSBundle mainBundle],
                    @"Model",
                    @"Label for the line to enter or edit the Model of a car");
        self.carModelFieldLabel.text = [NSString
                                    stringWithFormat:labelFormat, local];

        local = NSLocalizedStringWithDefaultValue(
                    @"CarYearFieldLabel",
                    nil,
                    [NSBundle mainBundle],
                    @"Year",
                    @"Label for the line to enter or edit the Year of a car");
        self.carYearFieldLabel.text = [NSString
                                    stringWithFormat:labelFormat, local];

        local = NSLocalizedStringWithDefaultValue(
                    @"CarFuelFieldLabel",
                    nil,
                    [NSBundle mainBundle],
                    @"Fuel",
                    @"Label for the line to enter or edit the Fuel in a car");
        self.carFuelFieldLabel.text = [NSString
                                    stringWithFormat:labelFormat, local];

    NSString *carNumberText;
    carNumberText = [NSString stringWithFormat:@"%@: %d",
                    NSLocalizedString(                                    // 4
                      @"CarNumberLabel",
                      @"Label for the index number of the current car"),
                    [self.delegate carNumber]];
    self.carNumberLabel.text = carNumberText;
    ...
```

Here's what happens in the numbered lines in Listing 5-4:

1. Set up a default format string for labels that includes the separator character. This allows
   for later localization of the format string using the NSLocalizedString macros.

2. Set up a temporary variable used to store a pointer to each localized string object and then set the displayed string of a UI element. You could skip using a variable and set the interface string to the result of calling NSLocalizedStringWithDefaultValue.

3. Format all the labels.

4. Format the Car Number label. Use the same key as for the add/view scene.

Run the code again and confirm that all the strings are correct.

Multiple String Tables

Using one string table works for the CarValet app because it is relatively small. When you have larger projects with many localized classes, one monolithic file does not work as well. It is hard to maintain, hard to read, and provides little flexibility. In such situations, a better approach is to use multiple string tables. You can use one table per source file or per logical grouping, or you can choose other organizational units such as a scene.

You specify a table from one of three specialized localized string macros. Each one takes a tableName parameter, a string that specifies the name of the table. The table name @"Car" would add the localization to Car.strings. Tables are created if they do not exist. These are the three routines:

- NSLocalizedStringFromTable adds a table argument to NSLocalizedString.
- NSLocalizedStringFromTableInBundle lets you specify both a table and a bundle.
- NSLocalizedStringWithDefaultValue is the most flexible, letting you specify a table as well as a default value and bundle. So far, all calls in CarValet use nil for the table.

You can experiment with custom tables by adding them to a project. The files are created by genstrings. You need to add them to the project the first time they are generated. A call of the form genstrings -skipTable <table> tells genstrings to skip any strings for that table.

German Internationalization

German is a good target for internationalization for three reasons. First, there are many potential customers. Second, German has a different set of grammatical rules and includes gender and other modifications. And third, the language has compound words resulting in generally longer than English strings. Working with German is a good test to how well your UI adapts to long strings as well as a good source of possible downloads.

Before you start adding German words, make sure doubling of strings is off by unchecking the box next to the command-line argument in the scheme-editing pane.

Adding the German Locale

Now that you have set up localization, adding new languages is much easier. As you saw in the earlier section, "Redirection," and Figure 5-2, you add new languages using the localization area of the project info pane.

Follow these steps to add German:

1. In Xcode, select the CarValet project in the left-hand Navigator and make sure the CarValet Project is selected, not the CarValet Target. With the project selected, choose the Info tab of the CarValet project in the main view.

2. Find the Localizations area and click the + button.

3. Select German (de) from the resulting popup shown in Figure 5-6.

Figure 5-6   Language selection popup

4. In the localization items pane that appears, uncheck everything except the Base reference language `Localizable.strings` file. When the selection checkboxes look like those in Figure 5-7, click Finish.

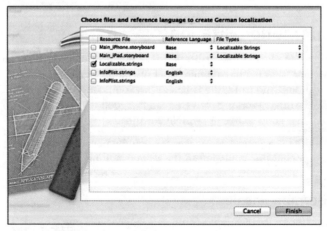

Figure 5-7   Localization items selection pane

In the Supporting Files group, `Localizable.strings` now has a disclosure triangle, with both Base and German versions. In the Finder, there is a `de.proj` folder with the strings file. If you left other files checked, the `de.proj` folder would also have a copy of those files. This is part of the redirection mechanism mentioned previously. Anything in the German project folder overrides something in Base. Note that accidentally leaving the storyboard checked can cause problems later on as changing the Base storyboard would not update the German one.

Localizing the App Name

There is one important string that is not in any of the code files you have worked with so far: the app name. In Figure 5-7, there is another strings file called `InfoPlist.strings` used for localizing application-level strings.

Localizing the app name requires two main steps. First, you have to add `InfoPlist.strings` to the German localization. Then, you update the file with the German app name. In general, it is a good idea to add this file when you create a localization. It was left out to show you how to add or remove files to a localization after a language has been added:

1. Select the `InfoPlist.strings` file in the project navigator.

2. Select the File inspector in the left-hand accessory pane. It should look something like Figure 5-8.

3. Check the box for German. Note that you could remove a file from a localization by unchecking a box for a language.

Figure 5-8   File inspector for a localizable file

When you check the box, the `InfoPlist.strings` item in the supporting files folder also has a disclosure triangle. Opening the items shows one strings file for English and another for German.

Adding the German App Name

To localize a project-based string, you need to know the real key used by the system for that item. Follow these steps to localize the string:

1. Select the `CarValet-Info.plist` file in the supporting files folder.

2. Find the key titled Bundle Display Name, the name that shows in the iOS app launcher, or home screen, of a device.

3. Press Ctrl or click the second mouse button anywhere in the Key, Type, or Value columns and choose Show Raw Keys/Values from the popup menu.

4. The name of the item you found in step 3 has changed to the actual key: `CFBundleDisplayName`. Make a note of the key or, better still, copy it to the Clipboard.

Create the localized launcher display name:

1. If you have not yet expanded the `InfoPlist.strings` to show the localization versions, click the disclosure triangle.

2. Open the German version of the file and update it so it looks like this (new content in bold):

```
/* Localized versions of Info.plist keys */

/* Name of the CarValet App in the App Launcher */
CFBundleDisplayName = "AutoParker";
```

Changing the Device Language

Shortly, you run the app in German, but first you need to know how to change the language of the simulator or device, even if it is running in a language you cannot read. This way, you do not get stuck in German or Arabic and end up resetting or even re-installing your device to get back to normal. These instructions are for the simulator, but they are easily adaptable to devices:

1. If you are running an application, go back home by choosing Hardware > Home or by pressing Ctrl-Shift-H.

2. Open the Settings app.

3. Choose General from the main Settings page on the iPhone/iPod touch or the left column on the iPad. It has a smaller version of the geared Settings icon. Note which item this is, as you may need to navigate with the unit in a different language. The name differs but the position stays the same.

4. Choose International, and again, note the position of the choice in the menu.

5. In the International screen that appears, choose Language, once again noting the position.

6. Choose any language from the list. Every language is shown in its localized format so your native one should be easy to spot. After you tap a language, you get a confirmation dialog in the current language. Tap the top-right confirmation button (no matter what it says). The screen goes black and tells you it is updating the language. The left button cancels changing the language.

Run the app in the simulator. When it is running, stop it in Xcode. Use the preceding steps to change the language to German. Find the screen containing the app, usually the second one, and you see that the name has changed to AutoParker. When you launch the app, no other strings are in German. Updating strings in the app is the next step.

Updating the German `Localizable.strings`

Open the German version of `Localizable.strings`, and you see that it looks identical to the English one. Change the right-hand strings to those in Table 5-2, make sure the simulator language is German, and run the app. The German version of the app should look as shown in Figure 5-9.

There is a chance your app will still show English strings. If that happens, the problem is that the `Localizable.strings` file is not a member of the CarValet target. To check and fix this, follow these steps:

1. Select the `Localizable.strings` file in the project navigator.

2. Show the File inspector on the left side of the Xcode window and look at the Target Membership area.

3. If the CarValet (top) target is not checked, check it.

If the CarValet target is checked, then your project is missing something from this chapter. You can go back over the chapter or look at the chapter sample code.

Table 5-2   **German Localization Strings**

String Key	German
CarFuelFieldLabel	*Kraftstoff*
CarInfoLabel	*Information zum Auto*
CarInfoMakeLabel	*Marke*
CarInfoModelLabel	*Modell*
CarInfoYearLabel	*Jahr*
CarMakeFieldLabel	*Marke*

String Key	German
CarModelFieldLabel	*Modell*
CarNumberLabel	*Nummer des Autos*
CarYearFieldLabel	*Jahr*
EditCarButton	*Bearbeiten*
NewCarButton	*Neues Auto*
NextCarButton	*Nächstes*
PreviousCarButton	*Vorheriges*
TotalCarsLabel	*Anzahl aller Autos*
UnknownMakePlaceholder	*Unbekannte Marke*
UnknownModelPlaceholder	*Unbekanntes Modell*

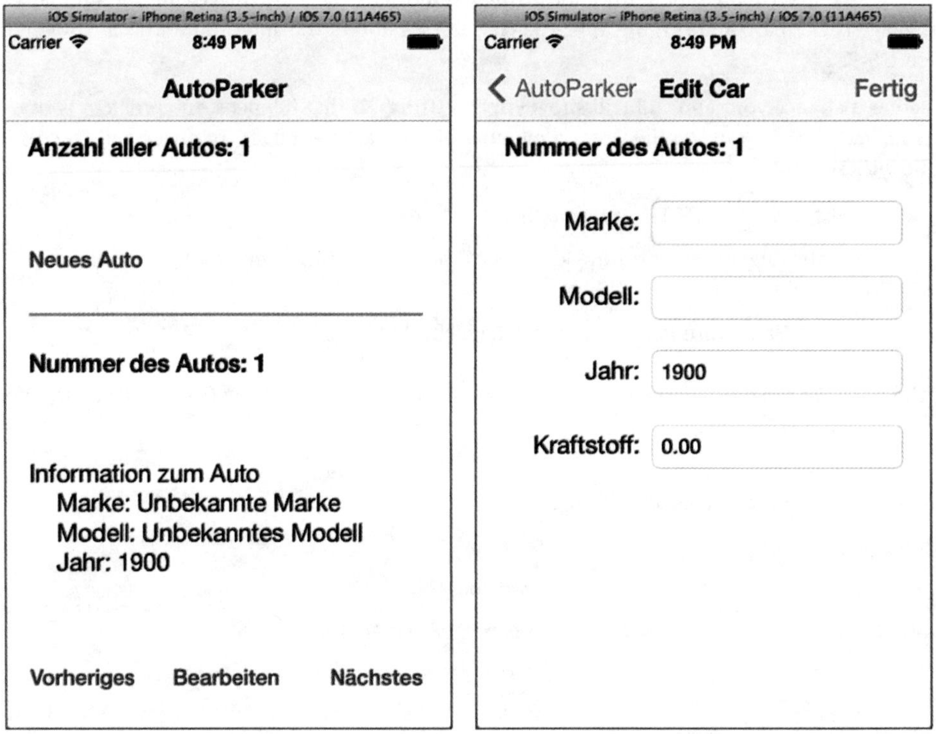

Figure 5-9   The CarValet app in German

There is one problem here: The title of the main screen is okay, but the edit screen is still English. The main screen worked because the default title is the name of the app, and that string is localized. Having said that, it is safer to control the strings.

Add the following code in `viewDidLoad:` for `ViewController.m`:

```
- (void)viewDidLoad {
    [super viewDidLoad];

    self.title = NSLocalizedStringWithDefaultValue(
                @"AddViewScreenTitle",
                nil,
                [NSBundle mainBundle],
                @"CarValet",
                @"Title for the main app screen");

    NSString *local;
    ...
```

Do the same for `CarEditViewController.m` but use the key `EditViewScreenTitle`, a default value of "Edit Car," and change the translator documentation to the "Title for the edit car screen." You have two choices for how to add new keys to the string table. First, you could manually create entries in the English and German tables. Second, and better, as it does not change work already done, is to replace the Base string table using `genstrings` and then copy the two new keys and comments to the German file. Then you can change the values to German. When you add another language, the new entries are copied from the Base table.

These are the additional German strings:

- `CarValet` is `AutoParker`
- `Edit Car` is `Auto Bearbeiten`

Changing Label Constraints

The app is now shown in German, but there is still one issue. To see this, run the app on the simulator and rotate to landscape. As you can see in Figure 5-10, the translated Total Cars label is too long.

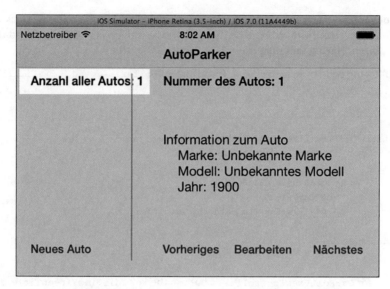

Figure 5-10   Translated label drawn outside of the container view

The core problem is the translated string is too large to fit on one line in the space provided by the add car group. Normally, you would expect to see a truncated string with a continuation character, something like *"Anzahl aller Au..."*.

The reason is the width of the label is not constrained to the width of its container. The resulting frame extends beyond the trailing edge of that container. You might expect the labels container view to clip the string...that is, to cut off any part of the label drawn outside of the frame of the add car grouping view. Views can clip their contents, but doing that requires setting a flag in IB or in code. Some types of view elements have that flag set by default, but not `UIView`.

Try setting the Clip Subviews flag for the add car group shown in Figure 5-11. When it is checked, run the app in landscape. The label is clipped but does not look good because part of a letter is missing. This is why the preferred way of showing strings that are too long is to truncate them using ellipses, the default behavior of labels, buttons, and other elements.

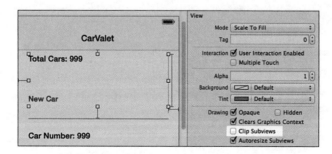

Figure 5-11   Clip Subviews flag in IB

In this case, there is a lot of vertical space between the label and button. You can change the label to allow multiple lines and modify the constraints as needed. Before you start doing this, make sure the Clip Subviews flag of add car grouping view is unchecked again.

As shown in Figure 5-12, running the app in landscape on a 3.5-inch screen shows one other issue: There is not enough room to show the total number of cars.

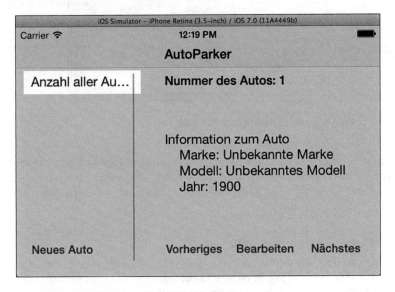

Figure 5-12   German Total Cars label clipped in portrait

The best solution is to find a set of constraints that resizes the Car Total label for any localized string in any orientation. You can do this by making it a multiline label by setting the number of label lines to 0.

Next, set new constraints for the label using these steps:

1. Select the total cars label, and choose Editor > Resolve Auto Layout Issues > Clear Constraints. You can also use the constraint resolution pane from the toolbar to do the same thing.

2. Set the leading, trailing, and top constraints to be adjacent to (0 points from) the leading, trailing, and top edges of the container.

3. Drag a connection between the label and button and set a vertical height constraint.

4. Double-click on the constraint and set the relationship to greater-than-or-equal-to and the constant to 0. Editing the constraint is shown in Figure 5-13.

5. Use the Size inspector to confirm that all the content-hugging priorities are set to 250 (the standard value) and all content compression resistance priorities to 750. If they are not, set them to those values.

6. Use the Attributes inspector to set the number of lines for the label to 0. That allows it to display multiple lines.

You might wonder why you set the constraint between the label and the button in step 3. This prevents the label covering the button. It says that the distance between the bottom of the label and the top of the label can never be less than zero. And since the button is fixed, the label does not grow any larger. If the text is too large, it gets truncated.

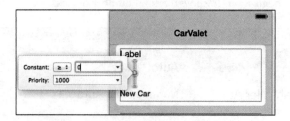

Figure 5-13   Setting a greater-than-or-equal-to constraint

Note that these settings are based on a recommendation from Apple, though they were not working with the beta version of iOS 7 used for this book. If they do not work with the version of iOS you are using, use the workaround described in "Caution: Multiline Labels and Auto Layout."

Caution: Multiline Labels and Auto Layout

As of the iOS 7 beta used for this book, the recommended constraints do not correctly resize the label. The root cause seems to be auto layout relying on the `preferredMaxlayoutWidth` property to find the horizontal size of a label. Preferred maximum width needs to be set before auto layout can successfully lay out the landscape view. Unfortunately, the system does not try to resize the label until after auto layout is done. The label never grows to show the text.

The solution is to wait until the view has completed laying out subviews and then set the preferred maximum width. Effectively, you have to wait until `viewDidLayoutSubviews` is done for all views and then set the preferred maximum based on the new width. The workaround code shown next uses a routine called `dispatch_async`, part of Grand Central Dispatch. That technology is beyond the scope of this book. For more information, see the Apple documentation or Chapter 18 of *iOS Components and Frameworks: Understanding the Advanced Features of the iOS SDK* by Kyle Richter and Joe Keeley.

The workaround fixes the problem for the Total Cars label by adding two methods to your view controller. Add the following methods below `viewDidLoad`:

```
// BEGIN WORKAROUND for labels not correctly updating during rotation
- (void)viewWillLayoutSubviews {
    self.totalCarsLabel.preferredMaxLayoutWidth = 0.0;
}

- (void)viewDidLayoutSubviews {
    dispatch_async(dispatch_get_main_queue(), ^{
        self.totalCarsLabel.preferredMaxLayoutWidth =
        self.totalCarsLabel.frame.size.width;
```

```
    });
}
// END WORKAROUND for labels not correctly updating during rotation
```

The solution works for one specific label. If there are other possible problem labels, add them to the methods, performing the same steps on each string. If there are a number of strings, you could create an `IBOutletCollection`, populate it with problem labels, and iterate through them.

Run the app again in German, and the landscape scene looks like Figure 5-14. Try rotating between portrait and landscape to make sure all the views are laid out correctly.

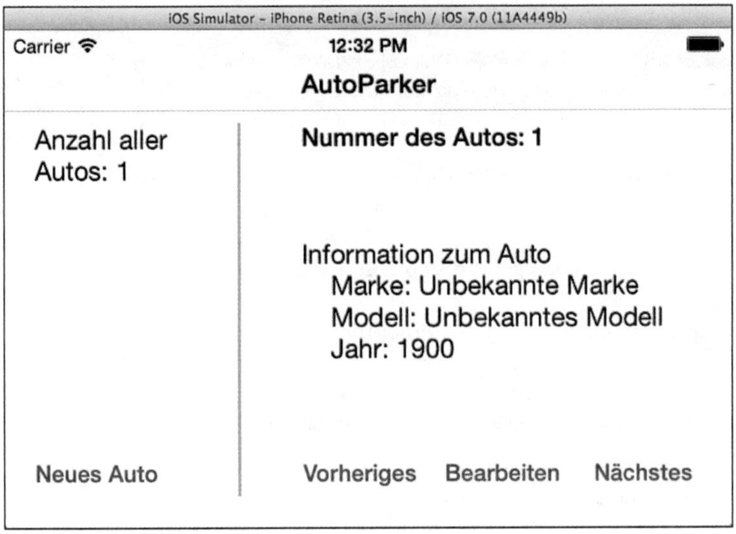

Figure 5-14   New landscape layout

Formatting and Reading Numbers

So far you have only localized strings in the CarValet app. Numbers and dates also vary in formatting from locale to locale. In iOS, the language and locale are set separately, as you saw in Figure 5-1. One simple example is a device using English for the language and Canada for formats.

As mentioned previously, German numbers reverse the period and comma separators. The number 1,234.56 in English is 1.234,56 in German. At the moment, you are showing the fuel amount using `stringWithFormat:` and reading it with `floatValue`. Neither of these methods works with localized numbers. For that, you need `NSNumberFormatter`, a class for both creating and parsing localized numbers as well as other formatting tasks. Creating a string uses either the class method `localizedNumberFromString:numberStyle:` or the instance method `stringFromNumber:`. Reading strings requires `numberFromString:` which, like `stringFromNumber:`, requires a bit more effort in setting up the formatter.

Adding localized number display and parsing requires only a few lines of code in `CarEditViewController.m`:

1. Display a localized fuel amount by replacing the line setting `self.fuelField.text` in `viewDidLoad` with this:

```
self.fuelField.text = [NSString localizedStringWithFormat:@"%0.2f",
                            self.currentCar.fuelAmount];
```

2. In `prepareForSegue:sender:`, replace the line that updates `self.currentCar.fuelAmount` with this:

```
NSNumberFormatter *readFuel = [NSNumberFormatter new];
readFuel.locale = [NSLocale currentLocale];
[readFuel setNumberStyle:NSNumberFormatterDecimalStyle];

NSNumber *fuelNum = [readFuel numberFromString:self.fuelField.text];
self.currentCar.fuelAmount = [fuelNum floatValue];
```

3. Make the same code change from step 2 in `viewWillDisappear:`.

The code in step 1 uses the localized version of the string with format call. `localizedStringWithFormat:` also uses indirection, though this time the system does the work for you. You specify a format string as normal, and the system will do whatever is required to show the localized versions of those formats.

The code from steps 2 and 3 allocates a number formatter, sets it to the current locale, and to work with decimal numbers. Next, it uses the formatter to get an `NSNumber` object from the localized entry in the text field, and finally, it converts that number to a `float` and assigns it to the fuel amount.

In final code, you would create a utility method for reading the field data. You might have a private instance variable for the number formatter and create it only once. Creating formatters for either numbers or dates is a relatively time-consuming operation.

To see the code working, run the app again with the device set to English language, with United States (or Canada, or United Kingdom, and so on) as your region format. Then do the following:

- Edit a car and enter a fuel amount of 1234.56. Note that the keyboard might block the field, so you should return to the main view and then return to the edit view to confirm that you entered the correct number.

- Go to the main screen and use Settings to set the region format, not the language, to Germany.

- Go back to the app and edit the same car.

You should see the fuel displayed as 1.234,56. Try making changes and confirm that the fuel is read and displayed correctly. You can also try switching to different region formats to make sure the fuel is displayed and edited correctly. Before moving to the next section, make sure you set your region back to your default. (This book uses United States.)

As you see later, you can localize dates by using NSDateFormatter.

> ### Caution: Balancing Display and Parsing
>
> When you use edit fields, it is very important to balance the use of localization. If you are localizing the display of a number or date, you must use a formatter to parse any changed value. Forgetting to do this can lead to unexpected values, sometimes resulting in errors.

Next, you learn how to localize the CarValet app for Arabic. If needed, you can start with the CH05 CarValet Arabic Starter project, which contains the final German internationalization.

Right-to-Left: Arabic Internationalization

Several of the constraints you have created use leading and trailing edges instead of left and right. This section shows you why.

Both English and German are left-to-right languages. This applies both to the flow of a sentence and the flow of each word. Changing "Mary had a little lamb." to right-to-left means flipping the complete sentence: ".bmal elttil a dah yraM" And even that does not catch the true difference, as there may be non-native words inside the sentence. If "Mary," a proper name, were foreign, the right-to-left version would be something like this: ".bmal elttil a dah Mary"

Note that everything from this section applies to any right-to-left language including Hebrew, N'Ko (African), Thaana (Maldives), and a few others.

The best way to understand all the issues with internationalizing to a right-to-left language is to do it.

Adding Arabic Strings

The first step in adding Arabic strings is creating the new localization with string tables for the interface and for the application name. You do this in much the same way you did German except you select both the Localizable.strings and InfoPlist.strings files in the localization pane.

When you have created the new localization, you need to run the app in Arabic. There are two ways to do this. First, you can use the settings app in the simulator as you did when you changed to German. Switching between languages in this way is useful when you want the whole device to behave as if it were in that language. If you want to switch languages in this way, the Arabic language choice looks like " العربــــية ."

A second option lets you run just your app in a different language but has no effect on the rest of the device. Generally, this is a faster way to check incremental changes. This option uses the `AppleLanguages` launch argument:

1. Open the scheme-editing pane to the Arguments tab.

2. Add two runtime arguments, one for setting the language to Arabic, and one for German. The two strings are:

   ```
   -AppleLanguages "(German)"
   -AppleLanguages "(Arabic)"
   ```

3. When you are done, the pane should look like Figure 5-15. Close the pane.

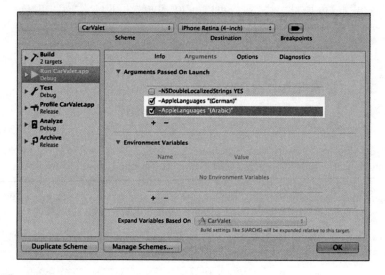

Figure 5-15   Scheme pane with Apple language arguments

When you closed the editing pane, both languages were checked, but what you want is Arabic. You can use a shortcut to show the scheme-editing pane as part of running the app. Option-click the run button and you will see the pane, though with Done and Run buttons in the lower right instead of OK. Uncheck German and press the Run button, and the app looks like the screen shown in Figure 5-16.

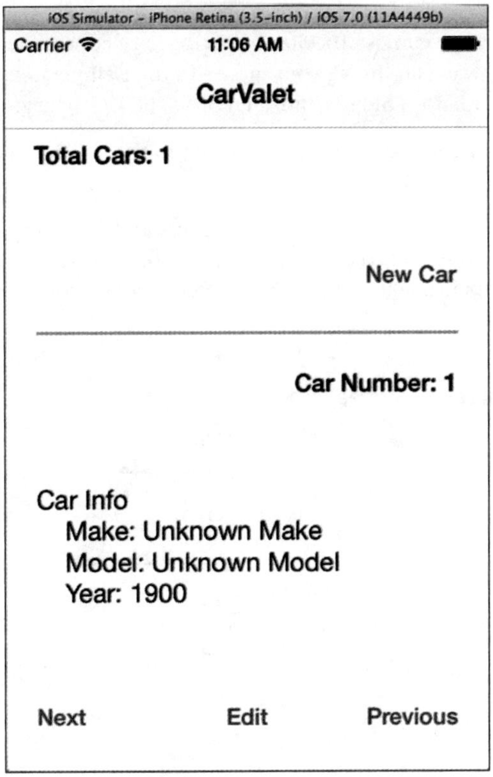

Figure 5-16   Arabic language, English strings

From now on, when you run the app, it will be in Arabic until you change the settings of the launch flags.

Leading, Trailing, and Language Direction

Because you used leading and trailing, the Total Cars and Car Number labels are aligned with the right-hand side of the screen. The same is true for buttons. New Car is on the right, and Previous and Next have been switched.

This is a significant savings in time compared to older ways of localizing. Without auto layout, you would need to add code to detect right-to-left languages and either manually change all the appropriate interface elements or use different storyboards. With auto layout, there is almost no work for you to do, and most of the work is done in the string table.

The only element not right-aligned in Figure 5-16 is the car info string. This is because the label has leading and trailing constraints that are up against the edges of its container. To make things work, remove the trailing constraint and resize the frame.

You can remove the constraint in at least two ways. Whichever way you choose, the first step is to select the view. After that, you use the Size inspector to select and delete the constraint using the gear icon. The other way is to move your mouse to the trailing area. Click to select the trailing constraint when the i-bar highlights and then press the Delete key.

Run the app again and you will see Car Info is aligned to the left side. There is a slight issue with indentation that you fix shortly.

Now use Table 5-3 to update the `Localizable.strings` and `InfoPlist.strings` files. To make this easy, you can copy and paste each string into the Arabic string table. If that does not work, check out the sample code for the book, which includes a completed Arabic string table you can use.

Table 5-3 Arabic Localization Strings

String Key	Arabic
AddViewScreenTitle	خادم السـيارة
CarFuelFieldLabel	وقـود
CarInfoLabel	معلومـات السـيارة
CarInfoMakeLabel	نـوع
CarInfoModelLabel	نموذج
CarInfoYearLabel	علم
CarMakeFieldLabel	نـوع
CarModelFieldLabel	نموذج
CarNumberLabel	السـيارة رقـم
CarYearFieldLabel	علم
EditCarButton	تحـرير
EditViewScreenTitle	تحـرير السـيارة
NewCarButton	سـيارة جديـدة
NextCarButton	تـالي
PreviousCarButton	سـابق
TotalCarsLabel	عمجمو السـيارات
UnknownMakePlaceholder	نـوع السـيارة غـير معروف
UnknownModelPlaceholder	نموذج السـيارة غـير معروف
CFBundleDisplayName (InfoPlist.Strings)	سـياس السـيارة

Run the app, and you should see something like the screen in Figure 5-17.

Figure 5-17   App with Arabic strings

The next step is localizing the numbers and the year.

Making Dates and Numbers Work

Figure 5-17 looks almost right. At first glance, it appears that the car counts and years are not correctly localized. However, it turns out they are. Look in the iPhone status bar at the top of the simulator, and you see that the time is still in English. This is because there are really four settings controlling full localization.

So far, you have only been changing the display language. Go to the Settings app and the International screen. In addition to selecting a language, you can also select a keyboard. For English, you can choose between some different software and hardware layouts. Other languages have more layouts, while some—such as Simplified Chinese handwriting—have just one. There might be several possible keyboards shown. Each time you switch to a new language, the keyboard settings for that language are added to the list.

The international settings screen has two more settings for controlling the region. The first is Region Format. This controls formats for various numbers, such as integers, floats, currency, and phones. It also controls how times and dates are displayed.

The other region setting is Calendar, and it controls how NSDate objects are converted to dates as well as date and time math. Some calendars, such as the Buddhist one, have 13 months.

The first step to seeing Arabic numbers and dates is to set the correct region. Keep the unit in English and use the Region Format to select Arabic > World. When you select World, you see the time in the status bar change. When you return to the International screen, the number of keyboards is in Arabic, as are the date, time, and phone number shown at the bottom of the screen. Now select Arabic as the main language and run the app.

None of the numbers on the main screen are in Arabic. Now go to the edit screen, and most of the numbers are in English. The exception is fuel. That is because earlier you changed `stringWithFormat:` to `localizedStringWithFormat:`.

The rule of thumb is to use the localized version, if you are displaying something in the interface and it contains something that could be localized such as numbers or formatting. Based on that, update the following two places to use `localizedStringWithFormat:`. Both update the numbers in labels:

- **CarEditViewController.m**—Look for `carNumberText` and update the assignment statement.

- **ViewController.m**—Modify the call in `updateLabel:withBaseString:count:`.

When you run the app, you see that the numbers in the labels for both screens are correct, but the date is not. Showing the localized year requires using a date formatter. You could argue that the year is user-entered data and should not be touched, but for now it is useful to see how to localize dates.

Creating a localized date from component parts is a multistep process. In this case, all you have is an integer for the year. These are the steps:

1. Create an NSDate object from any component(s) by using NSDateComponents.

2. Generate a format string for how you want to display the date (optional).

3. Create an NSDateFormatter that uses the format string or a standard format.

4. Generate the string for the displayed date from that date formatter.

Though this process might seem complex, you could easily encapsulate it in a utility method. For now, add the code from Listing 5-5 directly to `carInfo` in `Car.m`. (The new code is in bold.)

Listing 5-5 **Creating a Localized Date from the Year**

```
NSString *unknownModel = MyLocalizedStringWithDefaultValue(
                    @"UnknownModelPlaceholder",
                    nil,
                    [NSBundle mainBundle],
                    @"Unknown Model",
                    @"Placeholder string for an unknown car model");

NSDateComponents *dateComponents = [[NSDateComponents alloc] init];    // 1
[dateComponents setYear:self.year];                                     // 2


NSDate *yearDate = [[NSCalendar currentCalendar]                        // 3
                    dateFromComponents:dateComponents];


NSString *yearFormat = [NSDateFormatter                                 // 4
                    dateFormatFromTemplate:@"YYYY"
                    options: 0
                    locale:[NSLocale currentLocale]];
NSDateFormatter *yearFormatter = [[NSDateFormatter alloc] init];
[yearFormatter setDateFormat:yearFormat];                               // 5


NSString *localYear = [yearFormatter stringFromDate:yearDate];          // 6


        return [NSString stringWithFormat:
                @"%@\n    %@: %@\n    %@: %@\n    %@: %@",               // 7
                infoLabel, makeLabel,
                self.make ? self.make : unknownMake,
                modelLabel,
                self.model ? self.model : unknownModel,
                yearLabel, localYear];                                  // 8
}
```

Here's what happens in the numbered lines in Listing 5-5:

1. Allocate a date component object.

2. Set the year of the date component to the year of the car.

3. Use the current calendar to create a date from the date component object.

4. Set up a localized format to show the year.

5. Create a date formatter and set its format to the one created in step 4.

6. Generate the localized string for the date from the formatter.

7. Change the format string argument from a number to a string.

8. Replace the `year` attribute to the newly localized date string.

Run the new code, and you see the year displayed in Arabic on the main page.

Most of the time, you display full dates and/or times. This is much easier than converting to and from date components because `NSDateFormatter` provides a convenience class method `localizedStringFromDate:dateStyle:timeStyle:` that can generate various formats based on the current locale.

Like `NSNumberFormatter`, the date formatter class parses input using either `dateFromString:` or `getObjectValue:forString:range:error:`. This last method is supported in both the date and number formatters and is a safer way to parse input. Unlike the other methods, it returns a `BOOL` to indicate success or failure and sets an error object if problems occur.

> **Note: Using Custom Arabic Fonts**
>
> This chapter only uses built-in iOS fonts. It is possible to add custom fonts, and one of the reviewers for the book kindly pointed out that custom Arabic fonts might not work as expected. He recommended a library that worked well for his own app. You can find it at https://github.com/Accorpa/Arabic-Converter-From-and-To-Arabic-Presentation-Forms-B.

Text Alignment

The last issue is the Car Info label's text alignment. Although the text is shown right-to-left, the label itself uses left alignment. Things such as the Car Number label work because the label is just as big as it needs to be to show the text.

The car info area is larger than it needs to be and is left aligned, the default for all labels. Although the text direction is reversed, it still is aligned to the left, and the label is larger than just the size of the text.

There is no automatic way to correct for this. Auto layout has already updated the leading and trailing alignment of the label. You need to detect a right-to-left language and change the alignment of the car info view.

Add the code from Listing 5-6 to the `viewWillAppear:` in `ViewController.m`. The bold code detects the language direction and sets the text alignment for the label appropriately.

Listing 5-6   **Setting Text Alignment for Car Info in** `viewWillAppear:`

```
super viewWillAppear:animated];

NSLocaleLanguageDirection langDirection;
langDirection = [NSLocale characterDirectionForLanguage:        // 1
                 [NSLocale preferredLanguages][0]];

if (langDirection == NSLocaleLanguageDirectionRightToLeft) {     // 2
    self.carInfoLabel.textAlignment = NSTextAlignmentRight;      // 3
    self.totalCarsLabel.textAlignment = NSTextAlignmentRight;
} else {
    self.carInfoLabel.textAlignment = NSTextAlignmentLeft;
    self.totalCarsLabel.textAlignment = NSTextAlignmentLeft;
}

...
```

Here's what happens in the numbered lines in Listing 5-6:

1. Find the direction of the current language—that is, the language at the top of the preferred languages list. You might be tempted to use `currentLocale`, but that does not return the selected language.

2. Check whether the language is right-to-left.

3. If the language is right-to-left, change the text alignment of the car info label to right. Otherwise use left.

Run the code again, and this time the screen displays correctly, as shown in Figure 5-18.

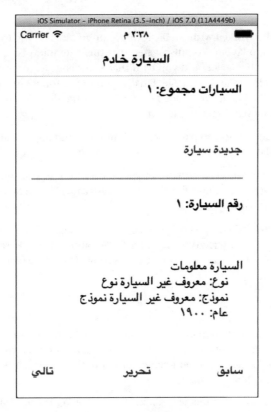

Figure 5-18   Arabic dates and car info correctly aligned

Summary

In this chapter, you created a truly international app, one that supports three languages: English, German, and Arabic. First, you explored the mechanisms iOS uses to make localization easy. You localized your app strings and used `genstrings` to make a string table. While doing that, you learned a handy way to double native strings and find places where you might need to change your layouts.

The first language you added was German, a language that typically has longer words than English. You learned the power of icons for both localization and looks and got some more practice with auto layout as you changed some buttons. You also found out the importance of continuing to test your app in all four combinations of screen size and orientation (or eight if you support iPad).

In this chapter, you also worked with Arabic localization to discover the true value of leading and trailing edges in auto layout. You discovered that there are four places to set the languages and display formats for the device, and you used that knowledge to correctly show numbers and dates in the user's locale and language. Finally, you found some cases where auto layout is not enough, and you need code. You added code to detect the direction of writing and used it to update button graphics and text alignment.

Along the way, you learned how to parse localized numbers and apply that knowledge to reading user-entered dates and times.

Before you leave this chapter, make sure to set your device back to your preferred language, region, and keyboard. This book uses English for the language, United States for the region, and the default English keyboard.

Your app can add, view, and edit cars in three languages, though editing can be a bit difficult, especially on small or rotated screens. In Chapter 6, "Scrolling," you add scrolling, which enables the user to show any field, and you also add some iOS user experience polish.

Challenges

1. Create a Pig Latin internationalization of the CarValet app. You can use another country or practice with regions using either the English–Canada or English–United Kingdom regional setting. Remember to set Region Format to the correct place in the Settings app, either United Kingdom or Canada.

    If you need to refresh your memory about the rules of Pig Latin, see http://en.wikipedia.org/wiki/Pig_Latin. And avehay unfay ithway isthay allengechay.

2. Change `carInfo` to add fuel on the main screen and use `NSNumberFormatter` to localize how fuel is displayed. Remember to localize the label.

3. Change the app to use a separate strings table for each screen. Update all the string localization calls to use the correct table—either `AddViewScreen.strings` or `EditScreen.strings`.Follow these steps to add German:

6

Scrolling

Sometimes you need to present more content than fits on the screen. You have already seen this on the car edit screen. When the keyboard is open, especially in landscape, you cannot show all the text edit fields. What you want is a virtual window onto larger content—a window the user can manipulate to show what he or she wants to see.

`UIScrollView` lets you do all that and more. In this chapter, you learn about and practice using the power of this versatile view. First, you learn the simple math behind scrolling and zooming and how easy it is to access. Then, you integrate a scroll view and change a single setting to add some bounce to your app. You delve deeper into scroll views by enabling scrolling to edit fields the user cannot see. Finally, you finish your scroll view exploration by creating a whole new controller for car images in the CarValet app—one that lets the user scroll and zoom.

By the end of the chapter, you will know how to add virtual space to your apps by using a scroll view. You will also know a standard way to shift views around as the keyboard comes and goes.

Scrolling Basics

Small screens make smartphones portable. They also limit the amount of information you can show. Sometimes information is bigger than the screen—for example a picture, a form with text fields, or a map.

On iOS, the solution is to scroll around. `UIScrollView` is a virtual window onto larger content. It provides all the support a user needs: dragging content around, zooming in and out, and all the other functionality an app might need.

The user drags or flicks a finger in a scroll view to slide the content around under a fixed "window." Figure 6-1 shows changing what part of the content is viewed. The blue rectangle is what the user sees on an iOS device screen. The larger image is contained by the scroll view. The left side shows the scroll view over the upper-left corner of the image. Then the user drags a finger diagonally from the top left toward the bottom right. The right side of Figure 6-1 shows the scroll view over a new part of the image. Note that the scroll view does not move. It is the content—in this case an image—that "moves" under a fixed visible area.

Figure 6-1 also shows two important UIScrollView properties. contentSize is the width and height of all the content inside the scroll view. contentOffset is the x and y location inside the larger content from the upper left of the visible scrolling window. On the left side of Figure 6-1, the x and y values of contentOffset are 0—that is, there is no offset. On the right side of the figure, both x and y are nonzero. The values of x and y are added to the top left of the content view to get the top left of the scroll view "window" on the content.

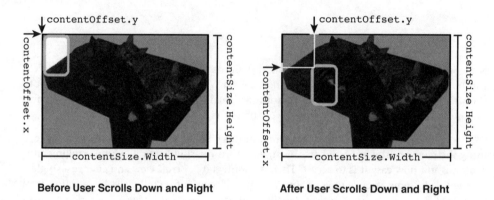

Before User Scrolls Down and Right   **After User Scrolls Down and Right**

Figure 6-1   Scrolling content

Scroll views also zoom in and out by scaling the content view. Figure 6-2 shows zooming in. The left side shows the content just before the user performs a zoom-in gesture by putting two fingertips close together on the screen and then moving them apart.

The right side of Figure 6-2 shows the result of zooming in. The most important property is zoomScale or the multiplier for the height and width of the content. The scale is 1.0 for a normal picture, larger for zooming in, and smaller for zooming out.

Once again, the visible area stays where it is, and the content is scaled. You can see by the numbers in the figure that contentSize and contentOffset are multiplied by the zoomScale. However, you should never scale content by directly manipulating the size or offset. Always use setZoomScale:animated: or zoomToRect:animated:. Later, you see that scroll view uses zoom scale for other purposes.

As you work your way through this chapter, you find out how to use scroll views to move, zoom, and even page through logical units of content.

```
        zoomScale = 1.0                    zoomScale = 1.4
   contentSize.width = 100           contentSize.width = 140
     contentOffset.x = 80              contentOffset.x = 112
```

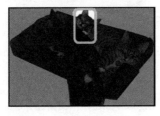 

Before User Pinch Zooms   **After User Pinch Zooms**

Figure 6-2   Zooming content

Bounce Scrolling

As users get familiar with iOS, they get used to scrolling. When experienced users get a new app, one of the first things they do is try to scroll the screen up and down. A screen with more content scrolls. But what about for screens that show everything? How does a user know that everything is shown?

One nice user experience feature is "bounce" scrolling of the screen—that is, moving down or up a little and then gently scrolling right back. The bounce feedback tells users they are seeing everything. In this section, you add bounce scrolling to the add/view car scene in the CarValet app.

Adding a Scroll View to the View/Edit Scene

The easiest way to set up a scroll view is to put all the content you want to scroll in one view. This new view becomes the scroll views content view. For the add/view scene, you need a `UIView` that contains the add car area, separator view, and view car area. Effectively this means the `view` of the `UIViewController` is the content view. But you cannot just drag in a scroll view and make it the root view of the view/add scene controller.

That leaves two choices. First, you can add a scroll view as a child of the root view and then add a `UIView` as a child of the scroll view and move all the content areas (add car, separator, and view car) into that new child. Unfortunately, you also have to redo all the layout, constraints, and property connections. That is a lot of work, and it's also a good way to introduce bugs.

A second way uses the same basic technique you used to embed the add car view controller in the navigation controller. But this time, you use Editor > Embed In > Scroll View. Unfortunately, it is not quite as easy as selecting the current top view and selecting the command.

This is because that view is the visual part of the add car view controller. Before using the embed command, you have to make a new top-level view. Doing that requires breaking the connection between the controller and its view.

Make sure you use the CH06 CarValet Starter project. As you see in the next section, the structure and constraints of the edit scene have been changed. Follow these steps to break the connection and embed everything in a scroll view:

1. Open the project and select Main_iPhone.storyboard. Make sure to uncheck the Arabic language Launch Flag in the scheme for this project. Also set the simulator back the United States region (or whatever region you have been using for your project).

2. Select the CarValet view controller from the left-hand list of view elements in IB and expand it to show the children of the root view.

3. In the project browser, change the name of the current root view to Content View.

4. Drag the root view from its current position to the list just below First Responder, as shown in Figure 6-3. The gray square and arrow show what is dragged and where.

5. Drag a UIView into the view controller where the old content view used to be.

6. Move Content View from the view controller into the newly added root view. Make sure the content view is inside the new root view and does not replace it. The easiest way to do this is to drag the content view onto the controller in the IB canvas.

   Ignore any problems with constraints for now. You will fix those later.

7. Select the new content view, and choose Editor > Embed In > Scroll View. A new scroll view appears in the hierarchy. The hierarchy now looks like Figure 6-4.

8. Fix the constraints. This takes a few steps:

   - First, choose the new scroll view and use the pin constraint popup to set a distance of 0 for all four edges (top, bottom, leading, and trailing) to its nearest neighbor... the root view of the controller. Make sure you choose the update frames of the new constraints option before adding the constraints.

   - Next, choose the content view and set the same 0 distance to the edges of the scroll view with the pin constraint popup. Do not choose the update frame option.

   - With the content view still selected, use the alignment popup to center it horizontally and vertically (the bottom two checkboxes), choosing update frames before setting the constraints.

   - There is one remaining issue. Select the add car group and pin the top edge based on whatever number shows in the popup.

- Pin the bottom of the view car group the standard distance from the bottom of its container and update frames.

- Select all the children of the view car group and update frames.

After you drag in the new top level view, the hierarchy on the left-hand list looks something like Figure 6-4.

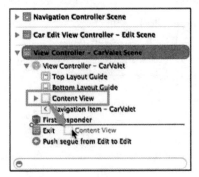

Figure 6-3   Adding a `UIView` after First Responder

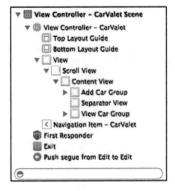

Figure 6-4   New hierarchy with scroll view

Run the app on both 3.5-inch and 4-inch displays. You should notice something is not quite right. The Total Cars label is too far from the navigation bar. Although this might seem like the wrong behavior, it is actually behaving correctly.

View controllers have an `automaticallyAdjustsScrollViewInsets` property that determines if scroll views will inset, or shrink, their content areas for navigation bars, toolbars, and other such items. The default value is `YES`, which means the scroll view is adjusting the height of the content view so the top is just below the navigation bar.

On the IB canvas, the constraint from the top of the content view to the top of the add car group extends under the toolbar. When the top of the content view is moved under the toolbar, the add car group is still 72 points below the content view. That means it is 72 points below the navigation bar, and not what you want.

There are two ways to fix this. The first is to change the 72 points to the standard distance. The only issue with this is, on the IB canvas, the top of the add car group moves under the navigation bar. It works if you run it on the simulator, but it is harder to maintain.

The second way is easier. Add the following line of code to `viewDidLoad` in `ViewController.m`, just below the call to the superclass:

```
self.automaticallyAdjustsScrollViewInsets = NO;
```

You now have an add/view scene with a scroll view but no bounce. You add bounce by selecting the scroll view, opening the Attributes inspector, and checking the Bounce Vertically check box.

Run the app in the simulator and bounce the main view. When the content view bounces, the areas underneath are white because the scroll view uses the default color. If you want to show the difference between the content view and empty space, change the background color of the scroll view to a different color.

Try changing it to light gray, run the simulator, and scroll. You see light gray above or below the edges of the content view when bouncing. If you were writing production code, this would be a good time to make sure the changes work in different screen sizes and orientations.

The bounce effect is there to provide feedback that the user has reached the edge of a scrollable area. So far, the content view and the scroll view are the same size, so any attempt to scroll bounces. Now, it is time to move on to the edit screen and add support for scrolling content. In this case, scrolling text fields into view when the keyboard is up.

Handling the Keyboard

You have not yet finished making the edit scene work in all screen sizes and orientations. The problem is that the keyboard sometimes covers at least one of the input lines, and there is no layout that works in all orientations and screen sizes with the keyboard open.

The solution is to put the view with the fields inside a `UIScrollView`. When the screen is big enough to show everything—that is, when the scroll view is large enough to show all the content—it only bounce scrolls (or not, if the Bounce Vertically check box is unchecked). The user cannot accidentally move the content off the screen. But when the keyboard opens, you resize the scroll view to be above the keyboard. The content view stays the same size, so the user can scroll through the input lines.

In this section, you do the following:

- Add the scroll view.
- Resize the scroll view, based on the height of the keyboard.
- Handle rotation.

While doing this, you learn how to set up the content area of a scroll view, resize scroll views, and listen for the keyboard opening and closing.

Adding the Scroll View

The starter project for this chapter has an updated edit view, as shown in the highlighted portions of Figure 6-5. Your first thought might be to simply embed the form view inside a scroll in the same way you added bounce scrolling to the add car scene. In this case, embedding is not what you want to do, and the reason is auto layout.

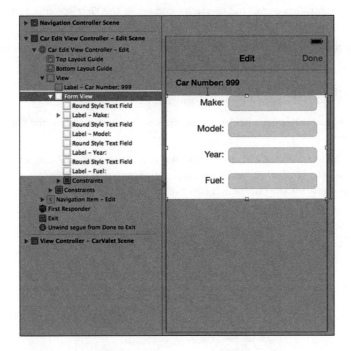

Figure 6-5   New edit view form and hierarchy

When the content view is the same size as the scroll view, it is possible to create a complete set of constraints for that content view in relation to its scroll view. This does not work when the size of the content inside the scroll view can be different from the size of the scroll view.

Remember that a scroll view works by offsetting the origin of the scroll view relative to its content... It is a window onto some larger view. Constraining the content to the scroll view means it has a fixed relationship with the scroll view—there is no scrolling.

Instead, you need the content view constraints to be independent of the scroll view, so the content view hierarchy lives in its own world. This can be done in two main ways. IB's pixel-perfect layout works if the size of the content view does not change. One example of this is an image, as you will see later in "Scrolling Through Content."

If the size of the content can change, you need some way to update both the content view and the `contentSize` property of the scroll view container. For the form view, even though the height is static, the width can change when the device rotates.

The easiest way to make this work is using code to add and manage the content view and the `contentSize` scroll view property. When you are done adding the scroll view, you no longer see the form view on the canvas, though it is available to the view controller. Follow these steps to add the scroll view:

1. Open `Main_iPhone.storyboard` and select the edit scene.

2. Move the Form View out of the hierarchy and under the First Responder. You do this the same way you moved the content view in Figure 6-3.

3. Drag a scroll view on the scene so that the top of the view is below the car number label.

4. Use the pin constraint popup to set the scroll view constraints. It should be 15 points from the car number label, 0 points from the edge of its container, and 200 points high. Figure 6-6 shows the popup for these constraints.

   When you add the constraints, the scroll view resizes and moves to the correct position in the view.

5. Open an Assistant editor with the `.h` file and create two properties: `scrollView` is a reference to the scroll view, and `formView` is a reference to the form view. You need to drag from the form view in the left-hand list to create the property.

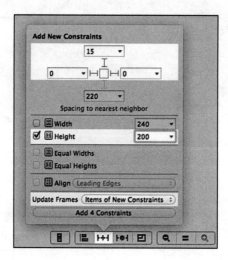

Figure 6-6   Pin constraints for scroll view

Tip: Easy and Maintainable Content Views

The sample code starter for this chapter came with the form view already created, but why was it created before adding a scroll view? In fact, why create it at all?

The answer lies in creating self-configuring content views. Ideally, the form view resizes based on the width of its container: The labels and text fields grow or shrink based on the available space. You could do this in code, calculating the position and size of each label and text field, changing their frames, and telling the view to update. But that is a fair amount of code (about 25 or so lines), and any change in content means changing the code.

A better idea is using auto layout to set things up for you, using the top-level form view as a grouping view. As long as none of the constraints of the children inside form view refer to something outside of form view, it acts as a self-contained view hierarchy. The constraints are complete.

Using the IB canvas is the easiest way to create the constraints. Adding form view to the existing hierarchy allows you to set up all the internal constraints and get it working correctly. While you are doing this, the form view is constrained relative to its parent. That is, the form view has its own constraints enabling it to adjust position and size. And that lets you test that the children behave correctly.

After you remove the form view from the view controller hierarchy, any constraints attached to that hierarchy are removed. Form view no longer has any external constraints. But all the constraints for the children remain. And if you need to change things at a later date, you can drag form view back onto the main view, constrain it, make your adjustments to the subviews, then remove it again.

This is a powerful technique for creating dynamically added grouping views that use auto layout for their children.

Adding, Configuring, and Updating the Form View

Now that you have a scroll view, you need to add the content (form) view and manage its size. When you change the size of form view, you also need to update the scroll view's `contentSize`.

Unlike auto layout and constraints, you set the frame of the form view and let the system do the rest. You still need to know the "constraints," that is, the rules governing how to set the bounds, and those rules need to be complete:

- The origin of the frame view starts from x and y coordinates of 0.
- The height of the frame view is fixed at `200` points, enough to enclose all the label/input field pairs.
- The form view is as wide as its parent, the scroll view.

The question is where to put the code to add the frame view to the scroll view, set the frame views size, and the scroll view `contentSize` property. The answer lies in how the edit car scene is shown.

The only way to open the scene is by tapping the Edit button. That means the car scene is recreated each time. Unlike the add/view scene, there is no way to leave and return to the same edit screen. Unlike the returning to the add/view scene after rotation problem you solved in Chapter 4, "Auto Layout," you can do everything in `viewDidLoad`.

Add the code from Listing 6-1 to `viewDidLoad` in `CarEditViewController.m`. New code is in bold.

Listing 6-1 **Adding and Sizing** `formView` **to** `scrollView`

```
- (void)viewDidLoad {
    [super viewDidLoad];

    self.formView.translatesAutoresizingMaskIntoConstraints = YES;           // 1

    [self.scrollView addSubview:self.formView];                              // 2

    self.formView.frame = CGRectMake(0.0, 0.0,                               // 3
                            self.scrollView.frame.size.width,
                            self.formView.frame.size.height);

    self.scrollView.contentSize = self.formView.bounds.size;                // 4
...
```

Here's what happens in the numbered lines in Listing 6-1:

1. The frame view does not have any constraints relative to the superview. Tell the system to create constraints using its current frame.

2. Add the form view to the scroll view.

3. Make sure the form view is as wide as the scroll view.

4. Set the scroll view `contentSize` so it can scroll if needed. (Refer back to Figure 6-1 for the relationship between the scroll view size and the `contentSize`.)

Resizing for the Keyboard

When the keyboard comes up, it might cover one or more of the input fields. A scroll view lets you move the fields into view so the user can see where he or she can input text. All you have to do is resize the scroll view so it is above the keyboard. The scroll view becomes smaller, but the content size does not change and the user can scroll the form view, and therefore, the fields.

When the keyboard opens and closes, iOS uses the built-in `NSNotificationCenter` to send events. You add code to listen for the correct events and change the size of the scroll view as needed. Doing this takes three steps:

1. Add methods responding to keyboard open-and-close events.

2. Register for keyboard open-and-close notifications when the view opens.

3. Deregister for keyboard open-and-close notifications when the view goes away.

The last step is important. If you fail to unregister, it is possible to get notifications when the view controller is off the screen but still allocated. At best, this results in setting the view to an undefined state. More likely it will crash the app.

Resizing the Scroll View

Resizing the scroll view means changing one or more of its constraints, as you saw when you added landscape in Chapter 4. The question is, what to change?

There are four constraints for the scroll view: align to the leading and trailing edges, a fixed distance from the Car Number label, and a fixed height. To change the height of the scroll view, all you need to do is change the numerical constant for the fixed height constraint.

You only need to change the constant in two circumstances. The first is when the keyboard shows and covers part of the scroll view. In that case, you need to reduce the height by the amount of overlap. That is, you need to figure out the amount of overlap and subtract that from the default constant for the height constraint.

The second time you need to change the height constraint is when the keyboard goes away. In that case, you change the constraint back to its original value. This means you need a reference to the height constraint and an instance variable for the original height constraint.

Add a property called `scrollViewHeightConstraint` referencing the height constraint. Put this just below the `scrollView` property you added earlier.

Change the `@implementation` statement in `CarEditViewController.m` so it looks like the following:

```
@implementation CarEditViewController {
    CGFloat defaultScrollViewHeightConstraint;
}
```

Initialize the default value in `viewDidLoad`, just after the call to the superclass:

```
defaultScrollViewHeightConstraint = self.scrollViewHeightConstraint.constant;
```

Now you need the amount of overlap, if any.

Finding Overlap: View Frames

The events sent when the keyboard opens and closes contain information about both the starting and ending frames of the keyboard. There is also a set of helper functions for coordinate math, including the intersection of rectangles.

An important thing to remember is that the `frame` of a view—that is, `<view>.frame`—is always given in the coordinate space of the parent of that view. The parent of the keyboard is the main window, so the frame of the keyboard is relative to the coordinate system of the main window. The frame of the scroll view is relative to the car edit view controller. And that might not be the same as the window.

Before you calculate any intersection, you have to convert the frames to use the same coordinate space. Generally, that means converting one of the frames into the other's space. To understand why this is important, look at Figure 6-7.

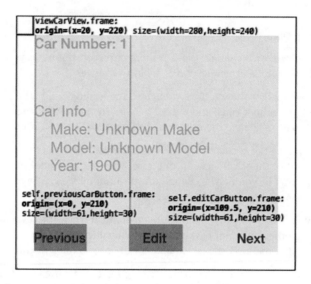

Figure 6-7   View frames

The frame of the view car group view is based on the coordinate system of its parent. The origin is (20, 220) relative to the parent. The frame for the Previous button (0, 210) is also in the coordinate system of the parent, but this time it is the view car group. It is clear from the x coordinate that the two frames are in different spaces, since the Previous button cannot be both at 0 and 20 points from the edge.

A bit of math would show you that the coordinates for the Previous and Edit buttons are offset by the origin of their parent, the view car group. But again, this is the frame of each button expressed in the coordinate space of the view controllers' root view.

The solution to converting between coordinate spaces is using the convertRect:forView: UIView message. Note that there are several variations of this message, including ones to convert points.

With a combination of the routines to intersect rectangles, the ability to convert view rectangles to the same space, and a variable for the default scroll view height constant, you have all you need to create the resizing code.

Add the keyboard open-and-close action methods shown in Listing 6-2 just below
`didReceiveMemoryWarning`.

Listing 6-2   Keyboard Open-and-Close Methods

```
- (void)keyboardDidShow:(NSNotification *)notification {
    NSDictionary *userInfo = [notification userInfo];                          // 1

    NSValue* aValue = userInfo[UIKeyboardFrameEndUserInfoKey];                 // 2

    CGRect keyboardRect = [aValue CGRectValue];                               // 3
    keyboardRect = [self.view convertRect:keyboardRect fromView:nil];

    CGRect intersect = CGRectIntersection(self.scrollView.frame, keyboardRect);// 4

    self.scrollViewHeightConstraint.constant -= intersect.size.height;        // 5
    [self.view updateConstraints];                                            // 6
}

- (void)keyboardWillHide:(NSNotification *)notification {                      // 7
    self.scrollViewHeightConstraint.constant = defaultScrollViewHeightConstraint;
    [self.view updateConstraints];
}
```

Here's what happens in the numbered lines in Listing 6-2:

1. Get the dictionary of information associated with the notification.

2. Look up the final view frame for the displayed keyboard.

3. Convert the value for the final view frame into a `CGRect` and convert the coordinate
   space from the device main window to the coordinate system used by the view car
   group—that is, to the root view of the edit scene view controller.

4. Find the rectangle defined by the intersection of the scroll view and the keyboard. If
   scroll view and keyboard do not overlap, the rectangle is all zeros.

5. Reduce the height of the scroll view by the amount of vertical overlap—that is, the
   height of the intersection rectangle. If there is no intersection, this subtracts zero.

6. Tell the view to update constraints as the scroll view height constant might
   have been changed. Note that you can wrap these last three lines of code in
   `CGRectIntersectsRect`. This function returns `true` if the rectangles intersect.

7. When the keyboard closes, set the height constraint constant back to the default and
   update constraints. Again, you could check if the height has actually changed before
   executing these two lines of code.

Next, register for keyboard open-and-close notifications by adding `viewDidAppear:` below `viewDidLoad`:

```
- (void)viewDidAppear:(BOOL)animated {
    [super viewDidAppear:animated];

    [[NSNotificationCenter defaultCenter]
        addObserver:self
        selector:@selector(keyboardDidShow:)
        name:UIKeyboardDidShowNotification
        object:nil];
    [[NSNotificationCenter defaultCenter]
        addObserver:self
        selector:@selector(keyboardWillHide:)
        name:UIKeyboardWillHideNotification
        object:nil];
}
```

Each of the calls registers for a particular notification with the default notification center. The call takes four arguments:

- An observer, or the object that is sent the registered notification method
- A selector—that is, the signature of a method called when the event triggers
- The name of the notification
- An optional object passed with the notification, which is useful when you are using a centralized object to handle notifications and need to differentiate the target

`UIKeyboardDidShowNotification` triggers after the keyboard finishes opening and results in a call to the registered `keyboardDidShow:` method. If you needed to animate views moving as the keyboard opens, you can register for `UIKeyboardWillShowNotification`, called just before the keyboard animates open. `UIKeyboardWillHideNotification` is triggered just before the keyboard animates closed and calls `keyboardWillHide:`.

The names of the methods are arbitrary; you can call them whatever you want. `UIViewController` has no standard keyboard notification methods. However, it is good practice to use a standardized naming scheme because doing so makes subclassing easier.

> ### Tip: Using a Superclass for Common Behavior
>
> Responding to keyboards is a common task for apps. To make things easier, you could create a subclass of `UIViewController` to encapsulate the behaviors associated with handling the keyboard:
>
> - Registering for keyboard notifications using an object to make the registration unique
> - Methods for handling open, close, and other keyboard messages that complete with any needed default behavior
> - Unregistering for keyboard notifications

> You can add an IBOutletCollection to the class of any views that need to be resized when the keyboard opens or closes. The default methods can go through the array and update views. This allows you to use IB to drag connections to views that need resizing.
>
> Any view controller that needs to work with the keyboard can inherit from the subclass.
>
> A more advanced technique is to create a category on UIViewController and then #import the category if you need to handle the keyboard. This works as long as you do not need any properties.
>
> For more information on these techniques, see the iOS developer documentation or Chapters 6 and 11 in *Learning Objective-C* by Robert Clair.

Finally, you remove the view controller as an observer of keyboard events. To do so, add the bold code to viewWillDisappear:

```
- (void)viewWillDisappear:(BOOL)animated {
    [super viewWillDisappear:animated];

    [[NSNotificationCenter defaultCenter]
        removeObserver:self
        name:UIKeyboardDidShowNotification
        object:nil];
    [[NSNotificationCenter defaultCenter]
        removeObserver:self
        name:UIKeyboardWillHideNotification
        object:nil];

    ...
```

The arguments to remove an observer are similar to those for adding an observer. The only difference is that you do not specify a selector. Other than that, the arguments must match those used in the call to add an observer. If you specified an object in the observe call, you must specify the same object in the remove call. If you don't, the call might silently fail, and your object will still be observing.

Run the app again and open the keyboard. Scroll the form view up and down. You can scroll through all the fields and have margins at the top and bottom. Change the orientation to landscape, and now it is possible to scroll the form view beyond the last field. Getting rotation to work requires one more change.

Adding Resizing

When the screen is rotated, both the scroll view and form view need to be resized. Then the contentSize property needs to be updated.

You already have code to resize the scroll view. Put breakpoints in keyboardDidShow: and keyboardwillHide: and run the app again. Rotate the screen and you see that each method is called. The system hides and shows the keyboard to set it to the correct size. Those methods also correctly set the size of the scroll area.

The form view is also resized when the screen rotates. This happens when the scroll view changes size and updates the layout for its children. All you need to do is update `contentSize` from the new form view frame. Add the following line of code at the end of both the `keyboardDidShow:` and `keyboardWillHide:` methods:

```
self.scrollView.contentSize = self.formView.frame.size;
```

Run the app in portrait, open the edit screen, and tap in one of the fields. Now change the orientation to landscape. The form view scrolls correctly. Rotate back to portrait, and everything still works.

Scrolling Through Content

This section shows you some of the most advanced features of `UIScrollView`. You add a new scene for paging through a set of zoomable car images. *Paging* means you scroll by units of content instead of smoothly through the content. In this case, each scroll gesture to the left or right moves by one car. To make this work, you do the following:

- Create a new view controller class for viewing car images.
- Add a new scene with a scroll view using the new class.
- Populate the scroll view with car images.
- Set up the scroll view to page through images.
- Add the ability to zoom a car image in and out.

You start by adding the car images (thanks to Sunipix.com for the free images!) to the project:

1. In the downloadable content for this chapter is a folder called `CH06 Assets CarImages`. Copy the folder into the `Base.lproj` folder of the current project.

2. In the left-side project browser, open the supporting files folder and make sure the folder is selected.

3. Choose File > Add Files to CarValet and add the folder you just copied. Make sure the option to create groups for added folders is selected.

4. Add a new view controller class called `CarImageViewController` and move the files for that class just above the Supporting Files group in the project browser.

5. In IB, drag a new view controller below the edit scene. You may need to zoom out to have enough space. Use the magnifying glass icons in the lower-right taskbar for zooming.

6. With the new view controller selected, go to the Identity inspector and set the class to `CarImageViewController`.

7. Select the add/view scene and drag a bar button item into the status bar (just as you did in Chapter 3, "Introducing Storyboards"; see Figure 3-23). Set the title of the button to Car Images.

8. Drag a push segue connection from the new bar button item to
   `CarImageViewController`. When the status bar appears in the new controller, give it
   the title "Car Images."

9. Copy the Car Number label edit scene to the car image scene. Put it in the same place
   by setting the constraints to 15 from the top and 0 from the leading edge. Make sure to
   update frames when setting the constraints.

10. Add a scroll view and set the constraints to place the top edge 15 points from the bottom
    of the car number label, and adjacent (that is, 0 points) to the leading, trailing, and
    bottom edges of the parent. Again, update frames when you add the constraints.

11. Ctrl-drag to add two properties to `CarImageViewController`: `carNumberLabel` for the
    label and `scrollView` for the scroll view.

Run the app and make sure you can go to the new car images scene and get back to the main
scene. Of course the scene is almost empty, so now you need to add some images.

Populating the Scroll View

So far, you have created content views using IB. Now you create the content view in code. In
this case, the content view is a `UIView` with a number of `UIImageView` children. In a real app,
the images would probably be pictures taken with the camera. In this app, the images are the
car pictures you added to the project.

Set the content of `CarImageViewController.m` to the code in Listing 6-3.

Listing 6-3   **Initial Code for** `CarImageViewController`

```
//
//  CarImageViewController.m
//  CarValet

#import "CarImageViewController.h"


@implementation CarImageViewController {
    NSArray *carImageNames;                                      // 1
}

- (void)setupScrollContent {
    NSMutableArray *imageViews = [NSMutableArray new];           // 2

    CGFloat atX = 0.0;
    CGFloat maxHeight = 0.0;
    UIImage *carImage;
    UIImageView *atImageView;
```

```objc
    for (NSString *atCarImageName in carImageNames) {                      // 3
        carImage = [UIImage imageNamed:atCarImageName];
        atImageView = [[UIImageView alloc] initWithImage:carImage];

        atImageView.frame = CGRectMake(atX, 0.0,                           // 4
                                       atImageView.bounds.size.width,
                                       atImageView.bounds.size.height);

        [imageViews addObject:atImageView];

        atX += atImageView.bounds.size.width;                             // 5
        if (atImageView.bounds.size.height > maxHeight) {                 // 6
            maxHeight = atImageView.bounds.size.height;
        }
    }

    UIView *carImageContainerView = [[UIView alloc] initWithFrame:          // 7
                                     CGRectMake(0.0, 0.0,
                                     atX, maxHeight)];

    for (UIImageView *atImageView in imageViews) {                        // 8
        [carImageContainerView addSubview:atImageView];
    }

    [self.scrollView addSubview:carImageContainerView];                   // 9
    self.scrollView.contentSize = carImageContainerView.bounds.size;
}

- (void)viewDidLoad {
    [super viewDidLoad];
                                                                          // 10
    carImageNames = @[ @"Acura-16.jpg", @"BMW-11.jpg", @"BMW-13.jpg",
                       @"Cadillac-13.jpg", @"Car-39.jpg",
                       @"Lexus-15.jpg", @"Mercedes Benz-106.jpg",
                       @"Mini-11.jpg", @"Nissan Leaf-4.jpg",
                       @"Nissan Maxima-2.jpg" ];

    [self setupScrollContent];
}

@end
```

Here's what happens in the numbered lines in Listing 6-3:

1. Set up a private instance variable for the array of car names. If the contents of the array can change, you can use NSMutableArray.

2. Set up a mutable array for adding the image views.

3. Go through each image file name, create a `UIImage`, and put it in an image view.

4. Change the starting x position of the image view frame so it is next to the previous image. You do this by setting the x origin of the first image to 0 and then adding the width of the previous images to the origin in step 5.

5. Add the width of the current image to the starting position for the next image (or to get the final width of the view if this is the last image).

6. Set the maximum height for the content view to the height of the tallest image.

7. Allocate a container view with a width of all the images and the height of the tallest image.

8. Add each image to the new container view.

9. Add the container view as the child of the scroll view and set the content size.

10. Initialize a static array of car image file names.

Run the app and tap on the Car Images button in the navigation bar. You can scroll through all the pictures, but you see that they vary in both width and height. A better experience is having all the images be the same width. After you resize the images, you can use paging to move from image to image.

Adding Paging

Paging works by moving the content in units of the width and/or height of the scroll view. The user experience is flipping horizontally through the car images. To accomplish this, each car image must be the width of the scroll view. And because each image is the same width, the size of the content view is the width of the scroll view times the number of images.

Replace `setupScrollContents` with the code in Listing 6-4.

Listing 6-4   Paging Version of `CarImageViewController`

```
- (void)setupScrollContent {
    CGFloat scrollWidth = self.view.bounds.size.width;                      // 1
    CGFloat totalWidth = scrollWidth * [carImageNames count];               // 2

    UIView *carImageContainerView = [[UIView alloc] initWithFrame:
                        CGRectMake(0.0, 0.0,
                                   totalWidth,
                                   self.scrollView.frame.size.height)];

    CGFloat atX = 0.0;
    CGFloat maxHeight = 0.0;
    UIImage *carImage;
```

```
    for (NSString *atCarImageName in carImageNames) {
        carImage = [UIImage imageNamed:atCarImageName];

        CGFloat scale = scrollWidth / carImage.size.width;            // 3

        UIImageView *atImageView = [[UIImageView alloc]
                                    initWithImage:carImage];

        CGFloat newHeight = atImageView.bounds.size.height * scale;   // 4

        atImageView.frame = CGRectMake(atX, 0.0, scrollWidth, newHeight);

        if (newHeight > maxHeight) {
            maxHeight = newHeight;
        }

        atX += scrollWidth;

        [carImageContainerView addSubview:atImageView];
    }

    CGRect newFrame = carImageContainerView.frame;
    newFrame.size.height = maxHeight;
    carImageContainerView.frame = newFrame;

    [self.scrollView addSubview:carImageContainerView];
    self.scrollView.contentSize = carImageContainerView.bounds.size;
}
```

Here's what happens in the numbered lines in Listing 6-4:

1. Get the width of the scroll view for setting the width of each image.

2. Calculate the total width for the container view.

3. Calculate a scale factor for making the current image the width of the scroll view.

4. Scale the image view based on the new height. Also check for a maximum height for setting the content view height.

Run the app and view the car image screen. Now each car image is small enough to fit on the screen. To add paging, open IB, select the scroll view, and check Paging in the Attributes inspector. This time, when you run the app and scroll left or right, you see a different car image.

Adding Zoom

Zooming is useful for helping the car valet see a license plate number or confirm that a particular scratch was already on a car. To enable a `UIScrollView` to zoom requires four main changes:

- Adopting the `UIScrollViewDelegate` protocol in the car image view controller
- Implementing the `viewForZoomingInScrollView:` protocol method
- Connecting the scroll view delegate to the view controller
- Specifying a maximum zoom level greater than `1.0` and/or a minimum level less than `1.0`

The following steps take you through the first two parts of adding zoom to the car images scroll view:

1. To adopt the `UIScrollViewDelegate` protocol in the car image view controller, make the changes shown in bold to `CarImageViewController.h`:

   ```
   @interface CarImageViewController : UIViewController
   <UIScrollViewDelegate>

   @property (weak, nonatomic) IBOutlet UILabel *carNumberLabel;
   ...
   ```

2. Create a private instance variable for the view that zooms, in this case the car image container view, by adding the line in bold to the private variables declared near the top of `CarImageViewController.m`:

   ```
   @implementation CarImageViewController {
       NSArray *carImageNames;

       UIView *carImageContainerView;
   }
   ```

3. Set up the new instance variable for the container view in `setupScrollContent`. The top of the method changes as shown in bold:

   ```
   - (void)setupScrollContent {
       CGFloat scrollWidth = self.view.bounds.size.width;
       CGFloat totalWidth = scrollWidth * [carImageNames count];

       carImageContainerView = [[UIView alloc] initWithFrame:
                               CGRectMake(0.0, 0.0,
                                          totalWidth,
                                          self.scrollView.frame.size.height)];
       ...
   ```

4. Add the following method below `viewDidLoad`:

```
- (UIView *)viewForZoomingInScrollView:(UIScrollView *)scrollView
{
    return carImageContainerView;
}
```

This is the scroll view delegate protocol method for returning the view to zoom. In this case, there is only one zoomable view—the view containing all the images.

That takes care of the first two parts of adding zooming. Now you need to connect the scroll view delegate. To do that, open `Main_iPhone.storyboard` and Ctrl-click on the scroll view. Figure 6-8 shows using the resulting connections popup to drag a connection from the delegate outlet of the scroll view to the view controller shown in the bar below the main view controller canvas window.

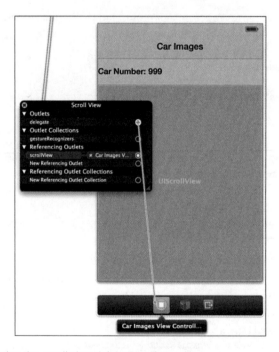

Figure 6-8   Connecting the scroll view delegate outlet

The final step to activate zoom is to change the maximum zoom level. Still in IB, select the scroll view and look at the Attributes inspector. Change the maximum zoom to 3.

Run the app, open the car image viewer, and zoom in. Hold down the Option key, and you see two dots appear on the simulator screen, as shown in Figure 6-9. Those represent where your fingertips will be if you press down on the mouse.

Figure 6-9   Pinch gesture in the simulator

Press the mouse and move the circles (your fingertips) apart. The image zooms. You are able to scroll around the image, and if you scroll too far left or right, you page to the next image. Notice that paging works correctly even though the view is zoomed in. As you come to the right or left edge of one car image, the scroll view snaps to an edge of the new car. This is because paging uses the scale factor to determine the new page size.

Zooming out uses the opposite gesture from zooming in: You pinch. However, it is easy to see that most of the time, the car valet is zooming in. Zooming out is an extra effort, especially when most of the time the user will try to get the image back to the original size. This would be a good behavior to provide through an interface element.

To do this, add a Reset Zoom button to the navigation bar. Tapping that button resets the scale to 1. The button is disabled unless the image is zoomed. Follow these steps:

1. Drag a bar button item into the status bar of the car image screen and change the title to Reset Zoom. Use the Attributes inspector to make sure it is initially disabled.

2. Create a property in `CarImageViewController.h` for the Zoom button called `resetZoomButton`.

3. Create an `IBAction` for the Zoom button called `resetZoom:` by Ctrl-dragging into the `.h` file and selecting the type Action instead of Outlet.

4. In `CarImageViewController.h`, add the code below to `resetZoom:`

```
[self.scrollView setZoomScale:1.0 animated:YES];
```

Run the app. The button is in there, but when you zoom, it is not enabled. You need to detect when the content is zoomed and enable or disable the button depending on the scale factor. You can use `scrollViewDidEndZooming:withView:atScale:`, another scroll view protocol method called anytime the scroll view finishes zooming content. The zoom can be a user pinch or a message. Add this method just below `viewForZoomingInScrollView:`

```
- (void)scrollViewDidEndZooming:(UIScrollView *)scrollView
                       withView:(UIView *)view
                        atScale:(float)scale {

    self.resetZoomButton.enabled = scale != 1.0;
}
```

The single line of code sets the enabled state of the button based on the current scale. If the scale is not `1`, the button is enabled; otherwise, it is not.

Run the app, scale an image, and reset the scale. Everything should now work. If it does not, make sure the button is sending the `resetZoom:` message.

One small thing to notice is the Reset Zoom button is enabled when you first open the car images screen. Fix that by adding the following line to `viewDidLoad`, just below the call to the superclass:

```
self.resetZoomButton.enabled = NO;
```

Rotation

The only thing not working correctly is changing orientations. If you change to landscape, the images are not resized, and the scroll view pages based on its wider size. That means the paging is off.

You need to regenerate the content view when the screen rotates. Make two changes to make rotation work. First, add the following method below `viewDidLoad`:

```
- (void)willAnimateRotationToInterfaceOrientation:
                  (UIInterfaceOrientation)toInterfaceOrientation
                                  duration:(NSTimeInterval)duration {
```

```
[super willAnimateRotationToInterfaceOrientation:toInterfaceOrientation
                                  duration:duration];

[self setupScrollContent];
}
```

Then change `setupScrollContent` to remove a container view if one already exists. Add the code in bold to the top of `setupScrollContent`:

```
- (void) setupScrollContent {
    if (carImageContainerView != nil) {
        [carImageContainerView removeFromSuperview];
    }

    CGFloat scrollWidth = self.view.bounds.size.width;
...
```

Run the app again on a 3.5-inch screen, and you see that rotation works, though it is not ideal. The car images are too high for the available space to make paging work in the horizontal direction. It is possible to scroll them down, but paging causes it to be a jerky vertical scroll. Since zooming already works, a simple fix is to allow making the image smaller as well as larger. Use IB to change the minimum zoom to `0.75`. Run the app again, and everything should work correctly in both orientations. (You create a better fix in Challenge 3 at the end of the chapter.)

What Car Is This?

The final thing you need to do with the car image scene is to correctly set the car number. With paging enabled, you know how much width each car takes. You also know the location of the scroll view in the content. To find the number (not the index) of the car, find the number of page widths.

You need to add the methods in Listing 6-5 above `viewDidLoad:`. The methods update the label and find the current car index. The car index is `0`-based, so add `1` before displaying.

Listing 6-5 **Updating the Label Using the Index of the Current Car Image**

```
- (void) updateCarNumberLabel {
    NSInteger carIndex = [self carIndexForPoint:self.scrollView.contentOffset];

    NSString *newText = [NSString stringWithFormat:@"Car Number: %d",
                            carIndex + 1];

    self.carNumberLabel.text = newText;
}

- (NSInteger)carIndexForPoint:(CGPoint)thePoint {
```

```
        CGFloat pageWidth = self.scrollView.frame.size.width;

        pageWidth *= self.scrollView.zoomScale;                          // 1

        return (NSInteger)(thePoint.x / pageWidth);                      // 2
}

- (void)scrollViewDidScroll:(UIScrollView *)scrollView {
        [self updateCarNumberLabel];                                     // 3
}
```

Here's what happens in the numbered lines in Listing 6-5:

1. Multiply the scroll view width by the zoom scale to get the actual page width.

2. Convert the result of a floating-point division to an integer. By casting the result—that is, telling the system to turn the result into an NSInteger—the system effectively uses the floor function, rounding it down to the nearest integer.

3. Update the Car Number label whenever the scroll view scrolls. scrollViewDidScroll: is another protocol method sent whenever the scroll view finishes scrolling content.

You also need to set the car number when the view first appears. Add a viewDidAppear: below viewDidLoad for the initial car update:

```
- (void)viewDidAppear:(BOOL)animated {
        [super viewDidAppear:animated];

        [self updateCarNumberLabel];
}
```

Summary

In this chapter, you have explored many parts of UIScrollView, from a simple bounce to scrolling and zooming.

You started by retrofitting the view/add screen and enabling a bounce to show the user that what shows on the screen is all there is (is the complete content view.) After retrofitting the edit view, you used the scroll view to give access to all the edit fields, even when the available screen area is too small for all of them. Finally, you used a new view controller to explore paging and zooming content.

Along the way, you found out how to enable and disable buttons, resize scroll views and their content area when the screen rotates, and figure out which item is shown as a user scrolls.

Now you can add a scroll view to your design toolkit. Your own apps can add some feedback with a bounce or let the user work with more information than can fit on a screen. You can also handle keyboards as they show and hide, and you can provide feedback on what buttons can and cannot be touched. And in case you forget to add the scroll view when you build the view, you have a reliable process for retrofitting later.

Even with three screens, controlling the navigation in your app is becoming more complex. In Chapter 7, "Navigation Controllers I: Hierarchies and Tabs," you use two key view controllers to tidy up navigation. One controller is perfect for presenting hierarchical content, just like looking at all the cars and then seeing the detail. The other makes moving between different groups of content, like the cars, car images, and a new about screen, a breeze.

Challenges

1. When the screen rotates from portrait to landscape, stay on the same car by aligning the left edge of the car image with the left edge of the screen. Doing this requires knowing how big an individual car is, what part of the content view is being shown, and how much width defines a car. Remember that zooming changes the paging width.

2. In the add/view scene, it is possible to view the data for a particular car. When the user opens the car image scene, start on the image that corresponds to the car currently being viewed. Because there might be more cars than images, use modulo divide to set the car number. % is the modulo operator for ints in Objective-C. Implementing this requires communication between the add/car scene controller and the car image scene controller. You have already done this for the edit scene. Use that code as a starting point. You might even be able to reuse something.

3. Add code to disable paging when the car image is zoomed. You need to detect when the content is zoomed in or out, and you need to set pagingEnabled for the scroll view.

4. Internationalize the screen. If you do not have access to native speakers, use an automated web translation site. A word of warning: It is very risky to ship code that uses automatic translations. The safest way is for native speakers to verify that the correct word or words are used, given the context. As of this writing, automatic translation sites are unable to correct for context. At best, the interface appears clunky, and it will more likely confuse, or even insult, your user.

Navigation Controllers I: Hierarchies and Tabs

Most apps have a main view leading to multiple screens, often with more than one way to move through them. You need to provide a way for your users to move around your app and some way for them to know where they are. Navigation controllers provide different ways to move between the parts of an app and the functionality those parts provide.

On iPhones and iPod touches, most apps using navigation controllers fall into two types. One uses a single main view that navigates through a series of screens showing progressively more or less detail. Contacts, Notes, and Settings are good examples. Others, such as Clock and Music, have several main views, each with different functionality or even their own hierarchy of content.

iOS provides controllers for managing navigation through each type of content. `UINavigationController` is for moving up and down hierarchies of information, and `UITabBarController` handles switching between multiple main views.

In this chapter, you explore both navigation controllers: what they are for, when to use them, and how to use them. You start by adding a `UINavigationController` to the CarValet app and connecting up the add/view and edit car scenes. You also use a toolbar and some color to add more polish to your app.

Next you work with `UITabBarController` for navigating among the car hierarchy, car images, and an About view. While doing this, you add tab bar items and hook them to the scenes they control. You also create and integrate a screen without using the storyboard.

As a result of all your work in this chapter, you will be able to use two powerful navigation controllers in your apps. You will know when and where to use them and how to make them work, as well as some more ways to make your apps stand out.

Navigation Controller

Think about using the Settings app. Better still, open it up and explore a little. You can lay out the content of the Settings app as an inverted tree, with the main screen at the top, and all the content screens as the leaves. Figure 7-1 shows a partial hierarchy with the leaf nodes in italic.

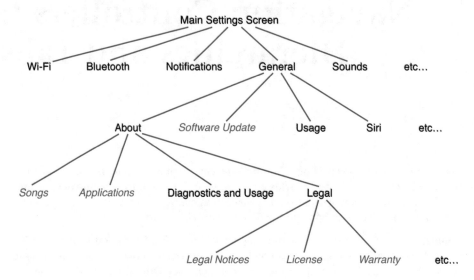

Figure 7-1   Partial settings hierarchy

This is a very common way to organize your content on iPhones and iPod touches. It elegantly solves how to show lots of content in a small space. Settings lets you modify hundreds of options for your iPhone and the apps it contains. Using a hierarchy to "fold" the content works well with both the screen size and how people are generally good at categorization and grouping.

Apps using hierarchies of content work in basically the same way. There is a top-level screen with an overview of the content, and then there are screens with more detail. The Settings app is a good example. You start at the top level with all the possible categories of settings, and you keep drilling down until you reach the detail for a particular setting.

UINavigationController is built to handle this type of navigation. It keeps track of the customer as he or she navigates the hierarchy of screens and provides default controls to get back. The controller does this by embedding all your content inside itself.

Figure 7-2 shows the parts of a navigation controller. At the top is a navigation bar. This is typically used for context and unwinding the current path. The title usually orients the user to what he or she is viewing. As you will see shortly, a left-hand back button enables the user to go back one step in the navigation path. An app can also have custom buttons on the navigation bar.

At the bottom is an optional toolbar that gives you another space to put controls, in this case an action button. Your view controller goes in the gray area. Somewhere in the current scene, you provide a way to open the next level of detail. In the add/view scene, for example, this is the Edit button.

Figure 7-2   Navigation controller

When you use a navigation controller, you start by connecting it to the first, or root, scene (a view controller). When the navigation controller opens, it opens this root scene. As you segue to a new scene (view controller), the navigation controller puts it on the current path and displays the scene.

The path is tracked as a stack of view controllers, with the root view on the bottom. Figure 7-3 shows the stack as you navigate to the Hebrew keyboard screen in Settings. You can see a back button in the navigation bar in each screen after the root view. The default is a less than symbol (<) followed by the name of the previous screen. If the name is too long, the screen name is replaced by the word "Back."

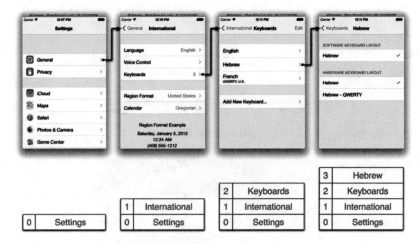

3	Hebrew

		2	Keyboards	2	Keyboards
2	Keyboards	1	International	1	International
1	International	0	Settings	0	Settings
0	Settings				

Figure 7-3   Navigation stack for license in settings

Navigation Controller Classes

All navigation functionality is provided through five main classes:

- `UINavigationController` coordinates all the components for the current navigation stack. In addition to managing the navigation stack and all transitions, it has references to the navigation bar and the optional toolbar.

- `UINavigationBar` is a view for the navigation bar at the top of the screen. It is used by `UINavigationController` to show the title of the current scene along with a button to return to the previous screen if needed. It can be used on its own, though that is not recommended.

- `UINavigationItem` manages the `UINavigationBar` for a particular view controller in the hierarchy. There are properties and methods for setting a title, and showing, adding, and hiding bar button items, including the back button.

- `UIBarButtonItem` provides an object for managing buttons in navigation and toolbars. You can create everything from system buttons such as Done, Cancel, and Action to text buttons, and more. Button items are not `UIButtons` or even a type of view. They are management items that can display something in the user interface. You can put a `UIButton` inside a button item.

- `UIToolbar` manages an optional toolbar, usually at the bottom of a screen. There are methods and properties for setting button items and appearance as well as a way to specify if it is placed at the bottom or top of the screen.

`UINavigationItem` uses the `title` property of the current view controller to set the text. Changing the `title` changes the text. You saw this earlier when you localized scene titles.

Figure 7-4 shows the navigation controller–related objects in the add/view scene of CarValet selected on the left-hand Interface Builder (IB) view element browser. The `UINavigationController` in the browser as well as on the left of the canvas includes the shared navigation bar.

The navigation controller manages the add/view scene in addition to others. Each managed scene has a `UINavigationItem` for setting the content of the navigation bar, including a title. The add/view title bar also has a bar button item to show the car images scene.

The scene has a special segue identifier for the first, or root view, controller as shown in Figure 7-4. Unlike push segues, this one looks like a line with two circles on each end. The root scene is the first scene presented by the navigation controller. The other connections on the storyboard show navigation paths between scenes. As an example, there is a connection between the add/view and edit scenes. Because there is nowhere else to go except back, the edit scene is a leaf node, just like those in Figure 7-1.

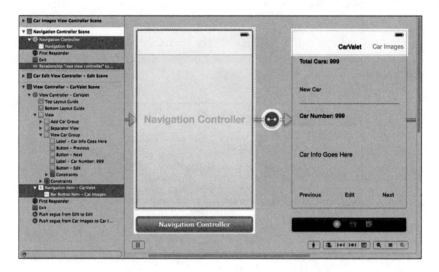

Figure 7-4   Navigation Controller items in the add/view scene in CarValet

Adding a Toolbar

Toolbars can give a more balanced feel to an app and do not need to be in every scene. A natural choice is to move the navigation and Edit buttons in the add/view scene into a toolbar.

The first thing is to add some icons to your project asset library. You can start with either the `CH07 CarValet Starter` project provided with the samples or continue to use your project from the previous chapter. Follow these steps:

1. Use the project navigator to select the `Images.xcassets` item.

2. Click the + button in the lower left of the image asset area to show the add assets popup, as shown in Figure 7-5.

3. Choose Import from the popup. In the file dialog that appears, select the CH07 Assets
   Toolbar Icons folder that comes as part of the sample code for this chapter and add it
   to the catalog.

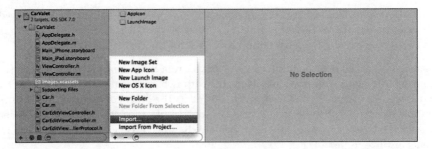

Figure 7-5   Asset catalog and asset addition popup

When you press OK, the contents of the folder in the Finder are copied to the asset catalog. A
new asset folder is created with the same name and is selected, showing the new icons. Your
catalog should now look like Figure 7-6.

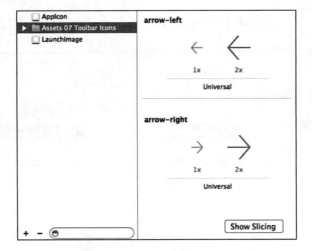

Figure 7-6   Asset catalog: imported items

The catalog provides a lot of flexibility for your application images and icons. You can see at a
glance if you have both retina (2x) and nonretina (1x) images. You can also slice images, something that is very useful if the image has to fill an unknown area.

Although slicing is not a part of this book, the basic idea is to designate which parts of your image can be duplicated and which ones are stable. A typical example is a solid background image with rounded corners. The rounded corners and edges stay static, but the middle can grow as much as it needs.

> ### Tip: Finding Icons
>
> Most great-looking apps have great-looking graphics. If you're not a graphic designer, it's a good idea to get help from those who are. There are several sources of icons and other elements on the web, as a search for "iOS icon graphics" shows. Be sure to take a good look before you buy.
>
> The button graphics used previously as well as other custom graphical elements you use later were kindly provided by Joseph Wain, one of those good designers. You can download his icons, both free and paid, at http://glyphish.com. Joseph also does custom work.

Populating the Toolbar

Now that you have the icons, it is time to add a toolbar to the add/view car screen. An important thing to remember is where you add the toolbar. You can always drag a `UIToolbar` into any view controller. But for toolbars that could be project wide, you set them up in the navigation controller. Here's how you do this:

1. Open the iPhone storyboard and select the Navigation Controller.

2. In the Attributes inspector, change Bottom Bar from Inferred to Opaque Toolbar. A toolbar appears at the bottom of the controller as well as of every scene on the storyboard.

3. Select the add/view car scene and drag three `UIBarButtonItems` into the toolbar. Then drag in a flexible space item between each pair of buttons. Figure 7-7 shows adding the second flexible space.

4. Select the middle bar button item, delete the title, and use the Attributes inspector to set the identifier to Edit.

5. Select the left bar button item, delete the title, and set the image to `arrow-left` and the button style to plain. As you start typing the name of the image into the field, Xcode uses autocomplete to show possible images.

   Do the same thing with the right-hand button, using `arrow-right`. These new icons from Glyphish give the app a more professional look.

6. Delete the original Previous, Next, and Edit buttons and constrain the bottom of the Car Info label flush with the bottom of the view car area.

7. Ctrl-drag from the new Previous and Next buttons to the view controller and select the same messages the original buttons sent. Note you can Ctrl-drag to the round yellow controller icon in the black bar below the scene on the canvas. This is faster than dragging to the left-hand list next to the canvas.

8. When you deleted the Edit button in step 6, you also deleted the segue to the edit scene. Add it back by Ctrl-dragging from the new Edit button to the edit scene and set up a push. Select the segue and set the identifier to EditSegue, the same as the segue using the original Edit button.

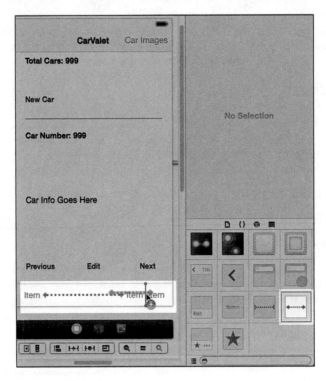

Figure 7-7   Adding a flexible space

Run the app in the simulator. Try adding a few cars and make sure the new Previous and Next buttons work. Now edit the car, and you will see a small problem. The toolbar shows up in the editor. In fact, it shows up in all scenes.

For some apps, you want a toolbar in some scenes but not in others. Luckily, there is an easy way to manage which scenes show toolbars and which do not. The `toolbarHidden` property of `UINavigationController` determines if the toolbar is shown (value is `NO`) or not (value is `YES`). When you add a toolbar using IB, the default is to show the toolbar in every scene—that is, toolbarHidden for the navigation controller is set to NO. This is different from adding one programmatically, as the documentation states the default value is YES, or hidden.

To make sure everything works as expected, add a line at the top of `viewDidLoad`, just after the call to `super` in each of the view controllers as follows:

- In `ViewController.m`, make sure the toolbar shows by adding:

  `self.navigationController.toolbarHidden = NO;`

- In `CarEditViewController.m` and `CarImageViewController`, add the following:

  `self.navigationController.toolbarHidden = YES;`

Run the app again and make sure the toolbar is only on the main screen.

Revisiting Localization

Now that the new toolbar buttons are working, you no longer need to localize their titles, nor do you need a reference to the Edit button. Make the following changes:

1. In `viewDidLoad` in `ViewController.m`, remove the lines reading and setting localized titles for the Previous, Next, and Edit car buttons. You can find the code just after the Add car button is localized.

2. Open `ViewController.h`, and remove the line with the `editCarButton` property.

3. Change the type of the `previousCarButton` and `nextCarButton` properties to `UIBarButtonItem`.

4. Open an IB canvas showing the main scene. Add an Assistant editor showing `ViewController.h` and connect the two modified properties with the new bar button items.

Before leaving the toolbar, you need to do a small update to localization. Run the app in Arabic using the `AppleLanguages` flag you set in Chapter 5, "Localization," in the section, "Adding Arabic Strings." Use the shortcut of Option-clicking the Run button to quickly modify the scheme.

The Arabic screen appears to be fine. All the text is still correctly aligned and the arrows appear to point the correct way. In fact, they do point the correct way, but the behavior is reversed. In Arabic, as in other right-to-left languages, the left-pointing arrow goes to the next item, not the previous one. The right-pointing arrow goes back.

The graphics are correct, but the behaviors are reversed. (See "Caution: Using Arrows in Buttons" for a variation of the same kind of problem.) Once again you can use the system language direction to fix the issue.

Replace the `previousCar:` and `nextCar:` action methods in `ViewController.m` with the code from Listing 7-1. Note that you could also abstract behavior into `changedDisplayedCar:`, but you would then need to make sure the method is only called from user actions.

Listing 7-1   **Updating** previousCar: **and** nextCar: **for Right-to-Left Languages**

```
- (IBAction)previousCar:(id)sender {
    NSInteger indexShift = -1;                                        // 1

    NSLocaleLanguageDirection langDirection;                         // 2
    langDirection = [NSLocale characterDirectionForLanguage:
                    [NSLocale preferredLanguages][0]];

    if (langDirection == NSLocaleLanguageDirectionRightToLeft) {
        indexShift = 1;                                              // 3
    }

    [self changeDisplayedCar:displayedCarIndex + indexShift];       // 4
}

- (IBAction)nextCar:(id)sender {
    NSInteger indexShift = 1;

    NSLocaleLanguageDirection langDirection;
    langDirection = [NSLocale characterDirectionForLanguage:
                    [NSLocale preferredLanguages][0]];

    if (langDirection == NSLocaleLanguageDirectionRightToLeft) {
        indexShift = -1;
    }

    [self changeDisplayedCar:displayedCarIndex + indexShift];
}
```

Here's what happens in the numbered lines in Listing 7-1:

1. Use a variable for the amount to change the index. Default to minus-one, or go backward for previous and plus-one, or go forward for next.

2. Get the current language direction.

3. If the language direction is right-to-left, reverse the send of the index change variable.

4. Call changeDisplayedCar: using the current index plus the localized index change.

Run the Arabic localization again and confirm the arrow toolbar buttons work correctly. Also note that the Edit button is localized. This is because you are using the system Edit button.

> **Caution: Using Arrows in Buttons**
>
> Using the arrows in the toolbar resulted in one type of issue: correct images but reversed behaviors.
>
> You can also run into the opposite problem. Imagine going back to the localization chapter before you added the toolbar. Now replace the Previous and Next button titles with the arrow images.
>
> Because the buttons use trailing and leading for alignment, running in Arabic correctly reverses the buttons. The button on the left goes to the next car, and on the right-hand one goes back. However, the graphics are reversed. The button on the left of the Arabic screen is the next button, the one with the right-pointing arrow.
>
> In a case like this, you have to reverse the graphics, not the behaviors.

Message-Based Navigation

So far you have used segues to navigate between scenes, including using the special exit segue. You have some control of passing data and modifying behaviors using `prepareForSegue:sender:`. Using `UINavigationController` properties and messages, you have full control. You can do things like push a new view controller to the stack, pop the current view controller, pop to the root-view controller, retrieve the array of view controllers for the current navigation stack, and even rearrange the array of view controllers.

You can use code-based messages to add an about scene to the CarValet app. Instead of adding another scene to the storyboard, you create the interface in a separate user interface resource file. In Xcode, these are called *XIB* files.

You can tell the navigation controller to open an XIB file by sending a message. Here's how you do all this:

1. Add a new Objective-C `UIViewController` subclass called `AboutViewController` and select the With XIB for Interface check box. Move the three new files to the CarValet group, just above Supporting Files.

2. Select `AboutViewController.xib`, and something that looks like the Storyboard editor opens. This is IB, without any support for storyboard functionality, such as segues and connections. Use the Attributes inspector for the view to set the top bar to an opaque navigation bar. You cannot set the title by double-clicking in the navigation bar.

3. Add some content to the view using labels, perhaps "CarValet, brought to you by <insert your name here>" and any other words of wisdom that take your fancy. In a shipping app, this would be a place to list your company and contact info, copyrights, support information, legal terms, and other related info. In fact, it might be just another step in the hierarchy of views such as About in Settings.

4. Open the iPhone storyboard, select the CarValet view controller, and drag a bar button item onto the left side of the button bar and set the title to "About."

5. Use the Assistant editor to Ctrl-drag the `aboutCarValet:` action from the new About button item to `ViewController.h`.

6. Open `ViewController.m` in the editor and import `AboutViewController.h`. Now fill out the body of the `aboutCarValet:` method with the code in Listing 7-2.

Listing 7-2   `aboutCarValet:`

```
- (IBAction)aboutCarValet:(id)sender {
    AboutViewController *nextController;

    nextController = [[AboutViewController alloc]                      // 1
                    initWithNibName:@"AboutViewController"
                    bundle:[NSBundle mainBundle]];

    nextController.title = @"About CarValet";                          // 2

    [self.navigationController pushViewController:nextController        // 3
                                animated:YES];
}
```

Here's what happens in the numbered lines in Listing 7-2:

1. Initialize the next view controller to an instance of `AboutViewController`. This call uses the XIB you created earlier for the view controller's interface.

2. Set the title of the About view. You could localize this string.

3. Tell the navigation controller to push the new view controller on the stack—that is, to open and transition to the scene.

Run the app making sure not to use Arabic; tap the Info button in the upper left and the About view opens. The navigation controller takes care of opening the instance of `AboutViewController`, animating in the new scene, and adding a back button to the navigation bar. Also note the toolbar shows up. Add the appropriate code to hide the toolbar for the About view.

A Bit of Color

As you look at the attributes of some items in IB, you sometimes see a Tint option. Using this option is a quick way to lend a colored theme to your user experience. Note that this is different from changing the Background color in the View area.

For `UINavigationController`, you can change the tint of the navigation bar, toolbar, and bar button items. Setting the tint of something that is managed by a navigation controller changes the color of that thing for every screen managed by that controller.

For instance, you are about to set the tint of the app's navigation bar. This one change in tint changes the navigation bar color for the entire hierarchy. This is because the navigation controller manages the navigation bar. The scenes shown by the navigation controller do not manage the bar.

A car app probably brings some colors to mind—perhaps a racy red, a cool midnight blue, or some other color. Whatever the color, change the theme for the navigation bar and toolbar using these steps:

1. Open the iPhone storyboard and expand the navigation controller in the left-hand column.

2. Select the Navigation Bar item and open the Attributes inspector. Look for a color picker labeled "Bar Tint" in the Navigation Bar section.

3. Change the tint to the color of your choice. Figure 7-8 uses Sky from the crayon palette accessed from the Other menu item in the popup. Notice as you change the tint in the navigation controller that it changes the tint for every navigation bar and any bar buttons.

4. Change the bar tint for the toolbar in the same way: Select the Toolbar item, which is usually below the Navigation Bar selected in step 2. You can use the same color as in step 3 or a different one, though the same color is better for a balanced look.

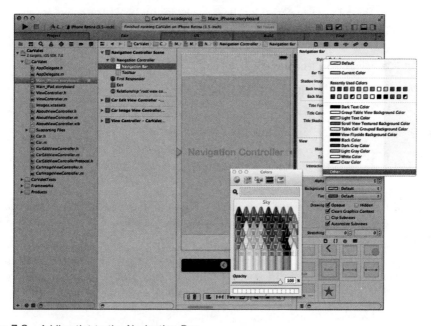

Figure 7-8   Adding tint to the Navigation Bar

Note: In Case Toolbar Bar Tint Does Not Work

In the pre-release version of Xcode used for this book, setting the tint color of a toolbar using IB did not work. If that is still the case, you can set it by adding the following code at the top of `viewDidLoad` just below the call to set `toolbarHidden`:

```
UIColor *sky = [UIColor colorWithRed:102.0/255.0
                               green:204.0/255.0
                                blue:255.0/255.0
                               alpha:1.0];
self.navigationController.toolbar.barTintColor = sky;
```

This sets the bar tint color to an RGB value. The method used to generate the color requires values from 0 to 1, so each RGB value is divided by 255.

Run the app, and you see that all the navigation bars and the toolbars are tinted with the new color, though the buttons and titles no longer look good.

One use of colors for bars, buttons, and titles is to give your app a consistent feel. Ideally, the colors should match some sort of branding. Doing this requires designing a color scheme, something best done by professionals. Buttons need to be noticeable as they are how the user performs actions, but not so noticeable that they overpower the content. Bars and titles should fade into the background.

Table 7-1 shows the color scheme used for the CarValet in this book. The colors are shown as both Apple Crayon colors and RGB (Red/Green/Blue) values.

Table 7-1   **CarValet Color Scheme**

User Interface Item	Apple Crayon Color	RGB
Bars	Sky	R: 102 G: 204 B: 255
Titles	Snow (White)	R: 255 G: 255 B: 255
Buttons	Mocha	R: 128 G: 64 B: 0

First, change the navigation bar title color. You do this with the same Attributes inspector you used to change the navigation bar tint. Further down, you see a Title Color attribute. Change that to white.

You could go through the app and select each button and bar button and change their colors, but that is subject to a lot of error. Instead, use the appearance protocol, a special addition to some classes that lets you modify how they look throughout your app.

All you need is a few lines of code.

Open `AppDelegate.m`. In the method `application:didFinishLaunchingWithOptions:`, replace the body of the method with the code in Listing 7-3. Note that the colors look different on the simulator and on a real device. The simulator colors depend on what monitor you are using. Always test color choices on real devices. It is the only way to know what they will actually look like.

Listing 7-3   Changing the Text Color of All `UIButton`s and `UIBarButtonItem`s

```
UIColor *mocha = [UIColor colorWithRed:128.0/255.0 green:64.0/255.0        // 1
                          blue:0.0 alpha:1.0];


[[UIButton appearance] setTitleColor:mocha forState:UIControlStateNormal]; // 2
[[UIBarButtonItem appearance] setTintColor:mocha];                         // 3

return YES;
```

Here's what happens in the numbered lines in Listing 7-3:

1. Set up a temporary mocha color using the Crayons palette—after all, we all need a good coffee sometimes.

2. Use the Appearance protocol to set all button title tint colors to mocha in their normal state.

3. Use the same protocol to set the tint color for all bar button item titles.

You can use the appearance protocol to set defaults for a lot more than button colors. You can use it for the navigation bar tint, background images for buttons and other items, and a lot more. If you want to know more, the Apple documentation on `UIAppearance` is a good place to start.

Before you go to the next section, save a copy of the current implementation. It is used as the base of two challenges at the end of the chapter.

Tab Bar Controller

A navigation controller is good for moving through related scenes. But what if you have different functionality or different categories of scenes? For that, you want a navigation controller that switches between different kinds of content. This is what `UITabBarController` provides.

A good example is the Clock app, shown in Figure 7-9. On the bottom of the app is a bar with four buttons, the tab bar. Each tab shows a different major function of Clock. Three of those areas have at least two screens: World Clock has a screen to add or edit a city, Alarm has one for adding or editing the details for an alarm, and Timer lets you specify a sound.

Each of the four areas has a different layout and performs different functions, though all have a similar color and font scheme.

Figure 7-9   Clock app

How the Tab Bar Works

With `UITabBarController`, each functional area or tab is a root view. In effect, the tab bar controller is the real root view of the application, as you can see in Figure 7-10.

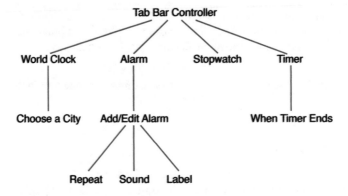

Figure 7-10   Clock hierarchy

When the user taps an item in the tab bar, the root-level view for that item is shown, even if it is the currently selected tab bar item. For example, on your own device, open Music, select Playlists, select a playlist, and then tap the Playlists tab at the bottom. The app returns to the list of all playlists.

Figure 7-11 shows the parts of a tab bar controller. This tab bar, shown in white, has two items: the first with a circle icon and the second with a square. Each tab shows a different root-level controller view. The tab bar controller contains the current root-view controller along with the tab bar. The tab bar contains the bar items and manages changing between root-level views.

There is no navigation bar for a title or buttons. Adding one can be as simple as using a UINavigationController for the root view of a particular tab, as two of the Clock tab items do. It is also possible to add a navigation bar manually, though then you need to add the methods and protocols to manage it.

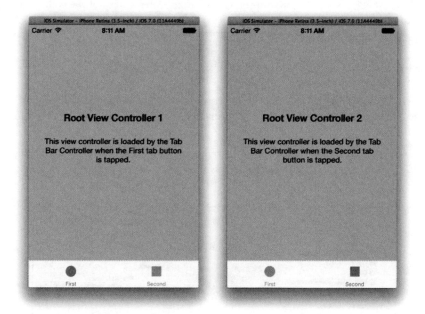

Figure 7-11   Tab bar controller

A tab bar controller uses three main classes:

- UITabBarController manages the view controllers shown by the items in the tab bar. It also manages user interaction with the bar, including handling selection. If there are more than five items, it includes a More button. It also manages accessing the extra tab buttons and rearranging the order of the tabs.

- UITabBar is a view for presenting one to five tab bar items. Each item represents a different root view for the app. If there are more than five items, a special More item is included on the right.

- UITabBarItem is an individual item in the tab bar and includes properties for both the title and image, as well as properties to customize how the image behaves during selection.

CarValet: Adding a Tab Bar

For a storyboard, you add a tab bar controller the same way you add a navigation controller: Select the root-view controller or controllers and then select Editor > Embed In > Tab Bar Controller. The selected view controllers all have to be at the same level of an application. This means you cannot select both a navigation controller, such as the add/view scene controller, and a subview of that controller, such as the car image scene controller.

Next, you add a tab bar controller to the CarValet app and include tabs for the add/view, car image, and about scenes. First, add the tab bar controller:

1. Add the `CH07 Assets TabBar Icons` folder that comes as part of the code for Chapter 7 to the `Images.xcassets`.

2. Open the iPhone storyboard and select the top-level navigation controller.

3. Choose Editor > Embed In > Tab Bar Controller. You now have a tab bar controller with one item.

4. In the browser, expand the new tab bar controller and open the Attributes editor for the tab bar. Change the image tint and bar tint to be consistent with the current colors in your app.

5. Expand the navigation controller in the browser and select the Tab Bar Item. Change the Title to Add/View and set Image to `car`, as shown in Figure 7-12.

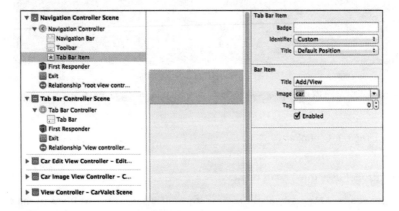

Figure 7-12   Setting the navigation controller tab bar item to `car`

Run the app in the simulator. At the moment, it is not very interesting, as there is only one choice. Since the root-view controller of the first item is a navigation controller, all the navigational elements are there, and navigation through the app works.

Moving Car Images to the Tab Bar

The next part of integrating the tab bar is removing scenes from the navigation controller and adding them to the tab bar controller. Follow these steps to add the car images scene as the second tab item:

1. Remove the Car Images button from the add/view scene. When you do this, you also remove both the segue to the images scene and the navigation bar from the images scene.

2. Ctrl-drag a connection from the tab bar controller to the car images view controller. In the popup that appears, select view controllers from the Relationship Segue category.

   This tells the tab bar that the chosen view controller is one of the items in the tab bar.

3. Set the title of the tab bar item in the car image view controller to Car Images and the Image to `photo`.

After you do this, notice a yellow constraint problem indicator in the left-hand column. This makes sense because the car number label used to be constrained to the navigation bar, and that is gone. To fix this, follow these steps:

1. Choose the label, and then choose Update Frames from the constraint fixing popup.

2. Choose the label, and then choose Clear constraints for the constraint fixing popup. This is the item next to the pin constraint popup.

3. Now use the pin constraint popup to set the constraints to 15 from the nearest top and bottom view and the default distance from the leading edge.

Run the app and tap the Car Images tab bar item. You are taken to the images scene, and all functionality still works. However, there is no way to reset the zoom. Follow these steps to add a graphical Reset Zoom button:

1. Open `CarImageViewController.h` in the editor and change the type of `resetZoomButton` from `UIBarButtonItem` to `UIButton`.

2. In the iPhone storyboard, select the `CarImageViewController` and drag a normal button into the top-level view and change the title to Reset Zoom.

3. Constrain the new button to the system distance from the top and trailing edges of the superview.

4. Drag a connection from the button to the `resetZoomButton` instance variable in the `.h` file.

5. Drag a connection from the button to the car image view controller to send the `resetZoom:` message.

6. In the Control section of the Attributes editor for the new button, set it to be disabled by default.

Run the app and go to the images screen. This time there is a Reset Zoom button. When the images screen first opens, the text is light gray and the button cannot be pressed. When you zoom the car, the text color changes, and the button is enabled. Resetting the zoom or manually changing the zoom back to 1.0 disables the button.

Car Valet: Moving Info

As with the navigation controller, you can modify the behaviors of a toolbar by using methods and properties. You can change the order of tab items, change the tab items, and find or set the currently selected tab.

In this section, you create a tab for the About view. Note that you could do all this in the storyboard, but going through the following steps gives you a chance to dynamically update the tab bar items:

1. Remove the About button from the navigation items in the main add/view scene by selecting the bar button item in IB or the browser and deleting it.

2. Open ViewController.m and remove the import of AboutViewController.h. Also remove the aboutCarValet: method implementation from the file, as well as the declaration from the .h file.

3. Open AppDelegate.m and import AboutViewController.h. Then add the bold code in Listing 7-4 to the beginning of application:didFinishLaunchingWithOptions:.

Listing 7-4 **New** application:didFinishLaunchingWithOptions:

```
- (BOOL)application:(UIApplication *)application
    didFinishLaunchingWithOptions:(NSDictionary *)launchOptions {
    UITabBarController *tabBarController =
                    (UITabBarController*)self.window.rootViewController;  // 1

    AboutViewController *aboutViewController =                            // 2
                    [[AboutViewController alloc]
                        initWithNibName:@"AboutViewController"
                        bundle:[NSBundle mainBundle]];

    UITabBarItem *aboutItem = [[UITabBarItem alloc]                       // 3
                        initWithTitle:@"About"
                        image:[UIImage imageNamed:@"info"]
                        tag:0];
    [aboutViewController setTabBarItem:aboutItem];                        // 4

    NSMutableArray *currentItems = [NSMutableArray                        // 5
                    arrayWithArray:tabBarController.viewControllers];

    [currentItems addObject:aboutViewController];                        // 6
    [tabBarController setViewControllers:currentItems animated:NO];      // 7
    ...
```

Here's what happens in the numbered lines in Listing 7-4:

1. Get a reference to the tab bar controller. Since `Main_iPhone` is set as the main storyboard for the project, the tab bar is already set as the root-view controller of the window by this point in the app life cycle.

2. Create an about view controller from the XIB file.

3. Create a tab bar item for the about scene, and give it an appropriate title and image.

4. Set the `tabBarItem` of the about view controller to the new tab bar item. The tab bar controller looks for this property when setting up the items in the tab bar.

5. Create a mutable array based on the view controllers managed by the tab bar controller. In this case, they are the ones you set up on the storyboard.

6. Add the about scene to the end of the view controller array. The items in the tab bar are displayed in the same order as in the array.

7. Update the array of items with no animation as the app is launching. If you do this while the app is running based on some user action, you are likely to animate changes.

Run the app in the simulator. There are now three tab bar items. The About item brings up the about view controller.

Summary

The controllers you have explored in this chapter make your app behave and look more like an iOS app. With `UINavigationController`, you added hierarchical navigation to viewing and editing cars. After you added the controller to the scene, hooked up the hierarchy, and set some properties, the navigation controller handled the extra interface elements and movement between screens.

You used `UITabBarController` to group related sets of content and made moving between content easy. It took just a bit of work in IB and a few lines of code. You also built a view controller outside the storyboard, using both IB and code. Then you integrated it into the flow of your app.

In addition, you used tinting to add more differentiation to your app, added a toolbar with buttons, and learned how to add graphical assets to your app.

Now you can add both kinds of navigation controllers to your own apps. You know how to design with and for them, as well as how to take a design to reality. And when you use some public domain code (source code for solving problems that others make available for general use) with a controller, you can integrate the screen into your app. You can even make your apps more colorful.

Although your app looks closer to an iOS app, there is still something missing. The add/view car scene still seems a bit clunky. It was great for learning basics, but a shipping-ready app really needs to show a table. And that is what Chapter 8, "Table Views I: The Basics," is all about.

Challenges

1. Implement the about scene using the Storyboard editor in both the navigation controller and tab bar controller cases. In addition to creating an about view controller on the storyboard, you need to remove all the code used and manually create it. You no longer need the XIB file, though you can quickly copy and paste the contents to the newly created storyboard view controller. Remember to set the class of the view controller you drag onto the storyboard to AboutViewController.

2. Add code to the UINavigationController-based implementation to show the last top-level scene the user was in. For example, if the user was in the car images scene, took the app out of memory, and then launched the app, the app shows the car images scene, not the add/view scene. To solve this challenge, you need to do the following:

   - Implement a way to identify what scene is active when applicationWillTerminate: is called and save that information. The easiest thing to do is set up a number where 0 is add/view, 1 is edit, 2 is car images, and 3 is about. Save that to the user preferences with the following code:

     ```
     // get the standard user defaults for this app
     NSUserDefaults *defaults = [NSUserDefaults standardUserDefaults];

     // set the preference for current scene
     // (assumes currSceneType is set elsewhere to the id for the scene)
     [defaults setInteger:currSceneType forKey:@"SceneType"];

     // make sure to synchronize so the defaults are saved
     [defaults synchronize];
     ```

   - Read the saved value in application:didFinishLaunchingWithOptions:

     ```
     NSUserDefaults *defaults = [NSUserDefaults standardUserDefaults];

     // Get the last viewed scene (0 if there was none)
     NSInteger lastScene = [defaults integerForKey:@"SceneType"] ;
     ```

   - Set the navigation view controller stack as needed. You only really need to set the stack if it is the car image or About view. In that case, the image or About view would be on top, and the add/view scene would be on the bottom. You can use setViewControllers:animated: to do this.

3. Add code to the tab bar–based implementation to restore the last viewed tab if the user removes the app from memory and launches it. The code to save and reload a preference is the same as that in Challenge 2. You can check or set the currently selected item of a tab bar controller by using the selectedIndex property.

Table Views I: The Basics

In previous chapters, the main screen showed only one car at a time. In iOS, it is more common to show several data items and scroll through them. You can see examples on the main screens of Contacts, Music, Settings, and many other apps that show tables of data items.

Table views are a key part of your toolbox for designing and creating apps for iPhone/iPod touch, where space is at a premium. When combined with a `UINavigationController`, table views make navigating through hierarchical data easy. A table gives your user quick access to a summary list of objects. Tapping moves the user quickly up and down the hierarchy to the required level of detail.

After you learn the basics of table view controllers, you create a small project to solidify and then refine what you have learned. Then you take the experience of building a table view and transform the add/view screen to gain valuable experience in converting existing projects to use new ways of presenting and navigating information.

Next, you implement a common way of adding objects to tables and enable the user to make new cars. Then you learn about editing tables and use that as another way to delete cars.

Then, you go deeper by changing how car details are viewed and adding a new scene showing car details using grouped cells, much as the Settings app does. Then you use a special way of presenting controllers to show one modally, forcing a user to do or cancel an action. You use modal presentation to build a couple of car attribute editors.

By the time you are finished with this chapter, you will have a good understanding of the basics of table views. You can use them in your own projects for showing lists of data. Combined with navigation controllers, your apps can move through hierarchies of detail. Editing parts of the data shown in the table can be done outside the hierarchy by using modals, enabling the user to make or cancel changes.

Introduction to Table Views

Table views are a workhorse for iOS. Even if an app does not use them for the main scenes, you are still likely to use them for preferences or an About screen. They provide all the infrastructure to show small or large numbers of individual data items that optionally use a hierarchy to view and/or edit detailed information. Yet using them for the simplest case requires only a few key classes and methods.

Figure 8-1 shows the basic parts of a table view. The table contains a number of individual table view cells, for items 2 through 12. It also has support for scrolling through and selecting cells. Other possible functionality includes adding headers and footers, sections, section headers and footers, and an index. You explore most of these in this book.

The cells in Figure 8-1 are very simple, showing just text. You can use one of the types of cells the system provides, or you can create fully customized cells.

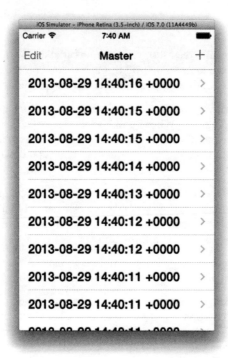

Figure 8-1   Table view parts

The code for Figure 8-1 requires three classes and two protocols:

- `UITableViewController` is the main view controller and has very few view properties and only one method. Most of the work is done by two protocols adopted by the controller. You implement methods from those protocols for displaying table cells and, in some cases, reacting to user interaction.

- `UITableViewDataSource` provides details about the data from the object to display in each cell to the number of sections and rows in the table. There are a number of optional methods that enable adding, deleting, and reordering cells.

- `UITableViewViewDelegate` supports the behaviors of a table view. You can do everything from configuring the height of an individual row or header to supporting editing and highlighting.

- `UITableView` implements all the functionality to configure and display the various parts of the table view. It has additional methods and properties for adding, moving, and deleting cells; updating data; manually scrolling content; accessing parts of the view; and configuring the index. As you will see, some of these things are best done in the data source (`UITableViewDataSource`) or delegate (`UITableViewViewDelegate`).

- `UITableViewCell` represents an individual item displayed in the table view. There are four system styles with various mixes of a title and subtitle, including the ability to add an image. In addition, you can create your own fully customized cells.

The general behaviors of a table view fall into four categories:

- **Setup**—Specify table view values for headers, footers, sections, section headers and/or footers, and number of cells in any visible sections.

- **Display**—Display the visible cells.

- **Scrolling**—Calculate what cells will become visible and load them. The table view manages creating versus reusing cell objects by keeping a pool of created cells and balancing which ones are reused as new data scrolls into view.

- **Selection**—Update the selection state of any cell or cells based on the table view's configuration. Call any delegate methods based on selection state.

Behaviors can occur at any time. For example, display occurs after setup and scrolling. Setup occurs any time the data is updated or the table is told to reload.

Project TableTry

The best way to understand table behaviors and the interaction between the five key classes is to create code. Follow these steps to create your own project and let the exploration begin:

1. In Xcode, create a new Empty Application called TableTry. Until now, you have used the Single View application template; this time you will choose Empty Application and only target iPhone. The created project has only one class defined for the app delegate. It has no user interface.

2. In `AppDelegate.m`, remove all but the last line of the `application: didFinishLaunchingWithOptions:` method. If you do not remove the code, every time you launch the app, you will see a white screen, no matter what changes you make in the storyboard you create in the next step. The revised method should look like this:

```
- (BOOL)application:(UIApplication *)application
    didFinishLaunchingWithOptions:(NSDictionary *)launchOptions {
    return YES;
}
```

3. Add an iPhone storyboard file by selecting File > New and then choosing the User Interface category. Save the file into the `TableTry` folder inside the main project folder.

4. Select the new storyboard file and drag a table view controller onto the storyboard. When you are done, it should look like Figure 8-2. Three entities have been added to your storyboard. First is the table view controller. Second is a table view, with the table view controller set as the data source (the object implementing the `UITableViewDataSource` protocol) and delegate (the object implementing the `UITableViewViewDelegate` protocol). Third is a table view cell to use as a prototype for the type of cell shown in the table.

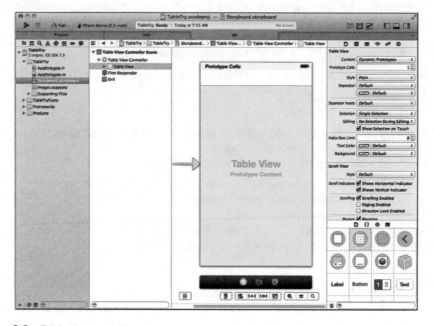

Figure 8-2   Table view controller

5. Open the Project editor and set the Main Interface for the TableTry target to the storyboard you just created.

Try running the app in the simulator, and you get a white screen with lines. The app is not broken; the table view is doing exactly what you tell it to do—in this case, showing placeholders for cells but not creating any.

The simplest thing you can do now is create some predefined cells:

1. Open the main storyboard and select the Attributes inspector for the table view.

2. In the Table View section at the top of the Attributes inspector, set the Content popup to Static Cells, and you see the table view on the storyboard change from the first image in Figure 8-3 to the second. Before you change from dynamic to static cells, the left-hand image in Figure 8-3 has a Prototype Cells header with just one prototype cell. After you change to static, the right-hand image has three static cells, all of which look the same.

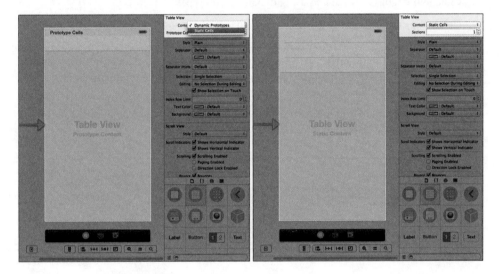

Figure 8-3   Creating static cells

Run the app again. Although it looks the same as before, each of the top three cells can be selected. Notice that the first cell is underneath the status bar. As you tap each of the top three cells, the one you tap is highlighted in gray. Tap the fourth cell, and nothing happens.

Creating Cells

Sometimes you want predefined cells. But more often, you want to show a list of data items that vary in number. The table view you just created used static cells. The number of cells and their basic look is fixed because you know the content in advance. They act like static views in the table. Sometimes you do not know how many cells you will show or how they will be organized. In such instances, instead of using static cells, you can use dynamic prototypes. Which one you choose depends on what you are trying to do:

- *Static cells* are useful when the table layout is fixed, such as most of the Settings app. You set up the number of cells, their content, and even the organization of the table at design time. You can change what information is shown at runtime by changing the contents of elements in the cell, but the basic organization of the table is fixed.

- *Dynamic prototypes* are handy when you do not know the number of data items you will show at runtime. A prototype is a template for what you want to show. At runtime, you can create as many cells as you need, using the prototypes. Each one has the same basic look but shows different data, such as an individual car. You can also have more than one prototype.

Continue exploring table views by converting your project to use dynamic prototypes. To do so, follow these steps:

1. Change the table view back to using dynamic prototypes.

2. Delete the extra two prototypes. Basically, change things back to the left-hand image in Figure 8-3.

3. Run the app, and you might see a warning that the prototype cell does not have a reuse identifier. This is something the table view controller uses to determine what kind of prototype cell to allocate or reuse.

   Open the storyboard and make sure the Attributes inspector is selected for the prototype cell. Set the reuse identifier to MyCell, as shown in Figure 8-4.

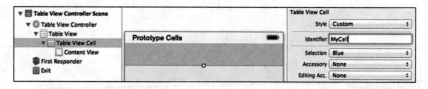

Figure 8-4   Cell reuse identifier

Now you need some code to tell the table view how many cells to create, and you need to populate those cells with data. You therefore need a UITableViewDataSource. In this case, you create your own subclass of UITableViewController, which implements the data source and delegate protocols for you. Follow these steps:

1. Choose File > New > File, select the Cocoa Touch category for iOS, and select the Objective-C class.

2. On the next screen, create a subclass of UITableViewController called MyTableViewController and save it in the project, making sure it is part of the TableTry target. (Note that this is the default behavior.)

3. Go back to the storyboard, select the table view controller, and use the Identity inspector to set the class to MyTableViewController.

You see a warning triangle in the navigation bar above the IB canvas. This tells you something is wrong, though the project should still build and run. You can look at all the warnings by clicking on the yellow arrow. In this case, the dropdown shows the warning is in MyTableViewController.m.

One way to find the errors is to open that file and look for the warning flag next to the line. Another is to click an item in the list of issues as you did in Chapter 4, "Auto Layout" (see Figure 4-23). A faster way is to click the black navigation triangles on each side of the yellow warning indicator. This opens the relevant file and takes you straight to the line with the problem. In the case of IB, it selects the UX element with the issue.

Both warnings were created when you created the class. The special #warning marker at the beginning of a line tells Xcode something needs work. Both warnings talk about incomplete implementations and serve as reminders that you have more code to write.

Sections and Rows

Each of the warnings tells you something about how the table view expects data to be organized. It is expecting zero or more sections of data organized into zero or more rows. It sounds strange to start at zero, but it is possible to have either an entirely empty set of data or just an empty section.

A good example is the Contacts app. It can have as many sections as the user has unique first letters for the last names of contacts. Each section has as many contacts as there are people whose last name begins with that letter. (For example, all friends with a last name starting with A.) But what happens if you have no contacts?

As it happens, the simulator version of the Contacts app can show you. Launch the app, tap Groups, and make sure only the Work group is selected. There is a table with the words No Contacts. As soon as you add one contact, such as John Adams, you see the contact, and No Contacts is gone. In this case, you have a table view with one section—contacts with a last name starting with the letter A—and that section has one row, for John Adams.

Your next job is to tell the table view how many sections of data there are and how many rows are in each section. In this case, you have one section with five data items. Follow these steps:

1. In MyTableViewController.m, replace the two methods shown next. The first method tells the table view how many sections of data, and the second tells how many data items for a given section. (Note the first method, numberOfSectionsInTableView: is optional and defaults to 1 if not provided.)

```
- (NSInteger)numberOfSectionsInTableView:(UITableView *)tableView {
    return 1;
}


- (NSInteger)tableView:(UITableView *)tableView
    numberOfRowsInSection:(NSInteger)section {
    return 5;
}
```

2. In the method tableView:cellForRowAtIndexPath: below the two methods you just replaced, change the CellIdentifier from @"Cell" to @"MyCell". This tells the table view what prototype to use for creating the new cell.

Run the app again. This time you have five cells you can click, though again, they are not very interesting.

Now it is time to add some data to each cell. In this case, you add a string with the section and row number of the cell.

Generating Cells and Index Paths

Before writing the code in this section, you need to understand what is meant by an index path in a table view. As you have seen, a table view shows data as one or more groups of *rows*. Each group of rows is called a *section*. Any cell in the table can be identified by a combination of its section and row. That combination is an *index path*.

Table views use a specialized version of the more general NSIndexPath object to represent the index path. It is composed of two integers: The first is the section, and the second is the row. Since it is an object, you can send messages or use dot notation to access parts. Table view uses a couple of special assessors, section and row, to make coding easier and more maintainable.

If you have an NSIndexPath called cellIndexPath in a table, you can find the section by using cellIndexPath.section and the row with cellIndexPath.row.

To generate a string in the form Section: <*the cell's section*> Row: <*the cell's row*>, you use the following:

```
NSString *myLabel = [NSString stringWithFormat:@"Section: %d  Row: %d",
                              indexPath.section, indexPath.row];
```

In fact, this is exactly how you generate unique labels for each of the five cells. Add the following lines in bold to tableView:cellForRowAtIndexPath:

```
- (UITableViewCell *)tableView:(UITableView *)tableView
        cellForRowAtIndexPath:(NSIndexPath *)indexPath {
...

    NSString *myLabel = [NSString stringWithFormat:@"Section: %d  Row: %d",
                                  indexPath.section, indexPath.row];
    cell.textLabel.text = myLabel;

    return cell;
}
```

Run the app and you see five cells, each with a section of 0 and a row of 0 through 4. Note that all index paths are 0-based, not 1-based. This works well with array-based data storage, though it can often be the source of "but I thought I coded it right" bugs.

Adding a Section

The next step is to add a section to the table. Doing so is as simple as changing the number returned from numberOfSectionsInTableView: from 1 to 2. Run the app, and there are two sections of five items each. But there are no section headings.

To add a section heading, you need to add an optional data source protocol method. Insert the following code below the numberOfSectionsInTableView: method:

```
- (NSString *)tableView:(UITableView *)tableView
titleForHeaderInSection:(NSInteger)section {
    return [NSString stringWithFormat:@"Section: %d", section];
}
```

When you run the app, you see that the code simply uses the section number to create a header. Notice that all you need to do to have the headers appear is add this method and return a non-nil value. That last part is key: You can prevent a header from displaying simply by returning nil from this method.

There is a slight issue with the section header being underneath the status bar. That is dealt with later in this chapter.

Experiment with adding more sections and/or more cells per section. Even if the numbers are quite large, the table view still works. Part of the reason is that the table view only keeps around the cells being viewed as well as some others for fast scrolling. If you created a table with thousands of data points, only a few tens would be in memory at a time—if that. A table view creates the cells it needs and recycles the ones no longer onscreen. That is what the reuse identifier you set above is used for.

Phase I: Replacing the Add/View Scene

To learn more about table views, you need cells with data. In this section, you create a car cell along with the code to populate it. You also add a way to create and remove cars. Along the way, you replace the add/view scene with a table view.

First you replace the add/view scene with a table view controller-based scene by following these steps:

1. Open the CarValet project. You can use an existing one or use the one provided in the CH08 CarValet Starter project.

2. Open the Storyboard editor, drag in a table view controller, and move the new view controller just above the existing edit/view scene.

3. Add two new Objective-C classes to your project just below Car.m: Base CarTableViewController on UITableViewController and CarTableViewCell on UITableViewCell. Make sure the classes are added to the CarValet target.

4. In the Storyboard editor, set the class of the table view controller to CarTableViewController, and set the class of the prototype table view cell to CarTableViewCell. While the prototype cell is selected, choose attributes and set the reuse identifier to CarCell.

5. Add a property for a Car object to a car cell. This is used for displaying data in the cell and, eventually, determining what car to view and edit. Open CarTableViewCell.h and add the code shown in bold:

```
#import <UIKit/UIKit.h>

@class Car;

@interface CarTableViewCell : UITableViewCell

@property (strong, nonatomic) Car *myCar;
```

6. Import `Car.h` into `CarTableViewCell.m`.

7. Open `CarTableViewController.m` and add the code shown in bold. In addition to importing the car model and car table view cell, you are declaring a data array for the cars, just as you did in `ViewController.m`:

```
#import "CarTableViewController.h"

#import "Car.h"
#import "CarTableViewCell.h"

@implementation CarTableViewController {
    NSMutableArray *arrayOfCars;
}
```

8. Copy the `newCar:` method from `ViewController.m` to the bottom of `CarTableViewController.m`, just above the `@end` statement. Then remove the call to `updateLabel:withBaseString:andCount:` from the pasted method.

9. In `CarTableViewController.m`, replace `viewDidLoad` with the following code from near the end of `ViewController.m` to allocate the car data array and add an initial car:

```
- (void)viewDidLoad {
    [super viewDidLoad];

    arrayOfCars = [NSMutableArray new];

    [self newCar:nil];
}
```

10. Change the number of sections to 1 and the number of rows to be the size of `arrayOfCars`:

```
- (NSInteger)numberOfSectionsInTableView:(UITableView *)tableView {
    return 1;
}

- (NSInteger)tableView:(UITableView *)tableView
 numberOfRowsInSection:(NSInteger)section {
    return [arrayOfCars count];
}
```

11. In `tableView:cellForRowAtIndexPath:`, make sure the `static CellIdentifier` is set correctly. The line of code should look like this:

```
static NSString *CellIdentifier = @"CarCell";
```

12. Switch to the storyboard and change where the navigation controller points by Ctrl-dragging from the body of the navigation controller in the Visual editor to the new car table view controller, as shown in the left part of Figure 8-5. In the popup that appears, choose the root view controller Relationship Segue. The navigation controller root view segue now connects to the car table view controller, as shown in the right half of Figure 8-5.

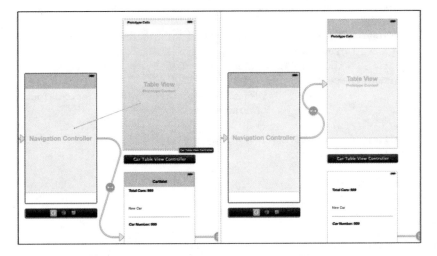

Figure 8-5   Setting a new root view controller

Run the app. The table view controller is now the add/view scene, and there is one car cell, though the only way you can tell is by selecting it. Before going on, change the title in the navigation bar to CarValet. You can do this directly or by copying the localization code from `ViewController.m`.

Adding a Car View Cell

You have the data for one car and a cell to represent it, but you don't have any view elements to display the data. The next step is to modify the prototype cell to show car data. Follow these steps:

1. Add the property `dateCreated` of type `NSDate` to the `Car` object. Set it to `[NSDate date]` in the base class initializer.

2. In the storyboard, open the Attributes inspector for the car table view cell and set it to the style Right Detail. The cell changes to show Title in black on the left and Detail in light gray on the right. Change the font size of Detail to 12 points.

   You change the font size by double-clicking the detail label, showing the Attributes inspector, and then using the Font area to change the size.

3. Add a publicly facing method called `configureCell` to `CarTableViewCell`, using the code in Listing 8-1. To make it public, you need to declare the method in the `.h` file.

4. Add code to `tableView:cellForRowAtIndexPath:` in `CarTableViewController.m` to set the car data for the cell. Then tell the cell to update itself. The changes are shown below in bold. Note that you have to change the class of cell you are creating so it knows about the `myCar` property and `configureCell` method:

```
- (UITableViewCell *)tableView:(UITableView *)tableView
        cellForRowAtIndexPath:(NSIndexPath *)indexPath {
    static NSString *CellIdentifier = @"CarCell";
    CarTableViewCell *cell = [tableView
                       dequeueReusableCellWithIdentifier:CellIdentifier
                       forIndexPath:indexPath];

    cell.myCar = arrayOfCars[indexPath.row];
    [cell configureCell];

    return cell;
}
```

Listing 8-1   `configureCell` in `CarTableViewCell.m`

```
- (void)configureCell {
    NSString *make = (self.myCar.make == nil) ?                    // 1
                     @"Unknown" : self.myCar.make;
    NSString *model = (self.myCar.model == nil) ?
                      @"Unknown" : self.myCar.model;

    self.textLabel.text = [NSString stringWithFormat:@"%d %@ %@",   // 2
                     self.myCar.year, make, model];

    NSString *dateStr = [NSDateFormatter                           // 3
                     localizedStringFromDate:self.myCar.dateCreated
                     dateStyle:NSDateFormatterShortStyle
                     timeStyle:NSDateFormatterShortStyle];

    self.detailTextLabel.text = dateStr;                          // 4
}
```

Here's what happens in the numbered lines in Listing 8-1:

1. The make or model of a car could be `nil`, so set it to a default value. You can also localize values here. (Chapter 5, "Localization," covers localization in detail.)

2. Set the main label to the year, make, and model of the car.

3. Get a localized version of the creation date, in as short a form as possible.

4. Set the detail text area to the shortened creation date.

When you run the code, you get a single car cell with data. Adding cars is the next step.

Adding New Cars

You already have a method to add cars. All you need is a user interface item to call it. Look at an app with table views that allow the creation of data items, such as Contacts. Apps like these commonly have an Add button in the navigation bar. Here's how you implement one in the CarValet app:

1. Open the storyboard and drag a bar button item into the navigation bar of the add/view scene.

2. Select the Attributes inspector for that button and change the identifier to Add. You see the button change to one with a + icon.

3. Ctrl-drag from the button to the car table view controller and choose `newCar:` under Sent Actions.

Run the app and tap the Add button. Nothing seems to happen. In fact, cars are added, but nothing is telling the table view to update the display. You do this by adding a call at the end of the `newCar:` method to tell the table view to completely reload itself:

```
[self.tableView reloadData];
```

Run the app again. Now each button tap results in a new car item, though the appearance of the new cell does not look as nice as it could. This is because you are telling the table view to redraw itself each time a new car is added. In addition, you are inserting the new cars at the end of the data array, so the most recent cars show up at the bottom.

It would be better to have new cars animate in from the top of the table. All it takes is a few changes to the `newCar:` method, shown in bold in Listing 8-2.

Listing 8-2   **Changes to** `newCar:` **for Animating Adding a Car**

```
- (IBAction)newCar:(id)sender {
    Car *newCar = [Car new];

    [arrayOfCars insertObject:newCar atIndex:0];                          // 1
```

```
NSIndexPath *indexPath = [NSIndexPath indexPathForRow:0 inSection:0];      // 2

[self.tableView insertRowsAtIndexPaths:@[indexPath]                        // 3
                 withRowAnimation:UITableViewRowAnimationAutomatic];
}
```

Here's what happens in the numbered lines in Listing 8-2:

1. Insert the car into the front of the data array.

2. Create an `NSIndexPath` object that specifies the location of the new cell—its section and row.

3. Tell the table view to insert an object at the new index path. This causes the table view to call the data source for the cell at section 0, row 0—in other words, the first element of the data array. Since the array has already been updated, the new cell is returned.

When you run the code and add cars, notice that they appear to slide in from the top, shifting the existing cells down. `insertRowsAtIndexPaths:withRowAnimation:` did the insertion animation for you. However, there is one very important point to remember: You must update the data before you update the table.

Try moving the call to `arrayOfCars` below the call to the `tableView` and then run the app. The result is a crash. The call to update the table tells the table view to insert a new cell at the specified index path. Then the table view asks for each of the cells, including the new one, so it can correctly update. Because the new car has not been inserted into `arrayOfCars` yet, when the table checks the number of rows, which in turn checks the number of items in the array, it then finds that `[arrayOfCars count]` is one less than it should be. And that crashes the app.

Removing Cars

You can add cars, but how do you delete them? It turns out that most of the code you need for simple deletion was created when you added the `CarTableViewController` class. To enable deletion, all you really need to do is uncomment and modify one of the provided methods.

Note that there is another related method, `tableView:canEditRowAtIndexPath:`, that allows you to optionally enable or disable editing for an individual cell. Although you do not use it in the CarValet app, you should know how to use it. Uncomment the method, and for now, have it return `NO` for any odd row.

There are many ways to do this. Perhaps the simplest is to use just one line with the modulo operation. Remember that the row index starts at 0, so line 1 has a row of 0, and the index number for odd rows is even (yes, you read that right):

```
return (indexPath.row % 2 != 0);
```

You might wonder why you are uncommenting methods with the word *edit* in their name. There are two possible types of editing for table view cells: deletion and insertion. For this project, you use only deletion. The combination of both methods allows re-ordering cells.

All you really need to support deletion is the method `tableView:commitEditingStyle:forRowAtIndexPath:`. Uncomment it and change it so it looks like the code below:

```
- (void)tableView:(UITableView *)tableView
    commitEditingStyle:(UITableViewCellEditingStyle)editingStyle
    forRowAtIndexPath:(NSIndexPath *)indexPath
{
    if (editingStyle == UITableViewCellEditingStyleDelete) {
        [arrayOfCars removeObjectAtIndex:indexPath.row];

        [tableView deleteRowsAtIndexPaths:@[indexPath]
                        withRowAnimation:UITableViewRowAnimationFade];

    }
//    else if (editingStyle == UITableViewCellEditingStyleInsert) {
        // Create a new instance of the appropriate class,
        // insert it into the array, and add a new row to the table view
//    }
}
```

Run the app, add a few cars, and then swipe left or right on an even cell. A Delete button appears. Tap the button, and the cell is removed. Tap outside the button, and the button goes away. Swiping on an odd cell does not show the button. All the behavior to show or hide the Delete button is handled by the table view and is enabled by implementing `tableView:commitEditingStyle:forRowAtIndexPath:`.

The most significant addition to the method committing the delete is the line in bold that removes the deleted car from the data array before the table view removes the cell. As with adding a row, it is very important to remove the data element first. If you do not, the table view removes the cell and then checks how many rows there are. Since the data source uses the array of data, and the data for the car has not been removed, the number of cells is one higher than it is supposed to be. Your app crashes. You can try changing the order of the code and running your app to see what the error looks like. Off by one or index out of bounds errors are ones you are very likely to encounter during your development career.

User-Initiated Editing

Swiping is nice, but a novice user may not know that gesture. It would be better to provide a user interface element for editing. To do so, follow these steps for adding Edit and Done buttons to the navigation bar:

1. Open the Storyboard editor and drag two bar button items into the browser for the table view controller below First Responder in the view element list. The bar button items do not show up in the graphical representation of the controller on the right side of IB.

2. Make one bar button item a system Edit button and the other a system Done button.

3. Make sure the Assistant editor is open and showing `CarTableViewController.h`. Ctrl-drag properties for each button: `editButton` for Edit and `doneButton` for Done.

4. Ctrl-drag an action called `editTableView:` from one of the buttons and hook the other button up to that action. Both buttons call the action.

5. Add the following line to the end of the `viewDidLoad` method:

   ```
   self.navigationItem.leftBarButtonItem = self.editButton;
   ```

6. Use Listing 8-3 for the `editTableView:` method.

Listing 8-3   `editTableView:` **Method for Editing Car Cells**

```
- (IBAction)editTableView:(id)sender {
    BOOL startEdit = (sender == self.editButton);                   // 1

    UIBarButtonItem *nextButton = (startEdit) ?                     // 2
                    self.doneButton : self.editButton;

    [self.navigationItem setLeftBarButtonItem:nextButton animated:YES];   // 3
    [self.tableView setEditing:startEdit animated:YES];            // 4
}
```

Here's what happens in the numbered lines in Listing 8-3:

1. Editing is starting if the Edit button is sending the message.

2. The next button to show is the item not showing: Done if Edit, and Edit if Done.

3. Animate the new navigation bar button.

4. Tell the table view to animate to an editing or nonediting state.

Run the app and try tapping the Edit and Done buttons. When you enter edit mode, you see red circles with lines in them, but only for each even row. This is because of the code in `tableView:canEditRowAtIndexPath:`. Change that method back to returning `YES` or simply comment out the method.

Rerun the app, and you should see something similar to Figure 8-6. The left-hand image shows the screen with a few cars before the Edit button is touched. After you tap the Edit button, the right-hand image appears. In this case, the delete wheel of the middle item has been touched. You should be able to delete as few or as many cars as you want. Tap Done, and the table returns to the normal state with the top button saying Edit.

Figure 8-6   Edit and Done buttons

So far you can create and delete cars. However, except for the creation date, every car is the same. You need to provide a way to view and edit the details of a car.

Before doing that, you need to clean up the storyboard. Since the old add/view and edit screens are no longer used, remove their controllers from the storyboard. Now move the new cars table view next to the navigation controller where add/view used to be. You do not need to remove the `ViewController` and `CarEditViewController` class files as there is still useful code there, such as for localization.

Finally, change the title of the title tab from Add/View to Cars. Remember that the tab bar item for Cars is part of the navigation controller, not the tab bar or table view controllers.

Phase II: Adding an Edit Screen Hierarchy

In this section, you add scenes to view and edit a car. You start by modifying car detail cells to show that there is more. Then you create a car detail scene with an associated class and connect it to a car cell. Next, you add some editing screens and any required classes, and you hook them up to appropriate car view detail cells. Along the way, you add the code for the full edit flow and learn about pickers.

The first step is to let the customer know there is more information. This is as simple as adding a disclosure indicator to the car data cell:

- In the storyboard, select the car cell prototype and use the Attributes inspector to set the accessory view to a disclosure indicator.

Run the app, and now every cell has a right-pointing chevron (which looks like a greater-than symbol) on the right side. This truncates the time and date area, but it won't matter later on, as you customize the cell in Chapter 10, "Table Views II: Advanced Topics." If you really want to modify things, modify `configureCell` to show a short format of only the date or time.

Adding a View Car Scene

You do most of the visual work for creating a car detail screen in the storyboard:

1. Drag in a table view controller and place it to the left of the new cars scene.

2. Select the table view and set the content to Static Cells and the style to Grouped. When you change the style, you see a setting for the number of sections. Give the table three sections.

The table view now looks as shown in Figure 8-7. The groups and cells appear both in the browser and on the storyboard. You can select groups and change the number of cells, and you can also edit each cell.

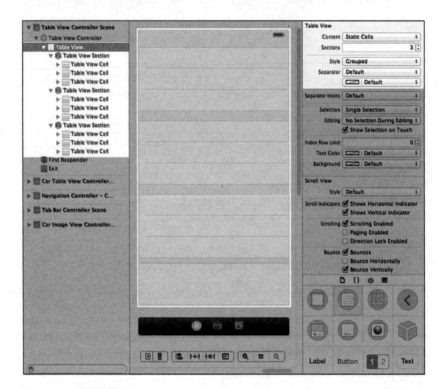

Figure 8-7   A grouped table view

Change the number of cells in each group, based on the number of data items to show for that group:

1. Select the first group, and the Attributes inspector changes to enable editing the number of rows, the header, and the footer. Leave the rows at three and set the header to Make, Model, & Year. The text for the header is added to the group on the storyboard.

2. Set the second group of one cell with a header of Fuel.

3. Set the third group's header to Date Registered and ensure that it has two cells.

4. For each of the cells, set the type to Basic and the content to the name of the data item it shows. For example, the three cells in the first group should be called Make, Model, and Year. The last group is split into Date and Time. When you are done, the view looks as shown in Figure 8-8.

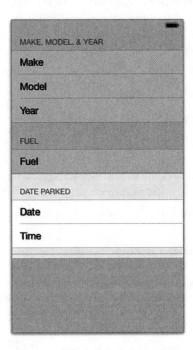

Figure 8-8   Detail view with cells

It is time to see how this view looks:

1. Ctrl-drag a push selection segue from the prototype car cell to the view car table view controller. Make sure you do not select an accessory segue, as they originate from cell accessory controls, not from selecting the cell itself. Also, make sure you are dragging from the cell, not any of the contents.

2. Select the segue and use the Attributes inspector to set the identifier to ViewSegue.

3. Set the navigation bar title of the car detail scene to View Car and run the app.

With very little effort, you have created a view that opens in response to tapping a cell. All the work of highlighting and unhighlighting a cell, transitioning the view, and creating a path back is handled for you.

Populating the View Car Scene with Data

To populate the view car scene with data, you need a custom class for the scene's view controller. Follow these steps:

1. Add the class `ViewCarTableViewController`, based on `UITableViewController`, and make sure it is included in the CarValet target. Set it as the controller class for the view car scene.

2. Add the following code shown in bold to `ViewCarTableViewController.h`:

    ```
    #import <UIKit/UIKit.h>

    @class Car;

    @interface ViewCarTableViewController : UITableViewController

    @property Car *myCar;
    ```

    This code should look very familiar. It is almost identical to the header for the prototype car cell. This is because the view car scene needs a `Car` object to view and edit.

3. Open the storyboard, select the static table view controller, and set its class to `ViewCarTableViewController`.

4. Open the Assistant editor and make sure it is showing `ViewCarTableViewController.h`. Ctrl-drag properties from each of the labels in the static cells to the `.h` file and name them `makeLabel`, `modelLabel`, `yearLabel`, `fuelLabel`, `dateLabel`, and `timeLabel`. Make sure the properties are of type `UILabel`. The easiest way to do this is to fully expand the table view in the left-hand browser by Option-clicking the triangle and then Ctrl-dragging from each label.

5. Open `ViewCarTableViewController.m` in the editor and import `Car.h`. Because this table shows static cells, you do not need any of the data source protocol methods, so remove them. Instead, you set up any dynamic content in the `viewDidLoad` method. Use the following code:

    ```
    - (void)viewDidLoad {
        [super viewDidLoad];

        self.makeLabel.text = (self.myCar.make == nil) ?
                            @"Unknown" : self.myCar.make;
    ```

```
        self.modelLabel.text = (self.myCar.model == nil) ?
                                @"Unknown" : self.myCar.model;

        self.yearLabel.text = [NSString stringWithFormat:@"%d",
                                self.myCar.year];

        self.fuelLabel.text = [NSString stringWithFormat:@"%0.2f",
                                self.myCar.fuelAmount];

        self.dateLabel.text = [NSDateFormatter
                                localizedStringFromDate:self.myCar.dateCreated
                                dateStyle:NSDateFormatterMediumStyle
                                timeStyle:NSDateFormatterNoStyle];

        self.timeLabel.text = [NSDateFormatter
                                localizedStringFromDate:self.myCar.dateCreated
                                dateStyle:NSDateFormatterNoStyle
                                timeStyle:NSDateFormatterMediumStyle];
    }
```

Again, most of this code should look familiar. The conditional assignment statements are the same as those used to create the main label in a car view cell. The date and time labels use the same method as a car view cell, but they use different styles of constants to show either more detail or no detail.

6. Import `ViewCarTableViewController.h` into `CarTableViewController.m` and add the following method above `viewDidLoad`:

```
- (void)prepareForSegue:(UIStoryboardSegue *)segue
               sender:(id)sender {
    if ([segue.identifier isEqualToString:@"ViewSegue"]) {
        ViewCarTableViewController *nextController;

        nextController = segue.destinationViewController;

        NSInteger index = [self.tableView indexPathForSelectedRow].row;

        nextController.myCar = arrayOfCars[index];
    }
}
```

You created a similar `prepareForSegue:sender:` method for `ViewController`. In this case, you are setting the `Car` object for the incoming `ViewCarTableViewController`.

Run the app, create a few cars, and tap one of them. The new view car scene opens. You are able to scroll the table, and rotation is handled correctly. In fact, both of the new scenes you created handle rotation, resizing their cells and scrolling as required. When you select a different car, the app shows a new car view screen with the correct data. Of course, the only difference between detail screens is the Date Registered area. Now it is time to add editing of the make, model, and year.

One thing you might notice is a white band at the bottom of both table views. This is the toolbar you added in a previous chapter. Since there is no need for the toolbar, you can remove it:

1. Open the storyboard and select the navigation controller.

2. Select the toolbar in the left-hand view and delete it.

3. Make sure the navigation controller is selected on the canvas, select the Attributes inspector, and set the bottom bar to none.

When you run the app, there is no white bar at the bottom.

Editing Data

Most of the data for a car can be edited. You need to provide scenes for editing the different attributes of a car starting with the make and model. Both items are text-based, at least for now, so both can use the same kind of scene. Follow these steps:

1. Drag a `UIViewController` to the right of the view car scene.

2. Add a `UINavigationBar` near the top and set the leading and trailing constraints to 0. Drag from the top of the navigation item into the top area. Depending on how high up the navigation bar is, you will either set the Top Space to Top Layout Guide, or the vertical space to the layout guide. Either way, make the connection and then change the value of the constraint to 0.

    Also, give the bar an appropriate tint. You can do this in the Attributes inspector for the navigation item.

3. Drag a bar button item into each side of the navigation bar. Make the left one a system Cancel button and the right one a system Done button.

4. Drag in a label and set the constraints to 20 points below the bottom of the navigation item and the system distance from the leading and trailing edges of the container.

5. Add a text field and set the constraints to the system distance below the label, and aligned with the leading and trailing edges (or 0 space from each edge).

6. With the field still selected, use the Attributes inspector to set the clear button to Appears While Editing. When you are done, the scene should look like Figure 8-9 (although the tints may vary).

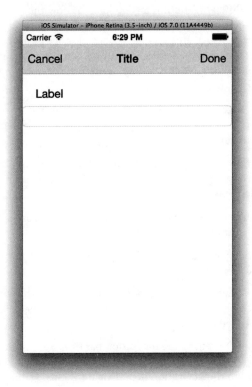

Figure 8-9   Make and model edit scene

Adding the `MakeModelEditViewController` Class

The new controller is for editing either the make or model of a car. This means the title, label, and field data need to be configured before the view is shown. There are two ways to do this: Either the view car scene can set up properties in `prepareForSegue:sender:` or you can use a protocol. Using a protocol is the preferred way since it gives greater flexibility and maintainability. It also means you can reuse the elements in other projects.

So far when you change the current screen, you are navigating up or down the hierarchy of views or switching to a new tab or set of views. In a hierarchy, you go from an overview of all cars to the detail on one car. Users see views sliding in from the right as they go deeper and out to the left as they move back up.

Sometimes you want to show something that is outside the hierarchy. Editing a particular attribute of a car is one example. Editing is not just the ability to change something; you also offer the chance to cancel a change, even if the user has already entered a new value.

This kind of operation is different, and it is a good idea to show the user that he or she is not just drilling deeper. You do this with a *modal* screen, which forces the user to make a choice. The user can either make a change and accept it or cancel. A user cannot navigate anywhere else in the app until that choice is made. Even the visual transition of a modal is different from usual. The default transition for modals is sliding in from the bottom and down and out when they are done.

In iOS, you can show any scene (or view controller) as a modal. You have choices in how you implement the transition. As you will see, you can use either a modal segue or a different call to the current navigation controller.

And when the user has finished, usually by touching either a Done or Cancel button, you need to go back to the scene that originally showed the modal. When you show the modal with a segue, going back is called *unwinding*.

Use the following steps to create the protocol for exchanging data, as well as turning the scene you just created into an editor for the make or model:

1. Create a subclass of a view controller called `MakeModelEditViewController` and set it as the class for the scene you just created.

2. Make sure the new make/model edit scene is selected in the storyboard and that the .h file is open in the Assistant view. Ctrl-drag properties from the label called `editLabel` and the text field called `editField`.

3. The final property is for setting the navigation bar title. Your initial thought may be to Ctrl-drag from the navigation bar. Although doing that works, it requires more code than connecting directly to the navigation item. Expand the navigation bar in the browser and Ctrl-drag from the navigation item to create a property called `myNavigationItem`. See the "Note: Why Connect to the Navigation Item?" for an explanation of why you are creating this property.

4. Ctrl-drag from each of the bar button items to create an action in the .h file: `editCancelled:` for Cancel and `editDone:` for Done.

5. Add a protocol called `MakeModelEditProtocol` and set the contents of the file to the code that follows. Each method in the protocol is used to set up a different part of the make/model edit scene, except for the final one, which is used to send the edited value back to the delegate:

```
#import <Foundation/Foundation.h>

@protocol MakeModelEditProtocol <NSObject>

-(NSString*)titleText;

-(NSString*)editLabelText;

-(NSString*)editFieldText;
```

```
-(NSString*)editFieldPlaceholderText;

-(void)editDone:(NSString*)textFieldValue;

@end
```

6. Import the protocol into `MakeModelEditViewController.h` and add the following property:

```
@property (weak, nonatomic) id <MakeModelEditProtocol> delegate;
```

7. Initialize the title, label, and text edit field using the protocol methods. Open `MakeModelEditViewController.m` and replace `viewDidLoad` with the code below, which sets each item in the user interface to whatever the delegate returns:

```
- (void)viewDidLoad
{
    [super viewDidLoad];

    self.myNavigationItem.title = [self.delegate titleText] ;

    self.editLabel.text = [self.delegate editLabelText];
    self.editField.text = [self.delegate editFieldText];
    self.editField.placeholder = [self.delegate editFieldPlaceholderText];
}
```

8. The only other methods required for the make/model controller are `cancelTouched:` and `editTouched:`. These methods transition back to the scene that opened the editor. In addition, if the user touches Done, the delegate is sent the current text field value.

   You need to close a controller opened from a modal transition and unwind the segue at the same time. You can use the `UIViewController` method `dismissViewController-Animated:completion:` to do this. Replace the two `IBActions` with the following code:

```
- (IBAction)editCancelled:(id)sender {
    [self dismissViewControllerAnimated:YES completion:nil];
}

- (IBAction)editDone:(id)sender {
    [self.delegate editDone:self.editField.text];

    [self dismissViewControllerAnimated:YES completion:nil];
}
```

9. Import the protocol into `ViewCarTableViewController.h` and add the code below just after the `@interface` declaration line:

```
<MakeModelEditProtocol>
```

   This code says that `ViewCarTableViewController` agrees to conform to the protocol.

10. Add the protocol methods to the bottom of `ViewCarTableViewController.m`, just above `@end`. The easiest way to do this is to copy the declarations from the protocol file, paste them into the `.m` file, and then go through each one replacing the ending semicolon (`;`) with an open curly brace (`{`) and press the Return key. For example, here is how the `titleText` method looks after pressing Return:

```
-(NSString*)titleText {
}
```

> ### Note: Why Connect to the Navigation Item?
>
> You might wonder why you created a property for the navigation item in the make/model edit view controller. After all, one of the default properties of a view controller is `navigationItem`.
>
> The reason is that the default navigation bar and item properties are set up and maintained by `UINavigationController`. In this case, your view controller opens with a modal, not a push segue. The edit view is opened using `presentModalViewController:animated`, which is a `UIViewController` method. It is not pushed on the navigation stack, so it is not managed by the navigation controller. You are responsible for adding your own navigation bar, setting up connections, and any required management.

Making View Car a `MakeModelEditProtocol` Delegate

The Make/Model editor is ready to edit something and let the delegate know the result. The next step is to prepare the delegate, in this case, `ViewCarTableViewController`. The one unusual part is keeping track of what data field is being edited.

The Make/Model editor really does not care what it is editing. In fact, it can edit any text item. All the context (title, label, placeholder text) is set by the delegate. That means the view car controller needs to keep track of what field is being edited. Follow these steps to complete adding editing of the car make and model:

1. Modify the top of `ViewCarTableViewController.m` to add a state variable and some state value constants by adding the following code in bold:

```
...
#define kCurrentEditMake   0
#define kCurrentEditModel  1

@implementation ViewCarTableViewController {
    NSInteger currentEditType;
}
...
```

2. In the storyboard, add a modal selection segue (not accessory action) from the make cell to the make/model edit scene. Select the segue and set the identifier to `MakeEditSegue`. While setting the identifier, make sure the style is Modal. Repeat the process using the model cell and an identifier of `ModelEditSegue`.

3. Set up the make/model edit controller using `prepareForSegue:sender:`. Use the method to set what data field is being edited and set the editor's delegate. Remember to import the header file for the editor, in this case, `MakeModelEditViewController.h`.

You created similar code for `CarTableViewController`. The first two lines of each `if` case get a reference to the incoming editor, the next sets the delegate, and the final one sets the state:

```
- (void)prepareForSegue:(UIStoryboardSegue *)segue
                 sender:(id)sender {
    if ([segue.identifier isEqualToString:@"MakeEditSegue"]) {
        MakeModelEditViewController *nextController;
        nextController = segue.destinationViewController;

        nextController.delegate = self;
        currentEditType = kCurrentEditMake;

    } else if ([segue.identifier isEqualToString:@"ModelEditSegue"]) {
        MakeModelEditViewController *nextController;
        nextController = segue.destinationViewController;

        nextController.delegate = self;
        currentEditType = kCurrentEditModel;
    }
}
```

4. Add the body of the protocol methods for setting up the make/model edit scene. Each method needs to determine what field is being edited and return the correct string; they will look almost identical. There are many ways to implement the behavior. In this case, you use a `switch` statement to give flexibility for adding more fields (as you do later in the book). The `titleText` protocol method looks like this:

```
-(NSString*)titleText {
    NSString *titleString = @"";

    switch (currentEditType) {
        case kCurrentEditMake:
            titleString = @"Make";
            break;

        case kCurrentEditModel:
            titleString = @"Model";
            break;
    }

    return titleString;
}
```

Use this as a template for all the other setup protocol methods. Table 8-1 gives the values for the make and model strings for each method, including `titleText`.

5. Update the detail field with any new value from the `editDone:` protocol method. Note that no action is required if the user cancels the edit, and even if the user taps Done, there might be no change. Use the code in Listing 8-4 for the protocol method.

Table 8-1 **Return Values for** `MakeModelEditProtocol` **Text Setup Methods**

Protocol Method	kCurrentEditMake	kCurrentEditModel
titleText	@"Make"	@"Model"
editLabelText	@"Enter the Make:"	@"Enter the Model:"
editFieldText	self.mycar.make	self.mycar.model
editFieldPlaceholderText	@"Car Make"	@"Car Model"

Listing 8-4 **View Car Implementation of the** `editDone:` **Protocol Method**

```
-(void)editDone:(NSString*)textFieldValue {
    if (textFieldValue != nil &&
        [textFieldValue length] > 0) {                              // 1
        switch (currentEditType) {
            case kCurrentEditMake:
                if ((self.myCar.make == nil) ||                     // 2
                    !([self.myCar.make isEqualToString:textFieldValue])) {
                    self.myCar.make = textFieldValue;               // 3

                    self.makeLabel.text = textFieldValue;           // 4
                }
                break;

            case kCurrentEditModel:
                if ((self.myCar.model == nil) ||
                    !([self.myCar.model isEqualToString:textFieldValue])) {
                    self.myCar.model = textFieldValue;

                    self.modelLabel.text = textFieldValue;
                }
                break;
        }
    }
}
```

Here's what happens in the numbered lines in Listing 8-4:

1. Update only if there is new text. If the text field was initially set to `nil` by `editFieldText` and is still `nil`, nothing has changed. It could also be an empty string.

2. There is some text from the edit field. Update if there is no current value or if the new value is different from the old value.

3. If there is an update, change the `Car` object.

4. Change the label in the car view.

Why Not Use an `enum` for `currentEditType`?

If you have done much coding in Objective-C, C, or C++, you might wonder why I did not use an `enum`—that is, an enumerated type—for `currentEditType`.

The main reason is because it is a simple two-state variable. Defining and using an `enum` would at least double the code. On the other hand, if I expected the number of states to grow, using an `enum` would make sense, especially when combined with a `switch` statement.

To learn more about `enum`s and how to use them, see *Learning Objective-C 2.0: A Hands-on Guide for Mac and iOS Developers* by Robert Clair.

Run the code, open the car detail view, and try editing the make and model fields. You should test the different cases:

- Edit a field and cancel. No change should happen.
- Edit a field with no set value, shown as "Unknown" in the interface. Make no change and tap Done. No change should happen.
- Edit a field, make a change, and tap Done. The car view should update.
- Edit a field, make a change, and then tap Cancel. The car view should not change.

Making this kind of list is a way of specifying test cases for an application. Test cases help you make sure that what you want to happen is what actually happens. Getting practice at turning desired behavior into test cases that confirm that behavior is an important skill. By using test cases to regularly test your code, you can catch bugs early in the process and also catch problems that get introduced. Also note that, while testing on the simulator catches most bugs, testing on a physical device is the only way to know if your app really works.

When you have edited a make and model, go back to the car table. You should find a bug: The cars list doesn't update with the new information.

Adding a `ViewCarProtocol`

There is nothing that links the view car controller back to the cars table controller. The only communication happens in `prepareForSegue:sender:` when `CarTableViewController` sets `myCar` for the incoming car view. You need a protocol so the two view controllers can communicate.

The protocol needs two messages: one for setting which car to view and one to tell the delegate if there are any changes to the data. The last part means view car has to track whether there are any changes. That is a good place to begin:

1. In `ViewCarTableViewController.m`, add another state variable of type `BOOL` below `currentEditType`. Call it `dataUpdated`. Initialize `dataUpdated` to `NO` just below the call to super in `viewDidLoad`.

2. Set `dataUpdated` to `YES` any time you update `self.myCar` in `editDone:`.

3. Add a new protocol called `ViewCarProtocol` just below `ViewCarTableViewController.m` and add the following bold lines:

   ```
   ...
   #import <Foundation/Foundation.h>

   @class Car;

   @protocol ViewCarProtocol <NSObject>

   -(Car*)carToView;

   -(void)carViewDone:(BOOL)dataChanged;

   @end
   ```

4. Import `ViewCarProtocol.h` into `ViewCarTableController.h` and add a line declaring a delegate that conforms to the protocol:

   ```
   @property (weak, nonatomic) id <ViewCarProtocol> delegate;
   ```

5. Set the `myCar` property in `ViewCarTableController`'s `viewDidLoad` method by adding this line just below the one initializing `dataUpdated`:

   ```
   self.myCar = [self.delegate carToView];
   ```

6. Set up `CarTableViewController` to be a delegate by importing `ViewCarProtocol.h` into the `.h` file and adding the following line of code just below the `@interface` line:

   ```
   <ViewCarProtocol>
   ```

7. Add the protocol methods to `CarViewTableViewController.m` just above `newCar:`. Leave `carViewDone:` empty. You no longer set the value of `myCar` in `prepareForSegue:sender:`. Enter the code you need so `carToView` looks like this:

   ```
   - (Car *)carToView {
       NSInteger index = [self.tableView indexPathForSelectedRow].row;

       return arrayOfCars[index];
   }
   ```

8. Set the cars table as the delegate for view car by changing the body of prepareForSegue:sender: to this:

```
if ([segue.identifier isEqualToString:@"ViewSegue"]) {
    ViewCarTableViewController *nextController;
    nextController = segue.destinationViewController;

    nextController.delegate = self;
}
```

Catching the Transition Back to the Main Cars Table

Figure 8-10 shows the current transitions and how they occur. You explicitly connect three segues: the push from the cars table to view car and both modal ones from view car to make/model edit. You also explicitly unwind the segue from make/model edit back to view car by using dismissControllerAnimated:completion:.

You use the editTouched: protocol method to communicate changes from make/model edit back to view car. But how can you communicate from view car back to the cars table?

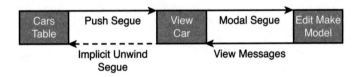

Figure 8-10   Scene transitions

The transition from view car to the cars table is an implicit unwind of the original push segue originating from a user interface element you do not control. The user taps the back button in the navigation bar, and the segue is unwound, with no storyboard or segue calls.

However, there is another mechanism. The back button is managed by the navigation controller. Each time a view controller is pushed on or popped off the stack, the navigation controller looks for an optional delegate and can send messages both before and after the transition.

To catch the transition from the car view back to the cars table, all you need to do is make the correct controller a delegate of the navigation controller and then implement the appropriate message. The current protocol is centered on the view car table view, so that is the place to listen for the transition:

1. Make the view car table view controller a delegate of the navigation controller by adding the code in bold in ViewCarTableViewController.h:

```
@interface ViewCarTableViewController : UITableViewController
<MakeModelEditProtocol, UINavigationControllerDelegate>
```

2. Set the view car table controller to the navigation controller delegate. In
   `ViewCarTableViewController.m`, add `viewWillAppear:` below `viewDidLoad`:

```
- (void)viewWillAppear:(BOOL)animated {
    [super viewWillAppear:animated];

    self.navigationController.delegate = self;
}
```

3. Add the following method to the top of `ViewCarTableViewController.m` to send the
   delegate a `carViewDone:` protocol message as long as data has been updated and the
   incoming view controller is the delegate. Also unregister as the delegate by setting the
   navigation controller's `delegate` property to `nil`:

```
- (void)navigationController:(UINavigationController *)navigationController
        didShowViewController:(UIViewController *)viewController
                  animated:(BOOL)animated
{
    if (viewController == (UIViewController*)self.delegate) {
        if (dataUpdated) {
            [self.delegate carViewDone:dataUpdated];
        }

        navigationController.delegate = nil;
    }
}
```

If you don't unregister as the delegate, you can end up with messages to deallocated
objects.

4. Finally, implement `carViewDone:` in `CarTableViewController.m`:

```
-(void)carViewDone:(BOOL)dataChanged {
    if (dataChanged) {
        [self.tableView reloadData];
    }
}
```

Run the app, add a few cars, and edit one. When you return to the cars table, the values are
updated. You can try this for a few cars to make sure the code is viewing and editing the correct
car.

Some Update Finesse

When you use `reloadTable` in `carViewDone:`, you are telling the table view that all the
content in every cell is *dirty*—all its content is out of date. This causes the table view to update
at least all the cells that are visible to the user (and usually more). In your app, this is quite
fast because the data is simple. But imagine an app that takes longer to figure out the content
of each cell, perhaps because of a lot of calculation or even the need to communicate with a
server.

Instead, you could just tell the table to update only the cells that have changed. `reloadRowsAtIndexPaths:withRowAnimation:` updates just a specified set of cells. To use this method, you must know the index path for the cell being viewed—that is, the selected cell. And you can get the index path for the selected cell by using `indexPathForSelectedRow`. Follow these steps:

1. Add a state variable below `arrayOfCars:` with this code:

   ```
   NSIndexPath *currentViewCarPath;
   ```

2. Set the value by changing `carToView`:

   ```
   - (Car *)carToView {
       currentViewCarPath = [self.tableView indexPathForSelectedRow];

       return arrayOfCars[currentViewCarPath.row];
   }
   ```

3. Finally, change `carViewDone` to only update the cell being viewed and only if it was changed:

   ```
   -(void)carViewDone:(BOOL)dataChanged {
       if (dataChanged) {
           [self.tableView reloadRowsAtIndexPaths:@[currentViewCarPath]
                               withRowAnimation:YES];
       }

       currentViewCarPath = nil;
   }
   ```

Before you run the app, you should make a small user experience tweak that makes it easier to use. The make/model edit scene has only one text field, so there is no need to make the customer tap to open the keyboard. Therefore, in `MakeModelEditViewController.m`, add the following line of code at the end of `viewDidLoad`:

```
[self.editField becomeFirstResponder];
```

Now run the app and try the full editing path. The keyboard automatically opens when you enter the edit screen, and all data updates. When you return to the cars table, if you modified the car, the new data animates in.

Editing the Year

Make and model are both text-based. You could use text for the year and only show a numeric text keyboard. But that does not help you make sure the user is entering a four-digit year that is within a particular range of years. Instead, you can create a picker-based edit view that is specific to Gregorian dates. (You can even internationalize the picker if you'd like to explore that.)

`UIPickerView` lets you present longer lists of individual choices or even several side-by-side lists. One place you can find pickers is when you set dates and times for Calendar appointments. Those use the `UIDatePicker` subclass.

A picker looks like a slot machine with rotors and a number of positions on each rotor. You specify the number of rotors and the number of positions on each rotor. You set up the rotors by implementing the methods in the `UIPickerViewDataSource` protocol.

You also need to set up the content of each position. It can be as simple as a string or as complex as a custom view with a specified width and height. You set this with methods in the `UIPickerDelegateProtocol`. The delegate also informs you when rows are selected, which is useful for dynamically updating choices or other parts of the user interface.

Setting Up the Year Editor

Unlike a slot machine, you need only one rotor. You need to put the picker view in a view controller for the Year editor, so follow these steps:

1. Drag a view controller onto the storyboard just below the make/model edit view controller.

2. Add a navigation bar to the top, and also add Cancel and Done bar button items. Set tints as desired.

3. Place a picker view constrained to the leading, trailing, and bottom edge. When you are done, the view controller should look something like Figure 8-11.

Figure 8-11   Year edit scene

4. Add a `YearEditViewController` class, inheriting from `UIViewController`, and make it the class of the new scene.

5. Add the same messages for the Cancel and Done buttons you did for `MakeModelEditViewController`, but do not fill out the body of the methods yet.

6. Add an `editPicker` property for the picker view.

Implementing the Model Year Picker

The model year of a car is a bounded number: It is no larger than the year after the current one and no smaller than the first production car. And even then, how many people drive a Model T around?

Before making changes to the Year editor, update the `Car` object with the new earliest model year:

1. Add the following line of code below the import of `Foundation.h` in `Car.h`:

   `#define kModelTYear 1908`

2. Change the `init` method to use `kModelTYear` for the year instead of `1900`.

3. Import `Car.h` into `YearEditViewController.m`.

To generate the picker, you must specify the number of components, the number of rows, and the content for each row. Since the picker is a list of years, there is only one component. How do you calculate the number of rows?

Picker Math

The displayed range can be from 1908, the year of the first mass-produced car, to the year following the current one. If the current year is 2014, the maximum year is 2015—after all, it feels good to buy next year's model. The number of rows is the maximum year minus the earliest year plus 1. If this were 1910, the math would be $(1910 - 1908) + 1$, or 3. A formula for that looks like:

`NumberOfRows = (MaximumYear - EarliestYear) + 1`

The maximum year is whatever this year is plus 1. You can get that by looking at the current date and adding 1 to the current year, as shown in Listing 8-5.

The picker calls a delegate method for the content of each row—in this case, the text of the year. Row indexes start from 0 at the top, to the number of rows less 1 at the bottom; rows are zero-indexed. A slight twist is that you want the maximum year to appear at the top of the picker, at index 0.

The year for any row is the maximum year minus the current row. Using 1910, the value for the second row, or row 1, is $1910 - 1$, or 1909. You do not have direct access to the maximum year, but you do have access to the total rows as a 1-based number, and you know the earliest year. Therefore, this is the formula:

```
YearForRow = ((EarliestYear + TotalRows) - 1) - CurrentRow
```

The final thing you need is the maximum year. You get it by adding 1 to the year of the current date. Doing this requires the integer value of the year for an NSDate, which you can get by breaking the date into components. Listing 8-5 is a method for returning the integer year from the date.

Listing 8-5 `YearEditViewController.m getYearFromDate:`

```
-(NSInteger)getYearFromDate:(NSDate*)theDate {
    NSCalendar *gregorian = [[NSCalendar alloc]                         // 1
                           initWithCalendarIdentifier:NSGregorianCalendar];

    NSDateComponents *components;

    components = [gregorian components:NSYearCalendarUnit fromDate:theDate]; // 2

    return components.year;                                             // 3
}
```

Here's what happens in the numbered lines in Listing 8-5:

1. Finding the year requires breaking a date into components, and that requires a calendar. This method works only with Gregorian dates, although you could use the current system calendar to localize the returned value.

2. Return a date component's object initialized with the year from `theDate`.

3. Return the `year` component.

Now you have enough information to add the protocol methods. Here's what you do:

1. Adopt the two picker protocols by adding this line below the `@interface` call in `YearEditViewController.h`:

   ```
   <UIPickerViewDataSource, UIPickerViewDelegate>
   ```

2. Add the method from Listing 8-5 as the first method in the `YearEditViewController.m`.

3. Insert the data source methods for the number of components and number of rows below `viewDidLoad`. Remember that the maximum year is the year after the current one:

   ```
   - (NSInteger)numberOfComponentsInPickerView:(UIPickerView *)pickerView {
       return 1;
   }
   ```

```
- (NSInteger)pickerView:(UIPickerView *)pickerView
numberOfRowsInComponent:(NSInteger)component {
    NSInteger maxYear = [self getYearFromDate:[NSDate date]];

    maxYear += 1;

    return (maxYear - kModelTYear) + 1;
}
```

4. Return the display value for each row by implementing the string title–based delegate method. Put the method just below the two you just created:

```
- (NSString *)pickerView:(UIPickerView *)pickerView
            titleForRow:(NSInteger)row
            forComponent:(NSInteger)component {
    NSInteger totalRows = [pickerView numberOfRowsInComponent:component];

    NSInteger displayVal = ((kModelTYear + totalRows) - 1) - row;

    return [NSString stringWithFormat:@"%d", displayVal];
}
```

5. Use the storyboard to connect the `dataSource` and `delegate` outlets of the spinner to the year edit view controller. The easiest way to do this is to Ctrl-drag from the picker to the controller below the view and use the popup picker, as shown in Figure 8-12.

Figure 8-12   Connecting the picker view data source

Before you can test the changes, you need to create a segue to open the Year editor:

1. Add a disclosure accessory indicator to the year cell.

2. Drag a modal selection segue named `YearEditSegue` from the year cell to the Year editor.

Run the app, view a car, and bring up the Year editor. The picker has all the years from 1908 to the year after the current one, with the highest year selected. Of course there is no way to remove the modal, so that is the next thing to do.

Adding the Year Edit Protocol

The protocol is very simple. The Year editor needs the year to show, and the delegate needs to know the year chosen when Done is selected.

Adding the protocol requires two key formulas. The first formula sets the initial picker row based on the existing year. The maximum year selects the top item, index 0. Your initial thought might be to take the target year and subtract the minimum year to get the row. Unfortunately, that does not work as the larger the year, the larger the difference and, therefore, index. You want to subtract the target year from the maximum year:

```
Row = MaximumYear - TargetYear
```

The second formula converts a selected row to a year. Again, this is an inverse problem. A row index of zero is the maximum year: the larger the index, the lower the year. In this case, the year is the maximum year minus the current row:

```
SelectedYear = MaximumYear - Row
```

This just leaves finding the maximum year, and that is simply the total number of rows plus the minimum year, minus 1:

```
MaximumYear = (MinimumYear + TotalRows) - 1
```

The last choice is what to show as a default year selection for the picker if none has been set—that is, if the car object has a year set to 1908. Since most people are driving cars within a few years of the current year, the best choice is to show that. You could display the default of 1908, but the chance of someone actually driving in a Ford Model T is astronomically small.

Follow these steps to create the protocol and associated properties and methods:

1. Add a new protocol called `YearEditProtocol` and add the following method declarations:

   ```
   - (NSInteger) editYearValue;
   ```

   ```
   - (void) editYearDone:(NSInteger)yearValue;
   ```

2. Import the protocol into `YearEditViewController.h` and add a property to conform the delegate, using the following line:

   ```
   @property (weak, nonatomic) id <YearEditProtocol> delegate;
   ```

3. In the .m file, initialize the year picker from `viewDidLoad`. You can set the selection of a picker by using the `selectRow:inComponent:animated` call:

```objc
- (void)viewDidLoad
{
    [super viewDidLoad];

    NSInteger yearValue = [self.delegate editYearValue];

    if (yearValue == kModelTYear) {
        yearValue = [self getYearFromDate:[NSDate date]];
    }

    NSInteger rows = [self.editPicker numberOfRowsInComponent:0];
    NSInteger maxYear = (kModelTYear + rows) - 1;
    NSInteger row = maxYear - yearValue;

    [self.editPicker selectRow:row inComponent:0 animated:YES];
}
```

4. Fill out the `editCanceled:` and `editDone:` methods:

```objc
- (IBAction)editCanceled:(id)sender {
    [self dismissViewControllerAnimated:YES completion:nil];
}

- (IBAction)editDone:(id)sender {
    NSInteger rows = [self.editPicker numberOfRowsInComponent:0];
    NSInteger maxYear = (kModelTYear + rows) - 1;
    NSInteger year = maxYear - [self.editPicker selectedRowInComponent:0];

    [self.delegate editYearDone:year];

    [self dismissViewControllerAnimated:YES completion:nil];
}
```

5. Import the year edit protocol into `ViewCarTableViewController.h` and add it to the existing protocols under the `@interface` line.

6. Open the `.m` file and import `YearEditViewController.h`.

7. Add a final `else if` condition to the `prepareForSegue:sender:` method so the last part looks like the following code. This sets the year editing delegate to the current view car scene:

```objc
} else if ([segue.identifier isEqualToString:@"YearEditSegue"]) {
        YearEditViewController *nextController;
        nextController = segue.destinationViewController;

        nextController.delegate = self;
}
```

8. Add the protocol methods to the `.m` file. When the year value changes, remember to update the value of the car, the label, and the data updated state variable:

```
- (NSInteger)editYearValue {
    return self.myCar.year;
}


- (void)editYearDone:(NSInteger)yearValue {
    if (yearValue != self.myCar.year) {
        self.myCar.year = yearValue;

        self.yearLabel.text = [NSString stringWithFormat:@"%d",
                                            self.myCar.year];

        dataUpdated = YES;
    }
}
```

Run the app in the simulator and try editing years. Everything should work. You can try adding more cars, as well as editing the make and model.

Summary

This chapter has equipped you to start using table views for lists of data. It has also shown you the power of adding navigation controllers for quickly moving up and down hierarchies of information.

After creating a simple project to explore table views, you converted the add/view scene to a list of cars. You completed the scene by using common patterns for adding and deleting items in a table view, in this case cars, as well as opening the detail for any car. You showed the detail by creating another table view, using a grouped style instead of a list. You created a couple screens to edit car attributes and used modal presentation of those screens to require the user to edit the attribute or cancel.

Along the way, you practiced using protocols for communicating data between controllers, and you were introduced to `UIPickerView`, a versatile element for picking numbers or choosing from a list.

With the basics of table views, you can design and create many of the standard kinds of iOS apps. You can show lists of objects and use a navigation controller to easily move through more or less detail. Modal presentation is a useful tool for editing attributes. And with `UIPickerView`, you can add combinations such as number picking and picking an item from a list of choices.

Even though adding and editing cars in CarValet is now easier, it still takes a lot of effort to populate the app with realistic test data. Every time you run the app, you have to start again. Chapter 9, "Introducing Core Data," introduces you to Core Data, which is not just a way to save your data but also a way to define it, search it, sort it, and much more.

Challenges

1. Add code that displays something when there are no cars. It can be as simple as the kind of label shown in the Contacts app. One approach is to include a view that you show or hide based on a condition. Also note that the user could delete the last car. The quickest way to test your code is to remove the initial car generated by `CarTableViewController` in `viewDidLoad`.

2. Add the ability to edit the fuel. You could do this using a new editor, or you could modify the Make/Model editor to work with numbers as well as text. If you take this approach, you need to add a configuration to specify text versus numbers and change what keyboard is brought up. You also need to add another current edit type so view car can do the right thing with the return value. The value is text, but the car object uses a float.

3. Instead of deleting cars, move them to a deleted section in the cars table. The easiest way to do this is to change `arrayOfCars` to a two-dimensional array. The first subarray is the active cars, and the second array is the deleted, or reclaimed, ones. You can use what you learned about multiple sections, headers for sections, and index paths. Finally, you need to choose what to do about deleting checked-out cars: Can they be deleted? If so, you need to modify the second array. If not, you can prevent cells from being deleted and the associated interface from showing. Take a look at the "Removing Cars" section earlier in this chapter, if you need a refresher.

9

Introducing Core Data

For many apps, presentation is just one key part of their value. Without data, there is nothing to present. And for many apps, the data has to persist. In the CarValet app, so far the data has been temporary: If you or the system removes the app from memory, the data is gone; build and download, crash, or reboot, and again the data is gone. You need a way to store data between app launches.

iOS offers several ways to do this: You can put the raw objects in a file, translate the objects and relationships into XML and put that in a file, or even create your own SQLite database. No matter which way you choose, there are a bunch of routines to write, including routines for saving a car, reading a car, finding a car, deleting a car, updating a car, and more. With a database, some of the basics are handled, but there is still a lot of work: You need to define the SQL data model, design and write the SQL queries, and even more.

Core Data, Apple's iOS and Mac storage technology, does most of the work for you. You use a visual editor to define the model—a set of objects that represent your data and the relationships between those objects. You have options of how and where the data is stored. Built-in routines handle initializing the data store (or stores); creating, updating, and deleting objects; and searching. With Core Data, you get access to even more: sorting, filtering ("just show me this year's Nissan Leafs, please"), and even a special class designed to work with table views. For the cost of a few lines of extra code, you get a multi-element relational database.

After getting a brief introduction to the basics of Core Data, you create the CarValet app's data model. Then you add the boilerplate code that any app needs, and you convert the cars table view and custom cell to use Core Data. After seeing the results of your work, you apply the same basic process to convert the detail table view.

When the CarValet app is using Core Data, you can make working with cars easier by updating the table to use `NSFetchedResultsController`, a special class designed to simplify using table views with Core Data. After you set up the fetched results controller, many of the table view delegate methods become simple calls to that controller.

When you are done with this chapter, you will be able to easily add data persistence to any app. And when the app uses a table, accessing and updating that data becomes even easier. First, you need to learn the parts of Core Data.

Introduction to Core Data

Core Data is Apple's technology for bringing persistence to an app's data model. It has all the power of a multistore relational database and adds specific areas of integration with the user experience on both iOS and Mac OS. Despite the power of Core Data, you need to do relatively little to begin taking advantage of it (see the "Note: From Basic to Full Use").

Note: From Basic to Full Use

The goal of this chapter is to get you started with Core Data. By the end of the chapter, you will be using it for adding, deleting, displaying, and editing cars. But this chapter only scratches the surface. To really take advantage of Core Data, you need to learn more about how it works; the associated classes, methods, and properties; and some typical use cases. You can learn all this and more in *Learning Core Data for iOS: A Hands-on Guide to Building Core Data Applications* by Tim Roadley.

Before looking at Core Data in more detail, it is important to understand where it fits in a typical application. For most applications, Apple recommends an overall architecture called Model–View–Controller (MVC).

The implementation classes are broken up into three areas of functionality. In MVC, the *model* is all about application data: creating, changing, deleting, and modifying. All this behavior is encapsulated into classes that are independent of any user presentation. When done well, anything to do with the model can happen from a command line or a graphical view. The presentation is up to the view layer.

The *view* layer is the visual user experience of the app. It includes everything that has to do with accessing and modifying the data, as well as any other visual app elements, such as preferences. The focus is on the look and the feel. What information to show comes from the model. The view layer is how the information is presented. In this book, the focus is on visual presentation. But you could also implement a view layer for printing, text-based, or even spoken output.

Controllers sit between the view and the model. They do everything from coordinate the behavior of the app and control the flow to acting as a go-between for the model and view. Controllers are usually the most complex part of an app. In addition to controllers that sit between the model and user experience, there might be other controllers interacting with the OS, dealing with communications, and a number of other things. And if your app has different view layers for printing or text, there might be other controllers for those specific views.

Core Data is focused on the model layer of MVC, with a few parts providing support for user interface controllers. As in most databases, the data-handling part of Core Data is broken up into three main layers: where the data is stored, the format of the data, and a data access environment. *Stores* are where the saved data is kept, and there can be more than one store. The data format is specified by a *managed object model*. Data is accessed through a *managed object context*, and there can be more than one context active at the same time.

These are the corresponding classes:

- `NSPersistentStoreCoordinator` coordinates all the stores used for your data. For iOS, there is usually just one on-device store.

- `NSManagedObjectModel` describes all the kinds of data objects you use in your applications. In database terms, this is the schema.

- `NSManagedObjectContext` is a manager for a set of data objects. The context includes the rules used for finding actual data elements in the stores, some number of the found data elements, and their current state. It is possible to have multiple contexts active at the same time, with the same objects in different states in each one. Contexts write back to the store only when they are saved.

Before you can create any data items, you need to describe them. In Core Data, an *entity* describes the parts of a data item: the names of the attributes, the attribute types, and any other special properties. In that way, an entity is like a class in Objective-C. In CarValet, there is only one entity: the car. If the app started supporting motorcycles, that would be another entity. There could also be an entity for the owner of the car.

Entities specify attributes and relationships. A car has attributes for the make, model, year, and so on. If CarValet added owners, a car would also have a relationship to an owner and vice versa. You rarely work directly with the system object for entities, `NSEntityDescription`; instead, you use Xcode to create the entities and their properties and relationships.

The parts of Core Data—the store coordinator, managed object model, managed context, and entity—form a stack, as shown in Figure 9-1.

Most of the time you are working with objects in a managed object context. Those objects are each a type of entity, and all possible entities are managed by the object model. At the bottom of the stack is the persistent store coordinator, which accesses objects in one or more stores.

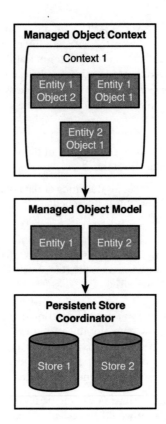

Figure 9-1   Core Data stack

Actual data items in a managed object context are based on NSManagedObject. This class handles all Core Data–related behavior, such as interacting with the entity description, handling updates, observing property value changes, and lazy loading of data from the store. Most subclasses of NSManagedObject are used to access attributes using dot notation. And subclasses are easy to create with a simple menu selection. Later, you do this for the car object to quickly access the make, model, year, and so on.

Moving CarValet to Core Data

The best way to understand Core Data is to use it. In the rest of this chapter, you convert CarValet to use Core Data. First, you add the model and then some boilerplate code to load and access it. Next, you convert the cars table and prototype cell. Then, you update the car data view and make sure any changes are updated. Finally, you learn a better way to use Core Data with data overview tables.

Before you can do any of that, you need to add the CoreData framework to your app. Follow these steps:

1. Open the CarValet project. You can start with your final code from Chapter 8, "Table Views I: The Basics," or use the CH09 CarValet Starter project provided with the sample code files for this chapter.

   Now open the CarValet target editing area by selecting the project at the top of the Xcode Navigator, looking for the Targets section in the Editor area (in this case, the Project Editor), and selecting the CarValet application target. (There should be only one item in the Targets list.) You can see the selected application target in Figure 9-2.

2. With the target selected, make sure the General tab is showing at the top of the Project Details area in the Project Editor. Now scroll the Project Details area down to Linked Frameworks and Libraries and use the + button to add the CoreData framework. Use the search box to help you find the framework as shown in Figure 9-2.

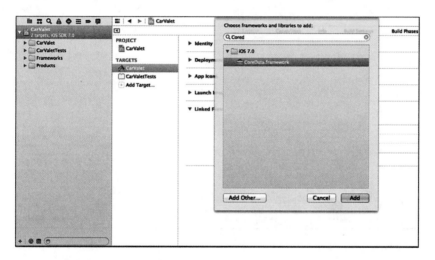

Figure 9-2   Adding the CoreData framework

Adding the CDCar Model

Next, you need to create the file that Core Data uses to set up entities and other configurations. The same description file and editor can be used for anything from a simple single-entity configuration like CarValet to very complex models including multiple entities, entity properties, default values, and relationships.

Adding the car model takes just a few steps:

1. Add a new file to the project by using the Data Model template from the Core Data category. Call the file CarValet and add it just above `Car.h`.

2. Open the new `CarValet.xdatamodeld` if it is not already there. You should see an editor similar to the one in Figure 9-3.

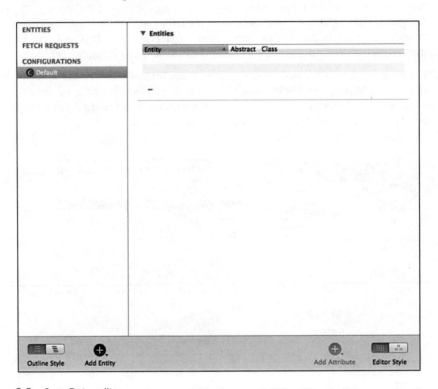

Figure 9-3   Core Data editor

3. Add an entity called `CDCar` by clicking the Add Entity button in the lower left.

4. Add an attribute for each existing property of the `Car` object, except `carInfo`. You can open `Car.h` in an auxiliary editor to make sure you get all the properties. As you add each property, set its type based on the current model.

The only attribute type that is not obvious is year. You can make that an integer 16, as year numbers are unlikely to get bigger than 32,767 for quite some time, no matter which calendar format you choose. When you are done, the attribute types should look as shown in Figure 9-4.

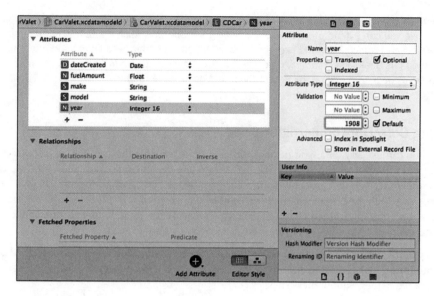

Figure 9-4   CDCar attribute types and year default

Your original Car data object set some default values in init methods. Core Data lets you do the same thing, although in some areas it is not very flexible. Set 1908 as the default for year using the Data Model inspector, also shown in Figure 9-4.

Now that the CDCar entity is defined, you can create a subclass of NSManagedObject to access properties using dot notation. The only caveat is that properties default to subclasses of NSObject. This means any integers, floats, Booleans, and so on are NSNumber. Although the step you are about to perform lets you use scalars such as NSInteger for primitives, there are some undesired results. In this case, Core Data turns the NSDate into NSTimeInterval.

With the Model editor still open, select Editor > Create NSManagedObject Subclass and, if prompted, choose CDCar and then save the file with all the other source files. If needed, put CDCar.h and CDCar.m below the model definition file. Although you can make changes to the generated files, any time you change the model and re-create the CDCar subclass, the old files are replaced.

Adding Code to Model Files

It is inevitable. You add some code to your generated managed object, and some time later, you regenerate the files. Your code is no more. But there is a way to avoid this problem using something called a category.

A *category* is not really a class, but an extension of an existing class. You specify the class to extend, have Xcode generate the files, and then add to the .h and .m files almost as normal. The one exception is that you cannot add any properties.

> Using categories, or class extensions as they are sometimes called, is a powerful technique because you can extend other classes, including system ones such as NSString. It is also a more advanced technique and is a good one to put on your "things to learn soon after I have finished this book" list. *Learning Objective-C 2.0: A Hands-on Guide to Objective-C for Mac and iOS Developers*, 2nd edition, by Robert Clair, is a good place to start.

Adding Core Data Boilerplate Code

Before you can use any data, you have to initialize Core Data for the app. You need objects for each of the three classes shown in Figure 9-1. When you become more familiar with Core Data, this is something you will probably do in your own helper class, as described in Chapter 1 of *Learning Core Data for iOS: A Hands-on Guide to Building Core Data Applications* by Tim Roadley. If you know your app will use Core Data before you create the project, some of the application creation templates provided by Xcode have a check box to use Core Data.

In this chapter, you use code based on the Master–Detail Application template from Xcode. The only modifications are adding an import of CoreData.h and two #defines for the model file and data file names. Follow these steps:

1. Open AppDelegate.m with AppDelegate.h in the Assistant editor. Now select File > Open to open the two CoreData_for_AppDelegate files in the CH09 Assets CoreData Files folder that is part of the code for this chapter. The quickest way to do this is to select the files in the Finder and choose File > Open or Cmd-O. That opens the files in Xcode.

2. Copy the #import and two #define lines from CoreData_for_AppDelegate.h and paste them under the existing import of UIKit.h in AppDelegate.h.

3. Replace the contents of the string for the MyModelURLFile #define with CarValet, the name of the Core Data model file you created earlier.

4. Replace the all-caps portion of the MySQLDataFileName #define with the name CarValet so the entire string is CarValet.sqlite. This is the name of the store managed by the persistent store coordinator, and it is an SQLite database. Do not access the database directly; see the "Warning: Store Files Are in a Proprietary Format."

5. Now copy and paste the @property and method declarations between the window property declaration and the @end statement.

6. Copy the three @synthesize statements from CoreData_for_AppDelegate.m just under the @implementation in AppDelegate.m. You need these statements to give read/write access to the read-only properties you just copied into the .h file.

7. Remove the methods applicationWillResignActive: and applicationWillTerminate: from AppDelegate.m.

8. Copy everything from applicationWillResignActive: down to the end of the file and paste it above the @end statement.

Warning: Store Files Are in a Proprietary Format

Do not use `CarValet.sqlite` directly in your app; always go through Core Data. Although `CarValet.sqlite` is a database and you can likely figure out how Core Data is storing information, all that is subject to change without notice. Relying on the format is a sure way to break your app in the future.

When you run the app now, it does not appear to do anything different. This is because all you have done is define the model and add code to prepare to use Core Data. There is no code creating or displaying a CDCar. That is the next step.

Making Code Easier to Read with `#pragma mark`

`CoreData_for_AppDelegate.m` contains two lines that start with a #pragma, a special statement used to give some information to Xcode. In this case, you are using it to bookmark different groupings of code.

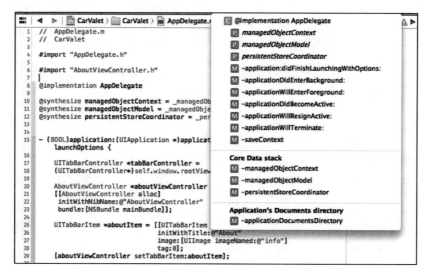

This screenshot is from `viewController`, with the boilerplate code integrated. You can see the two groupings of files near the bottom of the jump bar method dropdown. Each group has a line above the group and then a custom bolded title. Each of those items corresponds to one of the #pragma statements in the code.

Each line and title pair is from a #pragma statement. In this line:

```
#pragma mark – My Own Title
```

the dash (–) inserts a line, then the text is inserted in bold below the line, enabling easy grouping of methods. Both the dash (–) that generates the line and the text generating the bold title are optional.

Using #pragma marks is a good way to both quickly see the organization of your classes and quickly get to methods by using the jump bar.

Converting `CarTableViewController`

Using Core Data changes how data is accessed, created, deleted, and updated. To convert each part of an app, you need to identify those differences and add or change relevant code. Table 9-1 shows the differences and changes needed for `CarTableViewController`.

Table 9-1   **Changes for Core Data in the Cars Table View**

Change	Change for Core Data	Code Changes Needed
1	Use a managed object context.	Set a variable to the main managed object context in `viewDidLoad:` and make it available to the instance.
2	Access data objects through the managed object context.	Set up a fetch request to get appropriate entity data from the managed object context.
3	Let Core Data handle addition and deletion of cars.	Use Core Data calls for adding and deleting cars. Use the result of those calls to update `arrayOfCars`.
4	Use the new managed data object for data access.	Use `CDCar` instead of `Car`.
5	Change from primitive types to objects.	Change places that relied on the integer and float data types to use `NSNumber`.

Cars Table Change 1: Adding the Managed Object Context

The first change requires a reference to the managed object context. `AppDelegate` already has one, so all the cars table controller needs is a reference. Since the managed object context is used in many methods, it is worth setting up an instance variable, though a property is not required. Follow these steps:

1. Import `AppDelegate.h` and `CDCar.h` into `CarTableViewController.m` and remove the import of `Car.h`.

2. Create an instance variable by adding the following declaration just below `arrayOfCars` inside the curly braces below `@implementation`:

   ```
   NSManagedObjectContext *managedContextObject;
   ```

3. Add the following code to `viewDidLoad:` just below the call to `super` to set the managed object context:

   ```
   AppDelegate *appDelegate = [[UIApplication sharedApplication] delegate];

   managedContextObject = appDelegate.managedObjectContext;
   ```

Cars Table Change 2: Accessing Data with the Managed Object Context

Next, you need to set the contents of an array to the current CDCar objects. This requires a couple changes. First, getting the data from a managed object context requires describing the data you want in a fetch request. This can be as simple as specifying all objects of a particular entity type, or it can be a very complex filter and sort.

The fetch request is used as part of executeFetchRequest:error:, an NSManagedObjectContext method for retrieving an array of managed data objects. The same method is used to get an updated set of data objects whenever there is a change, such as an addition or a deletion. Since the cars array is updated from multiple methods in the cars table controller, the fetch request is another instance variable.

Finally, the method to execute the fetch request returns an array, not a mutable array. The variable type needs to be changed, so follow these steps:

1. Change the declaration of arrayOfCars from NSMutableArray to NSArray. At the same time, add the line for the fetch request below managedObjectContext:

   ```
   NSFetchRequest *fetchRequest;
   ```

2. Update viewDidLoad: to Listing 9-1. In addition to the bold code added for this step, some code has been removed.

Listing 9-1   viewDidLoad: in CarTableViewController.m

```
- (void)viewDidLoad {
    [super viewDidLoad];

    AppDelegate *appDelegate = [[UIApplication sharedApplication] delegate];

    managedContextObject = appDelegate.managedObjectContext;

    NSError *error = nil;
    fetchRequest = [NSFetchRequest fetchRequestWithEntityName:@"CDCar"];    // 1

    arrayOfCars = [managedContextObject executeFetchRequest:fetchRequest     // 2
                                                     error:&error];
    if (error != nil) {
        NSLog(@"Unresolved error %@, %@", error, [error userInfo]);          // 3
        abort();                                                             // 4
    }

    self.navigationItem.leftBarButtonItem = self.editButton;
}
```

Here's what happens in the numbered lines in Listing 9-1:

1. Set up the fetch request to look for all entities of class CDCar. Other methods and properties can be used to add filters, sorts, and even batching for loading objects.

2. Set the array of cars to all the managed objects in the context that meet the fetch request criteria—in this case, all cars.

3. An error occurred reading objects. Logging to a file is useful for learning, but it would be better to try to recover from the error, if possible; otherwise, inform the user what is going on and what to try.

4. The call to abort() is from the system-provided template. All it does is create a crash log and terminate the app. As the default comments say, abort is not a function you should use in a shipping application.

Cars Table Change 3: Using Core Data for Adding and Deleting Cars

The current way of adding cars simply allocates a new Car object and inserts it into a mutable array. The Car object takes care of setting any required initial values. Deleting is just one call to remove the Car object from the array. Using a mutable array assumes that memory does not run out, errors never happen, and session-to-session saving is done by something else.

Using Core Data brings persistence, error checking, and better memory management. There is some extra work, though mostly for error checking. To make the change for adding a car, replace newCar: with the code in Listing 9-2. The new code is in bold.

Listing 9-2   **Updated** newCar:

```
- (IBAction)newCar:(id)sender {
    CDCar *newCar = [NSEntityDescription                         // 1
                    insertNewObjectForEntityForName:@"CDCar"
                    inManagedObjectContext:managedContextObject];

    newCar.dateCreated = [NSDate date];                          // 2

    NSError *error;
    arrayOfCars = [managedContextObject executeFetchRequest:fetchRequest  // 3
                                          error:&error];
    if (error != nil) {                                          // 4
        NSLog(@"Unresolved error %@, %@", error, [error userInfo]);
        abort();
    }

    NSIndexPath *indexPath = [NSIndexPath indexPathForRow:0 inSection:0];
    [self.tableView insertRowsAtIndexPaths:@[indexPath]
                    withRowAnimation:UITableViewRowAnimationAutomatic];
}
```

Here's what happens in the numbered lines in Listing 9-2:

1. Create a new car in the current managed object context.

2. Initialize the car's creation date. See the following Note.

3. Regenerate the current array of cars to include the new car.

4. See #4 in Listing 9-1. This is not the recommended way to handle fetch errors.

> **Note**
>
> You could eliminate the line of code for initializing the creation date by creating your own cus-tom subclass for CDCar instead of using the automatically generated one. This topic is beyond the scope of this book. You could also add range checking and other validation criteria. For more information on both options, see *Learning Core Data for iOS: A Hands-on Guide to Building Core Data Applications* by Tim Roadley.

Deleting an object only needs one method call to the managed object context. That marks the object as deleted, although it is not actually removed from the store until the context is saved.

Use Listing 9-3 to modify the delete case of `tableView:commitEditingStyle:forRowAtIndexPath:`.

Listing 9-3   **Updated Delete Car Case**

```
if (editingStyle == UITableViewCellEditingStyleDelete) {
    [managedContextObject deleteObject:arrayOfCars[indexPath.row]];       // 1
    NSError *error = nil;                                                 // 2
    arrayOfCars = [managedContextObject executeFetchRequest:fetchRequest
                                              error:&error];

    if (error != nil) {
        NSLog(@"Unresolved error %@, %@", error, [error userInfo]);
        abort();
    }

    [tableView deleteRowsAtIndexPaths:@[indexPath]
                     withRowAnimation:UITableViewRowAnimationFade];
}
```

Here's what happens in the numbered lines in Listing 9-3:

1. Tell the managed object context to delete the CDCar object.

2. Add the code from Listing 9-1 to update the array of cars.

Cars Table Change 4: Changing to `CDCar` and Updating the Car Cell

All you need to do now is switch over to the new `CDCar` object class. There are three view controller classes using the `Car` object: `CarTableViewController`, `CarTableViewCell`, and `ViewCarTableViewController`.

For both `ViewCarTableViewController` and `CarTableViewCell`:

- In the `.h` file, change `Car` to `CDCar` in the `@class` declaration and for the `myCar` property.
- In the `.m` file, change the import from `Car.h` to `CDCar.h`.

Now change the return type of `carToView`:

- In `ViewCarProtocol.h`, change the `@class` declaration to use `CDCar` and the return type to `CDCar`.
- In `CarTableViewController.m`, modify the return type `carToView` to `CDCar`. This only requires changing the declaration line of the method:

  `- (CDCar*)carToView {`

Cars Table Change 5: Updating to Using `NSNumber`

You have probably seen the red error icon in the information area and navigation tab. As you are changing the app from using `Car` to `CDCar`, the project can no longer compile. The red hexagon with the exclamation mark not only confirms this, but also can be used to find out why.

Clicking on the error indicator in the navigation bar shows a list of files with warnings and errors. The dropdown will look something like Figure 9-5, though the list might be shorter or longer depending on the last time you built the project.

Selecting `CarTableViewCell.m` from that list opens the file and takes you to the first warning or error in that file. Xcode might even suggest a fix for the error or warning.

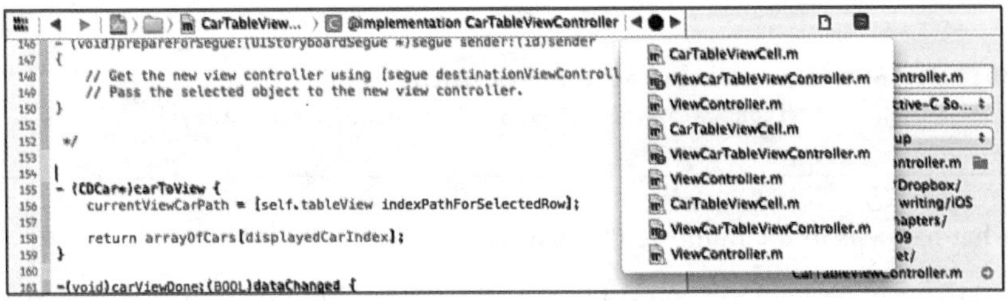

Figure 9-5   Error and warnings

Start by fixing the problems in `CarTableViewCell.m`:

- Use the suggested fix for the first problem in `configureCell`. This should replace the `%d` for `%@` in the call to set the `textLabel.text`. If the suggested fix is not showing, click the warning triangle on the left of the code, the one in the editor, not in the column on the right (changed item in the format string shown in bold):

  ```
  self.textLabel.text = [NSString stringWithFormat:@"%@ %@ %@",
  ```

Now move to `ViewCarTableViewController.m`:

1. Use the suggested fix for the year label.

2. For the fuel label, you need a different fix. Although changing from a format string of `%0.2f` to `%@` would work, it does not result in the format you want. The current format shows a float value with only two decimal places. Using the default fix shows more places.

   Instead, convert the `fuelAmount` `NSNumber` to a float. Make the changes shown in bold:

   ```
   self.fuelLabel.text = [NSString stringWithFormat:@"%0.2f",
                          [self.myCar.fuelAmount floatValue]];
   ```

3. Modify how `editYearValue` generates the integer return value (the modified code is bold):

   ```
   return [self.myCar.year integerValue];
   ```

4. Change how `editYearDone:` checks for a modified value and updates the car object and the displayed year (the modified code is bold):

   ```
   if (yearValue != [self.myCar.year integerValue]) {
       self.myCar.year = [NSNumber numberWithInteger:yearValue];
       self.yearLabel.text = [self.myCar.year stringValue];
   ```

After making that change, the errors go away. Run the app in the simulator and go through all the test cases. Verify that you can create and delete cars. Try viewing cars and then editing values. Make sure values are updated correctly. Try cancelling an edit and any other cases you have already tried or have thought of.

Stop the app from Xcode and then re-run it. There is no data. This is because you stopped the app from the simulator. The only places application data is saved are from `applicationWill-ResignActive:` or `applicationWillTerminate:`. Neither of these is called when the simulator stops the app.

Instead, before you close the app in the simulator, go to home. Do this either by pressing the simulated home button if one is present or using the Cmd-Shift-h key combination. This is an important step. Try this now by running the app, entering and editing some data, closing the app in the simulator, then re-running it from Xcode. Your data is saved.

The only change to the user experience in this chapter is that car objects are saved between application launches. All the code changes have been to convert the project to use Core Data. And as you are about to see, some of those changes were not necessary.

Reducing Dependencies Between Classes

When you architect, design, and write an app, it is a good practice to keep the dependencies between classes to a minimum. In CarValet, one example is using the Car data object. The only places that rely on the structure of the Car data object are the cars table and the view car table.

For example, the editors for make, model, and year do not use any sort of data model; they just edit a simple variable. More importantly, the value for the variable is exchanged using protocols. The editors are generic. The car model can change completely without requiring any changes to the editors.

This kind of compartmentalization is good coding practice, for both maintainability and reusability. The editors can be used in other projects with little or no change.

Easier Tables: NSFetchedResultsController

So far, after converting the CarValet app to Core Data, you have used a modified version of the car array to manage the table view. Each time there is a change to the data, a new array is generated. This has worked so far because there is not much data. However, it does not work as the number of cars gets larger—for example, if you keep a history of all cars parked. When there are too many data objects, at best you will have performance problems. More likely, you will have memory issues.

It also seems as if there should be less code. After all, if the managed object context can produce the array, it must have information on how many cars there are as well as an order for them. At the moment, you have code for calculating the number of sections and the number of rows in a section; which data item is at a particular index path; and updating the table based on changes to the data.

Instead of writing all that code, the system provides NSFetchedResultsController and associated protocols. They are designed to make tables that overview Core Data–based objects easy to manage by doing the following:

- Configuring the section and row count of a table
- Getting the data item represented by an index path
- Returning section header titles
- Tracking changes in the managed object context and enabling table updates using a delegate protocol
- Retrieving data in batches and optionally caching data to a file for increased performance

In this section, you convert the cars table to use a fetched results controller for basic table control and display. In Chapter 10, "Table Views II: Advanced Topics," you add sections, section headers, and sorting. Even when you do that, you only scratch the surface of an incredibly versatile mechanism. For more information, including how to implement a more generic managed table view class, see Chapter 5 of *Learning Core Data for iOS: A Hands-on Guide to Building Core Data Applications* by Tim Roadley.

Part 1: Integrating `NSFetchedResultsController`

You need an instance variable to hold the fetched results controller. Add the following declaration below the one for `fetchRequest` after the `@implementation` statement at the top of `CarTableViewController.m`:

```
NSFetchedResultsController *fetchedResultsController;
```

Now you need to initialize the fetched results controller. Doing so requires setting up an appropriate fetch request. This is because `NSFetchedResultsController` maps the result of applying a fetch request to a managed object context into index paths.

In Listing 9-2, you used a simple `NSFetchRequest` for returning all `CDCar` entities. A fetched results controller requires at least a filter and a sort. The filter can be `nil`, but a sort must specify at least one key.

Fetch requests can have an optional batch size, although that is not required for such a small amount of data. With larger data sets, a batch size limits how many data elements are read each time and, therefore, how many are in memory.

Initialize the fetched results controller by modifying `viewDidLoad` as shown in Listing 9-4 (the new code is bold).

Listing 9-4   **Initializing the Fetched Results Controller**

```
- (void)viewDidLoad {
    [super viewDidLoad];

    AppDelegate *appDelegate = [[UIApplication sharedApplication] delegate];

    managedContextObject = appDelegate.managedObjectContext;

    fetchRequest = [NSFetchRequest fetchRequestWithEntityName:@"CDCar"];

    NSSortDescriptor *sortDescriptor = [[NSSortDescriptor alloc]      // 1
                                 initWithKey:@"dateCreated"
                                 ascending:NO];

    [fetchRequest setSortDescriptors:@[sortDescriptor]];             // 2

    fetchedResultsController = [[NSFetchedResultsController alloc]    // 3
```

```
                                      initWithFetchRequest:fetchRequest
                                      managedObjectContext:managedContextObject
                                      sectionNameKeyPath:nil
                                      cacheName:nil];
        NSError *error = nil;
        [fetchedResultsController performFetch:&error];                    // 4

            if (error != nil) {
                NSLog(@"Unresolved error %@, %@", error, [error userInfo]);
                abort();
            }

        self.navigationItem.leftBarButtonItem = self.editButton;
    }
```

Here's what happens in the numbered lines in Listing 9-4:

1. Set up a simple sort on the creation time, with the most recent at the top.

2. Set the sort descriptors of the fetch request to the new sort. Note that you must set the sort descriptors to an array of descriptors, even if there is only one. That is why the statement uses the @[] array literal constructor.

3. Initialize the fetch results controller using the just-allocated fetch request and the managed object context from the app delegate. There is only one section, so no section names are needed. There is also no caching.

4. Tell the controller to read the initial set of data and deal with any error that might occur. As with comments in previous listings, the code that handles errors should not go in shipping apps.

Updating Basic Table View Data Source Methods

UITableViewDataSource implements three core methods used for returning the number of sections, returning the number of rows in a given section, and returning the cell for a given index path. Each of these methods can now use the fetched results controller. Update the methods by following these steps:

1. Replace the one line of numberOfSectionsInTableView: with this:

   ```
   return [[fetchedResultsController sections] count];
   ```

2. Replace the body of tableView:numberOfRowsInSection: with this:

   ```
   id <NSFetchedResultsSectionInfo> sectionInfo;
   sectionInfo = [fetchedResultsController sections][section];

   return [sectionInfo numberOfObjects];
   ```

3. Change the line in `tableView:cellForRowAtIndexPath:` that sets the car object of the cell to this:

```
cell.myCar = [fetchedResultsController objectAtIndexPath:indexPath];
```

As you can see, you can use a fetched results controller to access data objects based on index paths. This makes managing tables easy.

Updating Deleting and Viewing of Cars

When you run the app in the simulator, you should see any existing cars. However, trying to add or delete a car results in a crash. Viewing cars also gives unpredictable results. This is because the methods supporting those behaviors still use the old array-based management method and try to manipulate the table directly. Update to using the fetched results controller by following these steps:

1. In `tableView:commitEditingStyle:forRowAtIndexPath:`, change the code inside the `if` condition that deals with deletion to the following (with changed code in bold):

```
[managedContextObject deleteObject:[fetchedResultsController
                                    objectAtIndexPath:indexPath]];

NSError *error = nil;

[fetchedResultsController performFetch:&error];

if (error != nil) {
    NSLog(@"Unresolved error %@, %@", error, [error userInfo]);
    abort();
}
tableView deleteRowsAtIndexPaths:@[indexPath]
            withRowAnimation:UITableViewRowAnimationFade];
```

2. In `newCar:`, replace the line that generates the `arrayOfCars` with this:

```
[fetchedResultsController performFetch:&error];
```

3. Replace the return value of `carToView` with this:

```
[fetchedResultsController objectAtIndexPath:currentViewCarPath]
```

4. Delete the declaration of the `arrayOfCars` instance variable.

When you run the app, everything should work. You can add, delete, and edit cars. Remember to go home before you stop the app in Xcode. Next, you make changes in the car detail view in the cars table.

Part 2: Implementing `NSFetchedResultsControllerDelegate`

The code in this chapter works so far, but there is one potential problem. Each time the data in the managed object context is updated by an addition, a deletion, or a change, you send `performFetch:` to the fetch results controller. The call can result in far more work and time than simply updating only the changed data.

The fetched results controller has the ability to observe changes in the managed object context and call methods when those changes occur. All you need to do is support the `NSFetchedResultsControllerDelegate` protocol. You start by declaring support for the protocol:

1. Open `CarTableViewController.h` and add the following line of code just below the import of `UIKit`:

    `#import <CoreData/CoreData.h>`

2. Change the protocol declaration below `@interface` by adding the code in bold:

    `<ViewCarProtocol, `**`NSFetchedResultsControllerDelegate`**`>`

Adding the `NSFetchedResultsControllerDelegate` Methods

When you set `CarTableViewController` as the delegate of the fetched results controller, it sends messages to this delegate whenever a change occurs in the managed object context. In particular, there are three calls to make managing table updates easy:

-   `controllerWillChangeContent:` is called when some content is about to change but before the fetched results are changed.

-   `controller:didChangeObject:atIndexPath:forChangeType:newIndexPath:` is called after the change is complete and the fetched results are updated. The message is sent once for each change and might be called multiple times between the calls to `controllerWillChangeContent:` and `controllerDidChangeContent:`.

-   `controllerDidChangeContent:` is called after all changes have been complete and the fetched results are updated.

These calls work very well with one way of updating a table view. So far you have updated the table view from the same method that changed the data. This works for now because you are making only one change at a time. However, if you wanted to allow deleting multiple items, you would have to delete them one row at a time.

Instead, `UITableView` provides a way to show the results of any number of updates at the same time. If you wrap all the table updates in `beginUpdates` and `endUpdates`, all the updates and associated cell changes and animations occur at once.

Use the three delegate calls with the table view messages to update the content. You begin table updates when the content changes, change the table for each change, and end the table updates when content changes are done. Follow these steps to use fetched results controller delegate methods to update the table contents:

1. Set the current `CarTableViewController` instance as the fetched results controller delegate by adding the following line of code in `viewDidLoad`, just below the line that initializes `fetchResultsController`:

   `fetchedResultsController.delegate = self;`

2. Insert the following code just above `carToView`. The `#pragma` is used to easily find the new protocol support:

   ```
   #pragma mark - NSFetchedResultsControllerDelegate

   - (void)controllerWillChangeContent:(NSFetchedResultsController *)controller {
       [self.tableView beginUpdates];
   }
   ```

3. Now tell the table view that updates have finished and it should update. Insert this code below the `controllerWillChangeContent:`:

   ```
   - (void)controllerDidChangeContent:(NSFetchedResultsController *)controller
   {
       [self.tableView endUpdates];
   }
   ```

4. Use Listing 9-5 to add the protocol method that does the work of updating the table based on the type of change. It might be called multiple times between the `controllerWillChangeContent` and `controllerDidChangeContent` messages. Add the method after the two you just added.

Listing 9-5   **Updating the Table View**

```
- (void)controller:(NSFetchedResultsController *)controller
    didChangeObject:(id)anObject
        atIndexPath:(NSIndexPath *)indexPath
      forChangeType:(NSFetchedResultsChangeType)type
       newIndexPath:(NSIndexPath *)newIndexPath {

    UITableView *tableView = self.tableView;

    switch(type) {                                            // 1
        case NSFetchedResultsChangeInsert:                    // 2
            [tableView insertRowsAtIndexPaths:@[newIndexPath]
                        withRowAnimation:UITableViewRowAnimationFade];
            break;

        case NSFetchedResultsChangeDelete:                    // 3
            [tableView deleteRowsAtIndexPaths:@[indexPath]
                        withRowAnimation:UITableViewRowAnimationFade];
            break;
```

```
//      case NSFetchedResultsChangeUpdate:                        // 4
//          code to update the content of the cell at indexPath
//          break;

//      case NSFetchedResultsChangeMove:                          // 5
//          [tableView deleteRowsAtIndexPaths:@[indexPath]
//                      withRowAnimation:UITableViewRowAnimationFade];
//          [tableView insertRowsAtIndexPaths:@[newIndexPath]
//                      withRowAnimation:UITableViewRowAnimationFade];
//          break;

    }
}
```

Here's what happens in the numbered lines in Listing 9-5:

1. Determine what kind of update to make, based on the type of change.

2. When a new object is inserted, insert a cell at the appropriate place in the table.

3. An object is deleted, so remove the corresponding cell.

4. This type of change occurs when an object is changed or updated. Here you do anything required to refresh the cell that represents the data.

5. The final change is moving the data cell from one place in the table to another. Usually this means deleting the old cell and inserting a new one.

Neither of the last two change types needs to be supported. Although the update message is sent from edits in the car detail view, the changes occur while the cars table is offscreen, so modified cells will not animate. Of course, this might be what you want. The experience would be returning from the car detail view to a cars table that already reflects any changes.

Enabling Calling of the Delegate Methods

If you run the CarValet app now, the delegate methods are not called. You can see this by adding an NSLog statement or setting a breakpoint in controllerWillChangeContent: and then adding or deleting a car. The table updates, but not because of the delegate method.

Observers are informed of changes only when the managed object context is saved. The only place this currently happens is in the app delegate, when it enters the background or exits. Both of those events call a custom method saveContext, which sends save: to any changed managed object context.

To trigger the delegate methods, you need to save the context whenever you add or delete a car. tableView:commitEditingStyle:forRowAtIndexPath: deletes a car and newCar: adds one. In each of those methods, replace this line:

```
[fetchedResultsController performFetch:&error];
```

with this code:

```
[managedContextObject save:&error];
```

The original line refreshes all the fetched results controllers data, which can get more expensive as the amount of data grows. The new call saves only the changed cars, which in turn sends one message to the fetched results controller for each updated car.

The `save:` message triggers the delegate message flow: The initial `controllerWillChange-Content:` message, as many `controller:didChangeObject:atIndexPath:forChangeType:newIndexPath:` messages as needed, and then the final `controllerDidChangeContent:` message.

Running the code now and adding or deleting cars still results in a crash. Looking at the debugger output reveals the problem:

```
Terminating app due to uncaught exception 'NSInternalInconsistencyException', reason:
'Invalid update: invalid number of rows in section 0.  The number of rows contained in
an existing section after the update (3) must be equal to the number of rows contained
in that section before the update (3), plus or minus the number of rows inserted or
deleted from that section (0 inserted, 1 deleted) and plus or minus the number of rows
moved into or out of that section (0 moved in, 0 moved out).'
```

The exception tells you there is a mismatch between the number of rows the table view expects there to be and the actual number. This makes sense because both your original code and the new delegate methods are updating the table. There are two calls to add or delete the same object. To fix the error, follow these steps:

1. In `tableViews:commitEditingStyle:forRowAtIndexPath:`, remove the call to `deleteRowsAtIndexPaths:withRowAnimation:`.

2. Remove the last two lines from `newCar`:

   ```
   NSIndexPath *indexPath = [NSIndexPath indexPathForRow:0 inSection:0];
   [self.tableView insertRowsAtIndexPaths:@[indexPath]
                   withRowAnimation:UITableViewRowAnimationAutomatic];
   ```

Run the app, and everything should work. Try adding some cars, change one to a BMW, update another to something else, and delete a few. As you do this, the proper animations occur. Not only that, but everything is working with less code.

Summary

In this chapter, you learned how to add data persistence in your apps. After looking at the pieces of Core Data and how they fit together, you built a data model for the car object. You added some boilerplate code for setting up the Core Data environment and then used a repeatable process to convert first the car overview list and then the detail view to use the new data format.

You completed your exploration of the basics by using `NSFetchedResultsController` to significantly reduce the amount of code needed to manage a table view. Along the way, you learned how to recognize some common errors and make your code a bit more readable.

The ability to save and retrieve data adds many more possibilities for the kinds of apps you can create. Whether you are working with data created purely in an app or caching data from a server, Core Data gives you more flexibility, especially when combined with a fetched results controller.

With your data in a database, searching, sorting, and filtering become easier. In Chapter 10, you extend your knowledge of table views, adding searching, sorting, indexes, and even a custom cell to make your app look better.

Challenges

1. Add a new string attribute to the model called `name` and display it in the cars table. There are two things you need to know to make this work. First, any update to the model does not work with data created with earlier models unless you create migration code. Doing that is beyond the scope of this book. Instead, you need to delete the application and data from the simulator before running an app with a changed model. Second, to make it easier to display the name and date on the same line, you can use the Storyboard editor to change the prototype cell type from Right Detail to Subtitle. Then you can construct a string for the detail text label with the name followed by the date, in much the same way you do for the year/make/model label.

2. Add the ability to display the name in the car edit view. You need to use the Storyboard editor to add a cell for the name, use a property for the cell, and set the title of that cell in `viewDidLoad`.

3. Use `MakeModelEditViewController` and protocols to edit the name. Change the value of the name in the object so that when you return to the cars table, the cell updates.

4. Change the fetched results controller to sort by last name instead of creation date.

Table Views II: Advanced Topics

You started your table view journey in Chapter 8, "Table Views I: The Basics." But that was only part of the story for one of the central elements in building iOS apps. Many of the built-in Apple apps use more advanced table view features, such as custom cells, grouping, sorting, indexes, and searching. Contacts, Reminders, Mail, and other apps seamlessly integrate those features into the user experience.

In this chapter, you explore the more advanced features of table views, rounding out your ability to use this versatile element in your own apps. You start by creating your own car cell for the CarValet app, using the built-in basic one as a base. And now that app data is preserved, you will also be able to group and sort the table by various car attributes. To do that, you need to expand your knowledge of the fetched results controller and how Core Data makes the tasks easy.

As your app data grows in size, you then add some features to make it easier to get to the right car: adding an index down the right side of the table—not just an alphabetical one like Contacts creates, but one that can also move through the years. Finally, you wire up the table for search and discover the power of layered tables, as well as even more ways to use the fetched results controller.

By the end of the chapter, you will be able to create apps using the full power of tables. You will also know how to group, sort, and search your application data. Your journey into the power of table views begins by creating a custom cell for cars.

Custom Table View Cells

One of the tabs in the CarValet app lets you view images of cars. In a shipping application, those would be pictures of the cars taken with the device's camera. But you might not need to flip through full images; showing a thumbnail of the car image in the cars table might be enough to identify the car.

In this section, you customize the cell used to display the overview of a car. In addition, you learn how to use cells of a nonstandard height. You can start with an existing project or use the starter project from the folder CH10 CarValet Starter as a starting point for this chapter.

Your goal in this chapter is to create a custom cell that looks like Figure 10-1.

Figure 10-1   Custom car cell

There are a few things you can tell by looking at the desired cell:

- It is taller than a typical cell.

- There are three subviews: an image and two labels.

- The custom content needs to shift when the cell is in delete mode and a user either swipes or taps the Edit button.

- It uses a detail disclosure button.

So far you have not had to do any work to shift the content when a cell enters edit mode. This is because table view cells shift default types of content, including a property called the contentView. This is a UIView with all the content of the cell and, as Figure 10-2 shows, is already part of the prototype cells in IB.

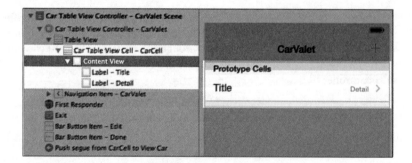

Figure 10-2   contentView in prototype cells

Creating your customized cell uses the same mechanism. In fact, any views you drag into a cell are put into the content view. Start by converting the current prototype cell to a custom one and setting the new size:

1. Select the current prototype cell and use the Attributes inspector to set the style of the cell to Custom, as shown in Figure 10-3.

Figure 10-3   Setting cell style to Custom

2. With the prototype cell still selected, choose the Size inspector, check the Custom box, and set Row Height to 68. This changes the cell height but not the height allocated by a UITableView. That number is set in the Size inspector for the table view.

3. With the Size inspector still active, select the table view and set Row Height to 68. You can see steps 2 and 3 in Figure 10-4.

Set Custom Cell Row Height

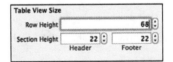

Set Custom Table View Row Height

Figure 10-4   Setting a custom row height

Adding the Custom Cell Visual Elements

With the row height set, you have enough room to add the visual elements. To lay out the cell, you need the car placeholder image for the cell, which you can find in the sample code for this chapter. Follow these steps:

1. Choose the `Images.xcassets` item in Xcode and add the `CH10 Assets Placeholder` folder included with the sample code for this chapter. You should have one item with two images.

2. Add a `UIImageView` to the container view and set the image to `placeholder`.

3. Use the alignment constraint popup to vertically center it in the container (though do not update frames yet).

4. Now, use the pin constraint popup to set the leading edge constraint to the standard distance and the width and height to 40. Set update frames and add the constraints.

5. Add a label roughly next to the image view. Set the font size of the label to 16 points and change the text to "Year Make Model."

6. Use the pin popup to set it the system distance from the leading and trailing edges. Then, select both the image view and the label and use the pin popup to align the top edges and update frames.

7. Duplicate the label, set the text to "Create Time," set the font size to 14 points, and the color to Dark Gray.

8. Set the constraints to be the system distance from the leading and trailing nearest neighbor and align the bottom edge with the image view. Once again, update the frames before applying the final alignment constraint.

9. Open the Assistant editor and make sure it is showing `CarTableViewCell.h`. When working with prototype cells or other kinds of nested views, it is important to make sure the right `.h` file is showing (if not, refer to step 1 of "Creating an Outlet" in Chapter 3, "Introducing Storyboards," just before Figure 3-6). The default file in this case is the one for the table view.

Now create the `IBOutlet` properties shown in Table 10-1 for the new view elements.

Table 10-1 `CarTableViewCell` **Properties**

Visual Element	Property Name
Image view	`carImage`
Top label with larger font	`makeModelLabel`
Bottom label in gray with smaller font	`dateCreatedLabel`

Populating the Cell

Modify `configureCell` in `CarTableViewCell.m` to populate the new visual elements. For now, you do not modify the car image. Here's what you do:

1. Modify the left-hand side of the line to assign the make, model, and year from `self.textLabel.text` to `self.makeModelLabel.text`.

2. Change `self.detailTextLabel.text` to `self.dateCreatedLabel.text`.

Run the app, and you see a cell similar to the one in Figure 10-1. Try creating, editing, and deleting cars. All this should work, and the new cells should display the correct values.

> **Note: If the Disclosure Indicator Is Not Showing**
>
> In the prerelease version of Xcode used for this book, the detail disclosure indicator did not show up when the cell was converted to a custom type. If this happens, try setting the accessory to None and then setting it back to detail disclosure.

Sections and Sorting

Your current table sort is not really set up with the end customer in mind. The valet might think in terms of time parked, but the end customer remembers his or her car. Helping the valet's customer, and therefore your customer, means adding the ability to sort by attributes of the car in addition to the park time. This makes four ways you could group the data: park time, car make, car model, or car year.

When you show groups, you need to make sure the sort order makes sense. Each of the four groups in this case has an associated sort: park time and car year are descending by time, and make and model are ascending.

In Chapter 9, "Introducing Core Data," you saw that a fetched results controller uses a fetch request to find data items. And a fetch request includes sort descriptors. Changing the sort in your table is as simple as changing the sort descriptors used by the fetch request. Try this:

1. Open `CarTableViewController.m` and go to the `viewDidLoad` method.

2. In the setup of `sortDescriptor`, change `initWithKey:` to `@"make"` from `@"dateCreated"`.

Run the app, and the list of cars is sorted by make, as shown on the left-hand side of Figure 10-5. The cars are sorted by model in reverse alphabetical order because `isAscending:` is still NO. You will fix this when you look more at how to sort a little later in this chapter.

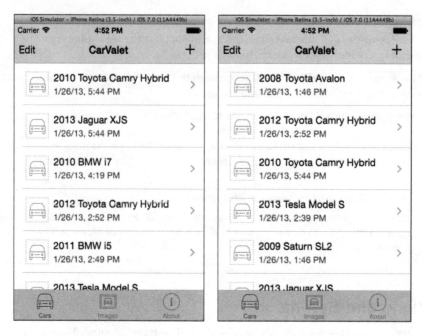

Sort on <code>createTime</code>   Sort on <code>make</code>

Figure 10-5   Changing sort descriptor key

Section Headers

Sorting is a good first step, though it is still difficult to find where each new car make begins and ends. This is a good place to use table sections and headers. The best way to think of a section is as a group of related data. In the contacts list, groups are based on the first letter of the last name (or first name, if that's what is set in the Settings app). In your app, all Chevrolets would be in one section, and all Mercedes would be in another.

In tables using a fetched results controller, you need to take only a few steps to show section headers. You already have a table sorted on `make`, so follow these steps to add the section headers:

1. Open `CarTableViewController.m` and go to `viewDidLoad`.

2. In the statement that allocates and initializes `fetchedResultsController`, change `sectionNameKeyPath:` to `@"make"` from `nil`.

3. Add the method in Listing 10-1 after `tableView:cellForRowAtIndexPath`.

Listing 10-1   Data Source Method for Section Titles

```
- (NSString *)tableView:(UITableView *)tableView
 titleForHeaderInSection:(NSInteger)section {

    id <NSFetchedResultsSectionInfo> sectionInfo;
    sectionInfo = [fetchedResultsController sections][section];   // 1
    return [sectionInfo name];                                    // 2
}
```

Here's what happens in the numbered lines in Listing 10-1:

1. Get the section information for `section` from the fetched results controller.

2. Base the name of the section on the value of the data in the `sectionNameKeyPath:` for every object in that section. In this case, it is the value of the `make` property.

Run the app in the simulator, and the cars are grouped by make. The header titles are the same as the name of the make for that group. One slight issue is that the table is sorted in reverse alphabetical order. Changing this is as simple as changing the ascending key in the sort descriptor from `NO` to `YES` in `viewDidLoad`. Run the app, and the sections are now in ascending alphabetical order.

Adding and Deleting Sections

Like rows, sections can be added and deleted. They are added when the first item in a section is created. For example, the cars table is currently grouped by make, and adding the first Chevrolet creates a new section. In the same way, sections are deleted when the last item for that section is deleted. Try this with your current app:

1. Find a section with only one car or, if needed, remove all but one car from a section.

2. Remove the last car from the section.

The app continues to work, but something like the following two errors are printed in the console (bold added for emphasis):

```
2013-08-30 17:02:47.831 CarValet[19648:a0b] *** Assertion failure in -[UITableView
_endCellAnimationsWithContext:], /SourceCache/UIKit_Sim/UIKit-2891.1/
UITableView.m:1310
2013-08-30 17:02:47.836 CarValet[19648:a0b] CoreData: error: Serious application
error.
An exception was caught from the delegate of NSFetchedResultsController during a call
to -controllerDidChangeContent:. Invalid update: invalid number of sections. The
number of sections contained in the table view after the update (6) must be equal to
the number of sections contained in the table view before the update (7), plus or
minus the number of sections inserted or deleted (0 inserted, 0 deleted). with
userInfo
(null)
```

The first error says something was not right after the table completed an animation—in this case, removing the last cell of a section. The second error sheds more light, as shown by the bold text. The problem is an invalid number of sections. Reading further, you can see that the fetched results controller returns the correct number of sections both before (7) and after (6) deleting the car. However, the table view is never updated, as you can see near the end of the second error: "the number of sections inserted or deleted (0 inserted, 0 deleted)."

You already update the table view when rows are added (inserted) and deleted by using `insertRowsAtIndexPaths:withRowAnimation:` and `deleteRowsAtIndexPaths:withRowAnimation:`. Now you can add the similar calls for sections by inserting the code in Listing 10-2. Put the code just below `controllerDidChangeContent:`.

Listing 10-2   Updating a Table When Sections Are Added/Deleted

```
- (void)controller:(NSFetchedResultsController *)controller
   didChangeSection:(id <NSFetchedResultsSectionInfo>)sectionInfo
          atIndex:(NSUInteger)sectionIndex
     forChangeType:(NSFetchedResultsChangeType)type {

  NSIndexSet *sections = [NSIndexSet indexSetWithIndex:sectionIndex];  // 1

  switch(type) {
      case NSFetchedResultsChangeInsert:                               // 2
          [self.tableView insertSections:sections
                      withRowAnimation:
                              UITableViewRowAnimationFade];
          break;

      case NSFetchedResultsChangeDelete:                               // 3
          [self.tableView deleteSections:sections
                      withRowAnimation:
                              UITableViewRowAnimationFade];
          break;
  }
}
```

Here's what happens in the numbered lines in Listing 10-2:

1. Create a set of the section to be inserted or deleted.

2. You are inserting a new section, so tell the table view to insert the section.

3. You are deleting an existing section, so tell the table view to delete the section.

The code you added also fixes a bug you did not encounter. Before you added the code in Listing 10-2, adding a new section would have caused a crash.

Run the app again and delete the last car from a section. No errors occur. However, there is another related problem. Change the make of a car in one section to the make of a car in a different section. Again, two errors are shown in the console, and although the app continues to run, it is in a strange state. In addition to the edited car not changing, some sections might be missing. Here's what you see onscreen (bold added for emphasis):

```
2013-08-30 17:07:09.271 CarValet[19705:a0b] *** Assertion failure in -[UITableView
_endCellAnimationsWithContext:], /SourceCache/UIKit_Sim/UIKit-2891.1/
UITableView.m:1326
2013-08-30 17:07:09.273 CarValet[19705:a0b] CoreData: error: Serious application
error.
An exception was caught from the delegate of NSFetchedResultsController during a call
to -controllerDidChangeContent:.  Invalid update: invalid number of rows in section 0.
The number of rows contained in an existing section after the update (2) must be equal
to the number of rows contained in that section before the update (3), plus or minus
the number of rows inserted or deleted from that section (0 inserted, 0 deleted) and
plus or minus the number of rows moved into or out of that section (0 moved in, 0
moved out). with userInfo (null)
```

Again, the clue is in the second error. This time, the invalid update text is not as helpful as the explanation of why the update was invalid. The rest of the error makes it clear that the change in section was not correctly reported to the table. That is, the index path for the moved data item was not updated to the new section. The code to update the table is already there, although it is commented out.

In `controller:didChangeObject:atIndexPath:forChangeType:newIndexPath:` uncomment the `NSFetchedResultsChangeMove` case. That code deletes cells from their old index paths—that is, sections—and adds them to their new ones.

This time when you run the app you can add, delete, and change cars without crashes.

Enabling Changing of Section Groups

Changing the groups shown in sections requires two main changes: an interface for the user to change the grouping and the code to update the sort and sections.

The interface presents four options: Parked, Make, Model, and Year. Parked corresponds to the default order on `dateCreated`. Using a `UISegmentedControl` is a good way to present a small number of options. Follow these steps:

1. Open `Main_iPhone.storyboard` and find the car table view controller.

2. Drag in a `UIView` between the bottom of the navigation bar and the top of the table view (the first prototype cell). Set the background color of the view to Mercury, and then use the Size inspector to set the height to 30 points.

3. Drag a `UISegmentedControl` into the new view, change the tint to magnesium, and set the number of segments to 4.

4. Set the constraints to the container to default for leading and trailing, and 6 for top and bottom. Update the frame when you update the constraints.

5. Change the segment names to Parked, Make, Model, and Year. You change a segment name by using the Attributes inspector for the segmented control. Select a segment from the Segment popup and then type in a new name and press Return. When you are done, the control should look as shown in Figure 10-6.

6. Show `CarTableViewController.h` in the Assistant editor and create an `IBOutlet` property called `tableHeader` for the `UIView` and another called `carSortControl` for the segmented control. Also, create an `IBAction` `carSortChanged:` that is sent when the value is changed, as shown in Figure 10-7.

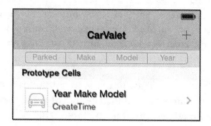

Figure 10-6   Sort selector for table view

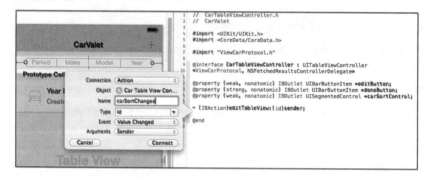

Figure 10-7   Adding `carSortChanged:` action

Adding Code to Change the Sort and Sections

Changing sections requires two code changes: creating a new sort descriptor using the correct data key and updating `sectionNameKeyPath` to correctly group the cars in the table view and set the section titles. Unfortunately, you cannot change the section name key path of a fetched results controller after it is allocated.

Because there is not a lot of data in this case, you replace the existing fetch results controller each time the sort order is changed.

> **Note**
>
> For applications with lots of data, creating a new fetch results controller when section group-ings change can be inefficient as the required fetch might take too long. In that case, you could create one fetched results controller for each key and switch between them. For more infor-mation, see Chapter 5 of *Learning Core Data for iOS: A Hands-on Guide to Building Core Data Applications* by Tim Roadley.

1. Open `CarTableViewController.m` in the editor and go to `viewDidLoad`.

2. Select the code starting with the line that allocates the `NSSortDescriptor` through the end of the `if` condition checking for an error with `performFetch:`, as shown in Figure 10-8.

3. Cut that code and paste it into the body of `carSortChanged:`.

4. In place of the code cut from `viewDidLoad`, type this line:

   ```
   [self carSortChanged:nil];
   ```

5. In `CarTableViewController.h`, add the following #defines above the interface declaration. These #defines map between the selected segment and the desired sort:

   ```
   #define kCarsTableSortDateCreated   0
   #define kCarsTableSortMake          1
   #define kCarsTableSortModel         2
   #define kCarsTableSortYear          3
   ```

6. Modify `carSortChanged:` so it looks like Listing 10-3. The code added after the paste is shown in bold.

```
- (void)viewDidLoad {
    [super viewDidLoad];

    AppDelegate *appDelegate = [[UIApplication sharedApplication] delegate];

    managedContextObject = appDelegate.managedObjectContext;

    fetchRequest = [NSFetchRequest fetchRequestWithEntityName:@"CDCar"];

    NSSortDescriptor *sortDescriptor = [[NSSortDescriptor alloc]
                                        initWithKey:@"make"
                                        ascending:NO];

    NSArray *sortDescriptors = [NSArray arrayWithObject:sortDescriptor];
    [fetchRequest setSortDescriptors:sortDescriptors];

    fetchedResultsController = [[NSFetchedResultsController alloc]
                                initWithFetchRequest:fetchRequest
                                managedObjectContext:managedObjectContext
                                sectionNameKeyPath:@"make"
                                cacheName:nil];
    fetchedResultsController.delegate = self;

    NSError *error = nil;
    [fetchedResultsController performFetch:&error];

    if (error != nil) {
        NSLog(@"Unresolved error %@, %@", error, [error userInfo]);
        abort();
    }

    self.navigationItem.leftBarButtonItem = self.editButton;
}
```

Figure 10-8   Selecting fetched results controller code

Listing 10-3   **Changing the Table Sections Based on Selected Sort**

```
- (IBAction)carSortChanged:(id)sender {
    NSString *sortKey;                                          // 1
    NSString *keyPath;                                          // 2
    BOOL isAscending;                                           // 3
    SEL compareSelector = nil;                                  // 4

    switch (self.carSortControl.selectedSegmentIndex) {         // 5
        case kCarsTableSortMake:
            sortKey = @"make";
            keyPath = sortKey;
            isAscending = YES;
            compareSelector = @selector(localizedCaseInsensitiveCompare:);
            break;

        case kCarsTableSortModel:
            sortKey = @"model";
            keyPath = sortKey;
            isAscending = YES;
            compareSelector = @selector(localizedCaseInsensitiveCompare:);
            break;

        case kCarsTableSortYear:
```

```
                sortKey = @"year";
                keyPath = sortKey;
                isAscending = NO;
                break;

        default:                                                    // 6
                sortKey = @"dateCreated";
                keyPath = nil;
                isAscending = NO;
                break;
    }

    NSSortDescriptor *sortDescriptor = [[NSSortDescriptor alloc]    // 7
                                        initWithKey:sortKey
                                        ascending:isAscending
                                        selector:compareSelector];

    [fetchRequest setSortDescriptors:@[sortDescriptor]];

    fetchedResultsController = [[NSFetchedResultsController alloc]   // 8
                                initWithFetchRequest:fetchRequest
                                managedObjectContext:managedContextObject
                                sectionNameKeyPath:keyPath
                                cacheName:nil];
    fetchedResultsController.delegate = self;

    NSError *error = nil;
    [fetchedResultsController performFetch:&error];                 // 9

    if (error != nil) {
        NSLog(@"Unresolved error %@, %@", error, [error userInfo]);
        abort();
    }

    [self.tableView reloadData];                                   // 10
}
```

Here's what happens in the numbered lines in Listing 10-3:

1. Specify a configuration variable for the property name used for sorting the cars.

2. Specify another configuration variable for the property name used for grouping cars into sections and for finding the section titles.

3. Determine whether the sort is ascending for alphabetical items or descending for time-based items.

4. For items that are based on strings, use a localized case-insensitive compare; otherwise, use the default `compare:` method.

5. Set up the configuration variables depending on how the table is sorted.

6. Setting `keyPath` to `nil` results in only one section with no title.

7. Set up the sort descriptor, using the configuration variables.

8. Set up the fetched results controller, using the configured key path.

9. Fetch the data from Core Data.

10. Tell the table to reload from the updated fetched data.

Run the app. If there are no cars with an unknown value for make, add one. Now tap the Sort by Make segment. You get an error something like this:

```
2013-08-30 19:40:15.396 CarValet[20992:a0b] CoreData: error:
(NSFetchedResultsController) A section returned nil value for section name key path
'make'. Objects will be placed in unnamed section
```

The error says some Core Data object is returning `nil` for the value of the property used to determine the section title, or the `sectionNameKeyPath:`, of the fetched results controller. In this case, the property key is `make`, and the object is the newly created car.

To solve this, give `make` and `model` default string values of Unknown. In addition to modifying the model, the only other change is to remove code that displays Unknown by checking for `nil`.

While the app is still running, for any car with an unknown make and/or model, either set them both to something valid or delete the car. Make sure the app saves data changes by exiting the app in the simulator using the Home button before using the inspector to stop the app. Use these steps to set the default values in the model and to update the app to use those values:

1. Open `CarValet.xcdatamodeld` in the Core Data editor.

2. Select the `make` attribute and show the Data Model inspector.

3. Change the default value to Unknown.

4. Do the same for the `model` attribute.

5. Search for all occurrences of Unknown in the project by selecting the Find icon in the Navigator and typing "Unknown", including the quotes, in the search box.

   You get a list of all occurrences of that string in the project, looking something like Figure 10-9.

6. In `CarTableViewCell.m`, remove the four lines assigning the make and model temporary strings and then modify the line that sets the `text` of the `makeModelLabel` (the new code is bold):

   ```
   self.makeModelLabel.text = [NSString stringWithFormat:@"%@ %@ %@",
   ```

```
[self.myCar.year stringValue],
self.myCar.make,
self.myCar.model];
```

7. In `ViewCarTableViewController.m`, replace the two conditional assignments in `viewDidLoad` with the following statements:

```
self.makeLabel.text = self.myCar.make;

self.modelLabel.text = self.myCar.model;
```

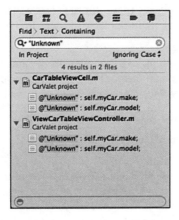

Figure 10-9   Results of a find in Xcode

Run the app and insert a new car. If the car data was saved earlier, you might have a car with a make and model of "(null)." That is a string representing a value of `nil`. You should either delete the car or change the make and model.

The app still shows Unknown for the new car's make and model. When you edit the car, the app also shows Unknown. Changing the sort order to make or model adds a section header and title for Unknown.

Adding an Index

A nice feature of the Contacts app is the quick A–Z index shown on the right side. Because you are using a fetched results controller, adding an index like this is as simple as adding the following two methods in `CarTableViewController.m` after `tableView:titleForHeaderInSection::`

```
- (NSArray *)sectionIndexTitlesForTableView:(UITableView *)tableView {
    return [fetchedResultsController sectionIndexTitles];
}

- (NSInteger)tableView:(UITableView *)tableView
        sectionForSectionIndexTitle:(NSString *)title
        atIndex:(NSInteger)index {
    return [fetchedResultsController sectionForSectionIndexTitle:title
                                                        atIndex:index];

}
```

Run the app, and you see A–Z indexes appear for the Make and Model sorts. Each index shows only the first letter of names that are in the table. If there are no cars with a make starting with Z, then Z is not in the list.

No matter what color scheme you picked, the index likely stands out, perhaps in a glaring fashion. Ideally, the index should be present but not overpowering. It should also be easier to see when a user is interacting with it. Three table view properties let you control those aspects:

- **sectionIndexColor**–The color of the text items in the index.

- **sectionIndexBackgroundColor**–The background color of the index view when not being touched.

- **sectionIndexTrackingBackgroundColor**–The background color when it is being touched.

One way you could configure the index is using the same combination you used for the header and sort order segment control: magnesium for the text and magnesium for the background. To keep the index from being overpowering, you can use a translucent version of magnesium using the alpha property of UIColor.

Add these lines to the end of viewDidLoad. Each set of statements sets up a color and then assigns it to one of the three index color properties:

```
UIColor *magnesium = [UIColor colorWithRed:204.0/255.0
                                     green:204.0/255.0
                                      blue:204.0/255.0
                                     alpha:1.0];
self.tableView.sectionIndexColor = magnesium;

UIColor *mercuryWithAlpha = [UIColor colorWithRed:230.0/255.0
                                            green:230.0/255.0
                                             blue:230.0/255.0
                                            alpha:0.1];
self.tableView.sectionIndexBackgroundColor = mercuryWithAlpha;

UIColor *mercury = [UIColor colorWithRed:230.0/255.0
                                   green:230.0/255.0
```

```
                              blue:230.0/255.0
                              alpha:1.0];
self.tableView.sectionIndexTrackingBackgroundColor = mercury;
```

Showing the Year in an Index

When you sort by year, you see only one or perhaps two index items. This is because the default title for an index is based on the first letter of whatever string is returned by the key. For the year property, the number is converted to a string, such as @"2012". Then the first character is added to the set of unique indexes. All the years in the current millennium are indexed by 2, and all from the previous millennium are indexed by 1. What you really want is to have the entire year used as the index title.

One way to do this is to create your own subclass of NSFetchedResultsController and specialize the implementation of sectionIndexTitleForSectionName: to return a custom string if the current sectionNameKeyPath is year.

Alternatively, you can modify the two methods you just added to return a different result for a table sorted by year. Which approach to take is a design decision and depends on both the reusability and maintainability of the code. Either way, the amount of code to add is small. For a subclass, you only need to define the one method. Changing the cars table also requires a small amount of code. In this case, you change the two methods you just entered.

When the table is sorted by year, the fetched results controller sections property contains the information for each section of grouped cars with the same year. Part of the property is the title of the section. You can use that title to construct the index list, as shown in the first method in Listing 10-4.

The second method is used to find which section is associated with a particular index. It is used to move the table to the correct section when the index is tapped. Implementing this method is easy to do because the passed-in index is the index of the section. See the second method in Listing 10-4.

Listing 10-4 **Creating an Index for Sorting by Year**

```
- (NSArray *)sectionIndexTitlesForTableView:(UITableView *)tableView {

    if (self.carSortControl.selectedSegmentIndex == kCarsTableSortYear) {   // 1
        NSMutableArray *indexes = [NSMutableArray new];                     // 2

        for (id <NSFetchedResultsSectionInfo> sectionInfo in               // 3
                fetchedResultsController.sections) {
            [indexes insertObject:[sectionInfo name]                         // 4
                    atIndex:[indexes count]];
        }

        return indexes;                                                     // 5
```

```
    }

    return [fetchedResultsController sectionIndexTitles];              // 6
}

- (NSInteger)tableView:(UITableView *)tableView
sectionForSectionIndexTitle:(NSString *)title
            atIndex:(NSInteger)index {

    if (self.carSortControl.selectedSegmentIndex == kCarsTableSortYear) {    // 7
        return index;
    }

    return [fetchedResultsController sectionForSectionIndexTitle:title      // 8
                                        atIndex:index];
}
```

Here's what happens in the numbered lines in Listing 10-4:

1. Check whether the table is sorted by year.

2. Set up a mutable array to hold the index titles.

3. The fetched results controller is sorted by year, so iterate through each section.

4. Insert the header string for the current section at the end of the titles array.

5. Return the array of year titles.

6. Getting to this line means the `if` condition at comment 1 failed. That means the table is sorted some other alphabetically based way, so return the default value.

7. If the table is sorted by year, the correct section number is just the index.

8. The table is not sorted by year, so return the default value.

Replace the current methods in `CarTableViewController.m` with the ones from Listing 10-4; then run the app and try each of the sorts. You see no index for the Parked sort, A–Z indexes for Make and Model, and the years for Year. Tapping on items in the index puts the section as close to the top of the table view as possible.

Searching Tables

The final functionality that could help the valet is to be able to search for a specific car. If the customer knows she has a BMW, filtering the content so that only BMWs show is a quick way to find her car.

Before you look at how to add searching to your table, it is useful to understand how searching works. In Figure 10-10, you can see the two stages of a search. On the left-hand side, the user

has tapped in the search field to bring up the keyboard and cover the main table with a translucent view. On the right-hand side, the current search results are displayed in a table below
the search field.

Figure 10-10   Search table view

Although the process of implementing a search seems like it might be complicated, most of
the hard work is done by `UISearchDisplayController`, an object associated with your own
view controller. When the user taps in the search field, the search display controller brings up
the keyboard and displays the black translucent view. It also creates a new table for any search
results, but it defaults to using your view controller's table data source and delegate methods.
This last part is very important to understand and is a source of confusion for many people
when they implement searching.

The first time a user types something into the search field, the following things happen:

1. Your controller gets a callback to update the search results.

2. The search results controller creates a search results table.

3. The new table view calls your view controller's table data source methods to build the
   search results table.

4. The search results table is displayed.

As the user updates the search text, callbacks are used to update the set of found items. When the number of items changes, the search results table updates.

Because the search results table uses the same data source and delegate, methods such as `numberOfSectionsInTableView:`, `tableView:numberOfRowsInSection:`, and `tableView:cellForRowAtIndexPath:` can be called for different tables. And even when these methods are called for the search results table, the main table view, `self.tableView`, is still valid. Figure 10-11 shows how this happens. The search results table (highlighted in red) is above the original table (highlighted in green) in the view hierarchy, so it covers the main table, though the main table is still there.

Search Results Table

self.tableView

Figure 10-11   Two table views for a search

Important: The Search Code Might Not Behave as Expected...

The beta builds of iOS 7 and Xcode 5 available when this book was written have at least one table view-related search bug that prevented the following code solution from working properly. There is another way to implement search combined with filtering using `UISearchBar`'s scope bar. However, that also was not working correctly in those builds.

If you find this code does not work, look at the errata for the book (available, if there is any, at www.informit.com/title/9780321862969). In addition, if a change in code is required, the sample code on GitHub will be updated with the correct way to implement the functionality, assuming the functionality is possible.

Adding Searching

When you add search capability to a table, you are really adding a few things:

- A `UISearchBar` for the user to enter search terms
- A `UISearchDisplayController` for managing the display of search results
- Methods from the `UISearchDisplayDelegate` protocol for updating the found items, as well as other state information
- Any required updates to the table view data source and/or delegate methods
- Any other required methods and/or variables for updating and maintaining state

You need to add the search bar and search display controller:

1. Open `CarTableViewController` in the storyboard.

2. Select the existing header view and change the height to 84 points. Make sure you have the header view selected. The best way to do this is using the left-hand list of scenes, controllers, views, and constraints.

3. Delete the top constraint from the filter segment control and move it down to the bottom of the new header. Ignore the constraint errors for now.

4. Look for a search bar with a search display controller, shown in Figure 10-12, in the objects shown in the utilities area. Drag it into the top of the header view, the one containing the filter bar.

Figure 10-12   Search bar and display controller

5. With the search bar still selected, check the option to show the Cancel button in the Attributes inspector.

6. Set the constraints for the search bar to be zero from the leading, trailing, and top edges of the container and its frame when the constraints are applied.

7. Select the filter segment controller and set a new vertical constraint of 6 points from the top of the segment control to the bottom of the search bar. Update the frame and the filter bar is now the correct size below the search bar.

Adding the Search Predicate

You are already using a fetched results controller for displaying data. You need to limit it to cars matching the search criteria. In addition to sorting cars, the fetch request can also filter the data. It does this using a predicate.

Predicates, or `NSPredicate`, provide a very flexible way to filter data on multiple criteria. You need a simple search, based on the current table grouping. For example, if cars are grouped by model, you look for any cars with a `model` attribute that contains the search string.

Whenever the search term changes, the search display delegate is sent a `searchDisplayController:shouldReloadTableForSearchString:` message. The method returns a `BOOL` that controls whether the search results table is updated. Update the predicate of your fetched results controller by following these steps:

1. Open `CarTableViewController.h` and add `UISearchDisplayDelegate` to the list of supported protocols.

2. In `CarTableViewController.m`, add the following just above `carToView`:

   ```
   #pragma mark – UISearchDisplayDelegate

   #pragma mark - ViewCarProtocol
   ```

3. Put the code in Listing 10-5 between the two #pragma marks you just added in step 2.

Listing 10-5   **Updating a Car Search Predicate**

```
- (BOOL)searchDisplayController:(UISearchDisplayController *)controller
        shouldReloadTableForSearchString:(NSString *)searchString {
    if (searchString && ([searchString length] > 0)) {            // 1
        fetchRequest.predicate = [NSPredicate predicateWithFormat: // 2
                            @"%K contains[cd] %@",                 // 3
                            [[fetchRequest.sortDescriptors         // 4
                               objectAtIndex:0] key],
                            searchString];                         // 5
    } else {
        fetchRequest.predicate = nil;                             // 6
    }

    NSError *error = nil;
```

```
[fetchedResultsController performFetch:&error];                    // 7

if (error != nil) {
    NSLog(@"Unresolved error %@, %@", error, [error userInfo]);
    abort();
}

return YES;                                                        // 8
}
```

Here's what happens in the numbered lines in Listing 10-5:

1. Check whether there is a search string with at least one character.

2. Set up a predicate based on the search string. Build the predicate using a predicate format string. Note that these are not the same as format strings. See the "Predicate Programming Guide" in the Apple documentation.

3. The string builds a predicate that checks whether the value of key, %K, contains the specified string %@. A key is the name of an object property. [cd] means use a case- and diacritical-insensitive comparison.

4. The name of the property, or key, is the same as the one used for sorting the data. For a table sorted by car model, the property is model.

5. Specify the search string to use for %@ in the predicate format string.

6. There is no search string, so clear any existing predicate.

7. Fetch any car objects that match the filter.

8. Tell the search results table to update.

Run the app, tap to sort the table by make, and then try to enter b into the search field. You get a crash report similar to the following (bold added for emphasis):

```
2013-08-30 20:48:01.641 CarValet[22058:a0b] *** Assertion failure in -
[UISearchResultsTableView dequeueReusableCellWithIdentifier:forIndexPath:],
/SourceCache/UIKit_Sim/UIKit-2891.1/UITableView.m:5184
2013-08-30 20:48:01.653 CarValet[22058:a0b] *** Terminating app due to uncaught
exception 'NSInternalInconsistencyException', reason: 'unable to dequeue a cell with
identifier CarCell - must register a nib or a class for the identifier or connect a
prototype cell in a storyboard'
```

The second error tells you where to look for the problem. The table view is unable to dequeue a cell with an identifier of CarCell because no such cell has been registered. You might wonder why this crash occurs because it worked fine until now.

Look at the line that allocates the cell in `tableView:cellForRowAtIndexPath:`

```
CarTableViewCell *cell = [tableView
                    dequeueReusableCellWithIdentifier:CellIdentifier
                    forIndexPath:indexPath];
```

The dequeue message is sent to `tableView`, whatever view is passed in to the method. In this case, `tableView` is the search results view, not the main table. `CarCell` is registered with the main table, not the search table.

Although there is a method to register a cell class with a cell identifier, that does not work for the search table. `CarCell` is based on the storyboard prototype custom cell you set up earlier in this chapter. Xcode associated the cell identifier with the prototype. You have no way to use that same mechanism for the search table. Instead, you can change the following line in `tableView:cellForRowAtIndexPath:` (the change is shown in bold):

```
CarTableViewCell *cell = [self.tableView dequeueReusableCellWithIdentifier:
                    CellIdentifier];
```

Make sure you remove the index path part of the dequeue call. When you have done that, run the app again, tap to sort by make, and type b into the search field. The search results table looks something like the left side of Figure 10-10, depending on your data.

All the correct data is displayed, but the custom cells do not fit. Once again, it is because the search results table is different. You need to set the `rowHeight` to 68 so it is high enough for the custom cell. Add the following method after the code from Listing 10-5:

```
- (void)searchDisplayController:(UISearchDisplayController *)controller
    didLoadSearchResultsTableView:(UITableView *)tableView {
    tableView.rowHeight = self.tableView.rowHeight;
}
```

The method is called the first time the search display controller creates and loads the search results table. The one line sets the row height for the new table to the row height of the main table.

Run the app, change the group and search, and now the search results table looks correct. Cancel the search, and you see another error:

```
2013-06-03 15:06:01.668 CarValet[14554:c07] *** Terminating app due to uncaught
exception 'NSRangeException', reason: '*** -[__NSArrayM objectAtIndex:]: index 2
beyond bounds [0 .. 0]'
```

Finding the source of this error requires setting a breakpoint for all exceptions, which is covered in Chapter 14, "Instruments and Debugging." When the breakpoint is set, run the app. You see that the app crashes in `tableView:titleForHeaderInSection:` and, more specifically, it crashes because the fetched results controller has only one section but is being asked for information on a second section.

This error occurs because the fetched results controller is used for both the main and search results tables. Searching can change the data, including the number of sections and the number of cars in each section. When the search is cancelled, no code is run to reset the fetched results controller back to the presearch state. The easiest way to do that is to set the fetch request predicate to `nil`, and that is already done in `searchDisplayController:shouldReloadTableForSearchString:` when the string is empty.

Add the following to the search display delegate methods:

```
- (void)searchDisplayControllerWillEndSearch:(UISearchDisplayController *)
            controller {
  [self searchDisplayController:controller
      shouldReloadTableForSearchString:@""];
}
```

`searchDisplayControllerWillEndSearch:` is called after the user ends the search but before the main table is updated. Using an empty string results in clearing the fetch request predicate and updating the fetch request controller.

Run the app again, change the sort, search, and then cancel. Everything now works. Search again and tap one of the found cars. There are no car details—or if there are, they are wrong.

Showing Details for a Found Car

The car detail view finds what car to display by calling `carToView`, a method from the `ViewCarProtocol`. The cars table uses the index path of the selected cell to look up the car in the fetched results controller. And that is the problem.

This is the current call:

```
currentViewCarPath = [self.tableView indexPathForSelectedRow];
```

Once again, the message is to the main table view when it needs to be to the search table.

The simplest solution is to track what table view is displayed to the user. You know that it is the main table view when the controller first appears. The only times the current table view switches are when the search display controller loads and unloads the search table. Both of those events have associated methods. Add the following code to track the currently active table:

1. Open `CarTableViewController.m` in an editor and add the following variable declaration to the ones in curly braces just after the `@implementation` statement:

   ```
   UITableView *currentTableView;
   ```

2. In `viewDidLoad`, set the current table to the main table by adding this line just before setting `tableHeaderView`:

   ```
   currentTableView = self.tableView;
   ```

3. Set the current table to the search results table by adding the following line to the end of `searchDisplayController:didLoadSearchResultsTableView:`

   ```
   currentTableView = tableView;
   ```

4. Set the current table back to the main table with this line at the end of `searchDisplayControllerWillEndSearch:`

   ```
   currentTableView = self.tableView;
   ```

5. Fix the two `ViewCarProtocol` methods, `carToView` and `carViewDone:`, by changing `self.tableView` to `currentTableView`.

Run the app, sort by make, search for a car, and then look at the details. The details show correctly. Now change the model information and tap Done. You get a crash with errors that look like this:

```
2013-06-03 17:07:12.874 CarValet[16312:c07] *** Assertion failure in -[UITableView
_endCellAnimationsWithContext:], /SourceCache/UIKit_Sim/UIKit-2380.17/
UITableView.m:1054
2013-06-03 17:07:21.106 CarValet[16312:c07] CoreData: error: Serious application
error.
An exception was caught from the delegate of NSFetchedResultsController during a call
to -controllerDidChangeContent:.  Invalid update: invalid number of sections.  The
number of sections contained in the table view after the update (1) must be equal to
the number of sections contained in the table view before the update (7), plus or
minus the number of sections inserted or deleted (0 inserted, 0 deleted). with
userInfo
(null)
```

You have seen similar problems where the sections are not in sync. In this case, the difference in the number of sections is quite large: 1 after the update and 7 before. There is also the name of the method where the failure occurred, `controllerDidChangeContent:`. A quick look at that method shows that it sends a message to the main table view. This particular update is occurring in the search table.

Searching the file shows that there are still 12 other occurrences of `self.tableView`. Not all of them need to change. Some are used to update the state of `currentTableView`, another occurs when the Edit button is touched, and yet another occurs when the table sort is changed.

Of the others, five are in `NSFetchedResultsControllerDelegate` methods, and all of them need to change. You therefore need to use the find and replace mechanism, as follows:

1. Choose Edit > Find > Find and Replace.

2. Type `self.tableView` into the top bar and `currentTableView` into the bottom bar. The search area looks like Figure 10-13.

3. Click the right arrow next to the top bar until `self.tableView` in `controllerWillChangeContent:` is highlighted, as shown in Figure 10-13.

4. Click Replace & Find four times.

5. Click Replace to change the occurrence in `controllerDidChangeContent:`.

Figure 10-13   Finding and replacing in the Xcode editor

You need to make one more change to get the full detail flow working. Run the CarValet app, sort the table by make, and use Find to select a car that was visible in the main table before the Find interface opened. Make a change to the model of that car, go back to Find, and cancel the find. The model is changed in the search results table but not in the main table. Although the data model is correct, nothing updated the main table when searching was done.

Add the following line at the end of `searchDisplayControllerWillEndSearch:`

```
[self.tableView reloadData];
```

Now the whole flow works correctly.

An Index for Searching

Earlier in the chapter you added an index for quickly navigating to different sections. Some apps show a magnifying glass at the top of the index that you can use to quickly go to the search area.

The magnifying glass is a special item defined by the system. Adding it to an index requires modifying the methods that return the section titles and finding a section for a given title and index.

Replace `sectionIndexTitlesForTableView:` with the code in Listing 10-6. Then replace `tableView:sectionForSectionIndexTitle:atIndex:` with Listing 10-7.

Listing 10-6   **Building the Array of Index Titles**

```
- (NSArray *)sectionIndexTitlesForTableView:(UITableView *)tableView {
    NSMutableArray *indexes;                                              // 1

    if (self.carSortControl.selectedSegmentIndex == kCarsTableSortYear) {   // 2
        indexes = [NSMutableArray new];

        for (id <NSFetchedResultsSectionInfo> sectionInfo in
```

```
                  fetchedResultsController.sections) {
                [indexes insertObject:[sectionInfo name]
                          atIndex:[indexes count]];
        }
    } else {
        indexes = [fetchedResultsController sectionIndexTitles].mutableCopy;  // 3
    }

    [indexes insertObject:UITableViewIndexSearch atIndex:0];                   // 4

    return indexes;                                                            // 5
}
```

Here's what happens in the numbered lines in Listing 10-6:

1. Use a mutable array of indexes for inserting the search item.

2. If sorting by year, build the titles from full year strings.

3. Otherwise it is an alphabetical sort, so let the fetched results controller build the index of titles.

4. Insert the search item as the first index item.

5. Return the modified indexes.

Listing 10-7   **Finding the Section Index for a Title or Title Index**

```
- (NSInteger)tableView:(UITableView *)tableView
            sectionForSectionIndexTitle:(NSString *)title
            atIndex:(NSInteger)index {
    if (index == 0) {                                                // 1
        [tableView setContentOffset:CGPointZero animated:NO];        // 2
        return NSNotFound;                                           // 3
    } else {
        index = index - 1;                                           // 4

        if (self.carSortControl.selectedSegmentIndex == kCarsTableSortYear) {
            return index;                                            // 5
        }

        return [fetchedResultsController sectionForSectionIndexTitle:title  // 6
                                                   atIndex:index];
    }
}
```

Here's what happens in the numbered lines in Listing 10-7:

1. An index of 0 means the user picked the search item (the magnifying glass icon).

2. Move the table to the top so the search bar is visible.

3. Let the caller know there is no corresponding section.

4. Otherwise, it is a valid section. To find the right section, subtract 1 from the index to remove the search item added in `sectionIndexTitlesForTableView:`.

5. If sorting by year, the modified index is the correct section.

6. The sort is alphabetical so let the fetched results controller return the result.

Run the app, and the magnifying glass appears. Tapping the item scrolls the table to the search bar. All the other index items work correctly as well.

Summary

Your journey through the main power of table views is complete. In this chapter, you subclassed the built-in cell class to build a custom cell and added sorting, grouping, searching, and even an index to your app.

You began by building a better car cell, using the storyboard. You used a larger height for better data presentation. You added a custom class to initialize the cell data and figured out how to show cells of different heights in a table.

You used the app data saved with Core Data along with a fetched results controller to sort the cars and add grouping to the table. Then you made navigating all the data easier by adding an index. Finally, you went deeper with Core Data and added searching. As you did that, you discovered that searching a table actually results in two tables, with both using the same delegate and data source. To deal with that, you modified the methods to work well with both your cars table and the search table.

Along the way, you worked with `UISegmentedControl`, a visual element for switching between choices. You also learned a bit more about debugging and the usefulness of `#define`.

Now you can create apps for iPhone and iPod touch, using three of the main controllers for a device that size. Your apps can include the full power of table views, especially when backed by Core Data. And your designs can incorporate a segmented control where you need to switch between a few states.

Of course, the handheld form factor is only about 50% of all possible iOS devices. Chapter 11, "Navigation Controllers II: Split View and the iPad," opens the world of tablets as you adapt CarValet to work on that form factor in addition to the iPhone/iPod touch form factor. You do that with one of the most-used iPad controllers.

Challenges

1. Add sections to the Parked grouping. Base the sections on the hour of the day the car was parked. For example, have all cars parked at 10 a.m. grouped into one section, sorted by time parked, with the latest at the top.

2. Update the index title for the modified parked grouping in Challenge 1 to show the hour, from 11 p.m. down to midnight. You can use 12- or 24-hour format.

3. For a greater challenge, add the owner's first name and last name to the CDCar, add them to the car cell, and add them to the detail. Then add an item to group by last name, ensuring that you can search on that key.

Navigation Controllers II: Split View and the iPad

iPads account for almost half of iOS devices. As of June 2013, there were more than 600 million total iOS devices. Depending on the statistics you look at, iPads account for anywhere from 40% to 60% of those units. All iPhone apps will run on iPad, but they do so in a special mode. For the user, the app screen is centered on the display at actual or double size. Either experience is less than optimal. Creating a universal app, one that uses appropriate screen layouts and graphics on both iPhone and iPad, gives you the best chance of reaching customers using either handheld or tablet devices.

If you have not used an iPad, or even if you have, you might wonder why you need to do something different for a tablet. The basic answer is that the screens are much bigger. They can show more stuff, so they do not have the same restrictions as the smaller phone screens. Currently, the CarValet app is optimized for small spaces; now you need to adapt your user experience for a larger screen.

For navigation-based apps like CarValet, iPad's `UISplitViewController` is the controller of choice. It takes full advantage of the iPad screen by maximizing the detail area, while still providing a place for navigation, typically a table view–based hierarchy. Settings, Notes, and Mail are just some of the many apps that use this versatile controller.

After becoming familiar with the basics of the split view controller, you add one to the iPad storyboard. Next, you focus on navigation, starting with the car list. You add the other app sections and some nice animations as the user moves between them. To complete your investigation of navigation, you add the code to work in both landscape and portrait.

With navigation done, you move on to adapting the detail screens for iPad. To do this, you both create new screens and reuse old ones. You learn ways to choose which approach to take. Finally, you hook it all together so the user can do everything in CarValet the same as on iPhone but in a way that suits the iPad experience.

Split View Controller

UISplitViewController is very simple, defining only three public properties and no public methods. Even the delegate protocol has only four methods. The power is in how split view controller manages two other view controllers: one for a master or menu view, and another for the detail.

Figure 11-1 shows these three controllers in the iPad Mail app. The split view controller, outlined in green, is the app window root view. Inside are the master view controller on the left outlined in red and the detail view controller on the right in blue.

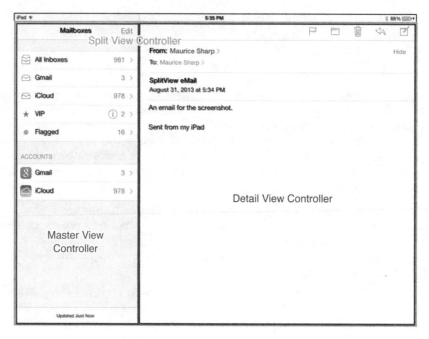

Figure 11-1   Split view controller

Figure 11-2 shows the same controller in portrait. On the left side, the master view controller appears to be missing, but it is still there, just not visible. Tapping the upper-left navigation bar button opens the navigation controller popover, as shown in the right-hand image. As long as you support the UISplitViewControllerDelegate protocol and write a little code, most of the work of showing and hiding the master controller is done for you. You can also choose to not show it or to show it all the time.

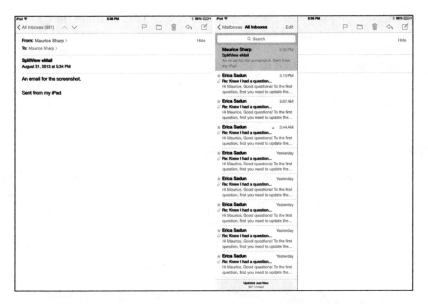

Figure 11-2   Portrait split view controller with master view hidden and shown

To use a split view controller, you need to do the following:

1. Create master and detail view controllers.

2. Set up master view navigation.

3. Implement the `UISplitViewControllerDelegate` protocol.

4. Show appropriate content in the detail view, based on the state of the master view.

Creating the master and detail controllers depends on what kind of content is displayed. Most of the time both are `UINavigationControllers`, enabling flexible navigation as well as adding navigation bars.

Master view navigation is easy to set up using a subclass of table view controller for the root. For navigation, you can use either segues or `tableView:didSelectRowAtIndexPath:` to push new table views. The navigation controller handles moving back in the menu hierarchy.

Unless you do not need to show the master view in portrait mode, you need to implement the `UISplitViewControllerDelegate` protocol. Minimally, it needs to allow showing the master view in both orientations. More likely, you will use it to manage the popover, including adding a navigation bar button for showing the popup.

The last step ties everything else together. When a user taps on a leaf node in the hierarchy, you need to update content in the detail controller. When the user taps a car, you show the car, and tapping About shows the About screen. The important thing to understand is that there is no default connection between the master and detail views. You have to do the work required to show appropriate detail, based on whatever is tapped, or change the detail when something else, such as a different car, is selected. And because the detail view is likely a navigation controller, you have to hide the Back button and make sure you are not accidentally pushing or popping too many view controllers.

The next section takes you through adding the split view and creating the master and detail view controllers, as well as some changes required to run the application.

Adding a Split View Controller

CarValet is already configured to be a universal app. At the moment, you cannot run it on an iPad, but as you will see soon, that is only because of some tab bar-specific code. Without that code, you would see a blank screen. This makes sense because the storyboard for iPad, added by Xcode as part of the initial project, is a view controller with an empty view.

You can make any new project universal by using the Device popup in Xcode, as shown in Figure 11-3.

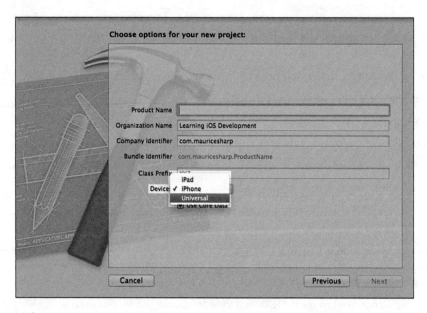

Figure 11-3   Creating a universal project

In this section, you add everything needed to show a split view controller with a basic menu and static detail content.

Although you can start from your own version of the project, it is better to use CH11 CarValet Starter, the project provided with the sample code for this chapter. Unlike previous chapters, it has changes beyond the end of Chapter 10, "Table Views II: Advanced Topics." All the changes are organizational, using Xcode's grouping feature to put related files into folders that indicate their purpose. Figure 11-4 shows the updated grouping. If you want to use your own project, the next paragraph and figure summarize the changes.

The Model folder contains the Core Data model and CDCar files. View contains the custom car table view cell. The Controller folder has the bulk of the files, including related storyboards, protocols, and XIB files. Some projects split this folder further by grouping related controllers into folders. Finally, the Old folder has files that were part of the older projects but are no longer used. In a real development project using source code control (or indeed the project used to create the sample code), these files would be deleted because they are archived. They are left in the samples in case you need to refer to something in those files. The Supporting Files folder is untouched.

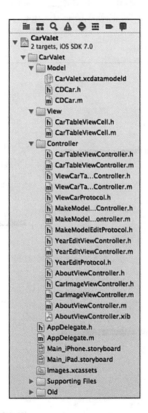

Figure 11-4   New project organization

To add an iPad group for the classes, follow these steps:

1. Select the CarValet project group folder.

2. Create a new group either by choosing File > New > Group, pressing Cmd-Option-N, or Ctrl-clicking the folder and choosing New Group.

3. Rename the folder iPad and move it below the Controller group.

Adding the Split View Controller

To add the split view controller, you need to first remove any existing controllers and then set up the split view, master, and detail controllers. Follow these steps:

1. Open `Main_iPad.storyboard` in the standard editor configuration.

2. Select the existing view controller and delete it.

3. Drag the split view controller onto the storyboard. Doing this adds four controllers and three relationships, as shown in the zoomed-out storyboard of Figure 11-5.

   The split view controller is added on the left. The top relationship is the master view controller. The current version of Xcode defaults to a navigation controller with a table view as the root. The bottom relationship is the detail view, which defaults to a simple view controller.

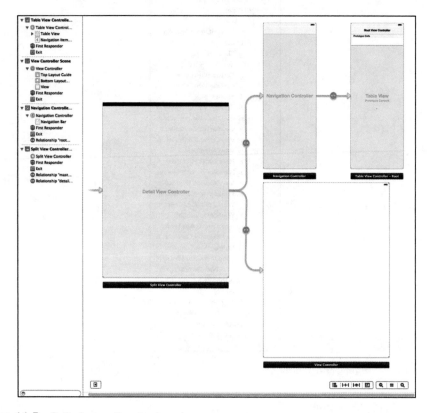

Figure 11-5   Split view on the storyboard

4. Replace the existing detail view controller shown on the lower right in Figure 11-5 with a `UINavigationController`. Removing the existing controller might require clicking outside any controller to deselect everything before selecting the detail controller. When selected, press the Delete key to remove it. Then drag out a `UINavigationController` from the object library.

5. Drag a connection from the split view controller to the new navigation controller and set it to a detail view controller relationship segue, as shown in Figure 11-6.

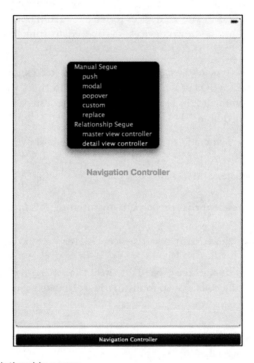

Figure 11-6   Detail relationship segue

6. Use the Attributes inspector to set the Size simulated metric of the new navigation controller to Detail. Now the Storyboard editor shows connected controllers in the correct size in portrait or landscape. You can see this by setting the simulated orientation of the split view controller to Landscape. Both the navigation controller and the root view controller change size. Change the orientation back to Inferred.

7. Delete the default table view controller added for the detail navigation controller.

8. Add a `UIViewController` and then set it as the root view controller for the detail navigation controller by dragging out a relationship segue.

You now have an iPad storyboard with a split view controller. Both the master and detail parts of the split view use navigation controllers, but neither has any content. Select the iPad simulator, make sure you have a breakpoint to catch all exceptions, and run the app. (If you are not sure how to set a breakpoint for all exceptions, see the "Another Useful Breakpoint" section in Chapter 14, "Instruments and Debugging.")

The CarValet app crashes in `application:didFinishLaunchingWithOptions:` while trying to set up a tab bar. But the iPad app doesn't use a tab bar. The solution is to set up the tab bar only for an iPhone. Your first thought might be to check the specific device your app is running on and compare that to known devices to see if it is an iPhone or iPad. That would only work as long as your list of known devices was up to date, something that's very hard to do.

Instead of checking for the type of device, what you really need to know is whether the interface is a kind of phone or not. iOS provides a utility routine to check the idiom, or kind, of interface. The call is in comment 2 in Listing 11-1. Follow these steps to set up the tab bar only on devices using the phone idiom:

1. Open `AppDelegate.h` and add the following line of code above the `@interface` statement:

    ```
    @class AboutViewController;
    ```

2. Define the `aboutViewController` property by inserting this line of code below the definition of `window`:

    ```
    @property (strong, nonatomic) AboutViewController *aboutViewController;
    ```

3. Change the top part of `application:didFinishLaunchingWithOptions:` in `AppDelegate.m` to the code shown in Listing 11-1. Updated code is shown in bold.

Listing 11-1 Checking for iPad

```
- (BOOL)application:(UIApplication *)application
    didFinishLaunchingWithOptions:(NSDictionary *)launchOptions {

    self.aboutViewController = [[AboutViewController alloc]          // 1
                              initWithNibName:@"AboutViewController"
                                       bundle:[NSBundle mainBundle]];

    if (UI_USER_INTERFACE_IDIOM() == UIUserInterfaceIdiomPhone) {    // 2
        UITabBarController *tabBarController =
                        (UITabBarController*)self.window.rootViewController;

        UITabBarItem *aboutItem = [[UITabBarItem alloc]
                              initWithTitle:@"About"
                              image:[UIImage imageNamed:@"info"]
                              tag:0];
```

```
    [self.aboutViewController setTabBarItem:aboutItem];

    NSMutableArray *currentItems;
    currentItems = [NSMutableArray
                        arrayWithArray:tabBarController.viewControllers];

    [currentItems addObject:self.aboutViewController];
    [tabBarController setViewControllers:currentItems animated:NO];
}

UIColor *mocha = [UIColor colorWithRed:128.0/255.0 green:64.0/255.0
                            blue:0.0 alpha:1.0];
...
```

Here's what happens in the numbered lines in Listing 11-1:

1. The about view is used on both iPhone and iPad, so always create it and assign it to a public property.

2. Set up the tab bar only if running on an iPhone (a phone-type device).

Run the app again and everything should work, though there is not much to see. Next, you start adding content by adding the main menu.

Tip: See the Whole Simulator

If you have a large enough screen, showing an iPhone 5 simulator full size works. On a laptop, that is a challenge. For an iPad retina, even a large screen can be too small. The secret is using the Window > Scale menu item to show a scaled-down version of the device. The default choices and their keyboard shortcuts are 100% (Cmd-1), 75% (Cmd-2), or 50% (Cmd-3).

Adding App Section Navigation

The CarValet app has three main sections: Cars, Images, and About. The iPhone uses a tab view for navigation between sections. You could use the same controller on an iPad, but it would not look very good. Tabs are designed for a small screen space. On iPad, each tab would be extremely wide, giving the screen a strange look.

This is one of the reasons the split view controller was created. It allows the same kind of section navigation but fits better in the larger screen. You already have a table view for navigation; the next step is adding the cells for each section.

The top-level menu stays the same, so you don't need to dynamically generate the cells. Instead, you can use a feature of `UITableViewController` for creating static cells (as you saw in Chapter 8, "Table Views I: The Basics"). It is a good idea for universal apps to have common elements between the iPhone and iPad versions since a customer could use both. You can use the images from the tab bar buttons for the menu table cells as well as the same section titles. When you are done with these steps, the menu should look as shown in Figure 11-7.

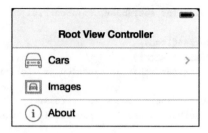

Figure 11-7   The main navigation menu

1. Open the iPad storyboard if it is not already open, and expand the contents of the table view controller in the left-hand list. Select the table view and open the Attributes inspector in the utilities area.

2. Change the content of the table from Dynamic Prototypes to Static Cells, as shown in Figure 11-8. A table view section, containing three cells, is added.

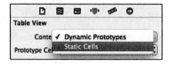

Figure 11-8   Setting a table to Static Cells

3. If there are more or fewer than three cells, select Table View Section in the left-hand list of view controllers and set the Rows to 3.

4. Drag a UIImageView into the first cell. Use constraints to set the width and height to 34 points, and then move the left edge so it is the system distance from the left edge of the cell. Finally, vertically center the image view. Make sure you update the frame.

5. Drag a label into the cell. Set the constraints to vertically centered in the cell, and the system distance from the image view and trailing container edge. Again, make sure to update the frame.

6. Select the image view and label, and Option-drag a copy into the next cell, using the same spacing. Do this once more for the final cell. Update the constraints in the last two cells to be the same as the first one.

7. Set the labels and images as shown in Table 11-1.

Table 11-1   **Main Menu Images and Labels**

Cell	Label	Image Name
1	Cars	car
2	Images	photo
3	About	info

8. The images look distorted because the display mode defaults to Scale To Fill, so for each image view, set the scale mode to Center, as shown in Figure 11-9.

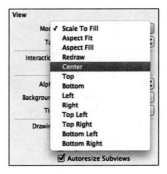

Figure 11-9   Setting the view mode to Center

9. Select the first cell and use the Attributes inspector to set Accessory to Disclosure Indicator.

    If you get the yellow warning for constraints or if the image and label disappear for the first cell, update the frames for the views in that cell.

Run the app, and if needed, rotate the device so it is shown in landscape. The three menu items are shown and selectable. Now it is time to add a bit more customization.

Tints, Title, and Generic Detail

The CarValet app still looks fairly generic. To change that, you can customize the navigation bar tint and add a title. Follow these steps:

1. Instead of manually changing the tint for each navigation bar, use the appearance mechanism you used for buttons. Open up `AppDelegate.m` and add this code to the bottom of `application:didFinishLaunchingWithOptions:`

```
UIColor *sky = [UIColor colorWithRed:102.0/255.0 green:204.0/255.0
                                blue:1.0 alpha:1.0];
[[UINavigationBar appearance] setBarTintColor:sky];
```

2. Clear the text in the title of the main menu navigation bar. Double-click the existing Root View Controller text and delete it.

3. Set the title of the detail controller bar to CarValet. The double-clicking trick does not work here because there is no text. Instead, select the navigation item from the left-hand list and use the Attributes inspector to set the title.

Now it is time to make the default detail view more interesting. Follow these steps:

1. Import the CH11 Assets Detail Default folder that comes with the code for this chapter into Images.xcassets. The image is a photo of the overflow valet parking tent outside Infinite Loop 1, the worldwide headquarters of Apple. Both normal and retina resolutions are included.

2. Open the iPad storyboard and replace the UIView in the root detail view with a UIImageView.

3. Set the image of the new view to Detail Default and the mode to Aspect Fill. If you do not set the mode, the image appears squished in landscape.

Run the app again. This time you should see the new colors and the nicer looking default detail view. Next, you add the about view and enable the portrait popover menu.

Adding About

Tapping a menu item should cause the CarValet app to behave similarly to tapping a tab bar item. If the content is not showing in detail, tapping should cause it to show. If the content is already showing, then unlike in the tab bar, tapping should do nothing.

Although you have only created three menu items, there are really five menu states, since Cars shows the list of cars. Table 11-2 lists what is in the detail view for each state.

Table 11-2   **Detail View Content for App States**

App State	Detail View Content
Nothing selected/initial launch	Default image
About menu item selected	AboutViewController
Images menu item selected	CarImagesViewController
Cars menu item selected	Default image (menu changes to cars list)
Individual car selected	Detail for the selected car

The detail view is a navigation controller, so you can push, pop, and even set the array of view controllers. Two of the detail items, About and Images, already exist, so there is no need to re-create them in the iPad storyboard. This means you do not use segues to transition.

Creating `MainMenuViewController`

Creating a custom class for a table using static cells is much easier than creating one using dynamic cells. The system handles all the methods to determine number of sections, determine number of rows, and create cells. All you need is `tableView:didSelectRowAtIndexPath:` for acting on user selections. Add the functionality for the main menu by following these steps:

1. With the iPad folder selected, create a subclass of `UITableViewController` called `MainMenuViewController`.

2. In the .m file, replace the contents with the following:

   ```
   #import "MainMenuViewController.h"

   #import "AppDelegate.h"

   @implementation MainMenuViewController

   - (void)viewDidLoad {
       [super viewDidLoad];

   }

   #pragma mark - Table view delegate

   - (void)tableView:(UITableView *)tableView
           didSelectRowAtIndexPath:(NSIndexPath *)indexPath {

   }

   @end
   ```

3. Add the following #defines to `MainMenuViewController.h` below the #import:

   ```
   #define kPadMenuCarsItem      0
   #define kPadMenuImagesItem    1
   #define kPadMenuAboutItem     2
   ```

4. In the Layout editor, select the table view controller and use the Identity inspector to set its class to `MainMenuViewController`.

5. Change `tableView:didSelectRowAtIndexPath:` to the code in Listing 11-2.

Listing 11-2   **Showing the About View**

```
- (void)tableView:(UITableView *)tableView
        didSelectRowAtIndexPath:(NSIndexPath *)indexPath {

  AppDelegate *appDelegate = [UIApplication sharedApplication].delegate;
```

```
UIWindow *mainWindow = appDelegate.window;
UISplitViewController *splitViewController = (UISplitViewController*)    // 1
                        mainWindow.rootViewController;
UINavigationController *detailController = (UINavigationController*)    // 2
                        [splitViewController.viewControllers lastObject];

UIViewController *nextController;

switch (indexPath.row) {
    case kPadMenuCarsItem:
        [detailController popToRootViewControllerAnimated:YES];    // 3
        break;

    case kPadMenuImagesItem:
        [detailController popToRootViewControllerAnimated:YES];
        break;

    case kPadMenuAboutItem:                                         // 4
        nextController = (UIViewController*)appDelegate.aboutViewController;

        if (![detailController.topViewController
                isMemberOfClass:nextController.class]) {            // 5
            [detailController pushViewController:nextController     // 6
                                        animated:YES];
        }

        break;
    }
}
```

Here's what happens in the numbered lines in Listing 11-2:

1. The split view controller is the root view controller of the main app window.

2. A split view controller has two view controllers. The first is the master, and the second, or last, is the detail controller.

3. If the user tapped the Cars or Images menu item, show the default detail image.

4. The user selects the about view, so get a reference from the app delegate.

5. Check if the about view is already showing. You can do that by looking at the class of the controller currently displayed in the detail navigation controller. If the class is the same as the about view class, then it is already being shown.

6. The about view is not shown, so push it into the detail area.

Run the app, make sure the simulator is in landscape, and try tapping the different menu items. Tapping the About menu shows the about view, and tapping on a different item either pops the about view off the stack or leaves the default detail image in place.

There are two issues with the navigation bar for the about view. First, there is no title. Second, the Back button appears. You can fix both these issues in `AppDelegate.m application:` `didFinishLaunchingWithOptions:` by adding the following `else` condition after the check for an iPhone (the new code is in bold):

```
    ...
    [tabBarController setViewControllers:currentItems animated:NO];
} else {
    self.aboutViewController.navigationItem.hidesBackButton = YES;
    self.aboutViewController.navigationItem.title = @"About";
}
```

Run the app again. This time the About item has the correct title and no Back button. Rotate the device to portrait, and the navigation bar still has no button to access the menu; that is the next thing you add.

Polishing Menu Images

In previous chapters, you used images for selections and there was not that much difference in the images. Whether it is a tab bar or the menu for the iPad, using a different image to indicate a selected state helps make things obvious. It is also good to show those using the right tint from the app color scheme.

There are two main parts to making selected images that use a custom tint work:

- Set the highlighted image.
- Update both images to use the template rendering mode.

The first part is adding images for the selected state:

1. Open `Images.xcassets` and import `CH11 Assets Selected Icons`.

2. In the iPad storyboard, select the car image from the menu table view. Use the Attributes inspector to set the highlighted image to `car-selected`.

3. Set the tint for the image to mocha (or whichever color you have chosen).

4. Set the highlighted image and tint for the two remaining menu cells. The highlighted image name is always the name of the regular image appended with "-selected."

Run the app in landscape and tap on each cell. You should see the image change, though it is still the same color as the source artwork. The next step is to change the tint.

Changing the Image Tint

The graphical data in an image can be used in two basic ways. The most typical way is to specify how to draw the image: the size, colors, opacity, and more. The other is as a template for showing something else. You have probably seen things like this as an image appears to change colors, or pulse, or other tricks. It is the same image and the same image data. It is just used in a different way.

In iOS, the renderingMode property of a UIImage tells the system how to use the image data. UIImageRenderingModeAlwaysOriginal says to show exactly what the image specifies. If it is a light blue stylized car, show a light blue stylized car.

UIImageRenderingModeAlwaysTemplate says to use the graphical data as a template, effectively allowing you to use the same light blue stylized car in whatever color, or tint in iOS, you want. The intensity and transparency of the color at any point on the image is the same, but it is displayed using the tint color.

The default, UIImageRenderingModeAutomatic, lets the system decide how to use the image. The idea is that you can use the same image for buttons and for other purposes. Whenever you set the image in IB, it is created with the default-rendering mode. Much of the time this does what you want, but not always.

The image views in menu table view cells are a good example. What you want is to set the rendering mode of the images. However, at this time there is no way to do that in IB, and the property itself is read-only.

With a small amount of code, you can replace the images with copies that are set as templates:

1. Open the Storyboard and an Assistant editor with MainMenuViewController.h.

2. Select the top car image and drag to the .h file as if you were going to create a property. When the popup comes up, set the type to an Outlet Collection, as seen in Figure 11-10.

   Name the property menuImages and make sure it is of type UIImageView.

3. Now Ctrl-drag from the other two image views to the new outlet collection.

   You can confirm all three images are in the collection by Ctrl-clicking on the controller icon in the bar below the layout window in IB. Look for an item called Outlet Collections and the property should be there and include all the image views.

4. Open MainMenuViewController.m and add the following code to the end of viewDidLoad:

```
for (UIImageView *atView in self.menuImages) {
    atView.image = [atView.image imageWithRenderingMode:
                    UIImageRenderingModeAlwaysTemplate];
    atView.highlightedImage = [atView.highlightedImage
                               imageWithRenderingMode:
                               UIImageRenderingModeAlwaysTemplate];
}
```

The code iterates through each image view in the outlet collection. For each of those views, it replaces both the image and the highlightedImage properties with a copy. The copy is made with imageWithRenderingMode:, a UIImage method that sets the rendering mode of the copied image.

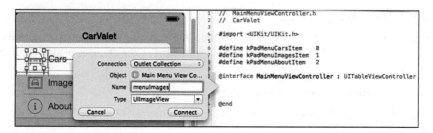

Figure 11-10   Setting an outlet collection

Run the code, and you can see tinted images that highlight when selected. This technique can be used on more than just image views in cells. It can also be used in tab bars, buttons, and bar buttons—anywhere you can specify an image and a highlighted image.

Accessing the Menu in Portrait

You can access the main/menu controller of a split view in portrait in one of two ways: always show the controller, as the Settings app does, or show a menu popover button for opening the menu, as in Mail and Notes. Either way requires implementing one or more methods of the `UISplitViewControllerDelegate` protocol.

All the methods support some stage of showing or hiding a menu popover. Always showing the menu is the simplest: You just return `NO` from `splitViewController:shouldHideViewController:inOrientation:`.

CarValet hides the menu in portrait, so you need a few more methods. What class do you use for the delegate? The Apple Xcode samples tend to use the detail view controller as the delegate. Other possibilities are the master view controller, the app delegate, or a custom class.

Using the detail controller makes sense when there is only one controller switching between different views. This app has four detail view controllers, not one: no menu item chosen, about, car images, and car detail.

`MainMenuViewController` is not a good choice because it shows a submenu based on the iPhone storyboard controller (car images). Using the app delegate adds code to an already code-heavy class, and it means you lose the opportunity to create a reusable class. A better choice is to use a custom object. One way to do this is to create an instance of the custom class and associate it with the app delegate. Then any object can access the delegate by using an app delegate property. But there is another way to implement coordination classes that need only one instance: Use a singleton.

A *singleton* is a special type of class that prevents the creation of more than one instance object. Instead of callers allocating and/or initializing an instance, they call a special class method that returns the single shared object. The same method usually creates the instance if it does not already exist. Typically, it looks as follows:

```
MySingletonClass *mySingleton = [MySingletonClass sharedMySingleton];
```

Implementing the `DetailController` Singleton

In addition to implementing the split view controller delegate protocol, the new class eventually manages the detail content. And even if it did not, most of the changes made by a split view delegate are to the detail view.

First, you implement the singleton functionality:

1. Add a new class called `DetailController`, based on `NSObject`, to the bottom of the iPad group.

2. Open `DetailController.h` and add the following line just above the `@end` statement. The + sign indicates a class method:

   ```
   + (DetailController*)sharedDetailController;
   ```

3. Set the contents of `DetailController.m` to the code shown in Listing 11-3.

Listing 11-3   **Detail Controller Implementation**

```
@implementation DetailController

#pragma mark - Singleton

+ (DetailController*)sharedDetailController                        // 1
{
    static DetailController *sharedDetailController = nil;         // 2
    static dispatch_once_t pred;

    dispatch_once(&pred, ^{                                        // 3
        sharedDetailController = [super new];
    });

    return sharedDetailController;                                 // 4
}

@end
```

Here's what happens in the numbered lines in Listing 11-3:

1. The declaration of the class method for returning the shared instance.

2. Create a static variable for holding the single instance after it is allocated.

3. Create the shared instance only once.

4. Return the shared instance.

> **Note: What Is** `dispatch_once`**?**
>
> `dispatch_once` is a handy routine which guarantees that the included code is executed only once. The `pred` argument is part of the mechanism which ensures that the code is executed once. The routine is part of something called Grand Central Dispatch (GCD), an advanced technology in both iOS and Mac OS.
>
> A discussion of GCD is beyond the scope of this book. For now, you can adapt this code wherever you need a singleton, replacing `sharedDetailController` with your own appropriate name.
>
> For more information, see the Apple documentation or *iOS Components and Frameworks: Understanding the Advanced Features of the iOS SDK* by Kyle Richter and Joe Keeley.

Adding `UISplitViewControllerDelegate`

Adding support for the split view controller delegate protocol takes three steps: Set up the `.h` file, add the required protocol methods, and set the instance as the split view delegate.

The `.h` file needs only two additions. The first declares that the class supports the protocol. The second declares a property for the split view controller managed by the delegate. Add these lines below the `@interface` declaration in `DetailController.h`:

```
<UISplitViewControllerDelegate>

@property (weak, nonatomic) UISplitViewController *splitViewController;
```

For now, you need to implement three of the four delegate methods. `splitViewController: shouldHideViewController:inOrientation:` determines whether the app should hide the menu. CarValet hides the menu in portrait itself. You add the navigation bar button to the active detail view controller.

`splitViewController:willShowViewController:invalidatingBarButtonItem:` is called when the split view controller rotates to an orientation that shows the menu. Use it to remove the navigation bar button for showing the popover menu.

You add support for the split view controller protocol methods by following these steps:

1. Open `DetailController.m` and add local instance variables for the navigation bar menu button, popover, and detail controller by inserting this code just below the `@implementation` statement:

   ```
   {
       UIBarButtonItem *menuPopoverButtonItem;
       UIPopoverController *menuPopoverController;
       UINavigationController *detailNavController;
   }
   ```

   `menuPopoverButtonItem` is the current menu bar button item, used for setting the left navigation bar button when the current detail controller changes. Tapping the button opens the `menuPopoverController`. `detailNavController` is the detail `UINavigationController`.

2. Add the following #pragma below the implementation statement to make it easy to see groupings of functionality in the Function dropdown:

```
#pragma mark — UISplitViewControllerDelegate
```

3. Add the following code below the #pragma statement:

```
- (BOOL)splitViewController:(UISplitViewController *)svc
    shouldHideViewController:(UIViewController *)vc
              inOrientation:(UIInterfaceOrientation)orientation {
    return UIInterfaceOrientationIsPortrait(orientation);
}
```

4. Continue by adding the code in Listing 11-4 to add the last two protocol methods.

Listing 11-4   Delegate Methods for Hiding and Showing the Menu

```
- (void)splitViewController:(UISplitViewController *)svc                      // 1
      willHideViewController:(UIViewController *)aViewController
         withBarButtonItem:(UIBarButtonItem *)barButtonItem
       forPopoverController:(UIPopoverController *)pc {
    barButtonItem.title = @"Menu";                                           // 2

    menuPopoverButtonItem = barButtonItem;                                   // 3
    menuPopoverController = pc;

    UINavigationItem *detailNavItem =                                        // 4
                  detailNavController.topViewController.navigationItem;
    detailNavItem.leftBarButtonItem = barButtonItem;
}

- (void)splitViewController:(UISplitViewController *)svc                      // 5
      willShowViewController:(UIViewController *)aViewController
   invalidatingBarButtonItem:(UIBarButtonItem *)barButtonItem {
    menuPopoverButtonItem = nil;                                             // 6
    menuPopoverController = nil;

    UINavigationItem *detailNavItem =                                        // 7
                  detailNavController.topViewController.navigationItem;
    detailNavItem.leftBarButtonItem = nil;
}
```

Here's what happens in the numbered lines in Listing 11-4:

1. Called when a rotation hides the main menu.

2. Set the title of the popover navigation bar button to Menu.

3. Set the local instance variables to the menu navigation bar button and popover controllers.

4. Find the navigation bar of the front-most detail controller and set the left button to the menu button.

5. Called when a rotation shows the main menu.

6. Clear the local menu navigation bar button and popover controller.

7. Remove the left navigation bar button item for the current detail controller.

Creating and Setting Up the Singleton

You need to set up the singleton before you can use it. The best place to do this is at application launch since all the view controllers already exist. Follow these steps:

1. Import `DetailController.h` into `AppDelegate.h`.

2. Change the `else` case in `application:didFinishLaunchingWithOptions:` to set up the detail controller and set the split view controller. Add the following code shown in bold:

```
} else {
    self.aboutViewController.navigationItem.hidesBackButton = YES;
    self.aboutViewController.navigationItem.title = @"About";

    UISplitViewController *splitViewController =
    (UISplitViewController *)self.window.rootViewController;

    DetailController *detailController = [DetailController
                                    sharedDetailController];
    detailController.splitViewController = splitViewController;
}
```

> ### Note: Setting Up and Accessing Singletons
>
> In reality, you do not need to set up a singleton by assigning it to an instance variable. A singleton is set up the very first time it is accessed using the `shared` class method. An instance variable provides a shorthand way to reference the singleton. You could just call the `shared` class method every time, including the first one.

Setting the `splitViewController` property solves only part of the problem, as `DetailController` needs a reference to the detail `UINavigationController`. `detailNavController` is not a public variable, so it can be set only from inside the instance or by creating a public method.

It would be nice to have the singleton set the variable whenever `splitViewController` is changed. That would cut down on excess calls by users of the singleton and make the code more reusable. Accessor methods are designed for this purpose. They are called whenever a property is accessed or set using either dot notation or a method call.

Table 11-3 shows the two types of accessors, getters and setters. Each does what the name implies: Getters get the value of a property; setters set the value. When you use `@property`, the getters and setters are created for you.

Table 11-3   **Method Call and Dot Notation Form for Getters and Setters**

Form	Getter	Setter
Dot notation	`if (object.variable == value) {`	`object.variable = value;`
Method call	`if ([object variable] == value) {`	`[object setVariable:value];`

You can override the defaults by creating your own getter and/or setter. Getter method declarations are always of the form:

`- (void) <propertyName>`

Setters look like this:

`- (void) set<propertyName>:(<ObjectType>)<propertyName>`

Add the `#pragma` and getter method in Listing 11-5 below the implementation and local instance variable declarations in `DetailController.m`.

Listing 11-5   `DetailController` **Setter for** `splitViewController`

```
#pragma mark - Setter

- (void)setSplitViewController:(UISplitViewController *)splitViewController {
    if (splitViewController != _splitViewController) {             // 1
        _splitViewController = splitViewController;                // 2
        detailNavController =                                      // 3
                        [splitViewController.viewControllers lastObject];
        _splitViewController.delegate = self;                      // 4
    }
}
```

Here's what happens in the numbered lines in Listing 11-5:

1. Change things only if the new split view controller is different from the current one.

2. Set the current split view controller to the new one. Note the use of the underscore form for the property. Using the dot or `set` form inside a setter is dangerous. (See the "Warning: Setters and Dot/set == Death.")

3. Set the private instance variable for the detail navigation controller.

4. Become the split view controller delegate.

Warning: Setters and Dot/`set` == Death

Setting the value of a property using dot notation or the `set` form of an accessor is normally safe. There are two exceptions. The first is in object initialization methods. The other case is when you use a setter. First, you need to understand that dot notation is just a shorthand way of specifying the `set`-based method call.

If you access a property inside the setter using the dot/`set` form, you are really just calling the setter. In the best case, the system detects the problem and throws an exception. More likely, you enter a recursive loop, calling the setter over and over and over until the system runs out of memory, shuts down your app, or your app crashes.

Whenever you declare an instance variable using `@property`, in addition to creating setters and getters, Xcode prepends an underscore (_) to the property name to create the real instance variable name. You can safely use the underscore version of the property name inside setters as it is the real memory pointer.

Run the app and rotate the simulator to portrait. The menu view controller disappears, and a menu button appears in the navigation bar of the current detail view. Tapping the menu button shows the menu controller, and tapping outside the menu controller dismisses it. You can also show and hide the menu controller by swiping right.

Use the menu to show different content in the detail area. There are two issues. First, the menu does not automatically dismiss when you select the item. Second, when you dismiss the popover, there is no button to open it again.

Consolidating the Code to Switch Detail Content

You might think you should add more code to `MainMenuViewController`. Although doing so works, as you add more view controllers, you get lots of repetitive code. Instead, you can consolidate all the work in `DetailController`.

Changing the current contents of the detail area requires running some code. You could do that by defining a special method in `DetailController`, or you could define a property and a setter. Follow these steps to use a setter for changing the current detail view controller:

1. Create a `strong` property called a `currDetailController` of type `UIViewController` in `DetailController.h`.

2. Add the code from Listing 11-6 after `setSplitViewController:` in `DetailController.m`.

3. Import `DetailController.h` into `MainMenuViewController.m`.

4. Replace `tableView:didSelectRowAtIndexPath:` with the code shown in Listing 11-7. As well as being cleaner and easier to read, the new method is only two-thirds the size of the original.

Listing 11-6   `DetailController` **Setter for** `currDetailController`

```
- (void)setCurrDetailController:(UIViewController*)currDetailController {
    NSArray *newStack = nil;                                          // 1

    if (currDetailController == nil) {                               // 2
        UINavigationController *rootController =                     // 3
                    detailNavController.viewControllers[0];

        if (detailNavController.topViewController != rootController) {  // 4

            newStack = @[detailNavController.viewControllers[0]];    // 5

        }
    } else if (![currDetailController isMemberOfClass:              // 6
                        [detailNavController.topViewController class]]) {

        newStack = @[detailNavController.viewControllers[0],         // 7
                    currDetailController];
    }

    [menuPopoverController dismissPopoverAnimated:YES];             // 8

    if (newStack != nil) {
        [detailNavController setViewControllers:newStack animated:YES];  // 9

        _currDetailController = detailNavController.topViewController;  // 10
        _currDetailController.navigationItem.leftBarButtonItem =    // 11
                                    menuPopoverButtonItem;
    }
}
```

Here's what happens in the numbered lines in Listing 11-6:

1. If the current detail changes, `newStack` is set to a replacement stack of view controllers.

2. Setting the new detail content controller to `nil` shows the default CarValet image.

3. The valet tent image is always the first, or root, controller.

4. Check whether the tent is already showing.

5. The tent is not showing, so set the new stack to just the detail controller that shows the tent image.

6. The new controller is not `nil`, so check whether it is already showing. Do this by checking whether the current and new controllers are the same class.

7. It is a new detail view controller, so change the navigation controller's stack. Put the tent view controller on the bottom and the new controller on top.

8. Dismiss the menu popover if it is showing. If it is not showing, this call sends a message to nil, so nothing happens.

9. Show the new detail content.

10. Set the current detail controller to the new one. Again, this is a setter, so use the underscore version.

11. Set the left button of the navigation bar to the menu popover button. If there is no popover button, leftBarButton is set to nil—that is, to no button.

Listing 11-7 **Updated** tableView:didSelectRowAtIndexPath:

```
- (void)tableView:(UITableView *)tableView
       didSelectRowAtIndexPath:(NSIndexPath *)indexPath {

    AppDelegate *appDelegate = [UIApplication sharedApplication].delegate;
    DetailController *detailController = [DetailController
                                  sharedDetailController];

    UIViewController *nextController;

    switch (indexPath.row) {                                      // 1
        case kPadMenuCarsItem:
            nextController = nil;
            break;

        case kPadMenuImagesItem:
            nextController = nil;
            break;

        case kPadMenuAboutItem:
            nextController = (UIViewController*)appDelegate.aboutViewController;
            break;
    }

    detailController.currDetailController = nextController;       // 2
}
```

Here's what happens in the numbered lines in Listing 11-7:

1. Set the next controller to the correct value or nil for the default tent picture.

2. Let DetailController handle changing or not changing the detail view, as well as dismissing the popover if one is shown.

After the changes, `MainMenuViewController` is handling behaviors associated with the table. `DetailController` implements behaviors specific to the split view, including showing and hiding the menu popover. Even when the menu view is shown in the popover, the menu controller itself should not care about where it is presented.

Run the app again, trying it in both landscape and portrait modes. Make sure everything behaves correctly, including switching between view controllers in portrait and landscape, showing and hiding the menu when rotating, and showing and hiding the menu button for the about and tent view controllers, depending on orientation.

The only thing that looks strange is the animation when changing detail content. This is because you are using the `UINavigationController` default animation. As an alternative, you can use core animation. Explaining the code is beyond the scope of this book. See "Recipe: Using Core Animation Transitions" in *Core iOS 6 Developer Cookbook* by Erica Sadun for more information.

Add the animation using these steps:

1. Import `<QuartzCore/QuartzCore.h>` into `DetailController.m`.

2. Add the `QuartzCore` framework to your project from Project Settings, just as you added `CoreData` in Chapter 9, "Introducing Core Data."

3. Update displaying the new navigation controller in `setCurrDetailController:` with the new code shown here in bold:

```
if (newStack != nil) {
    CATransition *transition = [CATransition animation];
    transition.duration = 0.3f;
    transition.timingFunction = [CAMediaTimingFunction
                                    functionWithName:
                                    kCAMediaTimingFunctionEaseInEaseOut];
    transition.type = kCATransitionFade;
    [detailNavController.view.layer addAnimation:transition forKey:nil];

    [detailNavController setViewControllers:newStack animated:NO];
```

The transition duration matches the iOS animation time for closing the popover. Make sure the navigation controller does not try to animate the change by setting `animated:` to `NO` in the call to `setViewControllers:animated:`.

This time when you run the app, the new detail content fades in. The animation is specified by the transition `type` property, as shown in Table 11-4. You can try experimenting with other transition types. Check the documentation for different subtypes by searching for `CATransition`.

Table 11-4 **Transition Constants**

Constant	Transition Effect
kCATransitionFade	The view fades as it is hidden.
kCATransitionMoveIn	The view slides over existing content. The direction is determined by the subtype property of the transition.
kCATransitionPush	The view pushes the existing content out of the way as it slides in. The direction is determined by the subtype.
kCATransitionReveal	The view is gradually revealed. The direction is determined by the subtype.

Adding Car Images

The car images view controller already exists on the iPhone storyboard, so you can load and show it. Doing this takes two steps: adding a storyboard identifier, and loading and preparing the controller, as described here:

1. Open `Main_iPhone.storyboard` in the Layout editor and select the car image view controller.

2. Set the Storyboard ID to `CarImagesViewController` in the Identity inspector, as shown in Figure 11-11.

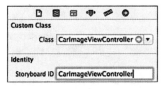

Figure 11-11   Setting the storyboard identifier

When a view controller has a storyboard ID, you can use the `UIStoryboard` method `instantiateViewControllerWithIdentifier:` to load an instance.

3. Open `MainMenuViewController.m` and update `tableView:didSelectRowAtIndexPath:` with the bold lines shown in Listing 11-8.

Listing 11-8   **More Updates to** `tableView:didSelectRowAtIndexPath`:

```
...
DetailController *detailController = [DetailController
                                    sharedDetailController];
UIStoryboard *iPhoneStory = [UIStoryboard                         // 1
                        storyboardWithName:@"Main_iPhone"
                        bundle:nil];


UIViewController *nextController;

switch (indexPath.row) {
    case kPadMenuCarsItem:
        nextController = nil;
        break;

    case kPadMenuImagesItem:
        nextController = [iPhoneStory                            // 2
                        instantiateViewControllerWithIdentifier:
                        @"CarImagesViewController"];

        nextController.navigationItem.hidesBackButton = YES;    // 3
        nextController.navigationItem.rightBarButtonItem = nil; // 4
        break;
}
```

Here's what happens in the numbered lines in Listing 11-8:

1. Load the iPhone storyboard.

2. Set the next controller to a car image controller loaded from the iPhone storyboard.

3. Hide the Back button.

4. Remove the existing Reset Zoom right navigation bar button.

`MainMenuViewController` does not need to worry if the car image detail view is showing or not. All it does is tell `DetailController` to set the detail area to the car image view. By using the `currDetailController` setter, `DetailController` takes care of checking the current detail view and loading the car image view if it is not already showing. This is a good example of using partitioning of responsibility to minimize the amount of code for adding a new behavior.

When you run the app, the car images controller shows correctly. But as usual, there appear to be a couple issues with adapting the controller to iPad. First, the car number is incorrect. Also, as shown in Figure 11-12, when you swipe through the cars, the car images become increasingly offset.

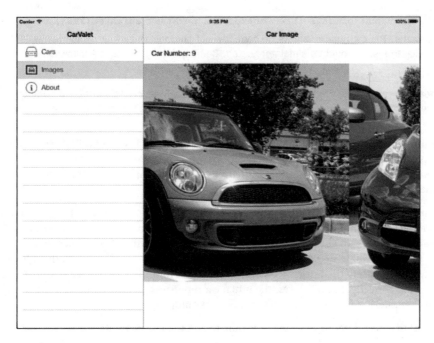

Figure 11-12   Offset car images

You might be tempted to look at what is happening and possible fixes, but in reality, there is only one issue. If you have access to an iPad, run the app on it. The car images still become increasingly offset; however, the initial car number is correct. There are differences between the simulator and devices, so it is a good idea to try code on a real iPad, especially when you encounter bugs that seem strange. See the "Tip: Why Did This Bug You?" to learn why the car number problem appeared to be simulator-specific.

Tip: Why Did This Bug You?

The first step in solving the car number problem is finding the source. The issue occurs only when the label is first shown, and that happens in `viewDidAppear:`. Use a breakpoint at the call to `updateCarNumberLabel` so you can step into that method and look at the state. The presenting issue is that `carIndex` has the wrong value, implicating `carIndexForPoint:`.

Instead of rerunning and breaking there, take a look at the relevant properties, and you see that there is an issue with `scrollView`. In the Debug Console, `po self.scrollView` quickly shows the issue: The frame is all `0`s. The scroll view is not being laid out.

Put a breakpoint in `updateCarNumberLabel` and let the app continue. Scroll to the next car, and you see that the frame is now initialized.

Now you can test your theory. You might notice that moving the car initializes the frame, so perhaps other movement would as well. Let the navigation controller animate, adding detail content in `DetailController.m`, by changing `NO` to `YES` in one line of the `currentDetailController` setter:

> ```
> [detailNavController setViewControllers:newStack animated:YES];
> ```
> This works. The car number shows up correctly, but so does an extra animation. This is the first clue the issue could be simulator-related. Confirm this by adding the following:
>
> ```
> [self.view layoutIfNeeded];
> ```
> before the call to updateCarNumberLabel in viewDidAppear:. Again, the car number label is correct. You can now try out the code on a real iPad, and when you do, you see that it works.

The source of the problem is mentioned in the "Tip: Why Did This Bug You?" Specifically, the scroll view frame is not initialized. Looking through the code, you see that setupScrollContent also relies on an initialized frame to set up the content correctly. And that is not the case during viewDidLoad.

The simple fix is to move both setting the scroll content and showing the initial label to the same view-based method. In this case, you change everything to use viewDidAppear:. In CarImagesViewController.m, cut [self setupScrollContent]; from viewDidLoad and paste it above the call to updateCarLabel in viewDidAppear:. Run the app in the iPhone simulator to make sure the images view still works. Then run it in the iPad simulator. The car images scroll correctly. In both cases, the initial car number is incorrect, but running the app on a device quickly shows you that everything works properly.

Now that Images and About are done, it is time to add the last menu item.

Adding Cars

Unlike About and Images, the first part of adding Cars updates the menu controller. On the iPhone app, the Cars tab has four functions: add cars, remove cars, view cars, and select a car to view detail. Only the last function, viewing a car, changes the detail content.

The first step is showing a car table when the Cars menu item is tapped. There is a car table on the iPhone storyboard, and you already know how to load a controller from there:

1. Add an identifier to the CarTableViewController on the iPhone storyboard.

2. Show the new controller in the menu view. Do this by changing the kPadMenuCarsItem switch case to the code shown in Listing 11-9.

Listing 11-9   **Showing a Car Table**

```
...
case kPadMenuCarsItem:
    nextController = [iPhoneStory                          // 1
                 instantiateViewControllerWithIdentifier:
                 @"CarTableViewController"];

        [self.navigationController pushViewController:nextController  // 2
```

```
                animated:YES];

    nextController = nil;                                    // 3
    break;
...
```

Here's what happens in the numbered lines in Listing 11-9:

1. Load the car table controller.

2. Make the car table the current menu controller.

3. Set the next controller back to `nil`. This is very important; if you did not do this, the last line of the method would load the car table into the detail area.

When you run the app in portrait, it does not quite do what you want. Open the menu popover, tap Cars, and the car table loads. However, the popup is dismissed. This makes sense because the current detail controller is always set, even if the next controller is `nil`. And every time the setter is called, the popover is dismissed. This behavior still makes sense; the problem is showing that the car table submenu should have no effect on the detail area.

The simplest solution is to make the call setting `currDetailController` conditional. A simple `BOOL` in `tableView:didSelectRowAtIndexPath:` is all you need:

1. Add the following line above the switch statement:

   ```
   BOOL newDetail = YES;
   ```

2. Change the last line in the `kPadMenuImagesItem` case to this:

   ```
   newDetail = NO;
   ```

3. Update the last line of the method, based on the bold code:

   ```
   if (newDetail) {
       detailController.currDetailController = nextController;
   }
   ```

Run the app in portrait and open the menu popover. Choose About, and it behaves correctly, with the popover closing and the detail area updating. Choose Cars; it works as expected, with the popover staying open and the car table showing in the menu area. There is just one problem: There is no way to get back to the main menu. The Edit button appears where the Back button should be.

Adapting the Car Table to iPad

There is no easy way to fix the issue of the Edit button appearing where the Back button should be. Although it is easy to show both the Back and Edit buttons by using `leftItemsSupplementBackButton`, this does not fix the deeper problem. Tapping a car cell uses a segue to open the detail in the same menu navigation controller.

There are three basic approaches to solving the issue. First, you could make an iPad-specific copy of the view controller class files and make the required changes. As part of this approach, you would also copy the iPhone view controller to the iPad storyboard and make appropriate changes. The second approach is a variant. You still copy the storyboard view controller, but you use subclassing to create an iPad view controller class with only the methods you need.

Because the iPad-specific visual changes are small, a better solution is to modify `CarTableViewController` to work with both iPhone and iPad. Doing this only requires three basic changes—adding a small protocol for finding the right car to show, adding a delegate to the main menu view controller, and adding or modifying three car table methods—as shown here:

1. Create a new Objective-C protocol file called `CarTableViewProtocol.h` below `CarTableViewController.m`.

2. Add an `@class` declaration for `CDCar` and one declaration to the new protocol:

   ```
   - (void) selectCar:(CDCar*)selectedCar;
   ```

3. Open `CarTableViewController.h` and import `CarTableViewProtocol.h`. Then declare a delegate property in the interface for the class:

   ```
   @property (weak, nonatomic) id <CarTableViewProtocol> delegate;
   ```

4. Only set the title in the navbar if there is no `delegate`. Add the following if condition around the call to set the title in `viewDidLoad` (the new code is in bold):

   ```
   if (!self.delegate) {
       self.title = NSLocalizedStringWithDefaultValue(
                       @"AddViewScreenTitle",
                       nil,
                       [NSBundle mainBundle],
                       @"CarValet",
                       @"Title for the main app screen");
   }
   ```

5. Open `CarTableViewController.m` and remove the `viewDidLoad` line that sets the left bar button:

   ```
   self.navigationItem.leftBarButtonItem = self.editButton;
   ```

6. Add `tableView:didSelectRowAtIndexPath:` to send `selectCar:` to the delegate if one exists. Eventually, this causes the delegate to update the detail content:

   ```
   - (void)tableView:(UITableView *)tableView
           didSelectRowAtIndexPath:(NSIndexPath *)indexPath {
       if (self.delegate != nil) {
           [self.delegate selectCar:[self carToView]];
       }
   }
   ```

7. Modify `editTableView:` to update buttons on the right side of the navigation bar if there is a delegate by replacing the call to `setLeftBarButtonItem:animated:` with the code in bold:

```
UIBarButtonItem *nextButton = (startEdit) ?
                    self.doneButton : self.editButton;

if (self.delegate == nil) {
    [self.navigationItem setLeftBarButtonItem:nextButton animated:YES];
} else {
    UIBarButtonItem *addButton = self.navigationItem.rightBarButtonItems[0];

    [self.navigationItem setRightBarButtonItems:@[addButton, nextButton]
                                animated:YES];
}

[self.tableView setEditing:startEdit animated:YES];
```

8. Create a `viewWillAppear:` method after `viewDidLoad`, using Listing 11-10. This method is called after the view is laid out but before it is shown, providing a chance to make final changes.

9. Add the code in Listing 11-11 above `prepareForSegue:sender:`. If there is a delegate, the method prevents the segue attached to car view cells from firing, resulting in the default table behavior that calls `tableView:didSelectRowAtIndexPath:`.

10. Add support for the new protocol in `MainMenuViewController.h` by #importing the file and adding the protocol name in angle brackets after the `@interface` statement.

11. Open `MainMenuViewController.m`, import `CarTableViewController.h` and `CDCar.h`, and add the following #pragma and method at the end of the implementation:

```
#pragma mark - CarTableViewProtocol

- (void)selectCar:(CDCar *)selectedCar {
    NSLog(@"\nSELECT a car: %@ %@ %@\n\n",
        selectedCar.make, selectedCar.model, selectedCar.year);
}
```

12. Add this code to `tableView:didSelectRowAtIndexPath:` in the `kPadMenuCarsItem` case, below where you instantiate `nextController` from the iPhone storyboard. In addition to setting the title, the code also sets the delegate:

```
nextController.navigationItem.title = @"Cars";
((CarTableViewController*)nextController).delegate = self;
```

Listing 11-10   **Car Table** `viewWillAppear:`

```
- (void)viewWillAppear:(BOOL)animated {
    [super viewWillAppear:animated];

    if (self.delegate == nil) {                                         // 1
        self.navigationItem.leftBarButtonItem = self.editButton;        // 2
    } else {                                                            // 3
        UIBarButtonItem *addButton = self.navigationItem.rightBarButtonItem;
        self.navigationItem.rightBarButtonItems = @[addButton, self.editButton];
    }
}
```

Here's what happens in the numbered lines in Listing 11-10:

1. Check whether there is a delegate.

2. If there is no delegate, put the Edit button on the left.

3. There is a delegate, so put both the Edit and Add buttons on the right. Note that the order of buttons in the array is from right to left. The Add button appears last, on the right of the navigation bar.

Listing 11-11   **Car Cell Conditional Segue**

```
- (BOOL)shouldPerformSegueWithIdentifier:(NSString*)identifier
                                  sender:(id)sender {
    if ([identifier isEqualToString:@"ViewSegue"]) {                    // 1
        if (self.delegate != nil) {                                     // 2
            return NO;                                                  // 3
        }
    }

    return YES;                                                         // 4
}
```

Here's what happens in the numbered lines in Listing 11-11:

1. You only need to check if this is a car table cell tap segue indicated by the string `@"ViewSegue"`.

2. Check whether there is a delegate.

3. There is a delegate, so do not fire the segue. When you stop the segue, the default table behavior takes over, calling `tableView:didSelectRowAtIndexPath:`.

4. Fire the segue because there is no delegate or it is a different segue.

Run the app on the iPhone simulator to confirm that the car table works correctly. When you make changes to a view or view controller that is used in multiple form factors, it is a good idea to test it on each form factor.

Now run the app on iPad. Everything works as expected: The Back button appears and goes to the main menu, Edit and Add work, and tapping a car prints something like the text below in the debugger:

```
2013-02-12 20:23:52.717 CarValet[1128:c07]
SELECT a car: Honda Accord 2012
```

Car Detail Controller

You already have a controller to show car detail on the iPhone storyboard. Better still, it uses a protocol to find what car to show and let a delegate know if there are changes. Follow these steps to show car detail:

1. Open the iPhone storyboard and set the `ViewCarTableViewController` storyboard ID so it's the same as the class name.

2. Open `MainMenuViewController.m` and import `ViewCarTableViewController.h`. Now add instance variables for a current car and current controller below `@implementation`:

   ```
   {
       CDCar *currentCar;
       ViewCarTableViewController *currentViewCarController;
   }
   ```

3. Add support for `ViewCarProtocol` to `MainMenuViewController` and copy the protocol methods to the end of the implementation:

   ```
   #pragma mark - ViewCarProtocol

   -(CDCar*)carToView {
       return currentCar;
   }

   -(void)carViewDone:(BOOL)dataChanged {
       NSLog(@"\ncarViewDone\n\n");
   }
   ```

   You have implemented these protocol methods once before for `CarTableViewController`.

4. Update the `selectCar:` method using Listing 11-12.

Listing 11-12   **Car Cell Conditional Segue**

```
- (void)selectCar:(CDCar *)selectedCar {
    NSLog(@"\nSELECT a car: %@ %@ %@\n\n",
          selectedCar.make, selectedCar.model, selectedCar.year);

    currentCar = selectedCar;                                    // 1
```

```
    if (currentViewCarController == nil) {                              // 2
        UIStoryboard *iPhoneStory = [UIStoryboard
                                    storyboardWithName:@"Main_iPhone"
                                    bundle:nil];
        currentViewCarController = [iPhoneStory
                                    instantiateViewControllerWithIdentifier:
                                    @"ViewCarTableViewController"];

        currentViewCarController.navigationItem.title = @"Cars";        // 3
        currentViewCarController.navigationItem.hidesBackButton = YES;
        currentViewCarController.delegate = self;
    }


    [DetailController sharedDetailController].currDetailController =     // 4
                                            currentViewCarController;
}
```

Here's what happens in the numbered lines in Listing 11-12:

1. Set the `currentCar` local variable to the selected car for use in `ViewCarProtocol`.

2. If there is no view car controller, load one from the iPhone storyboard.

3. Set up the new controller by giving it a title, hiding any Back button, and setting the `MainMenuViewController` as the delegate.

4. Tell the detail controller to show the detail car view.

Run the app on the iPad. It almost works. When the detail area doesn't contain a car detail controller, tapping a car in the table shows car detail. However, tapping a second car doesn't replace the information. This is because `ViewCarTableViewController` was designed for a single use. All the fields are set up in `viewDidLoad` instead of a different method. On the iPhone, changing a car happens when the car detail view controller is gone, so there is no notion of an information update.

No matter what the solution, you need to know when to tell the car detail to update. You do not want to update the first time the controller is shown. You therefore need to detect whether the current detail controller is car detail. If it is, you need to update the content. If it is not, you need to tell `DetailController` to load a new detail content controller. In `MainMenuViewController.m`, replace the last line of `selectCar:` with the following:

```
DetailController *detail = [DetailController sharedDetailController];

if ([detail.currDetailController
        isMemberOfClass:[ViewCarTableViewController class]]) {
    [currentViewCarController viewDidLoad];
} else {
    detail.currDetailController = currentViewCarController;
}
```

The `if` condition checks whether the current detail controller is a view car controller. If it is, `viewDidLoad` is sent. If it is not, a new view controller is loaded.

Now you can run the app on iPad and watch cars change in the detail view. Editing works, though the main menu view controller is not sent `carViewDone:` when cars change. It is possible for the main menu controller to detect when cars change, but this defeats the purpose of using a protocol.

You now have two basic choices. The first is to update `ViewCarTableViewController`, `ViewCarProtocol`, and `MainMenuViewController` to be more general. That would include changes to any other users of the protocol. But even if you do that, the presentation does not look good on the larger iPad screen. This includes both the detail view and all the editors. A better solution is to create a custom car detail view for iPad that correctly interacts with the menu.

Car Detail Controller, Take 2: iPad Specific

On an iPhone, the CarValet app is typically used in portrait, so information usually flows from top to bottom. On an iPad, the same is true for the master/menu view of a split view controller, but not for the detail view. The iPad is wider than the iPhone, no matter what the iPad orientation, and this opens up the possibility of using horizontal grouping of data items.

As with any other screen, there are many possible designs, depending on what you are trying to achieve. These are the goals:

- Visually group related information.
- Make the most relevant information easy to find.
- Easily enable both reading and editing.
- Use a more appropriate presentation of information, where appropriate.

`ViewCarTableViewController` has lots of wasted space, as you can see from the highlighted areas in Figure 11-13.

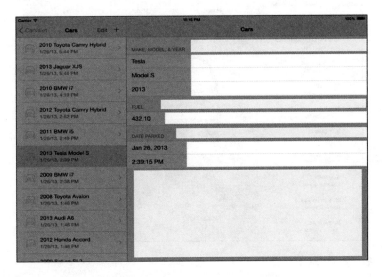

Figure 11-13   Ineffective use of iPad screen

There are four basic groups of information: make/model/year, car picture, time parked, and fuel. Because the iPad has a larger screen, you can show a larger picture. For a valet, the picture and time are likely to be important, and fuel is probably the least important for finding the car, though it is very important for returning it.

With most screens, the eye tends to start in the center. Therefore, the picture and time should be vertically centered. Next, the eye tends to do left-to-right scanning, usually from top to bottom. Since make and so on are the next most important items, they should appear at the top of the screen, going from left to right. Finally, fuel is at the bottom.

For the make/model/year items, the larger screen makes it possible to put a label on top and an edit field below. Using a label on the left of a field would either leave far too much whitespace on the right or create a crowded line that is hard to read.

For fuel, you can use a rotating picker similar to those used for dates and times. With this kind of presentation, there is no special parsing required for other locales. The only localization concerns are the separator, the language direction, and the characters for the numbers. You saw how to work with all these in Chapter 5, "Localization."

The car picture can be vertically centered in the most compact view. If you add the ability to take a picture or check the album, you could enable adding or associating an image by tapping. Time Parked goes on the left of the picture.

When you implement the changes described here, you get a screen that looks like Figure 11-14. The valet tent picture is used as a light background to enable a smooth transition from no car selected to showing car detail. You can try this yourself by hiding the background picture image view in the car detail controller, running the app, and then selecting a car. The transition from a screen with dense content (the empty detail area state showing the valet tent) to an area with lots of white space is visually jarring.

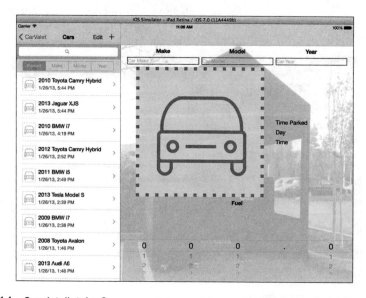

Figure 11-14   Car detail, take 2

Controller Layout on the Storyboard

The first step in building the car detail view controller for the iPad is creation and layout. This involves both adding elements and setting up appropriate auto layout constraints for both landscape and portrait. Generally, this involves three steps. First, put the elements you need in the controller in one orientation. Second, set up the constraints. And third, check the other orientation.

First, put the view elements in the controller roughly where you need them:

1. Open `Main_iPad.storyboard` and drag in a new `UIViewController`. With the new controller selected, use the Attributes inspector to set the size simulated metric to Detail and the orientation to Landscape. You can use these simulated metrics to test your layout in both portrait and landscape.

2. Drag a label in so it is the system distance from the top and left. Set the label text to Make and the alignment to centered. Set the font to System Bold 17.

3. Drag a text field and place it the system distance below the Make label and the system distance from the left edge. Use the Attributes inspector to set the text field placeholder to Car Make and set the Clear button to appear while editing.

4. Duplicate the label and edit field pair, and move it so it is centered horizontally in the parent view, with the label still the system distance from the top of the parent. Set the label text to Model and the placeholder to Car Model.

5. Select the new label and field, duplicate them, and move the duplicate pair so the right side is the system distance from the right edge and the label is the system distance from the top. Change the label to Year, the placeholder text to Car Year, and the keyboard type to Number Pad.

6. Drag in a picker view so the left, right, and bottom sides are flush with the parent. Duplicate the Make label, put the system distance on top of the picker and centered in the view. Change the text to Fuel.

7. Place an image view the system distance from the container's leading edge and the bottom of the Make Text entry field. Align the trailing edge with the trailing edge of the Model Text entry field, and set the bottom edge the system distance above the Fuel label.

   Set the background to Sky (to make it easy to see during development; you set it back later).

   Import `CH11 Assets Big Placeholder` into `Images.xcassets`. Set the picture for the image to `big-placeholder` and Aspect Fit.

8. Drag a label view so its leading edge is aligned with the leading edge of the Year Text entry view and roughly vertically centered with the picture. Then create two copies of that label, so they are the system distance apart vertically and their leading edges are aligned with the first label.

9. Change the top label to System Bold 17 and change the text to Time Parked. The next label is Day, and the one after is Time. The last two label changes are to help with layout. In the app, those fields are replaced with the date and time that the car records were created.

10. Select all three labels and vertically center the Day label with the car image.

11. Drag in an image view and resize it to fill the entire parent view. Set the image to Detail Default, the mode to Aspect Fill, and the alpha to 0.2. Use the left-hand list of view controllers to move the image view to the background, just below the top-level parent view.

Now it is time to add the constraints. Only update frames when instructed to do so:

1. Select the Make label and set it to the system distance from the leading and top edges of the superview and the system distance from the Model label.

2. Set the Model label to the system distance from the superview's top and Year label.

3. Set the Year label to the system distance from the superview's top and trailing edges.

4. The Make text field is system distance from the superview's leading edge, below the Make label and Model text field.

5. Model and Year text fields are similar—system distance from the label above them, and from their neighboring text fields, or for the Year, the trailing edge.

6. Now select all the labels and text fields, set them to equal widths, and update their frames.

7. Choose the picker and set leading, bottom, and trailing to zero from the container.

8. The Fuel label is system distance from the picker and horizontally centered in the container.

9. The placeholder image has the most constraints and is used to fill space between the top and bottom entry areas. It expands or shrinks as needed:

    - The leading edge is system distance from the superview.

    - The top edge is system distance from the bottom of the car Make text field.

    - The bottom edge is greater than or equal to the default space from the top of the Fuel label.

    - The trailing edge is aligned with the trailing edge of the Model text field but with a priority of High (750).

    - Reduce the Content Compression Resistance priority by 1 for each axis to 749.

10. The remaining three labels also have slightly complex constraints:

    - The Time Parked, Day, and Time labels are the system distance apart, with Time Parked on the top and Time on the bottom.

    - The leading edge of Time Parked is aligned with the leading edge of the Year text field.

    - Day and Time leading edges are aligned with Time Parked.

    - Day is vertically centered with the placeholder image view.

11. The background image is zero distance from the superview for all four edges.

This time, update the frames for the whole view controller. Do this by selecting the view controller (not the view) and choosing Editor > Resolve Auto Layout Issues > Update All Frames in View Controller. A similar choice is available from the resolution popup in the toolbar.

Use the simulated metrics to rotate to landscape. You might see some misplaced frames, but those are actually not an issue. Updating the frames in the controller shows little if any change. Now you can rotate between portrait and landscape and have all the elements align correctly.

Setting Up the Controller

You need a custom class for the new controller so you can populate the user interface elements and work with the picker view. Follow these steps:

1. Use the Navigator to select `MainMenuViewController.m` and then add a new class called `CarDetailViewController` that is based on `UIViewController`.

2. Open the Storyboard editor and set the custom class and storyboard ID of the new controller using the Identity inspector.

3. Set the fuel picker delegate and data source to the car detail view controller. You do this the same way you would for a table view controller: Ctrl-click the picker view and drag connections from the `dataSource` and `delegate` outlets to the car detail view controller.

4. Open the Assistant editor and drag connections to set properties as shown in Table 11-5.

Table 11-5 `CarDetailViewController` **Properties**

User Interface Element	Detail View Content
Car Make field	`carMakeField`
Car Model field	`carModelField`
Car Year field	`carYearField`
Car image view	`carImageView`
Time parked Day label	`dayParkedLabel`
Time parked Time label	`timeParkedLabel`
Fuel picker	`fuelPicker`

Now switch over to `CarDetailViewController.m`, and view the .h file in the Assistant editor. Before you can test the look of the new controller, you need to implement the fuel picker data source and delegate protocols. Follow these steps:

1. Forward declare the `CDCar` class in the .h file by placing the following line of code above the interface declaration:

   `@class CDCar;`

2. Add support for the `UIPickerViewDataSource` and `UIPickerViewDelegate` protocols.

3. Declare `myCar`, a weak, nonatomic property of type `CDCar` in the `.h` file.

4. Switch to the `.m` file and add a line for hiding the Back button to `viewDidLoad`:

   `self.navigationItem.hidesBackButton = YES;`

5. Add the code in Listing 11-13 for basic support of the fuel picker protocols. Put the code just below the end of `didReceiveMemoryWarning`.

Listing 11-13   Fuel Picker Support Protocols

```
#pragma mark - UIPickerView DataSource

- (NSInteger)numberOfComponentsInPickerView:(UIPickerView *)pickerView {     // 1
    return 5;
}

- (NSInteger)pickerView:(UIPickerView *)pickerView
            numberOfRowsInComponent:(NSInteger)component {                    // 2
    if (component == 3) {
        return 1;                                                             // 3
    }

    return 10;                                                                // 4
}

#pragma mark - UIPickerView Delegate

- (NSString *)pickerView:(UIPickerView *)pickerView
            titleForRow:(NSInteger)row
            forComponent:(NSInteger)component {                               // 5

    if (component == 3) {
        return @".";                                                         // 6
    }

    return [NSString stringWithFormat:@"%d", row];                           // 7
}
```

Here's what happens in the numbered lines in Listing 11-13:

1. Specify a method to return how many components, or "wheels," are in the picker: 5 for three places before the decimal, one after, and the decimal point.

2. Return the number of rows in a particular component.

3. This is the decimal point wheel, so return 1 for the number of rows.

4. Since the decimal point condition did not fire, this must be a number wheel. Return 10 for the numbers zero to nine.

5. Specify the title to show at a particular row on a given wheel.

6. Show **.** for the decimal point. Note that in an app with localization, you should use the locale to set the decimal separator. Refer to the "Formatting and Reading Numbers" section in Chapter 5 for how to do this.

7. For the number rows, the row number is the title. Return the row number converted to a string.

Modifying `MainMenuViewController`

Before you can run the CarValet app, you need to open the new car detail controller with `MainMenuViewController`. The current main menu controller opens the iPhone-based car detail in `selectCar:` instead of using `tableView:didSelectRowAtIndexPath:` to centralize menu selection behavior. To add opening the new detail controller, follow these steps:

1. Remove all but the `NSLog` statement from `selectCar:`.

2. Replace the import of `ViewCarTableViewController.h` with `CarDetailViewController.h` and then replace the declaration of `currentViewCarController` with this:

   `CarDetailViewController *currentCarDetailController;`

3. Change the `kPadMenuCarsItem` case in `tableView:DidSelectRowAtIndexPath:` to the code in Listing 11-14.

Listing 11-14 **Updated** `kPadMenuCarsItem` **Case**

```
case kPadMenuCarsItem:
    nextController = [iPhoneStory
    instantiateViewControllerWithIdentifier:@"CarTableViewController"];

    nextController.navigationItem.title = @"Cars";
    ((CarTableViewController*)nextController).delegate = self;

    [self.navigationController pushViewController:nextController
                                 animated:YES];

    if (currentCarDetailController == nil) {                        // 1
        currentCarDetailController = [[self storyboard]
                             instantiateViewControllerWithIdentifier:
                             @"CarDetailViewController"];
    }

    nextController = currentCarDetailController;                    // 2
    break;
```

Here's what happens in the numbered lines in Listing 11-14:

1. If there is no current detail controller, load one from the iPad storyboard.

2. Set `nextController` so `DetailController` can either show the new detail view or leave things if it is the existing detail view.

Now load the selected car into the new car detail by adding one line to the end of `selectCar`:

```
currentCarDetailController.myCar = selectedCar;
```

There is now enough code and IB work to show a car detail view, though not the details of any car. Run the app in the iPad and try both portrait and landscape. Update the constraints if needed to match the layout in Figure 11-14. Confirm that the fuel picker wheels have the correct range of values. Make sure the text fields have the correct keyboards: alphanumeric for the first two and a number pad for the year.

Preparing the Picker

The next step is to set values in and get values from the fuel picker. The picker shows a floating-point number as a series of individual digits. Setting the picker requires extracting the right positional digit for each wheel. Getting the fuel from the picker means compositing the positional digits back together. Follow these steps:

1. Import `CDCar.h` into `CarDetailViewController.m`.

2. Set up `#defines` for each component index by adding this code above the implementation statement:

    ```
    #define kFuelPickerHundreds 0
    #define kFuelPickerTens     1
    #define kFuelPickerOnes     2
    #define kFuelPickerDecimal  3
    #define kFuelPickerTenths   4
    ```

3. Add `#pragma` before the `@end`:

    ```
    #pragma mark — Utility Methods
    ```

4. Implement `getFuelValue`. This is the easier method for composing a float by adding each positional value multiplied by the base value of that position. For example, for the second wheel, or tens position, you would take the value of that wheel and multiply by 10. This is the code for that:

    ```
    - (float) getFuelValue {
        float fuel = 0.0;

        fuel = [self.fuelPicker selectedRowInComponent:kFuelPickerHundreds]
                * 100.0;
        fuel += [self.fuelPicker selectedRowInComponent:kFuelPickerTens]
                * 10.0;
    ```

```
        fuel += [self.fuelPicker selectedRowInComponent:kFuelPickerOnes]
                * 1.0;
        fuel += [self.fuelPicker selectedRowInComponent:kFuelPickerTenths]
                * 0.1;

        return fuel;
    }
```

5. Find the wheel values by using the highest remaining positional value and then subtract the result from the existing number. For example, if the fuel is 632.4, the 100s wheel value is the floor of dividing the fuel by 600. To get the 10s (second place) value, subtract 600 (or the 100s value multiplied by 100) and then use the floor of dividing by 10. Add the method in Listing 11-15 to the utility methods area.

Listing 11-15   **Setting Fuel Picker Fuel Component Values**

```
- (void)setFuelValues {
    float fuel = [self.myCar.fuelAmount floatValue];              // 1

    NSInteger currentValue;

    currentValue = (NSInteger)floor(fuel / 100);                  // 2
    [self.fuelPicker selectRow:currentValue                       // 3
                inComponent:kFuelPickerHundreds
                    animated:YES];
    fuel -= (currentValue * 100);                                 // 4

    currentValue = (NSInteger)floor(fuel / 10);                   // 5
    [self.fuelPicker selectRow:currentValue
                inComponent:kFuelPickerTens
                    animated:YES];
    fuel -= (currentValue * 10);


    currentValue = (NSInteger)floor(fuel);
    [self.fuelPicker selectRow:currentValue
                inComponent:kFuelPickerOnes
                    animated:YES];
    fuel -= currentValue;

    fuel *= 10;                                                   // 6
    currentValue = (NSInteger)floor(fuel);
    [self.fuelPicker selectRow:currentValue
                inComponent:kFuelPickerTenths
                    animated:YES];
}
```

Here's what happens in the numbered lines in Listing 11-15:

1. Get the current fuel level for the car.

2. Starting with the 100s position, divide `fuel` by `100` and turn the result into an integer with `floor`.

3. Set the 100s wheel to the integer value.

4. Subtract the 100s value from `fuel`. For example, if the fuel is 234.6, then step 3 sets the wheel index to 2. This step subtracts 200 from the current fuel, leaving 34.6 as the new value.

5. Use the same approach for the 10s and 1s.

6. To find the tenths, shift the value into the 1s position and use the same method to set the wheel index.

Loading a Car

In the CarValet app, showing the fuel happens when a car is loaded. You also need to set up the other fields and labels, as well as the picture. There is already a public property, `myCar`, for the car object. The simplest thing to do is to create a setter to update content if there is a new car.

Add the setter from Listing 11-16 just after the class implementation begins.

Listing 11-16   **Updating Car Data in the Detail View**

```
#pragma mark - Setters

- (void)setMyCar:(CDCar *)myCar {
    if (myCar != _myCar) {                                          // 1
        _myCar = myCar;                                             // 2

        self.carMakeField.text = _myCar.make;                      // 3
        self.carModelField.text = _myCar.model;
        self.carYearField.text = [_myCar.year stringValue];

        self.dayParkedLabel.text = [NSDateFormatter               // 4
                         localizedStringFromDate:_myCar.dateCreated
                         dateStyle:NSDateFormatterMediumStyle
                         timeStyle:NSDateFormatterNoStyle];

        self.timeParkedLabel.text = [NSDateFormatter
                         localizedStringFromDate:_myCar.dateCreated
                         dateStyle:NSDateFormatterNoStyle
                         timeStyle:NSDateFormatterMediumStyle];

        [self setFuelValues];                                      // 5
    }
}
```

Here's what happens in the numbered lines in Listing 11-16:

1. Check whether the new car is a different object from the current one. This includes setting a car when the current car is `nil`.

2. Set `myCar` to the new value. Remember to use the underscore version of a property inside a setter.

3. Set the make and model text fields from the corresponding car properties.

4. Use date formatters to set the time and date labels.

5. Call `setFuelValues`, the method written above, to set the fuel spinner.

Run the app and try looking at different cars in both portrait and landscape. All values should load correctly, though none save. This is also a good time to change the background of the car image back to the default—that is, clear.

Saving Cars

Several events could trigger saving, including clicking a Save button, changing a field or picker value, changing the car, or closing the car view. Value changes require code to detect them, and a Save button breaks the smooth user experience.

Follow these steps for saving the edited car when a new one is viewed or the controller moves from the detail content:

1. Add the `saveCar` method at the end of the utilities area:

   ```
   - (void)saveCar {
       self.myCar.make = self.carMakeField.text;
       self.myCar.model = self.carModelField.text;
       self.myCar.year = @([self.carYearField.text floatValue]);

       self.myCar.fuelAmount = @([self getFuelValue]);
   }
   ```

   The year is read from the text using `floatValue`, and fuel uses `getFuelValue`. `dateCreated` does not need to be saved because it is not editable.

2. To take care of saving when cars are changed, call `saveCar` in `setMyCar:` if the new car and old car are different:

   ```
   ...
   if (myCar != _myCar) {
       [self saveCar];

       _myCar = myCar;
       ...
   ```

3. To take care of closing the view or moving it offscreen, add `viewDidDisappear:` under `viewDidLoad` and call `saveCar` after invoking the method on the superclass:

```
- (void)viewDidDisappear:(BOOL)animated {
    [super viewDidDisappear:animated];

    [self saveCar];
}
```

This time when you run the app, the cars are saved, though the menu of cars does not reflect the change. In this version, updating the table requires viewing a different top-level menu item such as About and then viewing the Car menu.

Polishing the Car Detail Controller

You need to do four things to polish the car detail controller:

- Update the car table menu when the details change.
- Close the car detail content controller when dismissing the car table menu.
- Disable editing in the car detail controller when there is no current car.
- Change the popover menu behavior to stay open when Cars is selected and closed when a particular car is selected.

Updating a previous car table cell happens in one of three ways: The user selects a new car, goes back to the top-level menu, or changes the car table menu sort. All these actions happen inside CarTableViewController:

1. Open CarTableViewController.m and add the following bold code inside the if condition of tableView:didSelectRowAtIndexPath::

   ```
   if (self.delegate != nil) {
       NSIndexPath *previousPath = currentViewCarPath;

       [self.delegate selectCar:[self carToView]];

       if (previousPath != nil) {
           [currentTableView reloadRowsAtIndexPaths:@[previousPath]
                                   withRowAnimation:NO];
       }
   }
   ```

   Ensure that previousPath is not nil, or the reload call crashes.

2. Modify the carSortChanged: method to clear the current car index path for any current delegate. That means checking for a delegate and selected row, and if they both exist, updating the table and telling the delegate there is no selection. Do this by adding the following bold code to the top of the method below the variable declarations:

   ```
   SEL compareSelector = nil;
   ```

```
if ((self.delegate != nil) &&
    (self.tableView.indexPathForSelectedRow != nil)) {
        currentViewCarPath = nil;
        [self.delegate selectCar:nil];
}

switch (self.carSortControl.selectedSegmentIndex) {
```

Run the app and confirm that the cell values update as you move between cars, updating fields.

As you gain more experience with iOS, you'll see that there are better ways to keep multiple objects synchronized with changes in data. (See the "Note: A Better Way to Update.") However, they are beyond the scope of this book.

> **Note: A Better Way to Update**
>
> The best way to update the car table is by using an iOS notification mechanism. Doing so means every controller or object that cares about a change can register to be notified and take appropriate action. When you use this mechanism, you don't need to make multiple changes every time you add some code that can modify data.
>
> However, NSNotificationCenter and Key Value Coding/Key Value Observation (KVC/KVO) are more advanced uses of iOS and beyond the scope of this book. With KVC, the consequences of an incorrect implementation are sending messages to at best nil and more usually deallocated objects. These are some of the hardest bugs to track down. For more information, see *Objective-C Phrase Book* by David Chisnall or the Apple documentation.

Closing the Car Detail Controller

Closing the car detail controller when the user goes back to the main menu requires only a few lines of code in MainMenuViewController. When you do this, you are guaranteed the following:

- Tapping the Back button opens the main menu.
- The main menu is the only place that the car table menu is created.
- The main menu is the only place the car detail controller is created, and it will have a reference to that controller.

You can use one of the view life cycle methods for closing the detail controller. You need a message sent after the initial view is loaded, so it will be one of the Appear messages, either viewWillAppear: or viewDidAppear:. The big difference between the two is when the animation occurs. viewWillAppear: is called before the view appears but after everything is laid out. The other is called after the view is rendered on the screen.

Insert the code in Listing 11-17 in MainMenuViewController.m below viewDidLoad and try it. Then try the difference in timing using viewDidAppear:. You will find that the latter has too much lag time before the animation and is not balanced with originally showing the car detail content.

Listing 11-17   **Closing Car Detail Content**

```
- (void)viewWillAppear:(BOOL)animated
{
    [super viewWillAppear:animated];

    if (currentCarDetailController != nil) {                        // 1
        [DetailController sharedDetailController].currDetailController = nil;
        currentCarDetailController = nil;                           // 2
    }
}
```

Here's what happens in the numbered lines in Listing 11-17.

1. Update the detail content only if there is a current detail car controller.

2. `nil` out the local reference to avoid conflicts with the next controller. If you want to see the issue, comment out the line, select the car detail view, select the about view, and then go back to car detail view. The about view still shows.

Again, confirm that the changes work by running the app. It is a good idea to incrementally test changes as soon as possible.

Enabling and Disabling Editing Car Details

Preventing the user from interacting with any editable items is the fastest way to disable editing. Some views can be enabled and disabled, and for any that cannot, you can disable user interaction.

You want to disable editing whenever there is no car to edit, something that can happen in two ways. First, the controller might have just been shown and not had a car set. Second, you can explicitly set `myCar` to `nil`. Of course, you need to reenable editing when there is a valid car, and this suggests a method with an argument for the enabled state. Add the method in Listing 11-18 to `CarDetailViewController.m` below `saveCar`.

Listing 11-18   **Updating Car Detail's Editable State**

```
- (void)updateEditableState:(BOOL)enabled {                        // 1
    self.carMakeField.enabled = enabled;                           // 2
    self.carModelField.enabled = enabled;
    self.carYearField.enabled = enabled;
    self.fuelPicker.userInteractionEnabled = enabled;              // 3
}
```

Here's what happens in the numbered lines in Listing 11-18:

1. Use an argument to enable or disable editing.

2. `UITextField` has an enabled property.

3. Make sure the fuel picker enables user interaction so users can spin the wheels.

When the car detail controller is first created, it has no car to edit. Add the following bold line to viewDidLoad:

```
- (void)viewDidLoad
{
    [super viewDidLoad];

    self.navigationItem.hidesBackButton = YES;
    [self updateEditableState:NO];
}
```

The other time the car detail controller has no car to edit is when the car is changed and the new car is nil. Add the following bold line near the beginning of setMyCar:

```
...
if (myCar != _myCar) {
    [self saveCar];

    [self updateEditableState:(myCar != nil)];

    _myCar = myCar;
    ...
```

Popover Behavior Modifications

The last bit of polish you need to add to the CarValet app at this point is to refine the behavior of the popover menu in portrait mode. Currently, the detail controller is the only object controlling the popover, and it is the only one with a reference. Encapsulation recommends adding a public interface for hiding or showing the popover. Here's what you do:

1. Open DetailController.m, with the Assistant editor showing the corresponding .h file. Add the following method above the singleton #pragma:

   ```
   #pragma mark - Public Methods

   - (void)hidePopover {
       [menuPopoverController dismissPopoverAnimated:YES];
   }
   ```

2. Modify the declaration of the existing currentDetailController setter so that it looks like this:

   ```
   - (void)setCurrDetailController:(UIViewController*)currDetailController
                       hidePopover:(BOOL)hidePopover {
   ```

3. Replace the setter's call to [menuPopoverController dismissPopoverAnimated:YES] with a conditional call to the new method:

   ```
   ...
       }
   ```

```
    if (hidePopover)
        [self hidePopover];

    if (newStack != nil) {
    ...
```

4. To minimize required changes and maximize compatibility, add code for a new default setter that keeps the old behavior—that is, hiding the popover—and put the new method above setCurrDetailController:hidePopover::

```
- (void)setCurrDetailController:(UIViewController*)currDetailController {
    [self setCurrDetailController:currDetailController hidePopover:YES];
}
```

5. Add public method declarations for the two new methods to the end of the .h file:

```
- (void)setCurrDetailController:(UIViewController*)currDetailController
                    hidePopover:(BOOL)hidePopover;
```

```
- (void)hidePopover;
```

Test the changes and make sure there are no changes in behavior. So far, only the DetailController is calling the new methods, but that is still a good test.

There are two popover behavioral changes to implement. First, the popover should not close after a user taps the top-level Car menu item. Second, the popover should close when the user taps a particular car. MainMenuViewController can handle both of those cases using the methods just added to DetailController.

To keep the popover open, you need to use the new method with the BOOL argument. You also need to prevent the following last call in tableView:didSelectRowAtIndexPath: from setting the current detail controller as that closes the popup:

```
detailController.currDetailController = nextController;
```

To add code keeping the popover open, follow these steps:

1. In the tableView:didSelectRowAtIndexPath: method of MainMenuViewController.m, declare a Boolean above the switch statement to indicate whether currDetailController should be updated. This variable can replace newDetail, which is no longer required:

```
BOOL updateDetailController = YES;

switch (indexPath.row) {
```

2. Change the last line to conditionally update the detail controller based on the new variable:

```
if (updateDetailController) {
    detailController.currDetailController = nextController;
}
```

3. Modify the end of the `kPadMenuCarsItem` case to use the new setter so it looks like the following code. Note that the line to set the `nextController` to `nil` is gone. The new code is in bold:

```
...
if (currentCarDetailController == nil) {
    currentCarDetailController = [[self storyboard]
                                instantiateViewControllerWithIdentifier:
                                @"CarDetailViewController"];

    [detailController setCurrDetailController:currentCarDetailController
                                hidePopover:NO];
}

updateDetailController = NO;

break;
...
```

4. In the `kPadMenuImagesItem` case, remove the line that sets `newDetail` to `NO`.

5. Remove any lines of code from between the end of the switch statement and the `if` statement you modified in step 2.

6. Hide the popover when a car is selected by adding one line of code at the end of `selectCar`:

```
[[DetailController sharedDetailController] hidePopover];
```

Run the CarValet app and try all the combinations: navigating to car detail, trying to edit the blank detail content view, going back to the main menu, going to details, viewing different cars, changing values, making sure cells update when you navigate away, and so on. Also test the app on an iPhone and/or iPod touch since you made changes to a controller from that storyboard.

Summary

You have turned the CarValet app into a universal app, one that supports both iPhone/iPod touch and iPad. By doing so, you greatly increase the number of possible customers. As you went through this chapter, you learned some important information about designing for the iPad, including how to present information and how to use the split view controller for navigation-based apps.

You explored `UISplitViewController`, including how it uses master and detail controllers to make navigating hierarchies of data easy. You began adding a tablet experience by adding a split view controller to the iPad storyboard and adding code to check whether the app is running on an iPad.

Next, you added navigation to the master controller and got practice with a static table view. You added `DetailController` to make sure your app works in portrait and landscape. It manages presentation of the master controller in both orientations, including adding or removing a menu button. You learned that you can use singleton managers for many different tasks.

You moved on to implementing the detail screens in three different ways. In one case, you loaded the About screen from an XIB file. In another case, you loaded the car images from the iPhone storyboard, a useful skill for any developer. Finally, you created a targeted car detail screen and learned some design considerations for tablet versus phone screens. You solidified loading from other storyboards by creating an app navigation submenu for viewing a list of cars.

While adding the detail screens, you learned how to create a menu manager for transitioning between app sections. And you used an advanced way of doing view animations to make moving between sections look even better.

As you progressed through the chapter, you learned about singleton objects and why and when you might use them. You got some significant practice with accessor methods, as well as tips on designing classes. You increased your toolkit, adding `UIPickerView`, which is a new view element, and you learned a more refined way of transitioning between views using `CATransition`.

Now that you have finished this chapter, you can create apps for iPhone or iPad, or universal apps that work on both. You can now make key design decisions based on screen space. And for iPad, you can use the split view controller for navigation, as well as use your own detail and menu controllers to manage each activity. By using singletons, you can create managers and other kinds of objects where there can be only one instance.

You now have most of the pieces you need to create apps. There is one more piece that is central to the phone and tablet experience though: touch. Except for a few hardware buttons such as volume, almost all interaction and input from a user is by touch. In Chapter 12, "Touch Basics," you work directly with touches, including detecting system and custom gestures, as well as tracking movement.

Challenges

1. In `CarDetailViewController`, every time the car is changed, all the data is saved, even if it does not change. Update the controller to save data only when the data has changed.

2. In `CarDetailViewController`, entering the fuel is easy, but reading it is not. Add a label that shows the fuel and changes when the picker changes. Make sure the fuel area is visually grouped.

3. Add a new top-level menu item called Almost Blank that brings up a view controller with a label that says "This view intentionally left blank (except for this text)."

4. Practice setting an image for a car. This challenge requires the artwork in the CH11 `Assets Big Placeholder` folder from the sample code for this chapter. The basic steps to do this are as follows:

- Add a button to the car detail view centered over the car image view.

- Clear the button title and set the image for the default state to `big-placeholder`.

- Then change the State Config to Highlighted and set the image to `big-placeholder-selected`.

- Constrain the button appropriately so it shows up correctly.

- Now add code to detect if the button was pressed, and if so, set the image in the car image view to one of the pictures added in Chapter 6, "Scrolling." You also need to hide or show either the button or image view based on if a custom image is set.

Touch Basics

Gestures are everywhere. Tapping buttons, scrolling through lists, zooming images...most interactions with an iPhone or iPad are some sort of gesture. iOS provides lots of user interface elements with built-in gestures, but what if you want more?

That is what `UIGestureRecognizer` and related classes are for. They enable you to do things like attach a custom swipe or create your own recognizers. Setting up a recognizer can be as easy as writing an action method and making a few connections in Interface Builder (IB).

In this chapter, you add three recognizers to the CarValet app: One uses swipes to move through car details, another takes the iPad app back home, and the last one tracks a finger. First, you learn the basics of gesture recognizers—the common parts and the different types. Next, you implement swipes to navigate through car details. Then, you learn about creating a simple custom gesture recognizer and the importance of state. Next, you add a custom iPad gesture for resetting the interface. Finally, you create one more custom gesture for moving a view.

Gesture Recognizer Basics

From tapping buttons to moving a slider, many built-in interface elements implement their own gestures. But sometimes you need to do something different: swipe through cars, give a quick gesture to reset state, or move a view to a new destination. All these gestures are easy to implement using `UIGestureRecognizer` and related classes.

`UIGestureRecognizer` is an abstract superclass and encapsulates the properties and behaviors that are common to any recognizer: what view the recognizer is attached to, whether it is enabled, where the touch is happening, how many fingers are on the screen, and so on. Built-in recognizers as well as your own custom ones are all based on the abstract one.

Recognizers have a few common attributes. Every gesture has the following:

- The view the gesture recognizer is attached to
- The number of touches—both how many fingers are required and, during the gesture, how many are on the screen
- The current or previous touch location(s)

Gestures can have target/action pairs. A *target* is an object that implements an *action* method. The gesture sends the action method at appropriate points. When the message is sent depends on the gesture type: *single* or *continuous*.

A single gesture happens once—for example, a tap or a swipe. The action is called when the user performs the gesture. Continuous gestures, such as pinches and pans, call the action method throughout the gesture as well as at the end. This is an important difference. With a single gesture, the action message is called at the end, and only if the gesture is recognized. The method is not called if the gesture is cancelled or unrecognized. Continuous gestures send a stream of updates, and for the built-in gestures, have no notion of successful recognition.

iOS comes with six recognizer classes ready for you to use:

- `UITapGestureRecognizer` detects taps in a view. You specify how many touches, or fingers, are needed as well as how many times those touches need to happen. For example, you could require two fingers tapping three times. Tap is a single gesture, so the action message is sent only when the full gesture is recognized. Failed recognition sends nothing.

- `UIPinchGestureRecognizer` is a continuous gesture activated when the user pinches two fingers together or pushes them apart. You get messages when the fingers move and have access to a scale factor and velocity. These let you perform an action in time with the user. The built-in pinch gesture uses the scale and velocity to zoom in and out in time with the user.

- `UIRotationGestureRecognizer` happens as a user rotates two fingers. You get continuous messages with the amount of rotation as well as the velocity. You use these to match the onscreen rotation, or your own behavior, to user movement.

- `UISwipeGestureRecognizer` looks for a swipe in the specified direction with the required number of fingers. A swipe is a single gesture going up, down, left, or right, so you get a message only if the gesture is completed.

- `UIPanGestureRecognizer` starts when the user drags a particular number of fingers across the screen. You specify the minimum and maximum fingers and are continuously sent messages. The gesture includes the translation and velocity.

- `UILongPressGestureRecognizer` starts when the required number of fingers are pressed for the specified time without moving beyond a pixel boundary. You get continuous messages as the gesture is in progress.

Swiping Through Cars

People expect gestures to be a part of apps, so much so that they try gestures in places where they think they should work. One common navigation gesture is swiping through detailed content. The car images view of the CarValet app already supports swipes, but the detail view does not.

Most of the work of adding swipe gestures is in the supporting code for changing the displayed car. Very little is specific to the swipe. These are the general steps to get swipes working:

1. Add a method for moving back and forth through the cars: `nextOrPreviousCar:` in `CarTableViewController`.

2. Enable both car detail controllers to call the new navigation method.

3. Add action selectors for the swipe gestures to the iPhone and iPad car detail controllers.

4. Use the Storyboard editor to add and connect right and left swipe gestures for each car detail controller.

Moving Through Cars

You need to add a method to move to the next or previous car. The hardest part is figuring out the next row, especially because there can be multiple sections. Next should go to the first car of the next section or wrap around to the beginning of the first section from the last car. Previous should go backward through the list of cars, moving to the last car when a section changes or to the last car from the first car.

Use the project you were using for Chapter 11, " Navigation Controllers II: Split View and the iPad," or use `CH12 CarValet Starter` from the sample code from this chapter. First, add code for moving to the next or previous car. There are three routines to do this, shown in Listings 12-1, 12-2, and 12-3. You need to start by adding the following `#pragma` before the end of the class in `CarTableViewController.m` and then add each listing after the `#pragma`:

```
#pragma mark - View previous/next car
```

Listing 12-1 **Finding the Next Car**

```
- (NSIndexPath*)indexPathOfNext {
    NSInteger section = self.tableView.indexPathForSelectedRow.section;      // 1
    NSInteger row = self.tableView.indexPathForSelectedRow.row;
    NSInteger maxSection = [self.tableView numberOfSections] - 1;
    NSInteger maxRows = [self.tableView numberOfRowsInSection:section] - 1;

    if ((row + 1) > maxRows) {                                               // 2
        if (section > maxSection) {                                          // 3
            section = 0;
            row = 0;
        } else {
            if (section != maxSection) {                                     // 4
                section += 1;
            } else {
                section = 0;
            }
            row = 0;
```

```
        }
    } else {                                                        // 5
        row += 1;
    }

    return [NSIndexPath indexPathForRow:row inSection:section];
}
```

Here's what happens in the numbered lines in Listing 12-1:

1. Set up state variables.

2. Determine whether the next row is beyond the end of the current section.

3. The row is beyond, so check whether this is the last section, and if so, reset to the first row of the first section.

4. This is not the last section, so go to the first row of the next section if there is one.

5. This is not the last row, so go to the next row (increment by 1).

Listing 12-2   **Finding the Previous Car**

```
- (NSIndexPath*)indexPathOfPrevious {
    NSInteger section = self.tableView.indexPathForSelectedRow.section;
    NSInteger row = self.tableView.indexPathForSelectedRow.row;
    NSInteger maxSection = [self.tableView numberOfSections] - 1;
    NSInteger maxRows = [self.tableView numberOfRowsInSection:section] - 1;

    if (row == 0) {                                                 // 1
        if (maxSection == 0) {                                      // 2
            row = maxRows;
        } else {
            if (section == 0) {                                     // 3
                section = maxSection;
            } else {
                section -= 1;
            }
            row = [self.tableView numberOfRowsInSection:section] - 1;  // 4
        }
    } else {
        row -= 1;                                                   // 5
    }

    return [NSIndexPath indexPathForRow:row inSection:section];
}
```

Here's what happens in the numbered lines in Listing 12-2:

1. Determine whether this is the first row of the section.

2. This is the first row, so if there is one section, wrap the row to the end.

3. There is more than one section, so decrement or wrap the section number.

4. Set the row to the last item in the chosen section.

5. This is not the first row, so go to the previous one (decrement by 1).

Listing 12-3   **Moving to the Next or Previous Car**

```
- (void)nextOrPreviousCar:(BOOL)isNext {
    NSIndexPath *newSelection;                                      // 1

    if (isNext) {
        newSelection = [self indexPathOfNext];
    } else {
        newSelection = [self indexPathOfPrevious];
    }

    [self.tableView selectRowAtIndexPath:newSelection              // 2
                        animated:YES
                    scrollPosition:UITableViewScrollPositionMiddle];

    if (self.delegate != nil) {                                    // 3
        NSIndexPath *previousPath = currentViewCarPath;

        [self.delegate selectCar:[self carToView]];                // 4

        if (previousPath != nil) {
            [currentTableView reloadRowsAtIndexPaths:@[previousPath]
                            withRowAnimation:NO];
        }
    }
}
```

Here's what happens in the numbered lines in Listing 12-3:

1. Specify a variable for the index path of the new selected cell.

2. After finding the new path, tell the table view to show the new selection.

3. Check whether there is a delegate, like the iPad car detail.

4. If there is a delegate, update the delegate's car and update the table view cell for the old car.

Calling `nextOrPreviousCar:`

The iPad and iPhone car detail controllers need to send the new `nextOrPreviousCar:` method to their related car table menu. One way to do that is to make the new method public and then set a reference to the car table view in each detail view. An alternative is to expand the existing `ViewCarProtocol` and add a protocol-enabled delegate to the iPad car detail. Add the protocol and behavior by following these steps:

1. Add a new protocol message to `ViewCarProtocol.h` with the same signature as `nexOrPreviousCar:`, using the following lines:

   ```
   @optional
   - (void)nextOrPreviousCar:(BOOL)isNext;
   ```

   The message is optional because other classes support the protocol but might not need to move through cars. For example, `MainMenuViewController` on iPad supports the protocol but has no control over moving cars.

2. Open `CarDetailViewController.h` and import `ViewCarProtocol.h`.

3. Add a delegate that supports `ViewCarProtocol`:

   ```
   @property (weak, nonatomic) id <ViewCarProtocol> delegate;
   ```

4. Open `MainMenuViewController.m` and make the bold changes in Listing 12-4 for `tableView:didSelectRowAtIndexPath:`.

Listing 12-4   **Updates to** `tableView:didSelectRowAtIndexPath:`

```
UIViewController *nextController;
CarTableViewController *carTable;                                        // 1

BOOL updateDetailController = YES;

switch (indexPath.row) {
    case kPadMenuCarsItem:
        carTable = [iPhoneStory instantiateViewControllerWithIdentifier:
                    @"CarTableViewController"];

        carTable.navigationItem.title = @"Cars";
        carTable.delegate = self;

        nextController = carTable;
        [self.navigationController pushViewController:nextController
                                      animated:YES];

        if (currentCarDetailController == nil) {
            currentCarDetailController = [[self storyboard]
                                   instantiateViewControllerWithIdentifier:
```

```
                                      @"CarDetailViewController"];
        [detailController setCurrDetailController:currentCarDetailController
                                  hidePopover:NO];
        currentCarDetailController.delegate = carTable;                  // 2
    }

    updateDetailController = NO;
    break;
```

Here's what happens in the numbered lines in Listing 12-4:

1. Get a reference to the car table view controller, in case you need to create a detail view, and set its delegate.

2. Set the delegate of the iPad car detail view so it can send messages to move back and forth through the car detail view.

Adding Action Selectors

You now have almost all the code changes needed to support swipes: The car table can move to the next or previous car, and both the iPhone and iPad car detail views can call the new method. The last new code is the selectors used by the swipe gestures.

All the work for the iPad selectors is done by nextOrPreviousCar:, which contains code for updating the state of the delegate—in this case, the iPad car detail view. Add the code in Listing 12-5 above the utility method #pragma in CarDetailViewController.m.

Listing 12-5   iPad Car Detail Swipe Gesture Recognizers

```
#pragma mark - Gestures

- (IBAction)swipeCarRight:(UISwipeGestureRecognizer*)sender {      // 1
    [self.delegate nextOrPreviousCar:YES];                        // 2
}

- (IBAction)swipeCarLeft:(UISwipeGestureRecognizer*)sender {      // 3
    [self.delegate nextOrPreviousCar:NO];                         // 4
}
```

Here's what happens in the numbered lines in Listing 12-5:

1. Add an action method for the swiping right gesture. Note that you can quickly create any action method by using Xcode's completion feature. See the "Tip: Quickly Adding an Action Method."

2. Send YES to go to the next car.

3. Add an action method for swiping left.

4. Send NO for the previous car.

Tip: Quickly Adding an Action Method

You can quickly add action messages to your class files by using Xcode completion and the built-in templates. Here's what you do:

1. Place your cursor at the start of an empty line between the @implementation and @end statements, and outside the body of any method.

2. Type a dash (-), followed by an open parenthesis (() and then start typing ibaction. As you type, Xcode provides completions.

3. When you see a completion like the one in Figure 12-1, press Return.

Now you can fill in the selector and, if needed, the type of the selector. You can also change the argument name to make the code self-documenting.

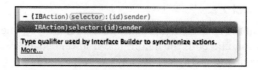

Figure 12-1   Xcode action method completion

Implementing the iPhone Action Selectors

Setting up the action selectors for ViewCarTableViewController in the iPhone detail view requires a bit of work. Because the car is set by car detail using a protocol method, you cannot use a setter to force an update. And, the delegate needs to be told if the current car needs to be saved.

This is the basic selector flow:

1. Tell the delegate to save the current car.

2. Move to the next or previous car.

3. Update the view content with the new car.

Make the following changes in ViewCarTableViewController.m:

1. Add the following skeleton method above titleText (the new code is bold):

```
...
#pragma mark - Utility Methods

- (void)loadCarData {
```

```
    }


    #pragma mark - MakeModelEditProtocol

    -(NSString*)titleText {
    ...
```

2. In `viewDidLoad`, select all the code except the call to `[super viewDidLoad]` and then cut and paste that code into the body of `loadCarData`.

3. Add a call to the new `loadCarData` method in `viewDidLoad`. Now `viewDidLoad` has only two lines of code.

4. Put the code from Listing 12-6 above the `Utility Methods` #pragma methods you just added.

Listing 12-6   iPhone Car Detail Swipe Gesture Recognizers

```
#pragma mark - Gestures

- (IBAction)swipeCarRight:(UISwipeGestureRecognizer*)sender {        // 1
    [self.delegate carViewDone:dataUpdated];                        // 2

    [self.delegate nextOrPreviousCar:YES];                          // 3

    [self loadCarData];                                             // 4
}
- (IBAction)swipeCarLeft:(UISwipeGestureRecognizer*)sender {         // 5
    [self.delegate carViewDone:dataUpdated];

    [self.delegate nextOrPreviousCar:NO];                           // 6

    [self loadCarData];
}
```

Here's what happens in the numbered lines in Listing 12-6:

1. Add an action method for the swiping right gesture.

2. Tell the delegate to update the current car.

3. Send YES to go to the next car.

4. Update the onscreen content.

5. Add an action method for swiping left.

6. Show the previous car by sending NO.

Adding the Swipe Gestures

You have written all the code for reacting to gestures. You now have a method for moving to the next or previous car, both car detail views can send the message, and there are selectors for the gestures.

The final step is to add the gestures and wire them in. You can do all this in the Storyboard editor for the iPhone and iPad. The steps are the same for either platform. The book shows iPhone and lets you update iPad for practice. Follow these steps:

1. Open `Main_iPhone.storyboard`.

2. Look for the Swipe gesture object in the Utilities area, or type `Swipe` into the Search area. Drag one into the bar below the View Car controller on the IB Canvas as shown in Figure 12-2. (The image uses a different search term to show all the gesture objects.)

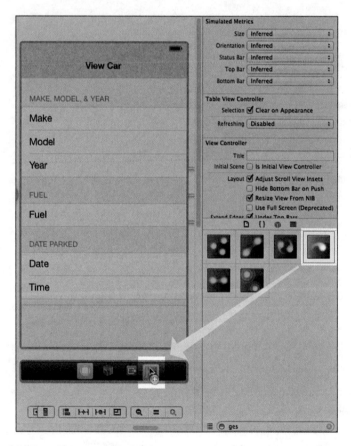

Figure 12-2   Adding a gesture recognizer

3. In the left-hand list, add `Right` to the end of the name.

As shown in Figure 12-3, set the action method for the swipe by Ctrl-dragging from the new swipe object to the view controller object. Then choose `swipeCarRight:` in the popup that appears.

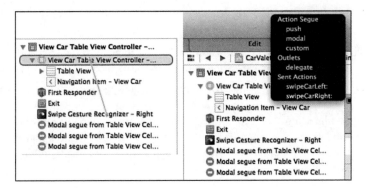

Figure 12-3   Setting the gesture selector

4. Open the connection popup for the table view and connect the `gestureRecognizers` outlet collection to the new recognizer.

5. Drag in another swipe gesture, but this time drag it onto the table view, as shown in Figure 12-4. Doing this adds the swipe to the table view's collection of recognizers.

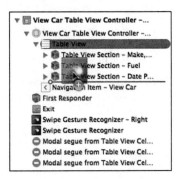

Figure 12-4   Adding a gesture to the table view

6. Set the selector for the new gesture to `swipeCarLeft:`.

7. With the gesture still selected, use the Attributes inspector on the left to set the swipe direction to Left, as shown in Figure 12-5.

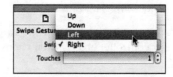

Figure 12-5   Setting the gesture direction

Choose an iPhone simulator and run the app. Make sure there are a few cars and then view the detail for one of them. Now you can swipe right to go to the next car or left to go back.

You can use similar steps to add swipes to the iPad. You should add the swipe objects to `CarDetailViewController` in the iPad storyboard. When you are done, choose an iPad simulator and run the app again. Try it in landscape to see both the menu of cars and car detail. Swiping right and left in the detail area should change the car detail and updates the highlighted cell in the table. Try different table sorts (such as make or model) and make sure the selected car moves between sections as expected.

Preventing Recognizers from Working

The iPad occasionally shows a car detail view with no information and disables interacting with any of the buttons, fields, or the picker. It does not disable the swipes. They do work, but the behavior might be unexpected.

You can disable recognizers in two ways. The first is to set a recognizer's `enabled` property to `NO`. Doing so requires a reference to the gesture. A second way is to set a gesture delegate and implement `gestureRecognizer:shouldReceiveTouch:`, as follows:

1. Open `Main_iPad.storyboard` and set the delegate for the swipe gestures to `CarDetailViewController`. You can do this by Ctrl-clicking a gesture recognizer and dragging a connection from the delegate outlet to the controller.

2. Open `CarDetailViewController.m` and add the following code after the last gesture action method. The method only allows gesture recognizers to receive touches if there is a car (that is, if `myCar` is non-nil):

```
-(BOOL)gestureRecognizer:(UIGestureRecognizer *)gestureRecognizer
    shouldReceiveTouch:(UITouch *)touch {
  return (self.myCar != nil);
}
```

Run the app and confirm that gestures are blocked when there are no car details shown and that gestures work when there is a car.

Custom Recognizers

In the last section, you added a built-in recognizer to the CarValet app. The next step is to add a custom recognizer. Before doing that, you need to understand more about how recognizers work.

Recognizers are state machines, flowing through four states for single-gesture recognizers and through seven for continuous ones. You update state and implement the gesture behavior by specializing one or more `UIGestureRecognizer` messages.

Recognizer States

Gesture recognizers are in one of four states—or seven, if they are continuously sending updates. Their default state is that the gesture is possible, even if there are no fingers on the screen. This might seem strange, but it is very important. When fingers touch down, the system only checks gestures that could recognize something (and are enabled). Therefore, `UIGestureRecognitionPossible` is the default state for all recognizers.

Single gestures track touch(es) until the gesture is either recognized, not possible to recognize, or cancelled. Continuous gestures add states for sending messages to their delegate and for resetting to some default state. Figure 12-6 shows the two different flows.

The top flow shows a single-gesture recognizer, and it is in one of three states. Possible is the default, and you are responsible for setting Recognized when appropriate. The Failed state occurs when the wrong number of touches occurs, the stroke pattern is wrong, the user lifts their finger(s) before the stroke is detected, or some other interruption occurs. The system resets the state to Possible after you finish processing a gesture.

Continuous flow is a bit more complicated. Failure usually occurs only for the wrong number of touches, although Cancellation takes care of the other failure cases. Unlike with a single stroke, the recognizer moves through a Began into a repeating Changed state. Began and Changed result in updates to the delegate. If there is an ending pattern, when it is detected, the state changes to either Recognized or, if the gesture was not close enough to the required one, Failed. The Failed state also occurs when there is a system interruption or the user lifts his or her finger before the gesture is completed.

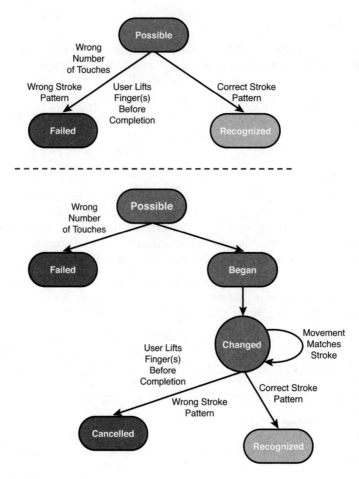

Figure 12-6　Stroke state diagrams

Table 12-1 shows the system state constants and briefly describes them.

Table 12-1　**Gesture State Constants**

System Constant	Description
Single or Both Types of Gestures	
UIGestureRecognizerStatePossible	The recognizer is either idle or checking for a match. This is the default state.
UIGestureRecognizerStateFailed	Failed to match the gesture. Could be because: the number of touches was wrong or the stroke did not match.

System Constant	Description
UIGestureRecognizerStateRecognized UIGestureRecognizerStateEnded	Successfully matched the gesture or there was no problem (for example, pinch is done).
Continuous Only Gestures	
UIGestureRecognizerStateBegan	Recognizer has received touches that could be part of the continuous gesture.
UIGestureRecognizerStateChanged	Gesture and/or touches are still valid. Update internal state and send a message to the delegate on the next event loop.
UIGestureRecognizerStateCancelled	Something has occurred to cancel recognition. Usually this is a system interrupt, such as a phone call. It also could be a particular gesture sequence or some other input, such as a time limit or bounds constraint.

Specializing Recognizer Messages

You can create a custom recognizer by subclassing UIGestureRecognizer and implementing one or more of the touch event handlers. You are also likely to implement other methods from the superclass, as well as your own logic and state variables.

The recognizer has two main jobs: Keep the gestures state up to date and recognize your custom stroke and/or perform your custom behavior. The main event handler methods follow the sequence of a stroke:

- touchesBegan:withEvent: is sent when the touches first occur—that is, when the user touches the screen.

- touchesMoved:withEvent: is sent each time the user moves one or more fingers.

- touchesEnded:withEvent: means the user has lifted his or her finger(s).

- touchesCancelled:withEvent: is an interruption by the system, such as a phone call. This event is not the same as the Cancelled state, though it might result in the gesture moving to that state. For example, if a drag is interrupted, you could reset the position or leave it where it was.

- reset is called by the system to reset the state of your recognizer. Typically, this is sent when the state changes to Recognized or End.

There are additional methods in both UIGestureRecognizer and UIGestureRecognizerDelegate for helping to coordinate with other gesture recognizers. For more information, see Chapter 1, "Gestures and Touches," in *Core iOS 6 Developers Cookbook* by Erica Sadun.

A confusing part of creating recognizers is that you do not end your own gesture. In other words, setting the state to Recognized does not stop the flow of events to `touchesMoved:withEvent:`, nor does it call `touchesEnded:withEvent:`. Instead, your recognizer might need some internal state variables to track whether the gesture is done. The only things that can stop the flow of touches are the user removing their finger(s) from the display or the system cancelling the gesture. Typically, you wait until `touchesEnded` to set the Recognized or Failed state. The best way to see how this works is to implement a recognizer, which you do in the next section.

iPad Go Home

Tapping a tab bar button in CarValet on the iPhone takes you back to the root view of that particular section. If you are viewing car details, tapping the tab button takes you back to the car table menu. On iPad, there is no similar control. Sometimes it is useful to set the iPad app back to a default state.

In this section, you implement a custom gesture recognizer for returning the iPad to its just-launched state: The master view shows the app sections menu, and the detail view has the default car valet tent picture.

For a gesture to work, the recognizer needs to be attached to a view. When the user taps in that view or any of its subviews, the system sends appropriate messages. The go home recognizer is attached to the current detail view. Since it makes no sense to activate the gesture until the main menu is up, `MainMenuViewController` sets up the recognizer and is the delegate. `DetailController` takes care of adding the gesture to the current detail view, if needed.

There are three steps for implementing and attaching the recognizer:

1. Create the custom `ReturnGestureRecognizer` subclass.

2. Add the gesture recognizer in `DetailController`.

3. Add a gesture callback action in `MainMenuViewController` and add the gesture recognizer to `DetailController`.

Creating the Return Gesture Recognizer

Before you create the gesture recognizer, you need to choose a gesture and determine how to detect it. Since it *returns* the iPad app to a known state, you can use a small letter *r*. The first challenge is determining how to recognize the character.

The easiest way to recognize a stroke is by breaking it down into components separated by transitions in x and/or y movement. As part of the events, you get both the current and previous touch points, allowing detection of changes in movement. The x value increases from left to right of the screen, and y increases from top to bottom. You can use comparisons between previous and current positions to determine changes in direction. If you needed other information such as velocity, you could use other data, such as time.

An *r* has two strokes, with four main components, as shown in Figure 12-7. The left side shows a completed lowercase *r*. The middle image is the two main stroke movements: a downward straight line followed by an upward-right hook.

The right-side image breaks the gesture down into strokes and shows the three main transitions. The first stroke is downward and starts the recognizer. The first transition happens when y reverses direction after moving down some minimal distance. Next, x increases and y decreases. Then x increases, and y moves relatively little. When this last phase happens, the stroke is recognized.

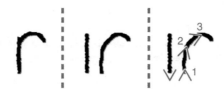

Figure 12-7   The *r* stroke

Creating ReturnGestureRecognizer

Before you start coding, you need to design any state variables. One obvious variable is the current stroke phase: Down is 0, the initial up is 1, the first turn is 2, and the final stroke is 3. The other variable comes from the need to have a minimal amount of down stroke. Tracking that requires knowing the initial touch. Implement the gesture recognizer by following these steps:

1. Use the Navigator to add a new group below iPad called Other. Select that group and add a new Objective-C class called ReturnGestureRecognizer, a subclass of UIGestureRecognizer.

2. Import the gesture recognizer subclass into ReturnGestureRecognizer.m:

   ```
   #import <UIKit/UIGestureRecognizerSubclass.h>
   ```

3. Add a #define for the maximum stroke wobble and add the state variables to the implementation (the new code is bold):

   ```
   #define kRStrokeDelta       5.0f

   @implementation ReturnGestureRecognizer {
       NSInteger   strokePhase;
       CGPoint     firstTap;
   }
   ```

4. Use Listings 12-7, 12-8, and 12-9 to add the recognition methods.

Listing 12-7   **Return Gesture Methods for Reset and Began**

```objc
- (void)reset {
    [super reset];                                              // 1

    strokePhase = 0;                                            // 2
}


- (void)touchesBegan:(NSSet *)touches withEvent:(UIEvent *)event {
    [super touchesBegan:touches withEvent:event];

    if (([touches count] != 1) ||
        ([[touches.anyObject view] isKindOfClass:[UIControl class]])) {   // 3
        self.state = UIGestureRecognizerStateFailed;
        return;
    }

    firstTap = [touches.anyObject locationInView:self.view.superview];    // 4
}
```

Here's what happens in the numbered lines in Listing 12-7:

1. Always call the superclass.

2. Reset the stroke phase.

3. If there is more than one touch/finger or the touch is in a control such as a button, the gesture fails.

4. There is only one finger, so set the location of the first tap.

Listing 12-8   **The Main** `touchesMoved:withEvent:` **Method**

```objc
- (void)touchesMoved:(NSSet *)touches withEvent:(UIEvent *)event {
    [super touchesMoved:touches withEvent:event];

    if ((self.state == UIGestureRecognizerStateFailed) ||      // 1
        (self.state == UIGestureRecognizerStateRecognized)) {
        return;
    }

    UIView *superView = [self.view superview];                 // 2
    CGPoint currPoint = [touches.anyObject locationInView:superView];
    CGPoint prevPoint = [touches.anyObject previousLocationInView:superView];

    if ((strokePhase == 0) &&                                  // 3
        ((currPoint.y - firstTap.y) > 10.0) &&
```

```
            (currPoint.y <= prevPoint.y)) {

        strokePhase = 1;

    } else if ((strokePhase == 1) &&                                    // 4

                ((currPoint.x - prevPoint.x) >= kRStrokeDelta)) {

        strokePhase = 2;

    } else if ((strokePhase == 2) &&                                    // 5
                ((currPoint.y - prevPoint.y) <= kRStrokeDelta) &&
                (currPoint.x > prevPoint.x)) {

        strokePhase = 3;                                                // 6
        self.state = UIGestureRecognizerStateRecognized;
    }
}
```

Here's what happens in the numbered lines in Listing 12-8:

1. If stroke detection has failed or is recognized, return. Remember, this method is called as long as there are fingers on the screen, even if the gesture is recognized.

2. Get the current and previous touch points in the same view coordinate system used by firstTap.

3. Check that the downward stroke is at least 10.0 points and then transitions to an upward stroke when the current y is less than the previous y.

4. Check for start of the stroke up and to the right, making sure the change in x is not too big.

5. The final stroke phase happens when x increases without too much movement in y.

6. The stroke is recognized, so set the phase and stroke state.

Listing 12-9   Return Gesture Method for Cancelled

```
- (void)touchesCancelled:(NSSet *)touches withEvent:(UIEvent *)event {
    [super touchesCancelled:touches withEvent:event];

    self.state = UIGestureRecognizerStateFailed;                        // 1
}
```

Here's what happens in the numbered line in Listing 12-9:

1. A system interruption sets the stroke state to Failed.

Adding the Gesture Recognizer to the Current Detail

Any time any detail view except the default one is shown, the return gesture recognizer is added. And even if it is accidentally added to the default detail view, the worst that can happen is returning the app to the default state, showing that same detail view.

`DetailController` manages showing detail content, so it is the logical place to add the gesture recognizer. However, it is not the best controller for responding to a recognized gesture. Although `DetailController` manages the detail, it does not manage the overall state of the app. That is done by `MainMenuViewController`, so this is where the recognized gesture action method goes.

You need to make a few small additions to the `.h` file and to `setCurrDetailController:`

1. Open `DetailController.h`, and add a public property to the interface:

   ```
   @property (strong, nonatomic) UIGestureRecognizer *returnGesture;
   ```

2. Open `DetailController.m`, import `ReturnGestureRecognizer.h`, and add the lines in bold to `setCurrDetailController:hidePopover:`. The code checks whether there is a return gesture and, if there is, adds one to any new detail controller:

   ```
   ...
   NSArray *newStack = nil;

   if (self.returnGesture && currDetailController &&
       (_currDetailController != currDetailController)) {
       [currDetailController.view addGestureRecognizer:self.returnGesture];
   }

   if (currDetailController == nil) {
   ...
   ```

Creating and Responding to the Gesture Recognizer

All you have to do now is add the action method, create the gesture recognizer, and add it to the detail controller. Follow these steps:

1. Import `ReturnGestureRecognizer.h` into `MainMenuViewController.m`.

2. Add the code in Listing 12-10 below `carViewDone:`.

3. Update `viewDidLoad` to allocate a gesture recognizer and then set the detail controller's `returnGesture` property. Add the following code to the end of the method:

   ```
   ReturnGestureRecognizer *returnGesture = [[ReturnGestureRecognizer alloc]
                                 initWithTarget:self
                                 action:@selector(returnHome:)];

   [DetailController sharedDetailController].returnGesture = returnGesture;
   ```

Make sure the recognizer sets the delegate to the main menu view controller and uses the action method you added in step 2.

Listing 12-10   **Responding to a Recognized Return Gesture**

```
#pragma mark - Return Gesture Action Method

- (IBAction)returnHome:(UIGestureRecognizer*)sender {
    [self.tableView                                              // 1
     deselectRowAtIndexPath:self.tableView.indexPathForSelectedRow
     animated:YES];

    if (currentCarDetailController != nil) {                    // 2
        [self.navigationController popToRootViewControllerAnimated:YES];
        currentCarDetailController = nil;
    }

    [DetailController sharedDetailController].currDetailController = nil;    // 3
}
```

Here's what happens in the numbered lines in Listing 12-10:

1. Deselect any highlighted cell in the main menu view table.

2. If there is another master menu showing, such as the car list, go back to the main menu.

3. Set the detail view to the picture of the valet tent.

Run the app on an iPad simulator, navigate to the About screen, and use your finger to make an *r* onscreen. Remember both the down and up portions of the stroke. When the stroke is recognized, the app should return to the initial state. Try this on other screens. Note that in the images scene, you might need to start the gesture in the upper area, outside of the car image. If you find that things are not working, make sure the code is entered correctly, and if needed, try debugging the stroke. See the "Tip: Debugging Strokes."

Tip: Debugging Strokes

Debugging strokes can be really difficult. You cannot set a typical breakpoint as that would interrupt the stroke. The best idea is to use `NSLog` statements in the various parts of the recognition routine, especially the state transition portions of `touchesMoved:withEvent:`.

There are even better ways, though, using more advanced breakpoint features. See Chapter 14, "Instruments and Debugging," for more information.

One More Gesture

A chapter on gestures wouldn't be complete without information on dragging a view around the screen. This section gives a bit more practice with custom recognizers. You add a custom drag view gesture and a yellow car that you can drag around the About screen. See Challenge 3 at the end of this chapter for another way to drag views using a system gesture.

Drag Gesture Recognizer

Dragging a view is a continuous recognizer. The action method is called repeatedly as long as the finger is down and the recognizer is in an appropriate state. As explained earlier in this chapter, in the section "Custom Recognizers," continuous recognizers have more states. Create your own continuous recognizer for dragging a view by following these steps:

1. Select the Other group in the Navigator and add the new class `DragViewGesture`, based on `UIGestureRecognizer`.

2. Import the gesture recognizer subclass:

    ```
    #import <UIKit/UIGestureRecognizerSubclass.h>
    ```

3. Add the methods shown here:

    ```
    - (void)touchesBegan:(NSSet *)touches withEvent:(UIEvent *)event {
        [super touchesBegan:touches withEvent:event];

        if ([touches count] != 1) {
            return;
        }

        self.state = UIGestureRecognizerStateBegan;
    }

    - (void)touchesEnded:(NSSet *)touches withEvent:(UIEvent *)event {
        self.state = UIGestureRecognizerStateRecognized;
    }

    - (void)touchesCancelled:(NSSet *)touches withEvent:(UIEvent *)event {
        self.state = UIGestureRecognizerStateRecognized;
    }
    ```

    There are two big differences from the previous custom recognizer. First, setting the state to `UIGestureRecognizerStateBegan` in `touchesBegan:` causes a callback to the target's action method. Second, `touchesCancelled:withEvent:` is added.

4. Add `touchesMoved:withEvent:` from Listing 12-11.

Listing 12-11   **Drag View** `touchesMoved:withEvent:`

```
- (void)touchesMoved:(NSSet *)touches withEvent:(UIEvent *)event {
    [super touchesMoved:touches withEvent:event];

    if ((self.state == UIGestureRecognizerStateFailed) ||          // 1
        (self.state == UIGestureRecognizerStateRecognized)) {
        return;
    }

    CGPoint currPoint = [touches.anyObject                          // 2
                        locationInView:self.view.superview];
    CGPoint prevPoint = [touches.anyObject
                        previousLocationInView:self.view.superview];

    CGRect newRect = CGRectOffset(self.view.frame,                 // 3
                                  currPoint.x - prevPoint.x,
                                  currPoint.y - prevPoint.y);

    if (CGRectContainsRect(self.view.superview.frame,              // 4
                           newRect)) {
        self.view.frame = newRect;
    }

    self.state = UIGestureRecognizerStateChanged;                 // 5
}
```

Here's what happens in the numbered lines in Listing 12-11:

1. Continue dragging only if the gesture is valid.

2. Get the current and previous points.

3. Create a new view frame by offsetting the current frame by the change in x and y.

4. Update the view frame only if it is completely inside the containing view.

5. Set the state to `UIGestureRecognizerStateChanged` so the target's action method is called in the next event loop.

In reality, there is no need to call back to a target. All the code to move a view is inside the drag gesture. The changes in gesture state that enable callbacks are shown to illustrate where such callbacks typically go.

Adding the Taxi View with Drag

Follow these steps to enable dragging the car view:

1. Open `AboutViewController.xib` in IB.

2. Add an image view above the text and set image to `placeholder` and the background color to lemon.

3. While you are in the XIB, fix the centering of the existing text so it works on the iPad. Select the label and set the constraints to horizontally and vertically centered in the container.

   Now set the taxi view constraints to the following: The bottom is the system distance from the top of the label, the width and height are fixed at `40`, and it is horizontally centered in the superview.

4. Select the image view and check User Interaction Enabled in the Attributes inspector. This flag enables the image view to receive gestures. Without it, placing a finger in the view does nothing.

5. Open the Assistant editor and create an `IBOutlet` to the new view called `taxiView`.

6. Open `AboutViewController.m` and import `DragViewGesture.h`.

7. Add the following lines of code to `viewDidLoad` to create a new drag view gesture and add it to the taxi view:

   ```
   DragViewGesture *dragView = [[DragViewGesture alloc] init];
   [self.taxiView addGestureRecognizer:dragView];
   ```

Run the app on iPhone and open the About tab. Note that if your app appears to crash, it is due to conflicting layout constraints. You will see something like this in the console:

When the app is running, you can touch the taxi view and drag it around the screen but not off the screen (though it is possible for the taxi to get stuck under the navigation bar, see Challenge 4). Now run the app on iPad and open About. Again, you can drag the taxi view around the screen but not off the screen. The use of `CGRectContainsRect` in `touchesMoved:withEvent:` forces all sides of the taxi view to stay inside its container.

Summary

In this chapter, you added gestures to the CarValet app. First, you learned about the basics of gesture recognizers, including ones provided by the system. Next, you added built-in swipes to move back and forth through the details for each car. You learned some shortcuts when adding gestures in the storyboard, as well as how to disable gesture recognizers.

Then you learned how to create custom recognizers, including details on how they work. Next, you applied your knowledge by implementing a custom recognizer to reset the state of the iPad app. While doing this, you learned a way to recognize more complex gestures by breaking them down into components and transitions.

Finally, you created a bonus continuous recognizer to drag a yellow taxi around the About screen. Along the way, you saw a quick way to create action methods in Xcode, as well as how to constrain a view to moving inside its superview.

You can use recognizers to add features that both engage and delight the customer. System gestures let you trigger app behaviors using swipes, taps, drags, and more. Custom gestures enable you to offer ways for the user to easily and naturally accomplish tasks.

Chapter 13, "Introducing Blocks," introduces blocks, a powerful extension of Objective-C and C++. You learn how to create blocks of code that are commonly used for method arguments. As you will see, blocks are very powerful, carrying with them properties and variables available in the environment where they were created.

Challenges

1. On iPhone, add a gesture to go back from the car detail view to the car table menu. The gesture should be a triple tap, using three fingers for each tap. Use a built-in recognizer.

2. Add two different ways to reset the taxi in `AboutViewController`. First, reset the car to its original position if the user puts a second finger on the screen. Resetting the car should also cancel the gesture so the taxi no longer moves, even if the user keeps moving a finger on the screen. Second, add a reset car view to `AboutViewController`. Dragging the car over this view should reset it and cancel the gesture.

3. Move the view in `AboutViewController` using `UIPanGestureRecgonizer` instead of the custom `DragViewGesture`. The pan gesture gives you more information, such as the translation amount. You need to determine how to use that to move the yellow taxi.

4. It is possible for the taxi view to get stuck under the navigation bar. This happens when you drag the taxi under the translucent navigation bar, and the notifications panel comes down. The best way to prevent this is to stop the taxi view from going under the navigation bar.

    Modify the code from Listing 12-11 so the first argument in the call to `CGRectContainsRect` also excludes the navigation bar from the superview's frame.

Introducing Blocks

Blocks are one of the most powerful and underutilized features of Objective-C. It is important that you understand blocks as more system calls start taking them as arguments. Blocks are part function, part method, and part variable. For many, blocks can appear magical, especially the way they seem to pull in the variables around them.

This chapter introduces you to blocks and helps you avoid the most common mistakes. You start by learning the basics of blocks: what they are and how to declare, use, and write them. Then you use your understanding of blocks to make the About taxi more inviting.

Next, you learn more about blocks, including other variables, their most powerful feature and the source of most mistakes. Then you see how to change those variables, not just read them. Finally, you integrate everything and replace part of a protocol. As you learn in this chapter, blocks give you a versatile way to share data and information between objects.

Block Basics

In many ways, a block is like an anonymous function: It can take arguments, it can return a value, and a symbol can be used to call a block. But blocks are much more than this. Using them is a way to pass inline "functions" as method arguments. And most powerfully of all, blocks have access to all the variables that are in scope at the time they are defined. Or put another way, a block is a closure that has access to any variable the creating method can access at the point when the block is defined.

Before you can use blocks, you need to know how to declare, use, and write them.

Declaring Blocks

Blocks use a modified function syntax. Like functions, blocks can take arguments and return values. This is the basic format of a declaration:

```
<ReturnType>(^<BlockName>)<(Arguments)>
```

- *ReturnType* is the variable type returned by a block, if any.

- *BlockName* is the symbol used for calling the block. The caret (^) is the system-wide indicator preceding the declaration of a block.

- *Arguments* is an optional list of arguments.

Here are a few examples of block declarations:

- `void (^simpleBlock)(void);`

  This is a simple block with no return value and no arguments.

- `NSString* (^returnsAStringBlock)(void);`

  This block returns a string and takes no arguments.

- `BOOL (^returnsABoolAndTakesTwoInts) (int first, int second);`

  This more complex block takes two integer arguments and returns a Boolean.

These declarations are used for blocks as variables or properties. You use a slightly different form for arguments to methods:

- `- (void)method1:(void (^) (void)) aSimpleBlock;`

- `- (void)method2:(NSString* (^) (void))aBlockReturningAString;`

- `- (void)method3:(BOOL (^)`
  `             (int first, int second))blockTakesTwoIntsAndReturnsABool;`

Using Blocks

You call blocks in much the same way you call functions. For a named block, this works just as you would expect:

`<ReturnVariable> = <BlockName>(<Arguments>);`

- *ReturnVariable* is an optional variable for holding the value returned by a block. If the block has no return value, you omit both ReturnVariable and the equals sign.

- *BlockName* is the symbol used for calling the block.

- *Arguments* is an optional list of arguments.

Note that a caret is not used for calling a block. It is used only for declaring and writing. For each of the blocks defined in the preceding section, here is an example of a call:

- `simpleBlock();`

- `NSString* returnString = returnsAStringBlock();`

- `BOOL isEqual = returnsABoolAndTakesTwoInts(1,2);`

Writing Blocks

Writing really has two parts: the return type and argument definitions, and the code for implementing its behavior. This is the definition format:

```
^(<ReturnType>)(<Arguments>){<Statements>};
```

- *ReturnType* is the variable type returned by a block, if any.
- *Arguments* is an optional list of arguments.
- *Statements* is the code implementing the behavior and can be anything you would normally write in Objective-C.

There is no block name in the implementation. Usually, you declare a block and assign it by using the definition. Here are the previous declarations, with sample block definitions:

- `void(^simpleBlock)(void) =`

     `^void(void){NSLog(@"simpleBlock called");};`

- `NSString*(^returnsAStringBlock)(void) =`

     `^(NSString*)(void){return @"Here is a string";};`

- `BOOL(^returnsABoolAndTakesTwoInts) (int first, int second) =`
     `^BOOL(int first, int second){return (first == second);};`

Some of the definitions seem a bit verbose, especially all the `void`s. There are two space savers you can use for defining blocks. First, you can omit arguments if there are none. That cuts out a little from the first two block examples. Second, the compiler figures out the return type by using the definition. Therefore, the definitions can change to this:

- `void(^simpleBlock)(void) =`

     `^{NSLog(@"simpleBlock called");};`

- `NSString*(^returnsAStringBlock)(void) =`

     `^({return @"Here is a string";};`

- `BOOL(^returnsABoolAndTakesTwoInts) (int first, int second) =`
     `^(int first, int second){return first == second};};`

Although the examples define and assign a block at the same time, the definition and assignment can happen in different places, even in different objects. This enables you to use blocks as arguments to methods or even class properties, providing lots of power and flexibility.

If you are the user of a class or method, you are not defining or using the block but are writing it:

```
[anObject aBlockBaseMethod:^{<your code goes here>}];
```

You have already done this with calls to `dispatch_async` in Chapter 5, "Localization," and to `dispatch_once` to create a singleton in Chapter 11, "Navigation Controllers II: Split View and the iPad." Both functions take a block of code and execute it either in the background or only once. They execute the code provided in a block.

If you look through the documentation, you see numerous examples of methods and system calls using blocks. One fun example is `UIView` animation.

Pulsing the About Taxi

In Chapter 12, "Touch Basics," you added a draggable yellow taxi to the about view. But how does the user know to tap it? One way you can let the user know is to show some text on the screen inviting the user to tap on the car. But that is fairly glaring, and it clutters up the screen.

A better way is to subtly pulse the view and perhaps even add a bit of movement. Doing that is easy with `UIView`'s block-based animation calls. The calls do the hard work for you. If you want to rotate a view, you can tell the system how long the animation should take and specify the new rotation. The system figures out the interim animation steps and draws them on the screen.

You can animate many properties of view. However, when you use auto layout, modifying some properties can result in unexpected behavior. The solution is to animate the constraints. For more information, see Chapters 5, 6, and 7 of *Auto Layout Demystified* by Erica Sadun.

Pulsing and View Constraints

How does pulsing translate into view constraints? Pulsing makes a view slightly larger and then returns it to normal size, while the center of the view stays at the same location.

Growing changes the height and width constraints. Staying in the same place depends on the constraints that affect position. The taxi is horizontally centered, with a fixed space between the bottom of the taxi view and the top of the label. If you change only the height and width, but not the space, the view moves to maintain distance from the label. And that is not what you want. Instead, you need to change the distance as well as the width and height.

You can continue using the project you used in Chapter 12 or use `CH13 CarValet Starter` provided with the sample code. Adding pulsing requires three main steps:

1. Change the view constraints to something more animation-friendly and get references to the animated constraints.

2. Create an animation call for pulsing as well as required state variables.

3. Stop the view pulsing when it has been dragged or pause pulsing if the about view moves offscreen.

First, you need to set up animated constraints and references:

1. Open `AboutViewController.xib`, select the taxi view, and view the constraints in the Size inspector.

2. Create properties for the width and height constraints named `labelTaxiSpace`, `taxiWidth`, and `taxiHeight`.

The pulsing animation is a repeating cycle with two stages. Stage one is two relatively quick grow/shrink cycles. Stage two is a longer delay, and then the cycle repeats. This continues until either the user drags the view or the about view moves offscreen. Of course, moving offscreen is different from completely stopping the animation. Stopping only happens when the user taps the taxi. Moving offscreen is a pause, not a stop.

Follow these steps to create a pulsing taxi:

1. Add support for `UIGestureRecognizerDelegate` to `AboutViewController.h`.

2. Open `AboutViewController.m` and add these variables below the implementation:

```
{
    BOOL        draggedOnce;
    BOOL        paused;
    NSInteger   pulseCount;
}
```

`draggedOnce` is true after the user has touched the taxi. `paused` is true when the animation should be paused. And `pulseCount` keeps track of the short and long pulse stages.

3. Initialize the state variables in `viewDidLoad` (the new code is bold):

```
[super viewDidLoad];

draggedOnce = NO;
paused = NO;
pulseCount = 0;

DragViewGesture *dragView = [[DragViewGesture alloc] init];
```

Strictly speaking, you do not need to initialize Booleans to NO or integers to 0, as these are their default states. However, it is good practice to initialize in case you choose new starting values later.

4. Add the gesture recognizer delegate method at the end of the class to set `draggedOnce` to YES when the user drags the view:

```
#pragma mark - UIGestureRecognizerDelegate

- (BOOL)gestureRecognizerShouldBegin:(UIGestureRecognizer *)gestureRecognizer {

    if (!draggedOnce &&
        [gestureRecognizer isKindOfClass:[DragViewGesture class]]) {
            draggedOnce = YES;
    }
```

```
        return YES;
    }
```

5. Start the animation in `viewDidAppear:` if the user has not dragged the taxi. Reset any state variables before starting the pulse:

```
- (void)viewDidAppear:(BOOL)animated {
    [super viewDidAppear:animated];

    if (!draggedOnce) {
        pulseCount = 0;
        paused = NO;
        [self pulseTaxi];
    }
}
```

6. Pause the animation if the about view goes offscreen:

```
- (void)viewWillDisappear:(BOOL)animated {
    [super viewWillDisappear:animated];

    paused = YES;
}
```

7. Finally, add the pulsing code from Listing 13-1.

Listing 13-1   **Pulsing the Taxi View**

```
#pragma mark - Pulse the Taxi

- (void)pulseTaxi {
    if (!paused && !draggedOnce) {                              // 1

        CGFloat pulseAmount = 6.0f;                             // 2
        CGFloat spaceAmount = pulseAmount / 2.0f;

        [UIView animateWithDuration:0.3f                        // 3
                       delay:0.0f
                     options:UIViewAnimationOptionAllowUserInteraction
                  animations:^{
                      self.taxiWidth.constant += pulseAmount;    // 4
                      self.taxiHeight.constant += pulseAmount;
                      self.labelTaxiSpace.constant -= spaceAmount;

                      [self.view layoutIfNeeded];                // 5
```

```
            pulseCount++ ;                                    // 6
        }
        completion:^(BOOL finished) {                         // 7
            self.taxiWidth.constant -= pulseAmount;           // 8
            self.taxiHeight.constant -= pulseAmount;
            self.labelTaxiSpace.constant += spaceAmount;

            [self.view layoutIfNeeded];

            if (!draggedOnce) {                               // 9
                NSTimeInterval delay = 0.1f;

                if (pulseCount > 1) {                         // 10
                    pulseCount = 0;

                    delay = 2.8f;
                };

                [self performSelector:@selector(pulseTaxi)    // 11
                           withObject:nil
                           afterDelay:delay];

            }
        }];
    }
}
```

Here's what happens in the numbered lines in Listing 13-1:

1. Animate only if the view is visible, !paused, and the user has yet to drag the taxi, !draggedOnce.

2. Set the view growth amount to 6 points and the distance to the top of the label view to half that. Remember that the growth amount is the total for both taxi sides in the horizontal or vertical direction.

3. Set up the animation call. A duration of 0.3 seconds is the same as many iOS animations. There is no delay, and you want the user to be able to drag the view during an animation. UIViewAnimationOptionAllowUserInteraction lets the view receive touch events. Forgetting this option is a common source of errors as doing so prevents any type of interaction, including button presses.

4. This is the start of the animation block. Increasing the constant for width and height increases the size of the view. Similarly, decreasing the space constraint reduces the gap.

5. If you forget to tell the view to lay out subviews, the animation either does not occur or is very jumpy. This is another common source of errors when animating constraints.

6. Pulse count tracks the animation stage.

7. The completion block is called after the animation is done. Anything you do in this block happens after the initial animation.

8. Reset the constant of each of the three constraints back to their original values, returning the taxi view to its original size while keeping it centered.

9. Check whether the view has been dragged, and if it has not, continue pulsing.

10. The next pulse delay depends on whether this is a first or second pulse. If it is the first pulse, there is a short delay. Otherwise, there is a longer delay, setting up a kind of heartbeat look.

11. Call the pulse method again after the short or long delay.

Run the app in both the iPad Simulator and iPhone Simulator. Try opening the About screen, watching a few pulse cycles, and changing to a different screen in the middle of a pulse. Go back to About and make sure the pulse cycle continues. Then try dragging the taxi and make sure the pulsing stops. Try starting the drag when the taxi is in the middle of pulsing and make sure it returns to normal. As soon as the view pulses, it snaps back to the original position.

Variable Scope

In the taxi pulsing example, you might have noticed something strange about the animation block. It uses `pulseAmount`, `spaceAmount`, and `self`. But how? If this were a function, each of those would need to be an argument. But the block takes no arguments.

This is one of the very powerful features of blocks. They have access to all the variables at the point where they were created. That is, they pull in all the variables from the current scope. One way to think about this is that they have access to the same variables that a line of code in exactly the same position would have. If you have used languages like Smalltalk and Lisp, you can think of blocks as closures.

Try the following example by adding the code to `viewDidLoad` for any controller showing on the screen:

```
int aNumber = 8;
void (^testBlock)(void) = ^{NSLog(@"\naNumber = %d", aNumber);};
testBlock();
```

When you run the app, `viewDidLoad` is executed along with the code you added, and a result like this is printed to the console:

```
2013-06-02 15:49:17.518 CarValet[12359:c07]
aNumber = 8
```

Now add these two lines of code after the first block call:

```
aNumber = 99;
testBlock();
```

Before you run the code, what do you expect to print in the console? If you said 99, you are in for a surprise and have been caught by the most common mistake made in using blocks.

Copying and Modification

You may have expected to see 99 printed in the console because in the pulsing example, you were able to successfully modify self.taxiWidth.constant. This has to do with how the block's execution stack is created. Figure 13-1 shows that the stack has a read-only (italicized) copy of each variable. The values are frozen at the time the block is created.

Although the block's copy of self is not modifiable, the value is still the address for the same aboutViewController object. The properties can still be changed, as can any part of those properties.

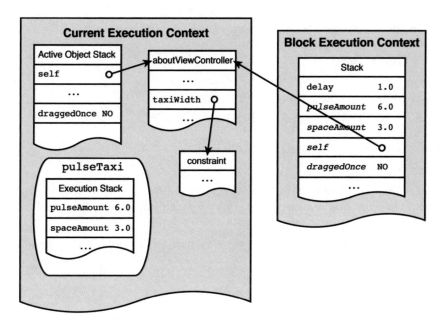

Figure 13-1   Block context variables

For the 99 example, aNumber is not a pointer; the value of the memory address is the value of the variable. The block's copy of aNumber is at a different address from the one outside the block. The value of this new variable is identical to the value of aNumber at the time the block was created. But since it is not a pointer, it is just a copy of the integer, not the actual variable from the method.

Modifying Scope Variables

Blocks are not able to modify the copied, or scoped, variables available to them. You can easily see this by changing the block to modify `aNumber`:

```
void (^testBlock)(void) = ^{aNumber = 5; NSLog(@"\naNumber = %d", aNumber);};
```

You get an error in the editor, and if you try to build, it fails with "Variable is not assignable."

If you need to modify a local variable inside a block, you need to add the __block modifier to the declaration. Change the declaration of `aNumber` to this:

```
__block int aNumber;
```

The error for the block disappears. More than that, changes to `aNumber` outside the block are reflected inside the block. Now execute this:

```
__block int aNumber = 8;
void (^testBlock)(void) = ^{NSLog(@"\naNumber = %d", aNumber);};
testBlock();
aNumber = 99;
testBlock();
```

The app prints the following at the console:

```
2013-06-02 16:17:21.936 CarValet[12647:c07]
aNumber = 8
2013-06-02 16:17:21.937 CarValet[12647:c07]
aNumber = 99
```

There are other issues around copying and not copying variables and objects into blocks, as well as more detail on how to create and use them. For more information, see Chapter 17 of *Learning Objective-C* by Robert Clair.

In the last part of this chapter, you practice what you have learned and replace a protocol with blocks.

Replacing a Protocol

Protocols enable one object to communicate with another, without either object knowing anything about the internals of the other. As you have seen, a protocol specifies a contract that the delegate implements the required methods conforming to the specification.

Like a protocol, a block is a contract. One object defines the return value and arguments. The other object writes a block matching the specification.

You have already done this in pulsing the taxi view. The animation call takes two defined blocks. One is a simple block with no arguments and no return value. The other takes one argument. `AboutViewController` implements the blocks as part of the method call, although you could just as easily define and write them elsewhere and use the block names in the method call.

In this example, you replace `ViewCarProtocol` with blocks. Note that a protocol can be more flexible than a single block. Protocols can have multiple methods for different purposes. They can also set methods as required or optional. A delegate declaring support for a protocol must support all the required methods, or the compiler generates an error. With blocks, you only know that implemented blocks conform, not that all required blocks are provided.

You replace the protocol in four general steps:

1. Update `ViewCarTableViewController` to use blocks instead of the protocol.

2. Modify `CarTableViewController` to set the new blocks.

3. Change `CarDetailViewController` to use blocks instead of the protocol.

4. Modify `MainMenuViewController` to set up blocks.

Step 1: Changing `ViewCarTableViewController`

Starting with the `.h` file, follow these steps:

1. Delete the import of `ViewCarProtocol.h`.

2. Change the delegate to `UIViewController *delegate`.

3. Add these block properties:

```
@property (copy, nonatomic) CDCar* (^carToView)(void);
@property (copy, nonatomic) void (^carViewDone)(BOOL dataChanged);
@property (copy, nonatomic) void (^nextOrPreviousCar)(BOOL isNext);
```

One thing to notice is that each block property is marked as `copy`, not `strong`. This is very important and is related to how blocks work with external variables. Again, for more information, see Chapter 17 of *Learning Objective-C* by Robert Clair.

Each of the properties declares a block that replaces the same protocol method:

- `carToView` returns a `CDCar*`.

- `carViewDone` takes one argument indicating whether the data has changed.

- `nextOrPreviousCar` takes a Boolean that indicates which way to move.

The next step is calling the blocks. The blocks are properties, so you need to get a reference to make the call:

```
self.<blockSymbol><Arguments>;
```

You could use the underscore version of the symbol name and skip using dot notation. However, if you do, you lose the flexibility of updating blocks dynamically.

Change `ViewCarTableViewController.m` to call blocks:

1. Update `navigationController:didShowViewController:animated:` with the new code shown in bold:

```
if (viewController == self.delegate) {
    if (dataUpdated) {
        self.carViewDone(dataUpdated);
    }

    self.navigationController.delegate = nil;
}
```

2. Change the body of `swipeCarLeft` as follows:

```
self.carViewDone(dataUpdated);

self.nextOrPreviousCar(YES);

[self loadCarData];
```

3. Make similar changes to the body of `swipeCarRight`:

```
self.carViewDone(dataUpdated);

self.nextOrPreviousCar(NO);

[self loadCarData];
```

4. Make one change in `loadCarData`:

```
dataUpdated = NO;

self.myCar = self.carToView();

self.makeLabel.text = self.myCar.make;
```

Most of the changes replace delegate method calls with block calls. There is still a delegate, but now it is only used to check whether the detail car view is returning to the cars table.

Step 2: Updating `CarTableViewController`

The changes to `CarTableViewController` are quite small: removing the protocol, making the existing protocol methods public, and setting the `ViewCarTableViewController` block properties.

To save time, each of the blocks is a call to the original protocol method. If you were starting the design from scratch, you would do the work in the blocks instead of calling methods. Here's what you do:

1. Open `CarTableViewController.h` and remove all references to `ViewCarProtocol`.

2. Add public declarations for each of the old protocol implementation methods:

   - `(CDCar *)carToView;`
   - `(void)carViewDone:(BOOL)dataChanged;`
   - `(void)nextOrPreviousCar:(BOOL)isNext;`

   At the moment, `MainMenuViewController` is the only caller for one of the methods. The declarations are there for flexibility. Again, if this were designed from scratch, you could create a better solution.

3. Open the .m file and insert the following lines in `prepareForSegue:sender:`

   ```
   nextController.carToView = ^{return [self carToView];};
   nextController.carViewDone = ^(BOOL dataUpdated)
                               {[self carViewDone:dataUpdated];};
   nextController.nextOrPreviousCar = ^(BOOL isNext)
                               {[self nextOrPreviousCar:isNext];};
   nextController.delegate = self;
   ```

The biggest change is in step 3. Here you set the block properties using simple calls to the existing methods. You could just replace the body of the block with the body of each method. For instance, this could be the `carToView` property:

```
nextController.carToView = ^{
    currentViewCarPath = [currentTableView indexPathForSelectedRow];

    return [fetchedResultsController objectAtIndexPath:currentViewCarPath];
};
```

Step 3: Modifying `CarDetailViewController`

Very few changes are needed for this class. Follow these steps:

1. In the .h file, remove all references to `ViewCarProtocol` and delete the delegate declaration.

2. Add a declaration for the `nextOrPrevious:` block property:

   ```
   @property (copy, nonatomic) void (^nextOrPreviousCar)(BOOL isNext);
   ```

3. In the .m file, use the new block in `swipeCarRight:` and `swipeCarLeft:`. Each call looks like this:

   ```
   self.nextOrPreviousCar(<BooleanArgument>);
   ```

   Replace BooleanArgument with either YES or NO, depending on the method.

All that remains is to update the iPad's main car menu.

Step 4: Updating `MainMenuViewController`

This class only uses the protocol for going to the next or previous car, so there are two simple updates:

1. In the `.h` file, remove the two uses of `ViewCarProtocol`.

2. In the `.m` file, `tableView:didSelectRowAtIndexPath:` has a small change. In the `switch` case for `kPadMenuCarsItem`, replace the line:

   ```
   currentCarDetailController.delegate = carTable;
   ```

   with this:

   ```
   currentCarDetailController.nextOrPreviousCar = ^(BOOL isNext)
                           {[carTable nextOrPreviousCar:isNext];};
   ```

   This change uses blocks copying in scope variables to include `carTable`, a reference to the master cars table menu. Since `carTable` implements `nextOrPreviousCar:`, and the copy points to the same object, it is used to call the method.

Run the app using the iPhone Simulator and the iPad Simulator, and make sure all the behaviors previously implemented by `ViewCarProtocol` still work. On iPhone, this includes displaying the correct car detail, updating the cars table when some detail changes, and going to the next and previous cars. On iPad, it is just the next and previous swipes.

With blocks, there is no need to create lots of similar protocols or use a protocol that doesn't quite match what you need. Providers don't need to check if a delegate has implemented optional methods. For classes that would use a protocol, instead of registering as a delegate and creating essentially empty protocol methods, you only create code for the things you need.

By replacing the `ViewCarProtocol` with blocks, you have started using a new and more versatile way to exchange information and trigger behaviors. This method is increasingly being adopted by the native iOS calls.

Summary

In this chapter, you have gotten an introduction to blocks. You started by learning how to declare, use, and write blocks. You also learned some shortcuts for writing blocks. Next, you added pulsing to the About screen's taxi and learned about animating view constraints.

Next, you learned about variable scope, one of the most powerful features of blocks. Then you learned about read-only versus read/write variables and why you can change parts of a copied object. Finally, you replaced the `ViewCarProtocol` with blocks.

Now that you understand blocks, you can use them for more than just arguments to system calls. Blocks provide an easy and powerful way to pass information and actions between objects of the same class or different classes. You can use them instead of protocols to increase the flexibility and reusability of your code. And as you go deeper into iOS, using blocks is a natural way to create small asynchronous actions.

There are just two chapters left before you are ready to launch into designing and building your own apps. No matter what apps you choose to build, there are two constants. The first is the need to tune performance. Instruments is an easy-to-use tool to find memory problems and make sure your app uses the limited resources in the best way. The other constant is that bugs happen. Chapter 14, "Instruments and Debugging," introduces you to Instruments, then takes you to the next level with the debugger. In addition to seeing some techniques to track down common issues, you learn about the versatility of breakpoints.

Challenges

1. Add movement as well as pulsing to the about view taxi. The movement should happen during the pulse to suggest that a tap will move the taxi. You can use the existing `labelTaxiSpace` constraint or introduce others to give the taxi more of a wobble.

2. `setupScrollContent` in `CarImageViewController.m` contains a `for` loop that iterates through image names:

   ```
   for (NSString *atCarImageName in carImageNames) {
   ```

   Replace the loop using the array block iterator `enumerateObjectsUsingBlock:`. The first few lines replacing the `for` loop look like this:

   ```
   [carImageNames enumerateObjectsUsingBlock:
    ^(id obj, NSUInteger idx, BOOL *stop) {
        carImage = [UIImage imageNamed:obj];
   ```

   You will also need to make other changes to make the block work.

3. Replace `YearEditProtocol` with blocks.

14

Instruments and Debugging

Apps are complex, with at least tens of classes, sometimes more. There are also storyboards, XIB files, resources, and more. The chances of getting so much code and work right the first time is very small. Issues can range from slowness in the interface to crashes. Luckily, Xcode provides powerful tools for checking your running application and for finding bugs.

Instruments provides a view into a running app, helping you find performance issues, memory use, leaks, and other useful information. The debugger lets you step through code, inspect variables, and even play sounds when lines of code are hit.

This chapter introduces you to these powerful tools. First, you explore Instruments and learn what kinds of information you can gather with it. Then, you dive into a time profile and optimize a slowly loading view controller.

Next, you learn about the debugger, looking at some ways it can help you find problems. You start with a tour. Then you learn about breakpoints, which, along with actions, form the heart of debugging. Finally, you use both Instruments and the debugger to track down an EXC_BAD_ ACCESS error, one of the hardest types to find.

Instruments

App performance is important. Users have little patience for apps that take too long to launch, are too slow to respond, or drain their batteries. Good design and coding practices can help, but they can only get you so far. And even when the app appears to work, how do you know?

Instruments is a tool for profiling parts of an app. You can use it to look at everything from execution time to memory use, network calls to battery usage—all the things that can affect the performance of an app.

Gathering data using Instruments is as simple as running your app for profiling and choosing your instrument(s). The available instruments check everything from execution time to memory use to network calls. You can use them to ensure the following about an app:

- It is fast and responsive.
- It uses memory efficiently.
- It has no memory leaks.
- It uses limited resources, such as the battery, wisely.

You can launch an app in Instruments in several ways:

- Choose Product > Profile.
- Press Cmd-I.
- Option-click the Run button and choose Profile.

Doing any one of these compiles your app and opens the Instruments application with your app as the target. When Instruments launches, you are presented with the Instruments template chooser, shown in Figure 14-1.

Figure 14-1   Choosing a profiling template

Notice that the section name is "iOS Simulator." If you launched instruments when building for a device, it would say "iOS." Where you run the app depends on two things: the current stage of optimization and the instruments you want to use. In general, you run on the simulator early in the cycle, to find general issues, or if you are using simulator-specific instruments.

The device tools are for fine-tuning as well as to run some of the most important checks, such as for timing and energy use. It's important to always check on a real device before finalizing your code. Preferably, you should check an app on different kinds of devices, especially the types you expect your customers to use.

Clicking Choose in the Instruments template chooser initializes a new document with the set of instruments included in the template. It also starts recording data from the simulator or device. Instruments is document-based. You can have multiple recording sessions in one document, as well as multiple documents, each with its own set of instruments. Saving a document saves all the recording session data. For now, though, click Cancel.

Templates and Instruments

When Instruments launches, you see a set of templates, not instruments. Templates are the tool's way of presenting task-based sets of instruments. For example, you can use Leaks to measure memory allocation and leaks, Time Profiler to see where the app is spending time, and so on.

Choosing a template creates a profiling document with the recommended set of instruments. For example, the Leaks template includes both memory allocation and memory leak instruments. The Allocations instrument shows the amount of memory you are using at any point. Leaks tries to find allocated memory with no references. Both instruments are important in finding leaks.

Table 14-1 lists the major templates, what they are useful for, and whether each is a tool that runs on a device, in the simulator, or both. The table does not include some special purpose templates such as Animation. Note that not all of the templates in the table are shown in Figure 14-1.

Table 14-1   **iOS Profiling Templates**

Template	Platform (Device, Simulator, or Both)	Use
Activity Monitor	Both	Finds possible areas for improving performance. A general tool that tracks activity including CPU, network, and memory.
Allocations	Both	Good for memory usage, once there are no leaks, as the Leaks tool tends to be slower. Tracks the amount of memory allocated. The most useful information is how much memory your app is using at any given time.

Template	Platform (Device, Simulator, or Both)	Use
Core Data	Simulator	Looks for issues using Core Data. Best for apps that use a lot of data. The effect of Core Data issues on smaller data stores is negligible. Shows activity related to Core Data, such as fetching, saving, and cache misses.
Energy Diagnostics	Device	Diagnoses how well an app uses battery.
Leaks	Both	Finds memory leaks and tracks the total amount of memory. The Leaks tool can be a bit slow.
Network	Device	Analyzes your network activity. One area is how well you are using the communications chip. Typically these chips have active, sleep, and low power settings. You want to concentrate activity to give the chip a chance to power down. Looks at network activity for various protocols, such as TCP, UDP, etc.
Time Profiler	Both	Finds where and why an app is slow by tracking the time taken by different user and system calls.
Zombies	Both	Finds calls to deallocated objects. This is not so much of an issue with ARC, although it can still occur.

The most commonly used templates are Leaks, Time Profiler, and Zombies. For apps that use communications, the GPS, or other battery-intensive features, Energy Diagnostics is also important.

You learn more about Zombies later in the chapter.

An Example Using the Time Profiler

The best way to learn how to use Instruments is through example. In this section, you use the Time Profiler instrument to improve the performance of the CarValet app. To do so, you need to use a real device. Although Time Profiler works on the simulator, the desktop is so fast that possible issues appear as small blips.

The slower the device, the easier it is to spot issues. The examples shown in this section were done using an iPhone 4, though they show up on any iOS device: iPod touch, iPhone, or iPad. After opening the CarValet project, either yours or the one provided with the chapter sample code, run the Time Profiler by following these steps:

1. Use a USB cable to attach an iOS device that is set up for development to your machine. If you do not have a development device, the first part of Chapter 15, "Deploying Applications," takes you through the process of setting one up.

2. Choose the device from the schema popup, as shown in Figure 14-2.

Figure 14-2   Choosing a target device

3. Profile the app by selecting Product > Profile, pressing Cmd-I, or Option-clicking the Run button and choosing Profile. When the profile window comes up, choose Time Profiler.

4. When the app starts running, go through the major functional areas of the app, paying attention to the profiling trace: viewing car details, swiping back and forth, making a change and going back, viewing car images, looking at the About screen, dragging the taxi, and so on. Stop the app when you see any high and long spikes after the initial app launch or if you see a noticeable delay in the interface.

The focus of this example is the time it takes to load the car images the first time the images screen is opened. The amount of time seems long, and the interface feels sluggish. Take a second recording, focusing on viewing the car images. You can do this either by profiling the app from Xcode or clicking the Record button in Instruments. Go straight to the car images scene and stop recording after the profile line settles down. You end up with a profile window that looks like Figure 14-3.

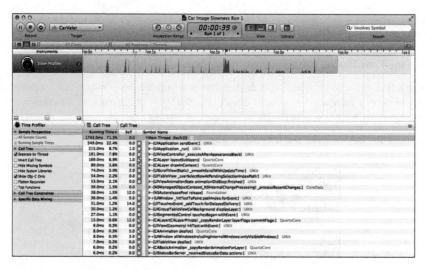

Figure 14-3   Car image slowness profile

The window has a few areas. The Toolbar on top provides quick access to common functions such as Record and showing the Extended Detail view. This is the unselected button in the View section.

Instruments lets you select the active instrument—that is, the one whose results are displayed in the lower area of the window. To the right of the selected instrument is a timeline that shows some sort of graphical representation of recorded data. When an instrument is expanded to show multiple runs using the triangle, the selected timeline is a darker color. In this case, it is the top, or second run.

The Call Tree view shows all the calls that are part of the selected timeline. The columns provide different data. In this case, Running Time is the most important column, grouping the call trees into the total percentage of time taken. The icons indicate what kind of call such as ones from UIKit, lower level system calls, or your own methods.

The lower-left window provides options for viewing the data. In this case, the call tree is showing only Objective-C calls.

You can insert a blue flag in the timeline by Option-clicking. This flag identifies an area of interest—in this case, opening the car images for the first time.

Finding the Problem

To find the problem, you need to focus on the time bump that happened when you were viewing car images. The best way to do this is in two stages: First, Shift-drag the cursor over the big bump in time in the second run. This zooms the data to fill the timeline, as shown in Figure 14-4.

Figure 14-4   Zooming the timeline

After zooming in, Option-drag over the larger time bump. You should see the contents of the call tree change. Now open the Extended Detail view, using the View selector in the toolbar. After you do that, your window should look something like Figure 14-5.

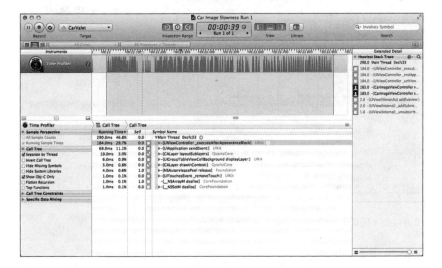

Figure 14-5   Focusing on the problem

The next phase is called call tree mining, and it is all about finding calls in your app that are taking too much time. Here's how you do it:

1. In the left-hand option area, uncheck Separate by Thread. The sample document in Figure 14-5 shows 184.0ms, or 29.7%, of the time taken by the first line, and 69.0ms, or 11.1%, taken by the second.

2. Next, you need to mine data, using one of two methods. One method is to look for app calls on the Extended Detail panel. In the right-hand column in Figure 14-5 are two calls with a black silhouette; they are app calls. The second method is to check the Hide System Libraries option, although doing this can sometimes cause you to miss issues.

3. Select the app call in Extended Detail, and the Call Tree expands and selects that line. It still shows 183.0ms, so this is likely the source of the performance problem.

4. Select the second line, and it shows the next level down in the call tree, with similar timing. There is another app call below the selected line, but it is less than 1% of the time. `setupScrollContent` looks like the culprit.

Now you could go into Xcode and see if you can figure out what is taking the time. But there is a better way. Double-click the line in the Call Tree, and it is replaced with the window shown in Figure 14-6. Not only do you see the code, you also see highlights with instrument-appropriate annotations. Since this is the Time Profiler, you see the percentage of time taken by that line.

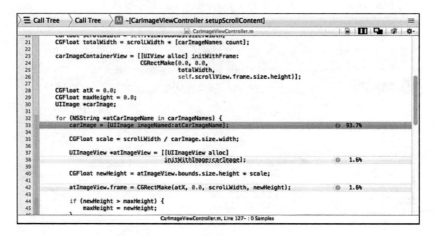

Figure 14-6   Problem code with percent of time taken

Now you can develop a hypothesis about what is taking the time. The routine uses the `imageNamed:` class call of `UIImage` to load each picture. That routine fetches the image from the app resources if it is not already in memory. The first time the user looks at car images, none of the images are loaded. The classic solution to this problem is to prefetch the images.

In a final app, there would be other ways to determine the size of the scroll view and number of images. Perhaps there would even be a more appropriate controller, such as a collection view, but that is beyond the scope of this book. For more information, see Chapter 10 of *The Core iOS Developer's Cookbook* (5th edition) by Erica Sadun and Rich Wardwell.

Fixing the Problem: Attempt 1

Prefetching means preloading the images. For now, all you need to do is call `imageNamed:` for each of the images before calling `setupScrollContent`. The first place to try this is in `viewDidLoad` for `CarImageViewController`. Follow these steps:

1. Click the small Xcode icon at the top right of the already open Instruments code view to open `CarImageViewController.m`. Add the following method to the top of the class:

```
- (void)prefetchImages {
    UIImage *carImage;

    for (NSString *atCarImageName in carImageNames) {
        carImage = [UIImage imageNamed:atCarImageName];
    }
}
```

The body of the method calls `imageNamed:` for each of the images.

2. Add a call to run `prefetchImages` in a background thread to the end of `viewDidLoad`:

```
[self performSelectorInBackground:@selector(prefetchImages)
                       withObject:nil];
```

3. Profile the app and view the car images. Stop when you are done. You can do either by pressing the Stop button on the left of the Instruments toolbar, or by quitting the app.

Use the previous techniques to zoom in on the part of the timeline for viewing car images and then focus the Call Tree by using Option-drag. As shown in Figure 14-7, at first glance, things appear a bit better. The prefetch is taking only 107ms, but `viewDidAppear` is still taking another 165ms, for a total of 272ms—worse than the original.

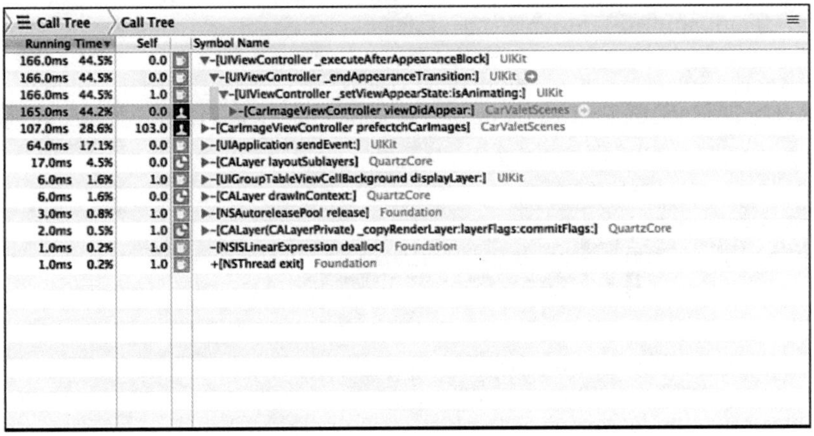

Running Time▼		Self		Symbol Name
166.0ms	44.5%	0.0		▼-[UIViewController _executeAfterAppearanceBlock] UIKit
166.0ms	44.5%	0.0		▼-[UIViewController _endAppearanceTransition:] UIKit
166.0ms	44.5%	1.0		▼-[UIViewController _setViewAppearState:isAnimating:] UIKit
165.0ms	44.2%	0.0		▶-[CarImageViewController viewDidAppear:] CarValetScenes
107.0ms	28.6%	103.0		▶-[CarImageViewController prefetchCarImages] CarValetScenes
64.0ms	17.1%	0.0		▶-[UIApplication sendEvent:] UIKit
17.0ms	4.5%	0.0		▶-[CALayer layoutSublayers] QuartzCore
6.0ms	1.6%	0.0		▶-[UIGroupTableViewCellBackground displayLayer:] UIKit
6.0ms	1.6%	0.0		▶-[CALayer drawInContext:] QuartzCore
3.0ms	0.8%	1.0		▶-[NSAutoreleasePool release] Foundation
2.0ms	0.5%	1.0		▶-[CALayer(CALayerPrivate) _copyRenderLayer:layerFlags:commitFlags:] QuartzCore
1.0ms	0.2%	1.0		-[NSISLinearExpression dealloc] Foundation
1.0ms	0.2%	1.0		+[NSThread exit] Foundation

Figure 14-7   Updating time attempt 1

The higher time makes sense when you realize what is happening. `viewDidLoad` starts a prefetch in the background. Prefetch starts loading images. Then `viewDidAppear:` is called and sends `setupScrollContent`, which in turn starts loading images. At best, each image is preloaded before it is needed, but you are still creating two `UIImage`s for each car picture, even if one is never used. If prefetching is the solution, it needs to happen somewhere else.

Fixing the Problem: Attempt 2

In a shipping app, the slowness you have found would either not be an issue, or there would be a different source of slowness. For this app, prefetching should work. It just needs to happen somewhere else. Since there is such a small amount of data, it can happen early on, when the app is launching. It is still a good idea to prefetch in the background. Otherwise, launching the app takes a lot longer. Here are the steps:

1. Open `CarImageViewController.m`, select `prefetchImages`, and cut `prefetchImages` from the file.

2. Open `AppDelegate.m` and paste the `prefetchImages` method at the top of the class inside the `@implementation` area.

3. Go back to `CarImageViewController.m` and copy the definition of `carImageNames` in `viewDidLoad`.

4. Open `AppDelegate.m` and paste the definition at the top of `prefetchImages`. Then modify it to look like this:

```
NSArray *carImageNames = @[ @"Acura-16.jpg", @"BMW-11.jpg", @"BMW-13.jpg",
                            @"Cadillac-13.jpg", @"Car-39.jpg",
                            @"Lexus-15.jpg", @"Mercedes Benz-106.jpg",
                            @"Mini-11.jpg", @"Nissan Leaf-4.jpg",
                            @"Nissan Maxima-2.jpg" ];
```

5. Cut the call to perform the selector in the background from the car image view controller and paste it into the app delegate before the last line of `applicationDidFinishLaunching:withOptions:`.

Profile the app, zoom in, and focus on the first view of car images. This time, it looks something like Figure 14-8. `setupScrollContent` has gone from 183ms to 5ms—a significant savings.

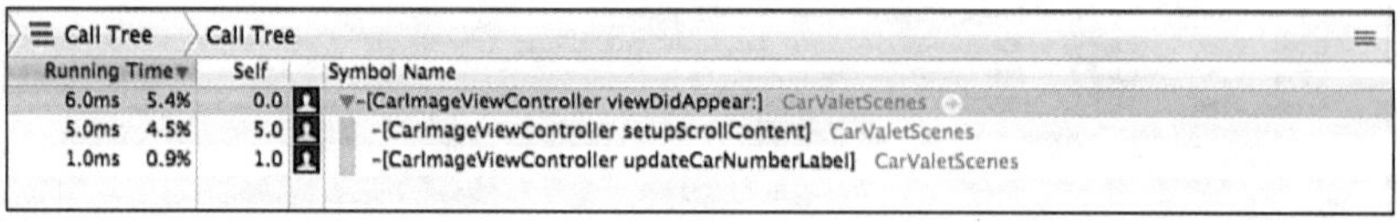

Figure 14-8   Prefetching in the app delegate

A Last Word on Instruments

The method for tuning the loading speed of the car images controller is basically the same method you use for any instrument:

1. Choose the performance area you want to investigate.

2. Profile your project using the appropriate template.

3. Search for places that indicate issues.

4. Zoom in and focus the call tree.

5. Use call tree mining to find possible issues.

6. Generate a hypothesis and update the code.

7. Profile and see if you fixed the issue.

8. Repeat these steps until you are satisfied.

One last word on Instruments: Exploring CarValet with other instruments is a good way to get an idea of how things should look. You should examine allocations to see what opening a new view controller looks like. You should also get a sense of the change in the amount of memory as you move through the app. You can do the same with the Activity Monitor template and other instruments to form a baseline for when you are troubleshooting.

> ### Tip: Testing Your App
>
> Testing your app is very important. You can use Apple's provided unit tests for automated testing of the logic and some basic things, but not for the user experience. There is an Automation template in Instruments, but that requires a combination of JavaScript and the Accessibility mechanism in your app.
>
> Using the Automation template is not a great solution for two reasons. First, it makes it next to impossible to add accessibility to your app. Second, it requires writing tests in a different language, JavaScript, and is executed in an atypical running application state.
>
> A better solution is to run automated tests, preferably from the same unit test framework provided by Apple. Telerik provides such a tool. You see more about Telerik and testing in Chapter 15.

The Debugger

Bugs are a fact of life. No matter what precautions you take, you will encounter bugs. The important thing is how long it takes to track down and fix bugs. That is where the debugger comes in.

The underlying debugger is LLDB, and although the console command line is important for some things, Xcode provides a user interface to three important features: viewing variables, breakpoints, and stepping through code.

When you hit a breakpoint or when a crash occurs, Xcode gives you access to a lot of information and tools. Figure 14-9 shows the CarValet app stopped at a breakpoint.

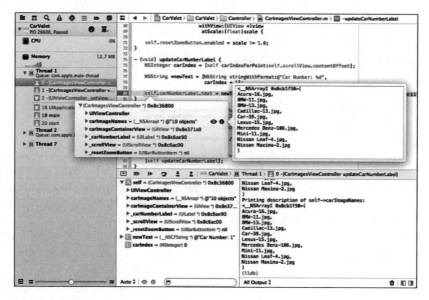

Figure 14-9   Xcode debugging information

On the left is the process view. Here you can see a list of active threads, with the one containing the breakpoint or crash showing the current call stacktrace. To the right is the code view, with the executing line highlighted in green. In this case, there is a breakpoint as well as a highlight.

You can show the code for any call in the stacktrace—including assembly, where available for system calls—by clicking. The icons next to the call tell you where it originated. Again, the human head and shoulder profile indicates the current method is one of yours.

When you hover over a variable in the editor, such as self halfway down the edit view in Figure 14-9, you see a dropdown. When you expand that dropdown, you see current values. Tap the info icon to get more detail for an object—in this case, the array of car images. You can use the eye icon to see a preview of the object, including images, as shown in Figure 14-10.

The variables view is on the bottom left next to the navigation panel. The bar above the variables panel enables you to control pausing, continuing, and stepping over/into/out of code. The framed dropdown arrow on the left of the panel controls what variables are shown. The default Auto setting shows you any variables that are relevant for the current line of code. You can also show just locals, or everything including globals and registers. Clicking the triangle next to a variable shows more information.

Figure 14-10   Previewing variable contents

Ctrl-clicking a variable opens a context-sensitive menu that lets you do anything from printing the value of the variable in the console, watching it, or looking at the raw memory. Context-sensitive menus are available all over Xcode and are well worth exploring. They can be significant time savers.

Also on the bottom is the console. Here you can type in LLDB commands to print objects or, as you have seen in previous chapters, access iOS debugging calls such as tracing auto layout.

Debug Gauges: Mini "Instruments"

In Figure-14-9, two items are at the top level of the navigation pane, CPU and Memory. These debug gauges are like mini instruments that are updated with statistics for your app. They introduce very little overhead and are a great way to spot when it is time to profile for more detail. Other gauges are available depending on the type of app and the target.

The CPU gauge, shown in Figure 14-11, is good for catching performance problems before they become problems. If you find performance a bit sluggish, take a quick look with the CPU gauge. Spikes indicate that you might need to do something more efficiently. Launching Instruments to hone in on the issue is as easy as clicking the Profile in Instruments button in the upper-right area of the gauge.

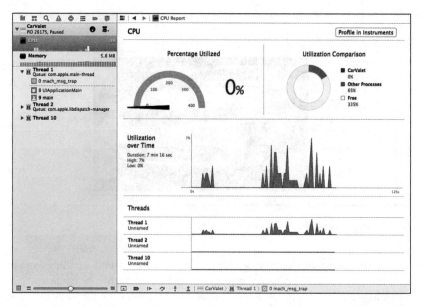

Figure 14-11   The CPU gauge

Figure 14-12 shows the Memory gauge. The ongoing memory graph is great for seeing both unexpected spikes and times when memory should free up but does not. Allocating a new scene should increase usage; closing that scene usually reclaims memory. Other events, such as allocating the array of car images, can increase usage. Look for bumps where not much is supposed to happen.

In addition to showing the ongoing memory usage, the meter in the upper left lets you know when memory use is becoming an issue. And once again, you can profile at the press of a button.

One last comment on the gauges: The navigation column shows a miniature form of the graphs for each gauge. If you need something else in the main window, you can keep your eye on these graphs. If things look like they need your attention, just click the relevant gauge.

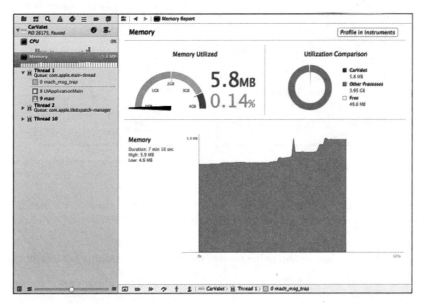

Figure 14-12   The Memory gauge

Breakpoints, and Actions, and Code...Oh My!

Using a breakpoint is a way to stop code execution at a place you choose, or when any problems occur. All you do is click in the line number next to a piece of code, and Xcode inserts a breakpoint. Figure 14-9 showed one in blue on line 80.

When running code (on both the simulator and real devices) hits a breakpoint, Xcode stops execution and enters the debugger. You can examine the call stack, look at variables, step over code, or even step into other methods. The variable window shows you values and even lets you change a BOOL from YES to NO.

Most people try to find issues by inserting an NSLog statement where they think the issue is, running the code, getting closer, putting in different NSLogs, and rerunning. They repeat this cycle until they can find a good place for a breakpoint.

But using this method is very inefficient and misses the real power of breakpoints. To see how powerful breakpoints can be, set one in your code by clicking on any line number to the left of the editor. Now Ctrl-click on that breakpoint and choose Edit Breakpoint from the contextual menu. You get a popup like the one shown in Figure 14-13.

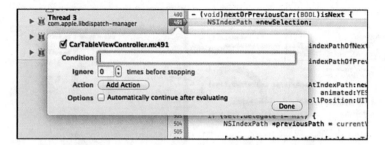

Figure 14-13   Edit breakpoint popup

Condition tells the debugger to trigger the breakpoint only when a condition is met. If you enter for !isNext as the condition, only the breakpoint for going to a previous car is triggered.

Ignore causes the debugger to ignore the breakpoint for a specified number of times.

Actions are the most powerful piece here. After clicking the Add Action button, you can choose from a few different actions. The most useful are logging a message, running a debugger command, and playing a sound. In combination with the option to automatically continue, you can replace NSLog statements with something much more powerful. More importantly, you do not have to compile and run your app. You simply add a new breakpoint and set the action.

A Practical Action Example

Let's look at an example that involves replacing NSLog. There are two ways to do this, and the one you choose depends on how much information you need. If you just need a simple string with basic information, the log message action might be enough. If you need detailed variable contents, the debugger command is better.

Say that you want to get an idea of how many times dragging the About screen taxi updates the frame. Follow these steps:

1. Open your latest version of the CarValet project or the provided CH14 CarValet Starter project in Xcode.

2. Open DragViewGesture.m and put a breakpoint on line 47.

3. Edit the breakpoint, add a log message action, and set its contents to Update Rect: %H. The last part prints a count of how many times the breakpoint has been hit.

4. Set the option for the breakpoint to automatically continue.

Now run the app in a simulator. Go to the About screen and start dragging the taxi. The console starts filling with Update Rect messages, with an increasing count.

Now say that you want to see the new rectangle. Leave the app running and follow these steps:

1. Edit the breakpoint.

2. Change the breakpoint to a debugger command and set the contents of the command to p (CGRect)newRect. In the debugger, this says print newRect as a CGRect.

Continue dragging the taxi, and the output in the console changes. You get the value. But there is more. On the same line as the action type popup are circles with a + and −. These let you add (or remove) more actions. Add a log action identical to the one you added earlier. Run the app, and now you see both the log message and the rectangle.

You made all these changes with the app still running. There was no need to rebuild and rerun. This time saving alone can be a huge benefit. And this is a very effective way of debugging strokes. If you need to confirm that the method is happening, you can set a sound and let the breakpoint automatically continue.

Another Useful Breakpoint

So far you have set breakpoints in your code. But there are two other types of breakpoints that help isolate problems. Figure 14-14 shows the breakpoint navigator and the dropdown from the Add button, showing each type of breakpoint.

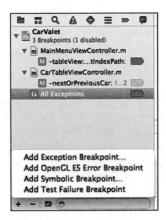

Figure 14-14   The breakpoint navigator

You use symbolic breakpoints when you do not have the source code. They enable you to stop on any symbol in a particular library. Although using them is beyond the scope of this book, a quick example will get you started. Say you know that a crash was caused by UINavigationController calling viewDidLoad:. Normally, you could not set a breakpoint because that is not your code. However, you can set symbolic breakpoints in that code. When you edit the breakpoint, look for the Symbol item and set it to the following:

```
-[UINavigationController viewDidLoad:]
```

The debugger stops every time that routine is entered. Of course, you will see assembly code, but it may get you closer to a solution.

Exception breakpoints are the other type. During active development, you should always have an All Exceptions breakpoint, though it may not always be enabled. This is a good way to catch errors as soon as they are introduced. The code stops as soon as the exception is encountered, giving you the best chance of finding the error.

Bug Hunt: Instruments and the Debugger

Every programmer dreads the crash...EXC_BAD_ACCESS. When this error occurs, you know that something has tried to access an object that is no longer allocated. These are the hardest problems to find because the code causing the problem usually happens at a very different place from the exception. And although ARC cuts down on these errors, it does not prevent them.

Tracking down this kind of problem is best done with both Instruments and the debugger. Instruments helps you find what object is causing the problem, and then you can use breakpoints to test your hypotheses about how the dead object is being accessed.

To get some practice tracking down this kind of problem, open the project in CH14 CarValet Bug and run it on an iPhone Simulator, following these steps:

1. View the detail of a car and go back and forth a few times.

2. Return to the top-level cars table menu.

3. Open the About tab.

4. Return to the Cars tab.

5. The app should crash. If it does not, repeat steps 1 through 4 until it does.

The current information in Xcode is not very useful. The code area is filled with assembly, and the stack trace has no app methods; in fact, it has very few items. The top one (item 0) is an Objective-C message send. This does not give you much help isolating the issue. But you can use both the Zombies instrument and the debugger to find what you need. The following sections show you how.

Starting with Zombies

Memory errors are difficult to find. Usually the source of the problem occurs long before the unexpected behavior or crash. When the system deallocates an object, that memory gets reused for some other object or primitive variable. The worst cases are when the memory does the following:

- Is not reused until after a few calls to the object and then is changed to something else. Everything appears to be working even though there is a lurking problem.

- Is reused for the same kind of object that likely has different values.

- Is reused for a primitive variable or a different class of object. A primitive value used as a pointer either points to some random place or might be an illegal value. A new object of a different class does not respond to messages or have the same instance variables.

When you suspect a memory error, or even if you do not, you can enable the memory management diagnostic tools provided by Xcode for your debug build. These tools work for both C and Objective-C memory allocations. For Objective-C, they turn any deallocated objects into Zombies. When your code references a Zombie, you get an immediate crash instead of getting a crash sometime later.

The Zombies Instrument template does all the necessary work to turn Zombies on. It is actually the Allocations instrument with the right checkbox checked. Figure 14-15 highlights the options panel and darkens the Zombie flag. Any time you see the Allocations instrument, you can turn Zombies on or off. The performance penalty is minimal.

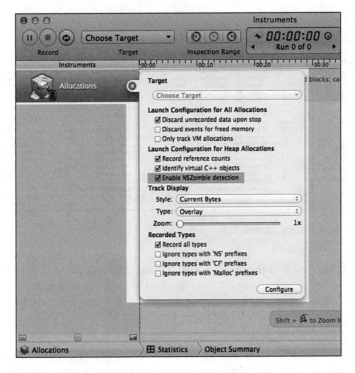

Figure 14-15   Enabling Zombies: Allocations Instrument options

Finding a Starting Point with Zombies

You need to profile the project from Xcode in Instruments and choose the Zombies template. Then you repeat the steps above until Instruments stops for Zombie access. You will see an automatically generated flag and popup much like the ones in Figure 14-16. When you click the circled arrow after the memory address, the bottom window changes to the history for the problem object.

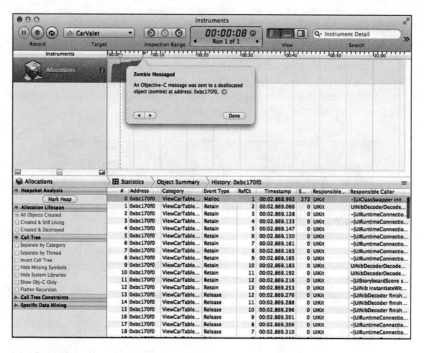

Figure 14-16   Instruments Zombie flag

The history can help you find the problem. First, the category tells you that the problem object is a kind of ViewCarTableViewController. This kind of makes sense because the car detail table should be released after you leave the car detail view. But this says something not only has a reference but also makes a call to the now-deallocated object.

The left-most column lists the originator and message at each step in the car detail table's history. Scroll down to the bottom and expand the Responsible Caller column. Figure 14-17 shows that UINavigationController called viewWillAppear: on the overreleased car detail table view.

	Statistics	Object Summary	History: 0xbc170f0						≡
#	Address	Category	Event Type	RefCt	Timestamp	S...	Responsible...	Responsible Caller	
116	0xbc170f0	ViewCarTableViewCo...	Release	1	00:05.558.099	0	UIKit	-[UINavigationController setDisappearingVi...	
117	0xbc170f0	ViewCarTableViewCo...	Retain	2	00:05.558.116	0	UIKit	-[UINavigationController navigationTransiti...	
118	0xbc170f0	ViewCarTableViewCo...	Release	1	00:05.558.125	0	UIKit	-[UINavigationController navigationTransiti...	
119	0xbc170f0	ViewCarTableViewCo...	Release	0	00:05.558.128	0	UIKit	-[UINavigationController navigationTransiti...	
120	0xbc170f0	ViewCarTableViewCo...	Zombie	-1	00:08.043.296	0	UIKit	-[UINavigationController viewWillAppear:]	

Figure 14-17   The Zombie call

Why is the navigation controller trying to send a message to car detail? The last user action for the cars tab was returning the cars table menu view. That should have popped the detail view off the navigation controller stack, but Instruments does not show what happened. It's time to move on to the debugger.

Moving On to the Debugger

Instruments showed a call to `viewWillAppear:`, a part of the view-opening cycle, and that gives you a place to start with the debugger. To be safe, put a breakpoint in both `viewDidLoad` and `viewWillAppear:` in `ViewCarTableViewController.m`. Optionally, you can practice editing breakpoints and set the ignore count to 1 since you know the first call works.

Run the app and reproduce the crash. If you did not set an ignore count, or if you have to try multiple times to reproduce the condition, continue using the keyboard shortcut Ctrl-Cmd-Y instead of the Product > Debug submenu.

The app crashes, but it does not hit one of the breakpoints. That gives you a possible clue. You need to look at what you know:

- `UINavigationController` is sending a message to a Zombie, which means it has a weak reference. If it had a strong reference, there could be no Zombie since strong means retain.

- None of the normal navigation flow, such as pops and pushes, use weak references; if there were weak references, there would be lots of crashes.

- Similarly, changing the navigation view stack only results in strong references as you are either setting a new array or adding objects to an array.

- Therefore, an object must be setting a weak reference in the navigation controller, and a good place to begin looking is in the Zombie class: `ViewCarTableViewController`.

For the next part of your investigation, follow these steps:

1. Open `ViewCarTableViewController.m` and search for `UINavigationController`. The only result is an argument type to a method, and that does not help.

2. Search for `navigationController`, the `UIViewController` property for the current navigation controller. There are only two real results. One clears the delegate in `navigationController:didShowViewController:animated:`. The other sets the delegate in `viewWillAppear:`.

3. Set breakpoints at the top of both methods you found in step 2 that modify the delegate.

Run the app and go through the steps that cause a crash. You know the issue is with the navigation controller, so focus your investigation there. At the debug prompt, type the following (and let autocompletion help you out with this):

```
po self.navigationController
```

This prints a valid navigation controller, the one managing the current view controller. Also look at the delegate property:

```
po [self.navigationController delegate]
```

This shows a `nil` value because you have not set the delegate. Step over lines with either the button in the debug control area between the editor and variables area or the F6 key until you pass the line that sets the delegate. Print out the delegate again, using the up-arrow key to repeat the previous command. Now you see the current view controller. You can confirm this by typing `po self` and checking that the object addresses match. Note that self is the current instance of `ViewCarTableViewController`, the currently active view controller.

Because you are at the end of the method, continue execution. At the next breakpoint, check the navigation controller's delegate and make sure it is the same object as the previous method. The body of the `if` condition does not execute because `viewController` is not the cars menu.

Continue once again, swipe through a few cars, and then return to the cars menu. At the breakpoint, check the navigation controller's delegate by using the up-arrow key to execute the previous command:

```
po [self.navigationController delegate]
```

You have not entered the `if` condition so have not cleared the delegate. Something is not right. The variables area shows that both method arguments have values and, more importantly, the `viewController` is a `CarTableViewController`. Check the delegate for the navigation controller sent in the method argument:

```
po [navigationController delegate]
```

This time, the delegate is correct. This says that the `navigationController` property for `self` has a problem. Print that out using the command:

```
po self.navigationController
```

You get `nil`! Step through the lines until just after the `if` condition sets the navigation controller's delegate to `nil`. Once again, check the delegate by using this method argument:

```
po [navigationController delegate]
```

The delegate is unchanged. Now you have the source of the bug. The detail view is dismissed, and the cars menu shows. At some point in the future, the detail view controller is freed up, but the navigation controller still has a weak reference. It has one because the method called `self.navigationController` instead of using the navigation controller sent as a method argument. (See the "Note: Why Did `nil.delegate = nil` Work?") The fix is to change the one line of code to the following:

```
navigationController.delegate = nil;
```

After you make this change, run the code and check the behavior using the breakpoint. You should see that the delegate is correctly set to `nil`. There is no more weak reference, and the app runs correctly.

> **Note: Why Did** `nil.delegate = nil` **Work?**
>
> You might wonder why the buggy line was not flagged. First, the compiler and linker have no way of knowing the right side will evaluate to `nil`. And in the runtime, sending any message to `nil` is valid, as is reading any property of `nil`. The result is always `nil`.

Summary

In this chapter, you learned how to check performance and find bugs. You started with Instruments, learning the types of information you can gather. Then you used Instruments to find and fix an app performance problem.

Next, you took a tour of the debugger and learned the power of breakpoints. Then you applied that knowledge in a practical example of editing breakpoints. Finally, you used the power of Instruments and the debugger together to solve one of the hardest types of bugs.

Along the way, you learned about call tree mining, a method for finding and fixing problems with Instruments, and the value of background tasks.

Your application toolkit is complete. You can design and implement apps for iPhone/iPod touch and iPad, and you can also create universal apps that run on both form factors. You know how to choose the most appropriate controllers, what view elements make sense and how to use them, how to save data, and how to tune and debug.

The last part of this process is making your app available and making sure you know how it is doing after it launches. Chapter 15 takes you through the process of moving your app from Xcode to the App Store. You also explore the other kinds of things you might want in your app—things like metrics and bug reporting. And, of course, learning is an ongoing journey, so Chapter 15 ends with suggestions on where to find more information.

Challenges

1. This is a timesaving challenge. Open the project `CH14 CarValet Challenge 1`. Profile the app using the Time Profiler and run through the app. Find and fix the performance issue. The performance issue is bad enough to show up on the simulator, though a device makes it much more obvious. All the fixes are in the new timesaving class, not `AppDelegate`.

2. This challenge is a debugger issue, another problem you are likely to encounter. Open CH14 CarValet Challenge 2, choose the iPad Simulator, and run the app. Look at the details on a car, and wait for the crash. Now use the resources at your disposal to find and fix the bug.

3. It's time to hunt your own EXC_BAD_ACCESS bug. Open the project in the CH14 CarValet Challenge 3 folder. Run the project in the iPad simulator and try rotating the screen. Find the bug using a combination of Instruments and the debugger.

Deploying Applications

The CarValet app is complete, performance is perfect, and the bugs have been found and squashed. Now you are ready to show your app to the world. Or are you? Ready on your machine is not necessarily App Store-ready. You need to take a few more steps before uploading your app.

In this chapter, you learn how to take your app from the simulator to the App Store. You start by learning about certificates, profiles, app IDs, icons, and launch images. Then you explore all the things you need to do before launch: doing better bug reporting, adding metrics, doing internal and external testing, and preparing for marketing.

Next, you learn the details of creating an app listing, uploading your app, and making it available, as well as some things to watch after the launch. The chapter ends with some pointers on where to go next.

Before you read any further, there is one very important thing you need to understand: Apple regularly changes things. Sometimes it makes small changes and sometimes significant ones. For some parts of this chapter, especially the section "Uploading and Launching," you can't rely completely on the screenshots. Focus is on the general process flow, along with the kinds of information you need to provide. This chapter gives you some idea of what the information is for and, where possible, guides you on how to craft it. When you get there in a few pages, make sure you read the "Caution: Sizes, Requirements, and Processes Change."

Certificates, Profiles, and Apps

To add an app to the App Store, you need to have six things in place:

- An Apple iOS developer account.
- Your distribution certificate and the associated private key.
- A development provisioning profile for installing your app on devices used for creating the app. (As you soon see, Xcode generates this for you as part of the certificate process.)

- An app ID you create with associated provisioning profile(s). (Again, Xcode can generate the profiles for you.)
- A distribution provisioning profile for your app.
- A profile for your app created in iTunes Connect.

Chapter 1, "Hello, iOS SDK," covers the different types of developer programs and registration. The next step is to generate a development certificate, a digital document used to uniquely identify you and your developer account/company. Note that you need to be a member of a paid developer program to do this.

A certificate is like an electronic car key. In addition to locking and unlocking the car, the key has a unique wireless code that is required for starting the car. Each code is unique to one car. You could not use your key to open and start someone else's car. Unlike car keys, certificates are used to generate, or sign, other forms of identification. A certificate can create a key for each of your cars.

A certificate has two parts: a private key that only you have and a public key that anyone can have. Signing uses your private key to generate a new key, based on some input. For apps, the input is the private key, app ID, and some other info, and the output is a *provisioning profile*. Code takes this provisioning profile and public key from your developer certificate and determines whether the profile is valid. Apple uses this to check whether an app should run on a device.

In other words, the private key is used to sign things, and the public key is used to check if it was really you that signed them. Your private key is a digital *you*, and should be protected. Anyone who has that key can create apps that appear to be from you. In addition, you need to make sure to back up your private key and keep it somewhere safe, such as an encrypted disk or partition. If you lose it, there is no way to regenerate it. You would have to generate a new certificate with new private and public keys, and all existing provisioning profiles would be invalidated (though any currently shipping applications using the old distribution profile will still work).

Caution: Sizes, Requirements, and Processes Change

The one constant in life is change. This applies to registration of app IDs, required icon sizes, default images, and even app submission. When Apple introduced iPhone 4, icon sizes changed. The same happened with iPhone 5 and the third-generation iPad with retina display. When submitting an app, the age rating was not always as detailed as it is now, and even registering an app ID changed when Apple introduced an updated developer portal.

Before you prepare and submit an app, it is a good idea to check the latest requirements in two very important documents. Both are available in Xcode as well as on the web.

For icon sizes, launch images, and similar things, check the *iOS Human Interface Guidelines*. In fact, read these guidelines regularly as they distill Apple's hard-won design knowledge in a form you can use to create better apps. In addition to the version in Xcode, you can find the latest version on the web at https://developer.apple.com/library/ios/#documentation/ UserExperience/Conceptual/MobileHIG/Introduction/Introduction.html.

For information on registering an app ID or uploading an app, see *iTunes Connect Developer Guide*. Again, this is available in Xcode, as a link on the home page of iTunesConnect. apple.com, and on the web at http://developer.apple.com/library/mac/#documentation/LanguagesUtilities/Conceptual/iTunesConnect_Guide/1_Introduction/Introduction.html.

Whether you are working with your first, fifth, or fiftieth app, checking these resources before you get too far can save you a lot of time and effort.

Generating a Development Certificate and Profile

Although generating certificates and profiles sounds like a complex process, it is easy to do and, in fact, Xcode can do most of the work for you. This is because you tell Xcode about your developer account (or in some cases, accounts) using the Accounts pane in Preferences, as shown in Figure 15-1.

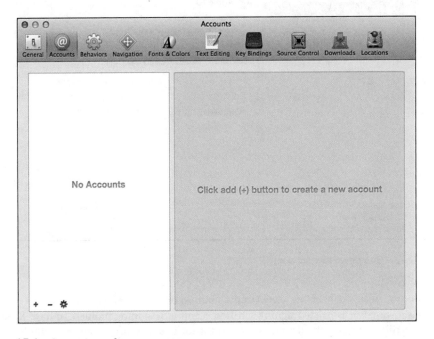

Figure 15-1   Accounts preferences pane

When you click the + button, you are prompted to enter the Apple ID and password used for your developer account. If you have not yet joined a program, you can click the Join a Program button and be taken to the signup page in Safari.

When you add a profile, the Accounts pane looks something like Figure 15-2. The next step is generating provisioning profiles, unless you already have some. If not, select your account in the right-hand column of the Accounts pane and then select the correct account member in the lower right. If you are an individual developer, there is only one.

The iOS column shows the role each member plays and is only important if you are using a company account or are part of some other team. The important thing is for the role to have permission to generate whatever kind of certificate or profile you need. This book assumes an individual account where you are the Agent, someone with full permissions.

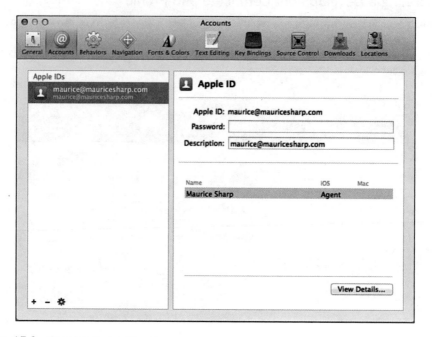

Figure 15-2   One developer account

With your role selected, click the View Details... button on the lower right. This brings up a window showing the associated signing certificates and provisioning profiles. To have Xcode generate certificates, press the Refresh button in the lower left. Shortly thereafter, another popover opens, enabling you to request both development and distribution certificates. Figure 15-3 shows the popover.

Figure 15-3   Requesting certificates

After a few moments, the spinner in the lower left stops and you see your certificates appear. Xcode has done all the work for you, including creating a private key. Better still, provisioning profiles are created at the same time.

Adding Devices to a Provisioning Profile

Provisioning profiles let you run development code on devices. If you try to run development code on a device that is not registered with your developer account, it will not work. Profiles contain a list of valid devices. If a device is not on that list, nothing works.

Adding a device takes only a few steps:

1. Plug a device into your machine using a USB cable.

2. Open the Xcode Organizer window, either from Window > Organizer, or by pressing Cmd-Shift-2. You see a window like that in Figure 15-4.

3. Select the device you want to add to your developer account.

4. Click the Use for Development button.

5. In the dropdown that appears, select the appropriate development team and press Choose.

Figure 15-4   Enabling a device for development from the Xcode organizer

Xcode now registers the device and regenerates your development profile. With a generic development profile, you can work on any app and have multiple development devices. With a distribution certificate, you can create, or sign, a profile for app distribution. Doing that requires an app ID.

App ID and Provisioning

A distribution provisioning profile is required for any beta/testing version you want to distribute more broadly, as well as for the final app. Generating the profile requires a distribution certificate, an Apple intermediate certificate (Xcode downloads that when certificates are generated), and an app ID. For test or ad hoc profiles, you also need a list of IDs for devices that you want to run the app.

You have the certificates, so now you need an app ID, which needs to be unique to your company and possibly to the app. Whether you need an app ID that's unique to the app depends on whether you are planning to use, or in the future add, any Apple services: in-app purchase, iCloud, push notification, game center, data protection, or passes. The safest choice is to use a unique ID for each app, which gives you the choice of adding services later.

Generating an App ID

Before you create an app ID, you need to know the bundle identifier for the app. This is a string in the form *com.domain.appname*. You can find the current bundle identifier by looking at the general tab for the project target in Xcode. It is at the top, though the final string in the profile is usually shown grayed out.

If you do not need Apple services, you can create a generic ID by using an asterisk (*), instead of *appname* (that is, *com.domain.**). You also need a text name to associate with the ID. This is important because portal operations such as creating a provisioning profile use this name, not the ID string. When you know this information, follow these steps:

1. Log in to your Apple developer account.

2. Click Certificates, Identifiers & Profiles in the upper right.

3. In the portal, select Identifiers. Here you should see a list of any existing IDs. This is also where you add Apple services.

4. Click the + button in the upper right. This takes you to the screen shown in Figure 15-5.

5. Enter the text name you chose earlier into the App ID Description field.

6. Choose any services your app uses.

7. If you need Apple services or you want a fully specified bundle ID, select Explicit App ID and type in the bundle name. Otherwise, select Wildcard App ID and enter the wildcard string.

8. Click Continue, check the details on the summary screen, and click Submit. Your app ID is created.

When you return to the app ID overview in the portal, you see the newly created ID.

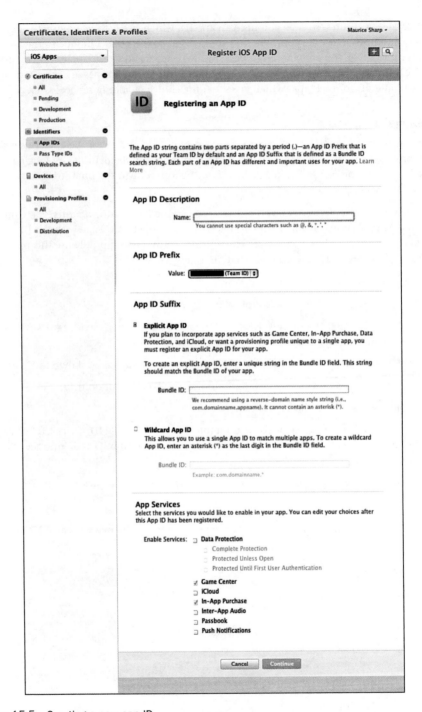

Figure 15-5   Creating a new app ID

Creating the App Distribution Provisioning Profile

Now that you have an app ID, the next step is to create a distribution provisioning profile. There are two types of profiles: ad hoc (or testing) and App Store profiles. You will use both of them. The ad hoc profile requires more information, so start there, with these steps (and remember, things might change):

1. Open the Certificates, Identifiers & Profiles area for your developer account and select Provisioning Profiles.

2. Click the + button and then select Ad Hoc, as shown in Figure 15-6.

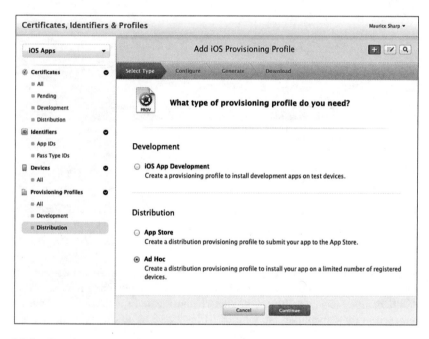

Figure 15-6   Creating an ad hoc profile

3. Click Continue, select the appropriate app ID from the list, and click Continue again to go to the next screen.

4. Select the distribution certificate for this app. Most of the time there is only one. Click Continue to go to the next screen.

5. Now select any testing devices. It helps to prefix testing devices for easy organization. For example, you can use *P* for personal, *F* for friend, or even codes for projects or apps. Click Continue to go to the final screen.

6. Name the profile something meaningful, such as <TYPE> <AppNameGoesHere>. For example, you could use `AdHoc CarValet`. Now click Generate.

7. Switch to Xcode and refresh your Provisioning Profiles the same way you did when creating your developer certificates. Refer to Figure 15-1.

If the new profile is not in the list, wait a few minutes and then refresh again. The Library area then includes the new profiles. Figure 15-7 shows an example.

Figure 15-7   Xcode Provisioning Profiles

There are three columns of information for each provisioning profile. First is the name, which corresponds to the original profile name field. Next is the profile Expiration date. And finally are any Entitlements associated with the profile. The entitlements are represented with the same icons used in the Capabilities tab for a target in Xcode. As an example, the last provisioning profile has three icons: The first is iCloud, the second is App purchase, and the third is GameCenter.

Generating a profile for the App Store is almost identical to generating an ad hoc profile, except you choose App Store in step 2 and do not need to specify testing devices (step 5). You are almost ready to build a distributable test app. First, you need to add some artwork.

Tip: What to Do When Things Go Wrong

Since I started development for iOS in 2009, I have encountered numerous problems with invalid/missing distribution certificates, inability to generate provisioning profiles, and related issues that bring on, as Erica calls it, "the yellow triangle of doom."

The first lesson I learned from all these occurrences (not to mention a love of British satirical sci-fi and fantasy) is "Don't panic." Usually the Xcode error will provide you all the information you need to fix the error. And if not, there are several things you can try, and there are places you can look to ask questions and get answers.

Surprisingly, one thing that sometimes works is "Do it again." Deleting everything in the profile library and using Refresh causes Xcode to go through all the steps, including ones you might have accidentally skipped.

If that does not work, here are a few things to try:

- Clear the list and then quit and reopen Xcode. Now click Refresh.
- Clear the list and quit, but this time restart your machine before relaunching.
- Clear the list, launch the Keychain application, and use the Keychain First Aid option. When the keychain is cleaned up, try Xcode again.
- If you're working on a new Mac, check whether you transferred both your public and *private* keys for your developer certificate. Of course, I always do this...well, usually.
- Use the Keychain application to make sure you have the required private keys. If not, add them or generate new certificates.
- Log on to the developer portal and check your certificates and profiles online. If they are there, you can manually download them. If not, and if Xcode is not cooperating, you can generate them using the portal.

If all this fails, you can go to the Apple developer forums. Look for similar problems or ask a question. You can also check with fellow developers and/or your local iOS/Cocoa developer group. Searching the web is another option. Use the resources at the end of this chapter as a guide for where to look.

And, as mentioned earlier, if all else fails, you can always regenerate your certificate. It means you need to regenerate your profiles, but at least you can get back to work.

Icons and Launch Images

Before you can distribute a test build, you need the required set of icons and launch images. Not every icon size and image is required; you need only those for the categories of devices and the orientations you support.

Except for the iTunes store artwork, the easiest way to check if you have all the images you need is by opening `Images.xcassets` and checking the `AppIcon` and `LaunchImage` items. Each one has slots for each icon size or image size you need.

Each item lists the kind of image (for example, iPhone App) as well as a point size. Because images are square, the point size tells you the width and height. Launch images list what screen they are for and in some cases which orientation, but they do not list sizes.

Table 15-1 shows the various images and sizes. Nonretina sizes are listed, though as of the writing of this book, the original iPad mini is the only iOS 7 capable device with a nonretina display.

Table 15-1   **Sizes for Icons and Launch Images**

Images	Nonretina	Retina	4" Retina
App Icons			
iPhone app icons	60×60	120×120	—
iPad app icons	76×76	152×152	
App Store Icons			
iTunes icon	—	1024×1024	—
Launch Images			
iPhone launch image	320×480	640×960	640×1136
iPad launch image (portrait)	768×1004	1536×2008	—
iPad launch image (landscape)	1024×748	2048×1496	—
Optional Icons			
Settings icon	29×29	58×58	—
Spotlight icon	40×40	80×80	—

In general, the names of the app icon or launch image files do not matter. The asset catalog manages that for you. Having said that, it is a good idea to use a convention to easily identify the target resolution of the image. Typically, an image with no special resolution or targeting an asset catalog 1x slot uses the plain image name. If it is for a 2x slot, the name is appended with @2x, and the R4 slot can use @R4. As an example, if the base image file is `MyLaunch.png`, that is the name for 1x resolution images; `MyLaunch@2x.png` is for 2x, or retina, slots; and `MyLaunch@R4.png` is for slots using R4. (Note that the iOS 6 version of this name would be `MyLaunch-568h@2x.png`.)

The iTunes icon name is `iTunesArtwork.png`.

Adding App Icons

Open the project you used for Chapter 14, "Instruments and Debugging," or use `CH15 CarValet Starter` provided in the sample code for this chapter. Follow these steps to add in the app icons:

1. Open `Images.xcassets` in the project, and then choose `AppIcon`. You see a set of empty asset bays shown on top in Figure 15-8.

2. In the Finder, open the folder `CH15 Assets App Icons` that comes as part of the sample code for this chapter. Select all the icons and drag them into the area with the empty assets. When you see some of the empty icon bays highlight, drop the icons. The area should look something like the bottom of Figure 15-8.

3. If all the icons for iOS 7 are not complete, drag in any remaining icons individually. In the bottom of Figure 15-8, the 2x iPad settings icon is missing. Drag Settings@2x directly into that box.

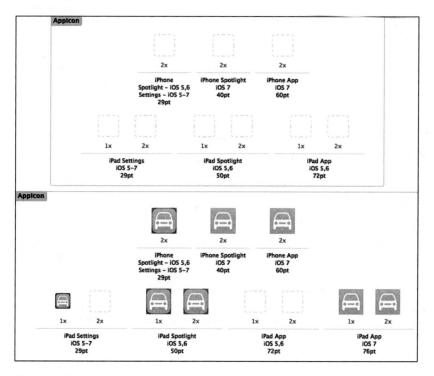

Figure 15-8   Adding app icons with the asset catalog

Run the app on different simulated screen types: iPhone (retina), iPad, and iPad (retina). For each device type, close the app and look at the icon. It will be the right size for that device. (If the new icon does not appear, you might need to clean the build by pressing Shift-Cmd-K and then the build folder by pressing Option-Shift-Cmd-K.)

Launch Images

After the user launches an app, it takes a bit of time before you can make any changes on the screen. During this time, the system shows the launch image. The default launch image is black and not very interesting.

Existing apps' launch images do everything from promote a brand to show a blank interface. Apple currently recommends showing the main screen of your app with no details. Spend some time launching applications making sure they are removed from device memory to see what other developers use for launch images. For CarValet, you use a variant of the no detail image from the iPad combined with the car from the app icon. Follow these steps:

1. Open LaunchImage in the Images.xcassets.

2. In the Finder, open the CH15 Assets Launch Images folder that came with the sample code.

3. Bring Xcode back to the front and make sure you can see the contents of the assets folder. Then drag each named image into the appropriate bay.

Now that you have a default launch image and icon, the next steps are to add some important extras to your app, do some external testing, and start marketing activities.

Prelaunch

Before your app is App Store-ready, you need to take care of four important details:

- Add bug reporting to your app.
- Include metrics gathering.
- Test with a wider audience.
- Start marketing activities. (Yes, this soon...and you should probably start sooner next time.)

All these processes could be done earlier in the development process, but not too early. Bug reporting can wait until you start outside testing. You can add metrics from the start. You usually wait to start outside testing until you have a solid beta. Marketing can make a huge difference in downloads, and even if you have existing customers, you still need to reach them.

Bug Reporting

The sad fact is that bugs make it into shipping apps. It's important to quickly catch and fix the ones in your shipping app that cause crashing and noncrashing exceptions. You can look at crashes by using iTunes Connect, but the data is limited and not well presented. What you really want to know is what crashes occur, how often, and on what device/OS, and you want a full stacktrace.

A few companies offer drop-in solutions with associated web services. Their software catches exceptions, anonymizes them, and reports to a server. You log on to their server and get the data. Solutions vary from do-it-yourself to full analytics, including seeing the steps that lead to the crash.

Most services are based on the open-source Plausible Crash Reporter project found at http://code.google.com/p/plcrashreporter/. You can use the code to capture bugs in your app. However, you need to create a back-end server and handle uploading bugs, along with many other details.

It is much faster to use an existing service. Most are free for basic reporting and then vary in cost, depending on features and/or number of incoming reports. The following are some of the existing major companies, in alphabetical order (see the "What Do You Use?" sidebar later in the chapter):

- www.atlassian.com/software/jiramobileconnect/overview
- www.bugsense.com
- https://www.crashlytics.com/
- www.crittercism.com
- www.flurry.com/flurry-crash-analytics.html
- http://hockeyapp.net
- pulse.io (performance only at this time)
- https://testflightapp.com

All the third-party bug-tracking software works basically the same way:

1. Go to the company's site and create an account.
2. Download the SDK.
3. Add the SDK to your app by following appropriate instructions. You usually need to add a static library to your project.
4. Include the company header in your app delegate, call a routine to start tracking and, optionally, set up more data and make more specific calls.

In addition to bug reporting, companies are starting to offer performance metrics including CPU use, memory, battery and, most importantly, network. Because so many apps rely on the network, knowing which performance issues are your app and which are the network is critical in tuning your product. And you can only do that with the kind of data you get after the app is shipped. One of the companies mentioned previously specializes in performance, though others in the list also offer services.

As you can see, adding reporting takes very little effort. Some providers have other calls you can make to send more details or even send custom reports. A few offer built-in user feedback and even communication to let a user know his or her bug has been fixed.

Note that it is up to you to make sure whatever you include does not violate any personal privacy information laws or your own app's statement of information use. See "Warning: Beware of Ever-Changing Privacy Laws" later in this chapter.

Warning: There Can Be Only One (Active Bug Reporter)

As mentioned, most, if not all, of the bug-reporting libraries use the open-source project for reporting exceptions. Because of the way `PLCrashReporter` works, there can be only one bug reporter, even if multiple services try to use it. If you use three services (for example, metrics, testing, and bug reporting), and all three can report bugs, only one will. And it might not be the bug-reporting service.

And these days everyone is offering to report bugs. For this reason, it is important to make sure any third party service has an option to turn off bug reporting. And not just preventing the bug report, but also stopping their library from initializing `PLCrashReporter`. If not, you might end up paying for a bug-reporting service that is never called.

Metrics

The App Store gives you some information about your shipping app: the number of down-loads and updates, user ratings, app rank, and a few more metrics. But the data can be hard to consolidate. And it does not tell you much about what users are doing or whether they are coming back to your app.

There are a few key questions in tuning your app:

- Are people downloading and using your app (first-time use)?
- What is the typical time using the product (engagement)?
- Are users staying around (retention)?
- What features are they using and not using (tuning the product)?
- Are they using new features (more product tuning)?
- Are certain locales adopting your app more quickly or slowly than others?
- For those paying for ads, which ads are working?

You can collect metrics yourself, but it takes a lot of effort. It requires capturing and sending data to a server, and you need software to analyze the data. Luckily, several companies offer plug-and-play solutions. You register on a site, add a library, make a call at app start, and the numbers start rolling in.

As with bug tracking, there are numerous providers in the metrics arena, though unlike with bug tracking, most are free. These companies are in the business of selling anonymous consoli-dated data, and your app provides just a small part of that data. Some companies also sell advertising, and others want you to advertise with them. Some of the large providers include other features (see the "What Do You Use?" sidebar later in the chapter). Check out the follow-ing companies that are active in the metrics space:

- www.appclix.com
- http://bango.com/mobileanalytics/
- www.flurry.com/index.html
- www.google.com/analytics/features/mobile.html
- www.localytics.com
- http://newrelic.com

Adding a metrics library is almost identical to adding a bug-reporting library. Unlike with bugs, you are highly likely to make many calls for different types of user events. Some services auto-matically capture moving from app screen to app screen. But that does not tell you what the user does on a particular screen.

> **Warning: Beware of Ever-Changing Privacy Laws**
>
> Any services, including metrics, bug reporting, and even ads, might capture some sort of PII: Personal Identifying Information. Protecting this information has become a priority in some countries and is currently the law in the European Union. If you use any services, make sure their use of such information (and yours) complies with the laws of any country where you distribute your app as well as your app's own privacy agreement.
>
> If you are not a lawyer, you can either accept the provider's assurance they comply, or you can hire your own lawyer to make sure. Breaking privacy laws can have serious consequences.

Quality Assurance Testing

There are many types of QA (quality assurance) testing, though for your purpose, you can focus on three: unit testing, automated functional testing, and integration testing.

Unit tests are usually created by the person writing the code, and they test that a particular feature performs as expected—for example, that correct input works and gives the right result and incorrect input fails appropriately.

Xcode comes with a unit-testing framework that is added to projects by default (at least as of the current Xcode 5 beta). With the addition of a Mac OS X server, you can run sophisticated continuous integration using unit tests and other tools such as static analysis. This is a powerful tool in finding problems while they are still small.

Functional testing checks that your app behaves as it is supposed to—for example, that touching buttons does the right thing, scrolling tables work, and proper errors are shown. This kind of automated testing can only test what you expect to happen and always in the same way.

Unfortunately, the existing Xcode automation tools do not support calls to the interface or communications layers. There are tools in Xcode for interface testing but they are quite limited. Many frameworks are available for automated interface testing, usually based on public domain frameworks. TestStudio from Telerik provides a professional solution, but there are costs for serious use.

Integration testing is done by real people trying to use your product, usually in ways you do not expect. Lack of this kind of testing is the source of most serious postshipping bugs.

Unit and Functional Testing

As mentioned earlier, Xcode includes a unit test framework for your projects. There are several other providers, depending on the kind of language you want to use for unit tests. For Apple, logic and model tests are written using Objective-C. Functional tests are written in JavaScript and use a special Instruments tool. Unfortunately, using the JavaScript tool makes it extremely difficult to effectively support accessibility, as they use the same user interface element properties to identify the elements. That makes it hard to have both accessibility and testing-friendly values for the properties.

Other providers use different languages and require different amounts of work. As of this writing, for functional testing, TestStudio by Telerik is the one best integrated with the Apple Objective-C-based unit test framework. Table 15-2 lists some of the many providers. (See the "What Do You Use?" sidebar later in the chapter.)

Table 15-2   Unit and Functional Testing Solutions

Solution	Language	Uses Accessibility	Link
Apple UnitTest	Objective-C	—	Built into Xcode
Apple Functional	JavaScript	Yes	Built into Xcode
TestStudio Functional	Visually specified and/ or Objective-C	No	www.telerik.com/automated-testing-tools/ios-testing/ios-application-testing.aspx
Monkeytalk	None or JavaScript	Recommended	https://www.gorillalogic.com/monkeytalk
KIF	Objective-C	Yes	https://github.com/square/KIF
Calabash	Cucumber and Ruby	No	https://github.com/calabash/calabash-ios
GHUnit	Objective-C	No	https://github.com/gabriel/gh-unit

Integration Testing

There is nothing like having real people test your app. It is the best way to discover memory and sequencing problems. It is also where you discover how customers really use your app.

Finding people to test your app can be challenging. Ideally, testers should know how to push your app to the limit and how to report bugs. It is possible to do integration testing on your own, if you do the following:

- Recruit testers who have either Xcode and a simulator, or a device.
- Set up an appropriate ad hoc provisioning profile that includes all the device IDs and distribute credentials for those using simulators.
- Build and distribute test (AdHoc) app versions, making sure testers keep up to date.
- Coordinate all the feedback and bug reports.

This is a lot of work, especially if you have no one else to do it for you. And that is where the various service providers can help. They vary from enabling easy distribution to doing the testing for you. Table 15-3 lists a few services. (See the "What Do You Use?" sidebar.)

Table 15-3   **Ad Hoc Testing Providers**

Provider	Services
https://testflightapp.com	Everything from distribution to reporting and testers.
http://hockeyapp.net	Everything from distribution to reporting and testers.
www.usertesting.com/mobile	Professional testing organization founded by people with mobile experience.
www.utest.com	Professional testing and more; can be costly, though for important apps, it is likely well worth it.
http://mobileappstesting.contus.com	Professional testing organization; requires doing a lot of upfront work.
www.mob4hire.com	Crowd-sourced testing; compatibility coming.
www.mobtest.com	Crowd-sourced testing; in beta at this writing.

One important thing to remember is that as a developer, you can only register a limited number of unique developer/testing device IDs in any one membership year. At this time it is 200, so if you had 199, added 1, and then removed 3, you would still have no new testing device slots until the beginning of your new membership year.

What Do You Use?

One question I get on a regular basis is "What service do you use?" The answer depends on the business importance of the app. If the importance is low, any of the free services will do, though Flurry offers both metrics and simple bug reporting.

For bug reporting and performance, it depends on the type of app. Assuming the revenue model supports it, Crittercism provides a well-rounded solution with both bug reporting and performance monitoring. For the more cost-conscious projects, a combination of Crashlytics and either New Relic or pulse.io can give you what you need.

No matter which service you use, you get data on bugs such as device type and OS, symbolicated stacktrace, frequency, custom metadata, and more. Some services offer breadcrumbs—that is, how the user got to the bug. Those can significantly reduce the amount of time to reproduce, and therefore fix, the bug.

For metrics, I like Flurry, for its in-depth analysis. And even though there appear to be limits on the number of cohorts (used for retention), a quick conversation usually results in the needed changes (though again, make sure this makes sense from a business/revenue perspective).

For unit and functional testing, I use Telerik's TestStudio. Scripting makes repetitive functional testing a breeze both in the simulator and on devices. And integration with Apple's UnitTest framework makes developer-driven and continuous integration testing easy, though this soon might require something like Jenkins (see later) to get working.

For early/alpha stage user testing, I think it's a toss-up between TestFlight and HockeyApp. Both are easy to integrate, make distribution easy, give access to a pool of testers, and have feedback mechanisms. For more important apps that require the human touch, usertesting.com is my service of choice based on the quality of service and its experience in mobile. (One of the founders used to work for Palm.)

One service not mentioned is the idea of continuous integration testing during development. The idea is to have automated testing as you build new versions of your app. Jenkins lets you do that and a lot more. When you have a build server set up, you can configure it to automatically build and run unit tests any time you check code into your source code repository. And Jenkins can do a lot more. Note that a build server can be the same machine you are using, though this is not recommended for teams. To find out more, visit their website: http://jenkins-ci.org.

Cloud storage and sharing is a service that is not really covered by this book but is becoming increasingly important. Apple provides a way to save Core Data into the cloud as well as game services through GameCenter. For a more general solution, I have found Heroku, https://www.heroku.com, a good place to start (and more), though there are several providers, some of whom have a strong client list (Parse, StackMob, and the Google cloud platform).

One extremely important service not mentioned is source code control. There is nothing worse than trying to fix an issue, discovering the change is much worse, and wanting to revert to the old code. Source code control lets you save incremental changes and go back to previous versions. I have used both SVN and Git, and all my source is stored somewhere in the cloud. GitHub is the standard place for public domain code and offers both free public and for-cost private storage.

Of course, over time, providers change. It pays to keep watching the various providers, old and new.

Marketing

Marketing can make the difference between a few downloads and thousands. There is no secret formula that guarantees success, but there are things you can do to increase your chances. Although marketing is covered in prelaunch, it really spans the lifetime of your app.

Before launch, the focus is on building infrastructure and interest. Infrastructure adds app functionality for easy rating and tell-a-friend functionality. Word of mouth can be a powerful and low-cost marketing tool.

There are many open-source projects for reminding a user to review and tell their friends. You can use them directly or as a basis to write your own. (And remember to contribute back if you make it better.) These are a few of the common ones:

- http://code.google.com/p/review-request/
- https://github.com/arashpayan/appirater
- https://github.com/nicklockwood/iRate
- http://ioscodesamples.com/testground/tell-a-friend/
- https://github.com/aporat/iTellAFriend

Interest

Interest is about contacting press, bloggers, and others who can increase awareness of your app. Remember that these people have thousands of developers contact them each day. You have a few words or perhaps an image or two to catch their attention. If you do, you get more time, but even that does not guarantee coverage.

Some very useful apps let people play with your app via the web. This can be a useful tool for marketing, though you need to make sure there is not too much utility, or why would they buy the app? One such tool is app.io, though others are appearing.

When your app ships, your listing is critical. It is the first thing a user sees.

A full treatment of marketing is beyond the scope of this book, but there are many books on marketing, covering everything from general principles to iOS-specific marketing. Here are a few to get you started:

- *iPhone and iPad Apps Marketing: Secrets to Selling Your iPhone and iPad Apps*, second edition, by Jeffrey Hughes

- *Pitch Perfect: The Art of Promoting Your App on the Web* by Erica Sadun and Steve Sande

- And since you are likely to need an app/company website: *The Ultimate Web Marketing Guide* by Michael Miller

Uploading and Launching

Your testing is done, your app is wired for bug reporting and metrics, and you are executing your marketing plan. The time has come to upload the app...almost. Before you do that, you need to create an app listing.

Remember that things change. April 2013 saw a complete redesign of the portal for accessing certificates, app IDs, profiles, and test devices. June 2013 streamlined certificates, profiles, entitlements, and other things with Xcode 5. It is only a matter of time before more updates occur. This section describes the flow involved in updating and launching. The screenshots were taken when this book was written. Tomorrow's websites could be different. Make sure you read the "Caution: Sizes, Requirements, and Processes Change" at the beginning of this chapter and keep an eye on the two important documents it talks about.

First, you need to add an entry for the app in the App Store:

1. Log in to https://itunesconnect.apple.com using your developer account e-mail and password.

2. If you have not already done so, sign the legal agreements that appear.

3. If you are going to sell apps, allow in-app purchase, or use iAd, Apple's ad framework, set up payment accounts. If you need to do this and you are not taken to that area when you log in, from the home screen go to the Contracts, Tax, and Banking section and provide any required information.

4. From the home screen, go to Manage Your Applications.

5. On the Manage Your Applications page, add a new app. You are prompted for the key app information. Figure 15-9 shows how this screen might look for the CarValet app. The alert in Figure 15-9 lets you know the bundle ID cannot be changed when the app is accepted or if you have set up Game Center. You need to make sure the app ID works for the entire life of the app. iOS uses the ID to uniquely identify an app, as well as associate it with data and settings. If you change the ID, there will seem to be two copies of your app on a device: one with all the old data and one without.

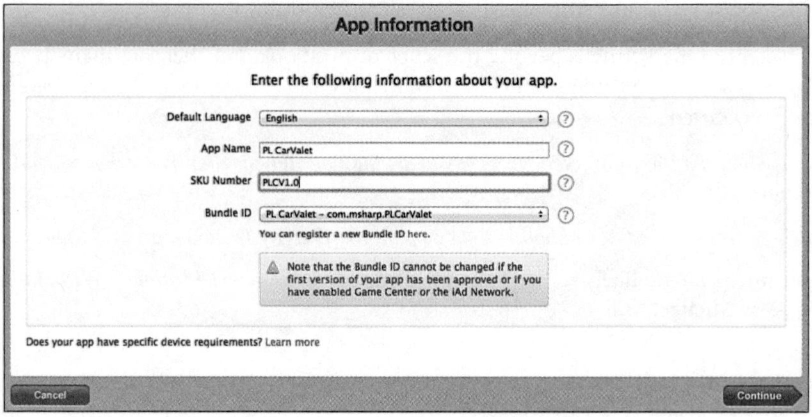

App Information

Enter the following information about your app.

Default Language	English
App Name	PL CarValet
SKU Number	PLCV1.0
Bundle ID	PL CarValet – com.msharp.PLCarValet

You can register a new Bundle ID here.

⚠ Note that the Bundle ID cannot be changed if the first version of your app has been approved or if you have enabled Game Center or the iAd Network.

Does your app have specific device requirements? Learn more

Cancel   Continue

Figure 15-9   New app page

6. Choose the name for your app that will appear at the App Store. This is a really important choice. Make sure you do not use an existing trademark or conflict with any existing app names. You have up to 255 characters for a name that makes a user want to get your app, or at least look at the listing for more information.

7. Set the stock-keeping unit (SKU) number to whatever you want it to be. Apple does not use it; it is for you.

8. When you are done setting the main app details, choose when the app launches, how much it costs, and decide whether to limit it to certain countries. Figure 15-10 shows how this screen could look.

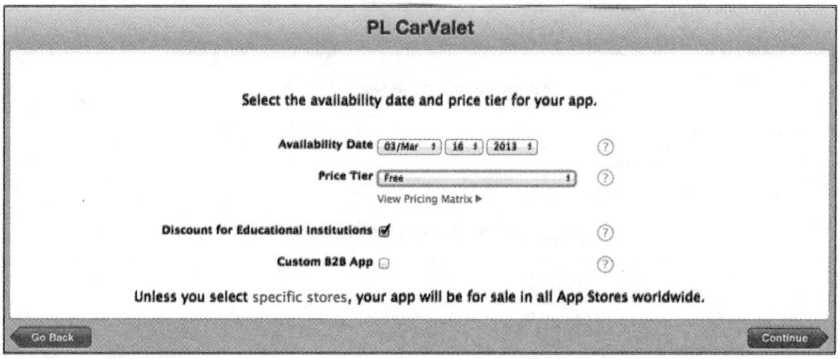

Figure 15-10   Launch date and price

The availability date is a guideline, and the actual date depends on when your app is reviewed and approved. As of this writing, the average time was about 1.5 weeks, though the time can vary widely. One source to check is http://reviewtimes.shinydevelopment.com. It shows a 30-day rolling average review time. Also note that the current developer program lets you request an expedited review once a year. This is not something to use lightly. Save it for a critical bug fix. When you use it, it is gone for the year...and "pretty please" does not work.

When picking a date, it is best to choose one at least a few months in the future, so you have control of the actual release date. When your app is approved, you can set up any required press activities and update the actual release date accordingly. When you start uploading updates, there is an option to hold the approved app until the developer releases it.

App Details

After you have set what, when, and how much for your app, you need to enter all the details needed to list and review your app. You need to worry about lots of pieces of information, starting with the version number, copyright holder and, most importantly, the category. Figure 15-11 shows the part of the page currently used to enter this information. (This is one of the most-likely-to-change pages.)

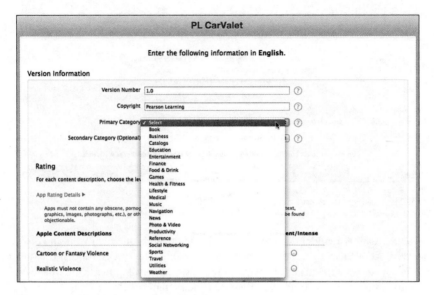

Figure 15-11   Choosing the primary app category

Choosing the right category makes a huge difference in the number of downloads. Customers use it as one way to filter what they look for. You can optionally choose a secondary category, but make sure your primary choice is the one users expect. Ask your possible users questions if you are not sure. Do some A/B testing.

After the category, you need to set the age rating. You need to tell users what kind of content your app contains in a number of different areas; Apple uses things like the amount of violence, horror, and alcohol use to set the rating, as shown at the top of Figure 15-12.

If your app is aimed at kids, make sure you check the Made for Kids box.

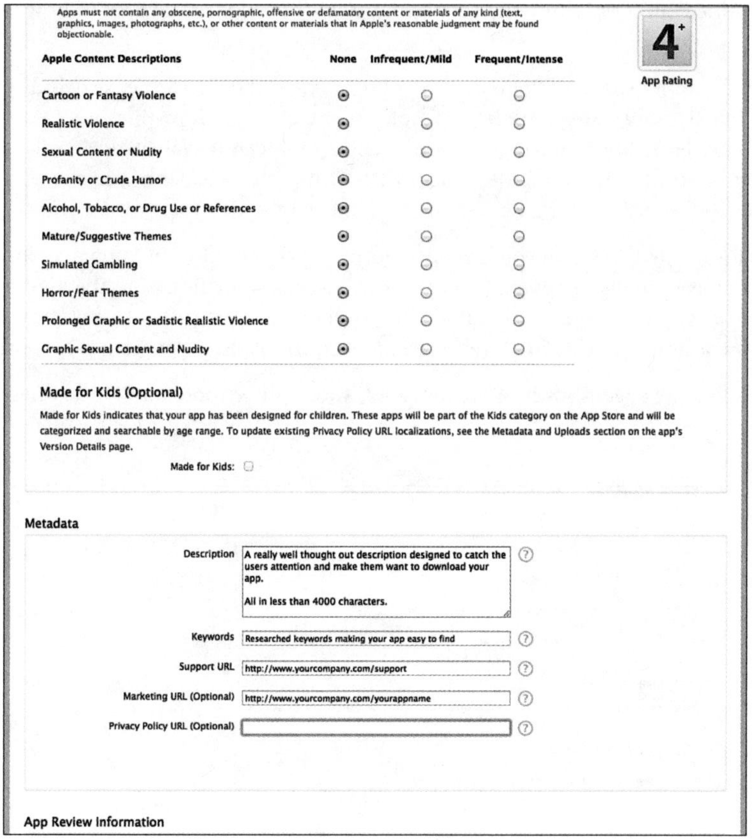

Figure 15-12   Content rating and metadata

Figure 15-12 also shows other important app information that is currently grouped under Metadata.

When you attract a user to your listing, the description has a strong influence on downloads. You have about three to five words to catch a potential user's attention and get the person to read more. And you need to keep the user engaged. Strike a balance between inviting and/or exciting prose and feature facts. Focus on why the app is valuable for the target audience. What problem does it solve? How will it make life better? Good marketing books and competent marketing consultants are worth their weight in gold.

It's a good practice to start reading through app descriptions. See which ones grip you and which ones make you want to move on. Look for patterns. For example, asterisks, pluses, and other characters can draw attention to key points when they are used sparingly. Conversely, listings using lots of long lines of these characters are distracting at best and deadweight at worst. The same goes for blasting the user up front with tons of reviews about how great the app is.

Keywords are another strong influence. When users search the App Store, keywords play, well, a key role. Unfortunately, Apple does not disclose precisely how they are used. There are people who specialize in optimizing keywords. These folks can be valuable. However, be aware that Apple is continuously tuning their algorithm. Optimization does not happen once. It is ongoing. A good sign something has changed is unusual trends in downloads.

The spaces for listing URLs give you a chance both to give more information and show that yours is a serious business. A company website with a section dedicated to the app, information on the company, as well as professional-looking support, can indicate a trustworthy company. You could use a service like Zendesk (www.zendesk.com) to add depth to app support.

The final part of the page, shown in Figure 15-13, shows three more main categories of information.

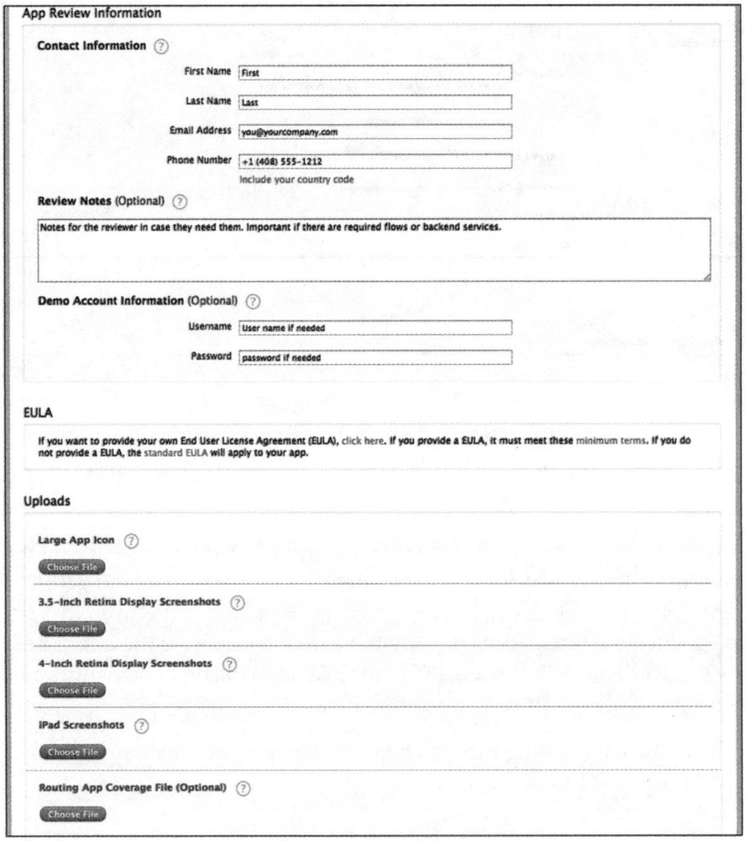

Figure 15-13   App review and other info

There are many reasons Apple might need to contact you. They might have simple questions because you have a typo somewhere, or they might need to warn you about a violation of naming or terms. Having the right contact information and person listed can save hours, days, or even weeks when issues occur.

Using the right EULA (end user license agreement) is critical. Whether you are an independent developer or just one person in a large company, EULAs both set a base level of expectation for users and provide some protection against legal action. You can choose to use Apple's default EULA or provide one of your own. Either way, you have to have one and make sure your app meets any conditions of the agreement. Take time to read the Apple default EULA if that is what you use.

Finally, you need to provide all the associated artwork.

The large icon used in the App Store is based on whatever you are using for the app, but it is much larger and has more detail. For CarValet, use the `iTunesArtwork.png` found in the `CH15 Assets iTunes` folder (and thanks again to Joseph Wain at Glyphish for the cool icon).

Any store listing includes one or more screenshots. These are another tool for convincing a user to choose your app. You must include at least one screenshot for each device and screen size you support. You can optionally include specific metadata and screenshots for any supported localization.

There can be up to five screenshots per device/screen size/localization, and they can make the difference between a download or not. Choose shots that illustrate your app solving problems, as well as showing how easy it is to use. Take a look at successful apps and see what they do. Some use simple screenshots, some use commented shots, and others are more innovative.

Save, Summary, and Setup

At some point, all the information is in, and it is time to commit the information. When you save it, you go to some sort of summary and management page for the new app. Figure 15-14 shows a possible screen. At this point, you can still modify most of the entered information, though not all of it. Do not be concerned if the icon is still a blank. It takes time to upload a large file, and when iTunes has it, the database has to get updated and the elves have to communicate the change.

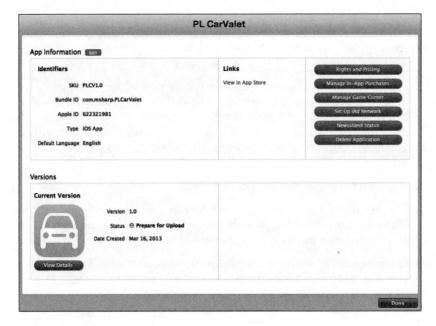

Figure 15-14   New app almost ready

Before you return to Xcode, you need to set up the App Store to receive your app. At this writing, you do that by selecting View Details under the icon for your new app. This takes you to a detail page that might look like Figure 15-15.

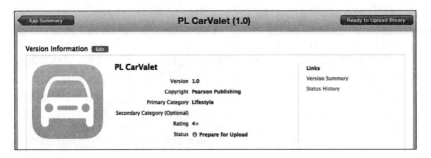

Figure 15-15   Ready to upload

Let the App Store know you are ready to upload the binary, answer the question on encryption, and head back to Xcode. Whatever e-mail address you used to register your developer account is notified that the app status is "Waiting for Upload."

Uploading to the App Store

You are almost there. The last stage is to build and submit your app to the App Store and then wait for Apple's review and approval. Almost all this can be done with Xcode.

Building an app for ad hoc testing and for the App Store are very similar. Both require building an archive; they only differ in the kind of distribution. To build the store archive, you need five things:

- A valid distribution certificate
- An app ID with an App Store distribution provisioning profile
- A complete App Store listing with a state of Ready to Upload Binary (see the previous section)
- A correctly configured project summary and build settings for the app target
- A project scheme for building a release-level archive

Note that distribution certificates are time-limited. Each certificate is valid for a period of one year, and when it runs out, you get an error saying you do not have a valid certificate. You can create a new one using the process shown earlier. Note that even if your certificate expires, any apps already out there still work as they contain a copy of both the distribution profile and the public part of the old distribution certificate.

You have already created an app ID and an App Store listing, and you have enabled Ready to Upload Binary. That leaves the project summary, build settings, and release archive scheme.

Configuring the Project

The project settings for Bundle ID and Version need to match the information in the App Store app record. Sometimes the bundle ID is set correctly because the app name is also the last part of the bundle string (for example, `com.msharp.CarValet`).

You use Xcode, as shown in these steps, to change the ID:

1. Open `CarValet-Info.plist` and look for the Bundle Identifier property.

2. Change the value to the same one in the app record—for example, `com.msharp.PLCarValet`. Make sure your development and distribution profiles match the new bundle string; this might require you to regenerate the profiles.

The version is set on the Summary tab for the app target. You can set both a version and a build number. You can also change the name as it appears on the iPhone. This can be very handy as you often want a different display name. Follow these steps:

1. In the Xcode Organizer, select the project.

2. Double-click the name of the target and change it to what you want. In this case, it is CarValet.

You access the settings in Xcode by selecting the project in the Navigator and then the summary for the app target, as shown in Figure 15-16.

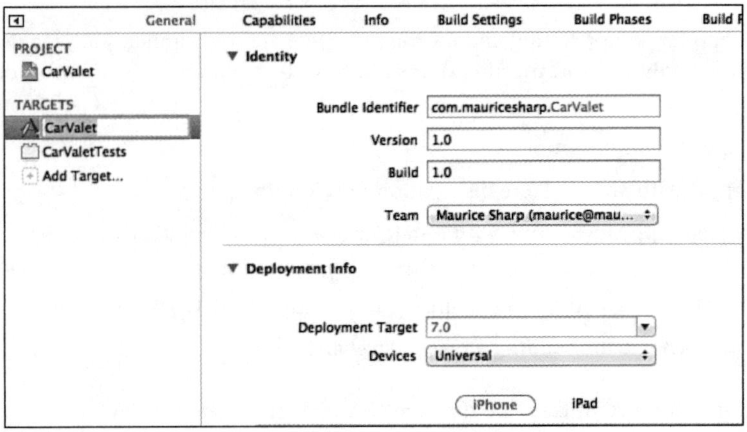

Figure 15-16   Changing the app name

Since you have made some basic changes, now is a good time to test the app in the simulator. If you have trouble, quit both Xcode and the simulator and then start Xcode and try again. If you close CarValet in the simulator, you see two versions: one with the old bundle ID and one with the new.

The bundle ID, not the app name, is a key part of identifying your app. This is why you have to make sure the app name does not conflict with any other. Nothing in the OS prevents many apps with the same name being present on a device.

Setting Up the Project Scheme

Before you can upload your app, you need to make sure you build the right thing. A distribution version is built as an *archive*—a bundled-up package containing the app and some supporting information, such as the distribution profile and symbol table. Archives are also useful for backups since they represent a shipping product.

Before you generate an archive, it is a good idea to ensure that the scheme generates what you want. Usually the same scheme is used as to create ad hoc builds that are sometimes based on debugging. Follow these steps to check the scheme:

1. Use the scheme/device popup in the Xcode Toolbar to select iOS Device as the scheme target and edit the scheme. You do not need a device attached to the machine, just the device target. The target controls the kind of code Xcode builds: a device target builds ARM code, a simulator target builds an app used in the Mac simulator.

2. Edit the scheme and select Archive. You get a dialog like the one shown in Figure 15-17. Make sure Build Configuration is set to Release. (You can instead set it to Ad Hoc to generate testing builds.)

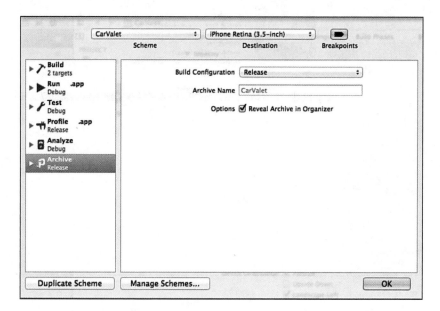

Figure 15-17   Checking the archive scheme

Tip: AdHoc and AppStore Schemes

You might have noticed a Duplicate Scheme button in Figure 15-17. You can use this button to create custom build schemes for specific purposes such as creating an AdHoc build or an App Store build. Another possible scheme can create a build for development but with debug turned off. Explore the schemes and settings to see the kinds of custom ones you can create.

Building and Uploading

The last step in submitting an app to the App Store is to create and upload the archive. You do both of these things with Xcode:

1. In Xcode, make sure the target is iOS Device and choose Product > Archive. After going through the build process, Xcode opens the Archives pane of the Organizer Window, as shown in Figure 15-18.

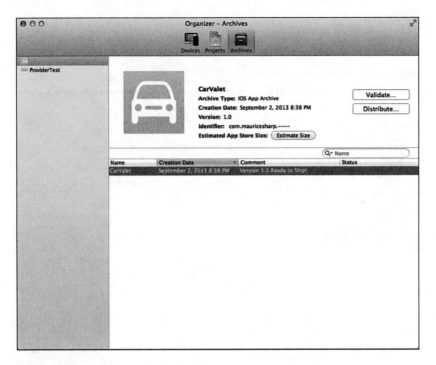

Figure 15-18   Archives pane: ready to ship!

2. Add a comment so you know what you are archiving. A good naming scheme will help later as you try to differentiate between individual test builds and shipping versions. The comment above is just for fun. A better one would be "Version 1.0 Build 2010.06.07.01." A test build might be "Beta 0.7 Build 2013.06.10.07." (See the "What Is a Build Number?" sidebar.)

3. Click the Validate button and make sure your archive is okay. Although validation is also run as part of distribution, it is better to catch and fix any errors before you do the final upload.

4. Enter your developer credentials on the next screen and then make sure the correct app and code signing identity are selected. Any problems are shown. Fix the issues.

5. Repeat the process of archiving, validating, and fixing until there are no issues.

6. To upload your app, click the Distribute button and choose Submit to the iOS App Store in the dialog. Enter your credentials, choose the app, and click Next.

Xcode uploads your app. When it is finished, you see a screen something like Figure 15-19.

Figure 15-19   Application uploaded!

You soon get a confirmation e-mail from Apple and can log into iTunes Connect to see the status. Other e-mails are sent when your app goes into review, and when it is approved or rejected. If by some chance it is rejected, you get more information on why and what you might need to do.

After you get the approval e-mail, go to iTunes Connect, view the app, and set the release date as needed. Then sit back and watch the downloads.

What Is a Build Number?

The target summary screen lets you set both a version and a build number. But what is a build number? The basic answer is whatever you want it to be. In practical terms, it is something you can use for tracking exactly when, where, and how a product is built.

Version numbers have limitations. If you are trying to ship version 1.0 of your application, the reality is you might have to go through four builds of your archive to make it work. It is all version 1.0, but it has gone through a few cycles, and any one of them could introduce something unknown.

Using build numbers is a way to set whatever meta-information you need for the particular build. The following are some possibilities:

- A number incremented by one for each build
- The date of the build in some format (for example, YYYY.MM.DD)
- The date of the build and the number of the build that day (for example, YY.MM.DD.BB, where a BB of 02 would be the second build on that day)

- The date and time of the build
- A hashed value including information such as date and time as well as some other identifiers such as location of build
- A number or hashed value indicating a source code repository identifier for the code used to build the app

The date with build number or source code identifier are the most common uses as they help QA and engineering isolate exactly what went into the build.

Some Things to Watch Postlaunch

When your app is in the App Store, there are still things to do. You need to do tasks like the following:

- Track downloads.
- Keep an eye on and, where appropriate, respond to feedback.
- Analyze the metrics and plan appropriate action.
- Monitor the bug reporting you added and respond to bugs.
- Keep up with marketing activities.

And, of course, plan your next great update or app.

Where to Go Next

You now have all the tools you need to design, build, and launch apps for iPhone, iPod touch, and iPad. As with any other endeavor, there is always more to learn. There are also many kinds of helpful resources, including books, websites, developer groups and conferences, and social media.

This book is just one in a series of iOS hands-on books. Your app might require you to have a deeper understanding of particular topics. Look for these other books in this series:

- *Learning Objective-C 2.0: A Hands-on Guide to Objective-C for Mac and iOS Developers*, second edition, by Robert Clair
- *Learning iOS Design: A Hands-on Guide for Programmers and Designers* by William Van Hecke
- *Learning iPad Programming: A Hands-on Guide to Building iPad Apps with iOS* by Kirby Turner and Tom Harrington
- *Learning Core Audio: A Hands-on Guide to Audio* by Chris Adamson and Kevin Avila
- *Learning Core Data for iOS: A Hands-on Guide to Building Core Data Applications* by Tim Roadley

- *Learning iOS Game Programming* by Michael Daley

- *Learning OpenGL ES for iOS: A Hands-on Guide to Modern 3D Graphics Programming* by Erik M. Buck

- *Learning iCloud Data Management: A Hands-on Guide to Structuring Data for iOS and OS X* by Jesse Feller

Other books go even deeper:

- *Xcode 4 Unleashed*, second edition, by Frederic F. Anderson

- *Programming in Objective-C* by Stephen G. Kochan

- *Effective Objective-C 2.0: 50 Specific Ways to Improve Your iOS and OS X Programs* by Matt Galloway

- *iOS Auto Layout Demystified* by Erica Sadun

- *Core Data for iOS: Developing Data-Driven Applications for the iPad, iPhone, and iPod touch* by Tim Isted and Tom Harrington

- *Test-Driven iOS Development* by Graham Lee

Recipe and pattern books are a great way to find solutions to coding problems or app features. They also give you ideas for new features. Try these:

- *The Core iOS Developer's Cookbook* by Erica Sadun

- *The Advanced iOS 6 Developer's Cookbook* by Erica Sadun

- *Cocoa Design Patterns* by Erik M. Buck and Donald A. Yacktman

Websites

This is a familiar conversation:

> Coder A: "Hey, how do I *<do some task/make some effect happen/...>*"

> Coder B: "Good question; did you Google it?"

Googling a problem can help, but how do you know what links to click? And when you get to a page, how do you know if the answer is a good one?

There are many resources on the web for solving coding problems, from Q&A to blogs. All of them can help you solve a problem or at least get you started. Here are a few good ones to get you headed in the right direction:

- Forums/QA sites:

    - https://devforums.apple.com/index.jspa

    - http://stackoverflow.com

- Blogs:

  - www.raywenderlich.com

  - www.cocoawithlove.com

  - http://iosdevelopertips.com

  - http://nshipster.com

- Aggregators:

  - www.cocoacontrols.com

  - http://maniacdev.com

Developer Groups and Conferences

Nothing beats face-to-face conversation, especially when the person you are talking to has already solved the same problem you're facing. And this goes not only for coding problems, but for the other areas that make an app successful: design, marketing, business, and so on. Conferences and local developer groups are great places to network with others.

No matter where you are, there are likely others creating iOS apps somewhere near you. Local developer groups exist all over the world. Finding them can sometimes be challenging, but the web can help. In addition to doing a simple search, you can look at a couple mobile group–aggregating websites:

- http://ios.meetup.com

- http://ios-development.meetup.com

- www.mobilemonday.net

Conferences

Apple's Worldwide Developer Conference (WWDC) is the most valuable iOS developer event. If you cannot get there (or even if you can), you can check out the session videos. They're well worth watching, often more than once. By only watching the videos, you miss the opportunity to talk to Apple engineers and the mass of attendees. Unfortunately, it has been very hard to get WWDC tickets in recent years; they usually sell out soon after sales start (70 seconds for WWDC 2013).

Luckily, there are many third-party developer conferences around the world. They range from fully produced events with top-tier speakers to semi-crowd-sourced hackathons. All of them can be valuable sources of learning and networking, as well as opportunities to meet vendors for metrics, testing, bug reporting, and so on.

Again, you can do a simple web search. And here are a few iOS-focused events and event aggregators to get you started:

- http://360idev.com
- http://cocoaconf.com
- www.iosdevcamp.org
- www.iosdevuk.com
- http://nsconference.com
- http://renaissance.io

In addition, there are a number of more general mobile conferences covering iOS as well as other platforms.

Other Social Media

You can find discussions about almost anything on social media, and iOS development is no exception. All the major services have groups, areas, and/or people. Again, you can do searches on your favorite places. And this section lists some to get you started.

LinkedIn has a number of dedicated and related discussion groups, some open and some moderated, including these:

- All the subgroups of "iPhone OS Developer Network"
- Cocoa and Cocoa Touch Developers
- CocoaHeads

Facebook has groups, though not a lot of them are technical, and some of them are the Facebook pages for websites. Here are a couple to get started:

- https://www.facebook.com/pages/iOS-Developers/137794742906132
- https://www.facebook.com/iOSDeveloperTips

Twitter has many good programmers and thought leaders contributing content. Some are feeds for website content, some for blog comments, and some are pure Twitter. Check out these:

- https://twitter.com/cocoacontrols
- https://twitter.com/ericasadun
- https://twitter.com/iOS_Dev_Tips
- https://twitter.com/jerols
- https://twitter.com/maniacdev
- https://twitter.com/mattgemmell
- https://twitter.com/rwenderlich

This is a good article on inspiring people for iOS developers to follow:

- www.appdesignvault.com/inspiration-35/

Summary

In this chapter, you took your app from an on-machine almost beta to waiting for review in the App Store. You started by learning about certificates and profiles and then generating your development credentials. You also learned how to generate your own certificate and profile, just in case Xcode has a problem. Next, you saw how to generate an app ID and provisioning profile and keep Xcode up to date. Then you added app icons and launch images, and learned all the different sizes.

The next step was learning about prelaunch activities. You saw several options for bug reporting, metrics, and quality assurance. Then you got an introduction to app marketing.

You moved on to creating an app listing for the App Store and learned the importance of bundle IDs, names, launch dates, app category, descriptions, and screenshots. Then you updated the app to "Ready to Upload Binary" status. With the App Store waiting, you learned how to configure the project to match the store information, change the on-device name, and check the project archive build scheme. Then you learned how to create and validate an app archive and upload it to the App Store.

Along the way, you learned about different types of quality assurance, reminding users to review and tell friends, and some things to watch after an app has launched.

Now it is time for you to design and build your own apps. As you encounter challenges, you can refer to explanations in this book. And as you get more experienced, the resources listed in this chapter can help you grow.

As you develop apps, there will be easy things and hard things, fun times and frustrating times. But through it all, remember to enjoy what you are doing.

Challenges

1. Create a full set of five screenshots for each screen size for the CarValet app.

2. Sketch out a high-level marketing plan for CarValet.

Index

C

D

M

Y-Z

More Resources for Mac and iOS Developers

Cocoa Programming
for Mac OS X,
Fourth Edition

Aaron Hillegass
and Adam Preble

ISBN-13: 978-0-321-77408-8

Effective
Objective-C 2.0

Matt Galloway

ISBN-13: 978-0-321-91701-0

iOS 6 App Development
Fundamentals
LiveLessons Part I
(Video Training)

Paul Deitel

ISBN-13: 978-0-13-293190-8

Objective-C
Advanced
Programming
LiveLessons
(Video Training)

Jiva DeVoe

ISBN-13: 978-0-321-90287-0

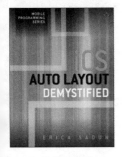

iOS Auto Layout
Demystified

Erica Sadun

ISBN-13: 978-0-13-344065-2

iOS UICollectionView

Ash Furrow

ISBN-13: 978-0-13-341094-5

Xcode and Instruments
Fundamentals
LiveLessons

Brandon Alexander

ISBN-13: 978-0-321-91204-6

Addison
Wesley

SAMS

For more information and to
read sample material, please
visit informit.com/learnmac.

Titles are also available at
safari.informit.com.

Developer's Library

informit.com/devlibrary

ESSENTIAL REFERENCES FOR PROGRAMMING PROFESSIONALS

The Core iOS 6 Developer's Cookbook, Fourth Edition

Erica Sadun

ISBN-13: 978-0-321-88421-3

The Advanced iOS 6 Developer's Cookbook

Erica Sadun

ISBN-13: 978-0-321-88422-0

Programming in Objective-C, Fifth Edition

Stephen G. Kochan

ISBN-13: 978-0-321-88728-3

Other Developer's Library Titles

TITLE	AUTHOR	ISBN-13
Objective-C Phrasebook, Second Edition	David Chisnall	978-0-321-81375-6
Test-Driven iOS Development	Graham Lee	978-0-321-77418-7
Cocoa® Programming Developer's Handbook	David Chisnall	978-0-321-63963-9
Cocoa Design Patterns Applications for the iPhone	Erik M. Buck / Donald A. Yacktman	978-0-321-53502-3

Developer's Library books are available at most retail and online bookstores. For more information or to order direct, visit our online bookstore at **informit.com/store**.

Online editions of all Developer's Library titles are available by subscription from Safari Books Online at **safari.informit.com**.

Addison
Wesley

Developer's Library

informit.com/devlibrary

Addison Wesley

REGISTER

THIS PRODUCT

informit.com/register

Register the Addison-Wesley, Exam Cram, Prentice Hall, Que, and Sams products you own to unlock great benefits.

To begin the registration process, simply go to **informit.com/register** to sign in or create an account. You will then be prompted to enter the 10- or 13-digit ISBN that appears on the back cover of your product.

Registering your products can unlock the following benefits:

- Access to supplemental content, including bonus chapters, source code, or project files.
- A coupon to be used on your next purchase.

Registration benefits vary by product. Benefits will be listed on your Account page under Registered Products.

About InformIT — THE TRUSTED TECHNOLOGY LEARNING SOURCE

INFORMIT IS HOME TO THE LEADING TECHNOLOGY PUBLISHING IMPRINTS Addison-Wesley Professional, Cisco Press, Exam Cram, IBM Press, Prentice Hall Professional, Que, and Sams. Here you will gain access to quality and trusted content and resources from the authors, creators, innovators, and leaders of technology. Whether you're looking for a book on a new technology, a helpful article, timely newsletters, or access to the Safari Books Online digital library, InformIT has a solution for you.

informIT.com
THE TRUSTED TECHNOLOGY LEARNING SOURCE

Addison-Wesley | Cisco Press | Exam Cram
IBM Press | Que | Prentice Hall | Sams
SAFARI BOOKS ONLINE

informIT.com
THE TRUSTED TECHNOLOGY LEARNING SOURCE

InformIT is a brand of Pearson and the online presence for the world's leading technology publishers. It's your source for reliable and qualified content and knowledge, providing access to the top brands, authors, and contributors from the tech community.

✦Addison-Wesley **Cisco Press** EXAM/**CRAM** **IBM** Press. QUe' ‡‡ PRENTICE HALL **SAMS** | Safari'

LearnIT at InformIT

Looking for a book, eBook, or training video on a new technology? Seeking timely and relevant information and tutorials? Looking for expert opinions, advice, and tips? **InformIT has the solution.**

- Learn about new releases and special promotions by subscribing to a wide variety of newsletters. Visit **informit.com/newsletters**.

- Access FREE podcasts from experts at **informit.com/podcasts**.

- Read the latest author articles and sample chapters at **informit.com/articles**.

- Access thousands of books and videos in the Safari Books Online digital library at **safari.informit.com**.

- Get tips from expert blogs at **informit.com/blogs**.

Visit **informit.com/learn** to discover all the ways you can access the hottest technology content.

Are You Part of the IT Crowd?

Connect with Pearson authors and editors via RSS feeds, Facebook, Twitter, YouTube, and more! Visit **informit.com/socialconnect**.

informIT.com
THE TRUSTED TECHNOLOGY LEARNING SOURCE

✦Addison-Wesley **Cisco Press** EXAM/**CRAM** **IBM** Press. QUe' ‡‡ PRENTICE HALL **SAMS** | Safari'

Try Safari Books Online FREE for 15 days

Get online access to Thousands of Books and Videos

Safari Books Online
FREE 15-DAY TRIAL + 15% OFF*
informit.com/safariebooktrial

> **Feed your brain**
> Gain unlimited access to thousands of books and videos about technology,
> digital media and professional development from O'Reilly Media,
> Addison-Wesley, Microsoft Press, Cisco Press, McGraw Hill, Wiley, WROX,
> Prentice Hall, Que, Sams, Apress, Adobe Press and other top publishers.

> **See it, believe it**
> Watch hundreds of expert-led instructional videos on today's hottest topics.

WAIT, THERE'S MORE!

> **Gain a competitive edge**
> Be first to learn about the newest technologies and subjects with Rough Cuts
> pre-published manuscripts and new technology overviews in Short Cuts.

> **Accelerate your project**
> Copy and paste code, create smart searches that let you know when new
> books about your favorite topics are available, and customize your library
> with favorites, highlights, tags, notes, mash-ups and more.

** Available to new subscribers only. Discount applies to the Safari Library and is valid for first
12 consecutive monthly billing cycles. Safari Library is not available in all countries.*

 Addison Wesley   Adobe Press   Cisco Press   FT Press   IBM Press   Microsoft Press   New Riders   O'REILLY

 Peachpit Press   PEARSON IT Certification   PRENTICE HALL   QUE   SAMS   vmware PRESS   WILEY   wrox

FREE
Online Edition

Your purchase of *Learning iOS Development* includes access to a free online edition for 45 days through the **Safari Books Online** subscription service. Nearly every Addison-Wesley Professional book is available online through **Safari Books Online**, along with over thousands of books and videos from publishers such as Cisco Press, Exam Cram, IBM Press, O'Reilly Media, Prentice Hall, Que, Sams, and VMware Press.

Safari Books Online is a digital library providing searchable, on-demand access to thousands of technology, digital media, and professional development books and videos from leading publishers. With one monthly or yearly subscription price, you get unlimited access to learning tools and information on topics including mobile app and software development, tips and tricks on using your favorite gadgets, networking, project management, graphic design, and much more.

Activate your FREE Online Edition at
informit.com/safarifree

STEP 1:   Enter the coupon code: CGABNXA.

STEP 2:   New Safari users, complete the brief registration form.
            Safari subscribers, just log in.

If you have difficulty registering on Safari or accessing the online edition,
please e-mail customer-service@safaribooksonline.com